Technical Factors in the Treatment of the
Severely Disturbed Patient

Peter L. Giovacchini, M.D.
L. Bryce Boyer, M.D.
Editors

NEW YORK   Jason Aronson, Inc.   LONDON

CLASSICAL PSYCHOANALYSIS AND ITS APPLICATIONS

A SERIES OF BOOKS
EDITED BY ROBERT LANGS, M.D.

THE FIRST ENCOUNTER: THE BEGINNINGS IN PSYCHOTHERAPY
*William A. Console, M.D., Richard D. Simons, M.D., and
Mark Rubinstein, M.D.*

PSYCHOANALYSIS OF CHARACTER DISORDERS
Peter L. Giovacchini, M.D.

TREATMENT OF PRIMITIVE MENTAL STATES
Peter L. Giovacchini, M.D.

A CLINICIAN'S GUIDE TO READING FREUD
Peter L. Giovacchini, M.D.

BETWEEN REALITY AND FANTASY: TRANSITIONAL OBJECTS AND
PHENOMENA
*Edited by Simon Grolnick, M.D., and Leonard Barkin, M.D.,
with Werner Muensterberger, Ph.D.*

SPLITTING AND PROJECTIVE IDENTIFICATION
James S. Grotstein, M.D.

EARLY DEVELOPMENT AND EDUCATION OF THE CHILD
Willi Hoffer, M.D.

STRESS RESPONSE SYNDROMES
Mardi J. Horowitz, M.D.

HYSTERICAL PERSONALITY
Edited by Mardi J. Horowitz, M.D.

BORDERLINE CONDITIONS AND PATHOLOGICAL NARCISSISM
Otto Kernberg, M.D.

OBJECT-RELATIONS THEORY AND CLINICAL PSYCHOANALYSIS
Otto Kernberg, M.D.

INTERNAL WORLD AND EXTERNAL REALITY
Otto Kernberg, M.D.

CHILDREN AND PARENTS: PSYCHOANALYTIC STUDIES IN DEVELOPMENT
Judith Kestenberg, M.D.

DIFFICULTIES IN THE ANALYTIC ENCOUNTER
John Klauber, M.D.

THE TECHNIQUE OF PSYCHOANALYTIC PSYCHOTHERAPY VOLS. I AND II
Robert Langs, M.D.

THE THERAPEUTIC INTERACTION 2 VOLS.
Robert Langs, M.D.

THE BIPERSONAL FIELD
Robert Langs, M.D.

THE THERAPEUTIC INTERACTION: A SYNTHESIS
Robert Langs, M.D.

TECHNIQUE IN TRANSITION
Robert Langs, M.D.

THE LISTENING PROCESS
Robert Langs, M.D.

SOURCE NOTES

Regression: Some General Considerations, Hans W. Loewald. Reprinted with the permission of *The Psychoanalytic Quarterly,* 1981, 50: 22–43.

Direct Presentation of Reality in Areas of Delusion, Margaret I. Little. Reprinted from *Transference Neurosis and Transference Psychosis.* New York: Aronson, 1981, pp. 93–108.

Object-Relations Theory and Psychotherapy with Particular Reference to the Self-Disordered Patient, Donald B. Rinsley. Originally published as "Application of Object-Relations Theory to Psychotherapy," *New Techniques in Psychotherapy, Part III.* Philadelphia: Smith, Kline and French Laboratories, 1981.

Helplessness in the Helpers, Gerald Adler. Reprinted with the permission of *The British Journal of Medical Psychology,* 1972, 45: 315–326.

The Meaning of Play in Childhood Psychosis, Rudolph Ekstein and Seymour Friedman. Reprinted with the permission of Grune and Stratton. In *Dynamic Psychotherapy in Childhood,* ed. Lucie Jessner and Eleanor Pavenstedt. New York: Grune and Stratton, 1959, pp. 269–292.

Library of Congress Cataloging in Publication Data
Main entry under title:

Technical Factors in the treatment of the severely
  disturbed patient.

  Includes index.
  1. Psychoanalysis. 2. Psychology, Pathological.
I. Giovacchini, Peter L. II. Boyer, L. Bryce.
[DNLM: 1. Psychopathology. 2. Psychoanalytic—Therapy—
Methods. 3. Mental disorders—Therapy. WM 460.6 T255]
RC506.T43   616.89′17   81-20587
ISBN 0-87668-429-0   AACR2

Manufactured in the United States of America.

CONTENTS

PREFACE

Since 1967, when Boyer and I undertook a venture similar to this book, the field of psychoanalysis has broadened in scope to include patients suffering from schizophrenic and characterological disorders. The varieties of psychopathology now treated by analysts are traceable to the earliest levels of psychic development.

Many psychoanalysts accept patients who fail to meet the criteria postulated by Freud for entering into psychoanalytic treatment, but they may not consider their work with such patients to constitute classical analysis. Classical analysis is still, in many circles, reserved for an elite group.

This distinction becomes ludicrous in view of the types of control patients often chosen by selection committees of psychoanalytic institutes for the purpose of teaching candidates in training how to conduct classical analysis. From conversations with colleagues, my own experience was not particularly atypical. My first patient was an active homosexual who heard persecutory voices. Another patient displayed sociopathic behavior and had a serious drinking problem which periodically led to homicidal rages. Of course the patients did not reveal these features when initially interviewed, but rather convinced the interviewer that they had qualities characteristic of the transference neuroses. However, despite these patients' serious underlying disturbances, both they and I survived the control analyses.

In the clinical setting outside the training context of psychoanalytic institutes, we sometimes encounter similar situations. When colleagues and I used data on patients suffering from characterological problems to support our technical recommendations, we were criticized by other analysts for having given the primitive elements of the psyche too much emphasis. In their judgment, what we witnessed stemmed from the oedipal level. These analysts could not accept our frame of reference.

The data that we receive from patients in psychoanalysis are never absolute and can lead to different formulations, depending on our perspectives and viewpoints. To arrive at a meaningful decision about whether a patient is oriented at an oedipal, pregenital, or presymbiotic level, we must have considerable information. In view of the types of patients who seek analysis, we have to sharpen our focus in order to determine whether we are dealing primarily with ego defects or with the outcome of repression and other defenses evoked by intrapsychic conflicts.

For example, some years ago I treated a patient who I believed suffered from an ego defect. To my mind, this young lady literally did not know how to mother. Before becoming pregnant, she insisted that there was nothing special about having children—any animal could have them. When she was pregnant, she read many books about child rearing as a person reads "how to" books in order to pursue a new hobby or a vocation. However, like the novice who has not started a pursuit early in life and made it part of his or her familiar world, she found such manuals difficult to understand. This was especially striking because she was very intelligent and capable of understanding technical and complex literature.

After her baby was born, she became utterly exhausted while taking care of him. She had no breast milk, so she bottle fed him. Feeding began early in the morning and ended late at night because she was so clumsy in preparing the formula and washing the bottles that it took all of her time between feedings. She felt similarly awkward relating to her son: she did not know what to "say" to him. She was afraid that he was not comfortable in her arms, and she had no idea how to play with him. She was astonished when a friend started playing "peek-a-boo" with him and claimed that she had never seen this game before.

In view of the unavailability of her own mother, and her inability to mother and to perform other related activities, I concluded that she suffered from an ego defect—a relative absence of a maternal introject. This defect was analogous to a person not knowing how to perform a particular function for which he or she has never acquired the necessary skills. For example, a person who speaks only English would find it awkward to communicate and relate in a society where only Sanskrit is spoken. Another patient with such a defect summarized his dilemma by stating that he lived in a world of calculus complexity, but he had only an arithmetic mentality. These patients had "lacunae," or inadequacies, in their psychic structures that made some important adaptations difficult, if not impossible, to achieve.

Some psychoanalysts have challenged these formulations about structural defects with the conjecture that my data could be explained on the basis of repression. This explanation would place my patient on a higher structural level, indicating that she really knew how to mother, but because of some guilt induced by oedipal rivalry with her mother, she had to repress this capacity. The explanation is plausible, but where are the data that would support such an assumption?

From a methodological viewpoint, it is always more difficult to prove that something that is not visible exists than to assert that it does not exist at all. Freud knew this well when he struggled to prove the existence of the dynamic unconscious, but he was able to show evidence of the effects of the unconscious on observable behavior. He also had dreams to support his hypothesis.

While repressed material always returns in some form, my patient showed *no* evidence of an aptitude for mothering. The "peek-a-boo" game failed to strike a note of even remote familiarity. Furthermore, she never dreamed of herself as a mother and her baby never appeared in her dreams. Repressed material strives for expression, but there was never any indication of such a striving in this patient.

Thus, we see how a structural defect may give rise to an oedipal interpretation. There are many similar situations in which the final decision will depend on the clinical course, as well as the past history, of the patient. I have heard arguments against the formulation of structural defects in patients who later displayed classical catatonic symptoms and who needed months or years of hospitalization.

In other instances, the bizarreness of the material creates an eerie effect and forces us to think in terms of primitive mental states. The patient of a supervisee dreamed that she was holding a baby in her arms. The baby became smaller and smaller until it was the size of an insect. Then the mother pulled off its appendages and threw the child away. The supervisor emphasized that having a baby represented the patient's oedipal triumph, but since the baby was hurt at the end of the dream, it also portrayed the patient's ambivalence and guilt. What had failed to impress the supervisor was the bizarreness of the dream's manifest content.

It is difficult not to have some reaction to such strange material. However, given the chiefly psychodynamic orientation of psychoanalysts, it is not surprising that they have given relatively little attention to the manifest content of dreams. Freud recognized the importance of manifest dream content for patients with structural defects when he postulated that certain elements in their dreams may represent psychic structure; for example, a house may depict the ego. It reasonably follows that defective psychic structure will, to some extent, determine the gestalt of the dream and contribute to its bizarre qualities. This is an area that requires further exploration.

The contributors to this book present patients who are undisputed examples of primitive mental states; often their behavior appears bizarre. I doubt that many analysts would interpret upward and consider these patients to be typical of the common (or perhaps more accurately, uncommon) neuroses. These are regressed patients who, for the most part, have serious structural defects. Some years ago, the overriding clinical reaction would have been to dismiss them out of hand as unsuitable for psychoanalytic treatment. Even today, analytic work with such patients is the exception; the general rule is to reject them for analysis and to use some other form of treatment, especially drug therapy.

My own long experience with case conferences convinces me that the attitude toward prospective analytic patients is still judgmental. Although patients have to meet certain analyzability criteria and the decision to analyze seems to be based upon certain scientific principles, I often feel that rejection is the outcome of the therapist's personal antipathy toward the patient. Of course, analysts need not openly accept everybody or feel obligated to work with all forms of psychopathology; they have their preferences and limits of tolerance. However, it would be best not to postulate a clinical axiom about the general treatability of patients based on a personal prejudice.

The authors in this volume remain strictly in a clinical frame of reference, free of tendencies to make moral evaluations. Their decisions about treatability are based on their understanding of psychic structure and processes. They offer their patients an analytic setting and let the patients make the decision as to whether they should be analyzed. As this book demonstrates, it is amazing how frequently patients accept such an offer.

Rather than dealing with indications and contraindications, this volume focuses upon specific technical issues of particular types of psychopathology. Each author presents his or her unique interactions with regressed patients. Yet many of these clinical episodes will seem familiar, as they are typical of the psychoanalytic treatment of primitively fixated patients. This book does not directly address the classification of the treatment of these patients, e.g., whether they are receiving psychoanalysis proper or intensive, psychoanalytically based therapy. Instead, the focus is on the clinical work itself. However, I would like briefly to consider the questions of what constitutes psychoanalysis and how we can be effective in a psychoanalytic context.

There has been considerable controversy as to how the treatment interaction of severely regressed patients differs from that of classical psychoneurotic ones, the idea being that these differences would determine whether the therapist was actually conducting analysis. Transference immediately comes to mind.

Freud's position was based on what he considered the lack of transference in "nonanalyzable" patients. In fact, he used the criterion of absence or presence of transference to classify patients. He distinguished between the narcissistic neuroses and the transference neuroses.

Since Freud's time, there has been ample evidence that even very primitively fixated patients form a bond or relationship with their therapist which is determined by their psychopathology and traumatic infantile past. This bond can be thought of as transference. Those who dispute this notion point to patients with severe disturbances, such as autistic children, who seemingly have no capacity to form any kind of relationship with anyone, including a therapist.

Some years ago at a meeting of the American Psychoanalytic Association, I recall being criticized by a colleague for my use of the concept of transference. She believed that since my patient had feelings toward others in the outside world which were not directed toward me, he had not established a transference. (The patient in question had directed angry feelings toward an employer and was dependently affectionate toward me.) According to this colleague, in order for a reaction to qualify as transference, *all* of the patient's feelings have to be directed toward the analyst. There can be no splitting. I reiterate the issue that I raised then: if my colleague was correct, transference can only be directed toward whole objects. But if transference, as defined, is also an archaic, infantile response based upon primary-process elements, how can such feelings be projected on whole objects? A primitive feeling at best would be associated with part objects; therefore all transferences would involve split objects. Some of the contributors to this book describe transferences—if that is still what we want to call them— which antedate object relations. In fact, Chapter 10 deals specifically with autistic children who have never been able to relate to external objects.

The authors present patients who bring the infantile world into the treatment relationship. Early preverbal orientations are re-enacted with the therapist. Whether we call these interactions "transference" is not particularly important. The therapeutic process proceeds in a fashion similar to that which has been postulated for the transference neuroses. It may seem to be enormously different because, instead of focusing upon sexual drives and oedipal triangles, these patients concentrate on issues of psychic survival and use archaic defenses such as denial and massive withdrawal. Still, in many instances, patients can be dealt with on an interpretative basis.

Not all interpretations are necessarily verbal ones. Regressed patients may derive considerable security from the knowledge that someone has understood them. This may be an experience they have never had before. Patients can be understood at levels that go beyond intellectual comprehension and verbal expression. Chapters 1, 3, 8, and 10 demonstrate how this occurs during crucial periods of treatment.

Insofar as patients reveal a need or a defect to the analyst, their reactions have a transference element. Although these patients may appear superficially withdrawn, they are intensely involved in the therapeutic relationship. Since they have few, if any, emotional involvements in the outside world, they invest heavily in the treatment relationship.

Regressed patients' intense need for therapy may be overwhelming and frightening. Furthermore, their fear of being traumatically rejected once again may cause them to pull back and not reach out for or respond to helpful ministrations. Nevertheless, they often have some hope that the treatment setting can provide them with the holding environment they so desperately need. This hope, minimal though it may be, creates transference readiness and, later, an intense attachment to the therapy.

This investment in the treatment is expressed in different ways and eventually leads to the creation of a relationship that recapitulates the infantile trauma. When it acquires some degree of organization, it becomes manifest as a repetition compulsion with some modifications. Patients repeat a past trauma but experience it as something current. Consequently, therapists usually confine their interpretations to the present interaction, stressing immediate feelings and attitudes, rather than making a genetic interpretation.

Since the treatment occupies more and more of the patients' life space, the analytic setting gains in importance. The analyst has to maintain the analytic setting and not let it become submerged in the infantile setting that patients may externalize into the consultation room. At such times, interpretations may consist of defining the analytic setting, usually attitudinally rather than directly. By implicitly emphasizing their interest in understanding the patients' thought processes, by not taking sides in patients' ambivalent struggles, and by not reacting to the content of patients' material, therapists show patients that they are worthy of understanding, that they do not have to elicit either horror or rage. Analysts should neither share their patients' hopelessness and misery nor feel compelled to rescue patients who feel terrified and vulnerable. These general principles are explicitly detailed in the following chapters.

Maintaining the analytic setting means establishing a holding environment. It represents an attempt to create a holding environment de novo for patients, since they never had such a security-inducing support in infancy. In very severe cases, some would advocate literally holding the patient to make up for an early deficit in the mothering relationship. However, with the exception of experiences with children, the following chapters do not record any treatment moments in which the therapist felt that it would be therapeutic to hold the patient. Furthermore, in thirty years of practice I have never touched a patient except to shake hands on rare occasions.

In analytic treatment, holding has to be symbolic even if the patient is not yet able to symbolize effectively. Otherwise, the analyst becomes immersed in the content of the psychopathology, and the infantile environment becomes dominant and replaces the analytic frame of reference. Analysts may feel patients' agitation within themselves and literally try to soothe patients because they themselves feel disrupted. When analysts hold patients under such circumstances, they actually are trying to contain their own disruptive excitement, which may have erotic overtones. Countertransference reactions are always significant, but in the treatment of severely regressed patients they are especially important.

Obviously, therapists cannot prevent themselves from reacting to such patients with disruptive feelings. What they can do is examine their responses constantly and distinguish between those that are chiefly motivated by their needs and those that are mainly the outcome of their patients' needs. Breaches in the analytic relationship are more apt to occur in the treatment of primitively fixated patients because the latter are especially adept at provoking therapists by forcing them to get in touch with the primitive parts of their own psyches. Many therapists have avoided delving into the deeper, more archaic elements of their characters by confining their work to patients with relatively intact psychic structures.

Often breaches in the analytic relationship become the crucial focal points of treatment, teaching both patients and therapists a good deal more about themselves. While these situations are unpremeditated and transient, there are occasions when patients want to maintain the breach and not let therapists return to the analytic frame of reference. Then we may be faced with an impasse and a psychotic transference.

What specifically is meant by a breach in this context? Breaches are situations in which the analyst, whether internally motivated or provoked by a patient, is forced to abandon the observational frame of reference of psychoanalysis and become involved directly in the patient's world. Holding a patient, as just discussed, would constitute such a breach. Feeling anxious about, protective of, or murderously angry toward a patient are familiar examples of nonanalytic reactions. To act on such feelings would represent an analytic breach, which with some patients is unavoidable. For example, a psychotic transference stimulates uncomfortable reactions in all analysts, although the amount of disruption it creates will depend upon the individual therapist's character and experience.

As good psychoanalytic treatment is nonjudgmental, so are the discussions of these issues in the following chapters. The authors frankly reveal their experiences and dilemmas, knowing that there is nothing unique about them. The reader who has had experiences similar to those presented in this book—and I conjecture there are many—should feel reassured to know that there are others who are working with the same clinical problems. Treatment with primitively fixated patients is trying and painful, as well as exciting and rewarding. Often we feel hopeless about the outcome. Sometimes we fail to reach such patients; but when we succeed, we experience the unique satisfaction that comes from knowing that we have helped others to begin to realize their potential as human beings.

P.L.G.

CONTRIBUTORS

Gerald Adler, M.D.   Training and Supervising Analyst, Boston Psychoanalytic Institute; Director of Medical Student Education, Department of Psychiatry; Coordinator of Psychotherapy Training, Massachusetts General Hospital; Lecturer in Psychiatry, Harvard Medical School.

L. Bryce Boyer, M.D.   Associate Director, Psychiatric Residency Training, Herrick Hospital and Medical Center, Berkeley.

Theodore L. Dorpat, M.D.   Clinical Professor of Psychiatry, University of Washington Medical School, Seattle.

Rudolph Ekstein, Ph.D.   Training and Supervising Analyst, Los Angeles Psychoanalytic Institute; Training and Supervising Analyst, Southern California Psychoanalytic Institute; Clinical Professor of Medical Psychology, University of California, Los Angeles.

Martin Fields, M.D.   Staff Member, Barclay Hospital, Chicago; private practice.

Alfred Flarsheim, M.D. (deceased).   Clinical Associate Professor of Psychiatry, University of Illinois College of Medicine; Professor of Psychiatry, Garrett Theological Seminary at Northwestern University; Consultant, Orthogenic School, University of Chicago.

Seymour Friedman, M.D.   Senior Faculty Member, Los Angeles Psychoanalytic Institute.

Peter L. Giovacchini, M.D.   Clinical Professor of Psychiatry, University of Illinois College of Medicine, Chicago.

Léon Grinberg, M.D.   Training Analyst, Madrid Provisional Psychoanalytic Association.

James S. Grotstein, M.D.   Training and Supervising Analyst, Los Angeles Psychoanalytic Society and Institute.

John A. Lindon, M.D.   Training and Supervising Analyst, Los Angeles Psychoanalytic Institute; Associate Clinical Professor of Psychiatry, University of California at Los Angeles Medical School.

Margaret I. Little, M.R.C.S., L.R.C.P., M.R.C. Psych.   Training and Supervising Analyst Emeritus, British Psychoanalytic Society.

Hans Loewald, M.D.   Training and Supervising Analyst, Western New England Institute for Psychoanalysis; Clinical Professor Emeritus, Yale University Medical School.

William W. Meissner, S.J., M.D.   Training and Supervising Analyst, Boston Analytic Institute; Associate Professor of Psychiatry, Harvard Medical School.

Thomas H. Ogden, M.D.   Director of Psychiatric Inpatient Residency Training, Herrick Hospital and Medical Center, Berkeley.

Donald B. Rinsley, M.D., F.R.S.H. (Lond.)   Associate Chief for Education, Psychiatry Service, Colmery-O'Neill VA Medical Center, Topeka; Clinical Professor of Psychiatry, University of Kansas School of Medicine.

Juan Francisco Rodríguez-Perez, M.D.   Training and Supervising Analyst, Madrid Provisional Psychoanalytic Association.

Harold F. Searles, M.D.   Training and Supervising Analyst, Washington Psychoanalytic Institute.

Vamik D. Volkan, M.D.   Medical Director, Blue Ridge Hospital, University of Virginia, Charlottesville; Professor of Psychiatry, University of Virginia Medical Center.

Part I

General Theoretical and Technical Issues

1

STRUCTURAL PROGRESSION AND VICISSITUDES IN THE TREATMENT OF SEVERELY DISTURBED PATIENTS

Peter L. Giovacchini

OVERVIEW

In the past fifteen years, there have been tremendous changes in clinicians' attitudes about what types of patients are psychoanalytically treatable. During this period of exploration, our understanding of character structure and psychopathology has expanded significantly. Since Boyer and I published our first book (Boyer and Giovacchini 1967) dealing with the treatment of schizophrenic and characterological disorders, there have been many books and articles written about this area of psychopathology. Kernberg (1976) and Kohut (1971) in particular have received considerable attention.

Both Kernberg and Kohut have provided us with a coherent organization that defines the clinical situations they are observing and provides a conceptual rationale for treatment. I have already published my critical judgments of Kohut's ideas (Giovacchini 1979). Regarding Kernberg, I believe he presents a comprehensive and ordered theoretical model which he can use to formulate a diagnosis that will then allow him to institute an appropriate treatment regime. In this regard, he is similar to Freud, who, after having made a diagnostic assessment, could then determine whether the psychoanalytic method would be appropriate for the treatment of that patient. He is different, however, in that the diagnosis is made on the basis of the patient's responses to confrontation, clarification, and interpretation. Furthermore, even when Kernberg decides that classical analysis is inappropriate, he still retains many analytic principles in his treatment and relies heavily on the transference in the "here and now" rather than on genetic reconstructions.

Kernberg presents us with a synthesis of other theoretical systems and in an interesting fashion he has brought two psychoanalysts together who would have been surprised to learn that they have been wedded to each other. In a delicate and skillful fashion, Kernberg has created a conceptual system which combines Melanie Klein and Heinz Hartmann's frames of reference. The floor on which they both stand was, of course, constructed by Freud.

In spite of Kernberg's careful organization and concise style, I find him difficult to read. Perhaps he is too organized in that he borders on the pedantic. In my opinion, his language seems too abstract if our focus is to remain with the clinical interaction. True, he does, from time to time, tell us about his experiences with patients, but his formulations often ignore his involvement, his countertransference responses to the patient from which the clinician might reach valuable insights about psychopathology. Searles (1978), in particular, has lamented this lack in Kernberg's expositions.

Wong and Rinsley (1980) give us a pithy, accurate overview of the historical development and current status of borderline and narcissistic patients. Their overview indicates that when psychoanalysts attempt to go beyond phenomenological description, there is still a strong tendency to make new formulations fit with well-established ones. For example, regarding mental mechanisms, analysts frequently emphasize splitting, projection, and projective identification; concerning developmental fixation points, clinicians such as Masterson and Rinsley (1975) rely heavily on Mahler's rapprochement subphase of separation-individuation (Mahler et al. 1975).

While this tendency to view phenomena in terms of established systems—even combined systems, such as Kernberg has done—

may prove valuable, it is also possible that the old wine bottle, no matter how great the vintage, may not be appropriate for the new wine. Our need to cling to what we have been taught may interfere with our capacity to understand the true significance of what the patient is trying to tell us.

I am not advocating abandoning Freud's psychoanalytic concepts and therapeutic approach. Indeed, I find attempts such as those that stress the replacement of metapsychology with systems theory, information theory, or, recently, Schafer's (1976) action theory, too esoteric and not clinically useful. Freud's theories have sufficient fluidity to enable analysts to move in and out of the theoretical frame, and thus to further their clinical understanding. In his technical papers, Freud (1911–1915) recommended that analysts suspend concentrated attention and the need to make immediate formulations in order to maintain an evenly hovering attention, the counterpart to the patients' free associations. Other approaches require a close attention to detail to determine where the patients' material fits into the preconceived system. However, many of these other frames of reference are too mechanistically constructed (e.g., information theory, which was designed to explain phenomena in a nonhuman environment in order to facilitate the construction of machines and computers) to permit the free-floating attention that Freud viewed as the sine qua non of analytic observation.

I believe we can make new formulations, involving both explanatory theory and technique, which represent extensions of Freud's theories. Still, these formulations, without necessarily introducing new terms as Kohut did, may not include familiar mental mechanisms or fixation points. They will retain and deal with concepts such as mental mechanisms, developmental stages, fixation, and regression, for example, but in these broad categories, we will find organizations that are not familiar to traditional psychoanalysis. Ego psychology, which Freud himself originated, is the first example of new concepts taken beyond the classical position. Similarly, in dealing with borderline and other patients, suffering from characterological psychopathology, we may have to go beyond what has been established; in this endeavor, we must avoid manipulating familiar frames of reference and/or introducing a new terminology without new ideas.

The study of the borderline state has become fashionable. The fact that it is an intriguing topic and has attracted the attention of many investigators, such as the contributors to this volume, can help augment our understanding of patients. Our investigations are the outcome of clinical necessity. However, the intense interest this subject has generated has also led to considerable confusion. Some question the very existence of the borderline state while many others dispute how it is to be defined.

Diagnosis is important because we need to establish what entities we are discussing. Elsewhere (Giovacchini 1979) I have proposed a nosological schema based upon a sequence of developmental fixation points, specific adaptive patterns, and even a tendency to provoke particular types of transference-countertransference constellations. Still, too much preoccupation with diagnosis can constrict us, involve us in useless pedantic controversy, and prevent us from exploring basic clinical issues that highlight analysts' dilemmas, confusion, and, in some instances, agitation.

BASIC CLINICAL ISSUES

Classification of the treatment of patients with structural defects is a basic clinical issue that has yet to be resolved. It is not clear whether the technical innovations required to treat such patients fall within the realm of psychoanalysis. We cannot resolve this issue until we can agree on what constitutes psychoanalysis as a treatment method, based on our expanded concepts about psychopathology.

Many of us agree that analysis mainly, or perhaps exclusively, involves the analysis of the transference, which is achieved through the vehicle of interpretation, beginning at the surface and proceeding downward into the more id-oriented layers of the personality. Precisely how this process works is still largely unknown. Though Freud (1914b) wrote about the working-through process, he dealt with generalities; this lack of sufficient detail must have contributed to his eventual dissatisfaction with the therapeutic aspects of psychoanalysis (Freud 1937). I believe that an understanding of the processes and transference-countertransference aspects of the treatment of borderline and other primitively fixated patients will teach us how psychoanalysis leads to the resolution of psychopathology. Whereas Freud wrote of the lifting of repression and the secondary-process elaboration of previously unconscious and primary-process dominated material, with our patients, we focus on the repetition of traumatic infantile elements and the healing of ego defects by the acquisition of new psychic structures. Are these objectives sufficiently different that the latter treatment must be seen as lying outside the realm of psychoanalysis?

Some clinicians do not feel that such a separation has to be made. One compelling reason is that analysts working with primitively fixated patients rely heavily upon the transference. In fact, stepping outside of the transference with such patients—that is, making an interpretation unrelated to transference projections or becoming involved with the patients' reality—often has disastrous consequences, with complications much more serious than might occur with better-structured psychoneurotic patients. I have been so impressed by these patients' demands for strict adherence to analytic principles that years ago I concluded that the treatment of choice for borderline patients was psychoanalysis (Boyer and Giovacchini 1967).

Nevertheless, it is important to reconsider some of our actions toward these patients and to ask ourselves if we behave differently with them than we do with patients who traditionally have been thought of as good candidates for analysis. For example, how do we respond when these patients demand things that we believe are "against the rules" or that make us uncomfortable for other reasons? Our responses to patients' demands are the outcome of many factors that go beyond purely technical issues. Beginning therapists, eager to build up their practice, may be very flexible since they do not want to lose patients. Older, more established therapists may not feel the same pressing need and may not want to treat certain patients. Thus, personal idiosyncrasies may make therapists unreceptive to patients with certain types of psychopathology; this is often the case with borderline and narcissistic patients.

Our reluctance to make therapeutic modifications sometimes makes it difficult to determine what is analytically feasible. It is easy to rationalize not wanting to give in to a patient's demands: we make a technical formulation that supports our reluctance rather than recognizing that for personal reasons we do not want to treat that patient on the terms he demands. However, in spite of personal motives, our formulations may be technically correct.

For example, on the telephone a middle-aged attorney indicated that he was very eager to be analyzed by me. Even then, I noticed a compulsive, concrete approach that made me wonder whether I wanted to get involved with him, given the difficulty of analyses with such patients and my own heavy schedule. Nevertheless, he insisted that he wanted to see me and agreed to wait whatever period I specified for an appointment. I finally agreed to see him in several months.

I will briefly summarize his demands and how I responded to him. I let him sit up during the first two sessions both because he had a need to go into endless detail about his background and because I didn't want to use the couch as a means of interfering with his recitation—that is, I didn't want to use the couch (or any element of the analytic setting, including interpretation) as a prohibition.

In any case, during the third session, he lay down on the couch and seemed eager to begin what he considered to be the formal elements of analysis. He talked freely for about half an hour and then he began to ask questions. At first, they were didactic questions about the nature of analysis, its rationale, and its theoretical foundations. In the context of a teaching seminar, they would have been fairly sophisticated, appropriate questions although many were framed in mechanistic terms. Then he asked questions about himself, firing them at me in the manner of a prosecuting attorney. I felt no inclination to answer his questions or to investigate his need to press me with such demanding questions. I also remembered how insistent he had been that *I* treat him; he had refused to accept a referral. I was beginning to find him oppressive, yet I did not want to throw his questions back at him, make an interpretation, or ask him why he was behaving as he was because any of these measures would have been attempts to stop his inquisition. I then decided that if I did not respond to him or, better still, if I could feel free to respond or not respond to him, I could maintain my analytic equanimity and view him as an interesting patient rather than an annoying burden. The patient felt an increasing exasperation at my silence and finally sat up, almost screaming his insistence that I summarize exactly where we were in the analysis at that moment and what progress, if any, we had made. He strongly implied that he expected progress. I replied that if I were to treat him, he would have to lie down; I added that since our time was up, I would see him at our next session. The patient left visibly angry and confused.

Afterwards, I reviewed my reactions and our interaction. I knew that I had found the patient's behavior offensive, but I also reminded myself that he was a patient and because of his character structure and defensive adaptations, he probably could not behave otherwise. Most likely, he was revealing fundamental ego orientations that would have to surface in analysis. I asked myself how I could respond to him without feeling that I was abandoning analysis and how I could remain silent without feeling that I was creating a power struggle. I also wondered whether all my deliberations might prove to be unnecessary as he had acted so dissatisfied at the end of the last session that it seemed doubtful that he would return.

However, he did return and he continued to ask questions about analysis and to demand evaluations of his progress. His agitation mounted as I remained silent. I realized that my lack of response represented exactly what I wanted to avoid, a power struggle. Therefore, to calm him (since I felt his agitation was getting out of hand) and to feel more comfortable myself, I told him that, as an analyst, all I wished to do was analyze him. I would view all of his material as if it were phrased in declarative sentences. I would feel free to answer or not answer, not because of any personal peculiarity, but because I needed this freedom to function as his analyst. Of course, if he wanted a therapist who answered questions, made evaluations, or gave him whatever he believed he should have, he was perfectly free to do as he pleased. It was his choice. I would preserve an analytic setting to which he could return if he decided to leave now. He chose to stay and did not feel impelled to change the content or style of his material because of this exchange. I, too, continued in my usual fashion and the analysis proceeded well.

I have had similar experiences with other patients who did not choose to remain in analysis. They sought other forms of treatment, However, in all such instances, I made it clear that I would preserve the analytic setting for them. Many of these patients did return, sometimes years later.

The example I have just given emphasizes adherence to the psychoanalytic method; the patient was not allowed to sabotage it. If I had modified my approach with this patient, I would have been abandoning analysis and I doubt that I would have been able to return to it. I wish to contrast this situation with that of severely disturbed patients who require modifications before analysis can be instituted. These modifications must be integrated into the analytic process. The following examples constitute general accommodations rather than specific responses.

A therapist whom I was supervising was treating a 24-year-old law student. The patient had seen ten different therapists since he had begun college, but he had left each one after a few sessions. The therapist saw this as a challenge and he was anxious to succeed in view of all the previous failures. However, for a person dedicated to the psychoanalytic method, this patient could be especially trying.

He introduced himself by stating that all he wanted was antidepressant drugs, meaning that he did not wish to discuss personal issues. The therapist did not immediately react, but felt puzzled, as the patient knew that he was dedicated to the psychoanalytic method and not psychopharmacology. Furthermore, the patient expected his session to last the full length of an analytic session rather than just the few minutes required to write a prescription and give the appropriate instructions and warnings. Although the therapist felt frustrated and wanted to dismiss him, he agreed to try it the way the patient demanded.

At first we tried to understand what the demand for drugs and limiting the treatment to just prescribing meant to the patient. We concluded that the patient had to establish control of the treatment relationship before he could allow himself to regress and reveal his helpless and vulnerable parts. We also formulated that the patient was imposing structure, as defined by limits such as excluding any personal material, with synthesizing potential so that he would not be submerged in the chaos of the amorphous elements of primitive ego states experienced as painful, disruptive agitation. In any case, we were trying to understand how the patient's initial needs might be preconditions for analysis.

The therapist prescribed imipramine and intended to confine his contact with the patient to discussing its pharmacological effects. However, it was understandably difficult to spend the entire session on this topic. The patient spontaneously began to reveal various facets of his current problems and gave a fairly comprehensive survey of his past life. By the time the therapist contacted me for supervision, the patient was no longer taking the antidepressant drug because it had had no effect on him.

The therapy continued on an analytic basis. It had its stormy moments, as might be expected for patients such as this young man, who had a borderline character structure with depressive features.

I tried to put myself in the therapist's position and wondered what I would do if this patient had come to me. It would depend upon many factors, including nontechnical ones, but I probably would have not given in to his demands. I was surprised when the therapist told me that he had asked two analysts who claim to adhere strictly to the classical position what they would have done and they replied that they would have prescribed drugs. Apparently, they did not consider such flexibility antithetical to analysis.

Now we have arrived at the final question, for which there is no absolute answer: Would it have been possible to conduct this analysis without any deviation, even a temporary one? At first we concluded that it would not have been possible. The patient's experiences with ten previous therapists—although we know little about these relationships—seemed to reinforce our conclusion. Later, however, we came to the startling realization that the patient probably would have remained in psychoanalytic treatment without any initial modifications. He revealed that part of him wanted the therapist to assert his superiority over drugs; that is, the patient wanted the therapeutic relationship to be a synthesizing force more powerful than drugs, strong enough to enable the analyst to survive the impact of the patient's projections.

We cannot be certain how to react when patients suddenly confront us with situations that we perceive as threatening to our analytic identity. I have referred to two interactions in which patients demanded a totally nonanalytic setting. In the first instance, I did not bend and we were able to conduct analysis; in the second case, the supervisee was flexible and again analysis was possible. Obviously, the dilemmas these patients created was related to their psychopathology, but they were not related to basic survival needs. By contrast, I believe that when we deal with certain borderline patients, real survival needs may be at stake and may necessitate certain relaxations in analytic standards.

Although many patients cannot survive an analytic relationship without expressing or experiencing adaptations that are the defensive outcome of the vulnerability generated by ego defects, other patients may be able to separate those symptomatic manifestations that are unacceptable to the analyst from the analytic setting.

An example of the latter is two patients of mine who smoke during sessions. Although I now do not allow smoking in my office, these patients started treatment with me many years ago when I smoked and paid no particular attention to patients' smoking habits. Ashtrays were plentiful and patients could use them if they wished. The activity of smoking had become incorporated into the psychoanalytic ambience and was a natural activity. Smoking became one of the soothing elements of the analytic setting. The therapy of both patients had reached the point of termination and treatment was discontinued on a satisfactory basis. Years later, long after I had given up smoking but they had not, they returned for further analysis. I was surprised, although I should not have been, when they lit cigarettes at the beginning of the session. I hurriedly unearthed an ashtray because I knew they could not have remained in treatment with me if at this late date I reversed my earlier position and imposed a "no smoking" prohibition. These patients, who had many borderline characteristics, did not have the flexibility to adapt to the new rules; thus, if treatment were to be instituted, I had to be flexible. However, adding cigarettes to the analytic setting did not change the setting fundamentally. By contrast, in the two cases discussed earlier, the patients attempted to replace the analytic setting with another type of interaction.

As a final example, I will discuss two female patients who attempted to modify, rather than eradicate, the psychoanalytic setting. These patients, who could be classified as narcissistic types, insisted on sitting up during their analytic hours. Freud (1914a) described such patients long ago, stating that these usually attractive women were in need of constant admiration and could only make narcissistic object choices.

My patients were attractive women who capitalized on their appearance to manipulate men. They demanded continuous attention from me at all times. Lying on the couch would mean losing eye contact, and thus, my involvement or admiration. Therefore they insisted on sitting up.

They sought treatment primarily out of their need for narcissistic gratification. As they grew older, they felt they were less effective in extracting from life what they needed. Basically, they felt empty and lonely; they attempted to fill their inner void by eliciting male confirmation of their desirability.

I decided to let one of these patients sit up, but not the other. In retrospect, I can speculate as to what was involved in this decision. The patient I allowed to sit up impressed me as being very fragile. She looked haggard and worn out and at times seemed on the edge of panic. I felt sorry for her; it seemed that the world that had supported her was crumbling all around her, abetted by the aging process. Rather than feeling manipulated, I felt I was responding to her helplessness.

With the other patient, my reactions were entirely different. She was imperious and made me feel as if I had to pay homage to her. I definitely felt manipulated and my first impulse was to reject her as a patient. Nevertheless, I was aware that underneath her icy veneer, this frustrated, angry woman was a vulnerable little girl who felt compelled to perform in order to be recognized as a person. During her childhood, others had used her attractiveness and precocious talents to enhance themselves. She was still being used in that fashion, particularly by her father. Now she was exacting a price, but she was feeling the absence of real emotional sustenance.

Despite my ambivalence toward this patient, in the initial session I decided that I could focus on the needy parts of the patient and not feel manipulated as long as I did not accede to her demand to sit up. Therefore, I insisted that she use the couch. The patient was furious at me, but in the second session she lay down on the couch.

I can see now that I was responding to different levels of these patients' character structure. With the first patient, I responded to her inability to hold a mental representation of me and to maintain a synthesis of her self-representation unless I was in her visual field and she felt my attention focused on her. With the other patient, I felt that she was trying to use me as she had been used and I did not believe I could maintain an analytic setting without certain formal conditions such as the use of the couch.

In view of the second patient's protests, I might have predicted that the analysis would end soon. However, in a manner reminiscent of the patient who demanded evaluations, she rather quickly accepted lying down and was able to understand that I needed her to do so in order to be able to analyze her.

By contrast, the first patient never formed an analytic relationship. She derived considerable support from the treatment and was able to feel more secure in the arrangement she had with her husband. They lived under the same roof but in separate bedrooms, and she was able to accept this. Still, with me there was very little regression and there were very few transference manifestations. She wanted to maintain our interaction at a conversational, advice-giving level. After several months, the patient felt satisfied; there was no reason to continue seeing me. It is difficult to predict whether I would have been able to get her into analysis if I had insisted on constructing the setting as I had wished. Of course, I had gone along with her in the hope that this would facilitate the formation of an analytic relationship, but it turned out otherwise.

With the exception of the patient who demanded I answer his questions and the one who wanted drugs instead of analysis, the clinical examples I have discussed involve additions to or alterations of the analytic setting rather than the eradication of the latter. Some of these patients did not absolutely require modifications to survive an analytic relationship. In fact, in the last example, giving in to the patient's request did not lead to the desired result.

The treatment of borderline and other primitively fixated patients teaches us that we have to maintain flexibility to be able to construct an analytic framework. On the other hand, in some instances we must remain inflexible and refuse to make compromises. All this does *not* mean that analysis is contraindicated or that we have to modify the analytic method. Unlike the clinical issues I have just discussed, the following issues, which relate specifically to the transference-countertransference axis, are indispensable technical maneuvers required for the survival of the analysis.

PRIVATION AND THE NEED TO BE "UNREASONABLE"

I will now turn to difficult treatment situations that may severely strain our capacity to preserve the analytic setting. As analysts, we believe that, within limits, patients should be provided with an ambience that will allow them to express associations and feelings that are manifestations of their psychopathology. Under the pressure of the repetition compulsion, they will create a milieu in analysis that is similar to the traumatic infantile environment. However, as we will see, patients will also attempt to make themselves less helpless and vulnerable as they repeat their initial traumatic situations. As Freud (1920) pointed out, repetition can represent an attempt at mastery. This can be done by converting an early passive experience into an active one; that is, patients who through the course of development have acquired adaptive and defensive techniques that they did not have during infancy may, during the transference repetition, use these defenses against assaultive and threatening imagos that may have been projected into the analyst.

Although the transference repetition is essential for analytic resolution, in some cases its very nature seems to preclude analysis. This is true of patients who assert the right to be "unreasonable," and, looked at in a certain light, this is reasonable but it can be hard to keep that in mind.

For example, from the outset of treatment, a young, married patient could not tolerate the idea of my ever leaving the city, for whatever reason. During one of our first sessions, she told me that she needed me to be around; if I absolutely had to leave, she would have to know far ahead of time and even then the pain would be unbearable. I told her about my next trip, which was several months away, and she was both angry and anxious about it. As the time approached, she spent more and more time talking about my projected departure to the point that she talked about nothing else during the sessions two weeks before my trip. Although my absence would entail missing only one session, the patient was furious.

The same pattern continued, with her feelings gradually becoming less intense. I had not appreciated the full meaning of her anguish until the following incident occurred. At the time, I was seeing the patient daily, except for Sunday. Quite unexpectedly, I had to go out of town. I had not told the patient ahead of time since I myself did not know until the last minute. Furthermore, I saw no reason to tell her because it made no difference in our schedule. I would be leaving after her appointment on Saturday morning and would return Sunday evening. I also realized that I wanted to be spared her abuse.

When she came in for that Saturday morning session, she immediately asked me where I was going. I was dumbfounded and wondered how she knew. She replied that as I was better dressed than usual, I had something better to do than see her. Furthermore, I had the look of anticipation of someone who was going to be involved in an activity different from my usual routine. She then went on to lecture and scold me for not understanding that she simply could not tolerate my being away and, if I insisted on thwarting her, she had to know exactly where I would be. With exasperation, I retorted that her attitude required that I remain in one place twenty-four hours a day, seven days a week. She calmly replied, "Of course."

Somehow, her natural response forced me back into a therapeutic frame of reference. I realized that from her viewpoint she was quite reasonable. This was a woman whose structural defects made it difficult for her to form and hold mental representations without the reinforcement of the external object. The external percept of me in my office was one that she could structure in her memory system, but having me away from the familiar environment caused a decathexis of myself as an internal object representation. This loss, which was equated with infantile abandonment, could lead to uncontrollable rage and overwhelming terror.

She experienced both my departure and my return as painful. It is understandable that the loss of a mental representation would be painful. However, my return was at least as painful. Then my presence was felt as assaultive and intrusive. She found it difficult to form an internal object representation of me for two reasons. First, having lost what we might call the analytic mental representation, she no longer had any internal frame of reference that would permit her to integrate within her ego external percepts of the analytic interaction. Thus, she viewed me as a stranger and an intruder, much as infants react with stranger anxiety to people for whom they do not have corresponding internal object representations. In a sense, my presence was incomprehensible, since it took time and trust for it to be integrated into her ego system.

Second, the holding quality (Winnicott 1960b) of the analytic interaction was also lost. For the infant, the holding environment produced by primary maternal preoccupation (Winnicott 1956) is unwavering and constant. It surrounds the infant completely and is timeless. In fact, its continuity is assured because of its constancy. Any departure of the sustaining person is experienced by the infant as an irreparable breach of fundamental support. Even if this patient could accept my return, she would never feel secure that I would not abandon her again because of the unpredictable abandonments of her infantile environment.

Winnicott's concepts of privation and deprivation (Winnicott 1963) are also pertinent at this point. Simply stated, privation refers to an ego organization that has not internalized a satisfactory, gratifying nurturing experience. The infant does not have a mental representation of good maternal care. Deprivation, on the other hand, assumes that there has been "knowledge" of gratification. In order to feel deprived, one has to know what it means to be gratified. Consequently, a person who experiences the frustration of deprivation must have had some endopsychic registration of relatively satisfactory nurture. Of course, there can never be total privation, as the infant cannot survive without some satisfactory nurture. Later, I will discuss the interplay between privation and deprivation, but now I wish to discuss the connection between partial privation and patients' "unreasonableness."

My patient frequently asserted her "right to be unreasonable." In her outside life, this often created problems. For example, once at a party she locked herself in the bathroom and refused to leave. On another occasion, she cut her blouse into strips and then locked herself in a closet. In such instances, she insisted on remaining in a setting where it was unreasonable to expect to stay indefinitely. The need to be unreasonable was eventually understood as a reaction to early ego levels characterized by privation. This privation caused her to seek some constancy in her life. Her inability to hold my mental representation also could be explained as the outcome of privation: I had come to represent the patient's nurturing source, which had no effective internal correspondent.

This patient made innumerable demands both within and outside of the analysis. She constantly wanted to be "given to." This usually meant asking for directions and advice as to how to run her life, but at times she even demanded instructions as to how she should feel. I sometimes had the impression that she was asking me to breathe for her, and once she brought me a dream in which I had supplied her with a respirator and was responsible for its operation. In the dream, I literally was breathing for her. She also had her friends constantly doing things for her (e.g., driving her around, feeding her lunch or dinner, shopping for her), but she never seemed to be satisfied. The patient recognized and stated that her needs were insatiable.

She reminded me of other patients who had described themselves as being "empty" and unable to fill the void they felt within themselves (Giovacchini 1975). These subjective states reflect the nature of the patients' self-representations and their comparative lack of psychic structure. Another patient, who was not as overt in her expression of voracious needs, summarized her psychic state in terms of privation. She stated that if one had never experienced gratification from a nurturing mother during infancy, it would require an immense amount of giving to make up for this primal deficiency. Together we were able to formulate the situation with an elementary mathematical analogy. If we wanted to convert zero into a quantity such as the number one, we would have to multiply it by infinity. That is, if we tried to get something out of nothing, we would have to fill in nothing with everything. In terms of psychic structure, this zero-infinity sequence expresses how the ego turns to the external world to cope with privation. The lack of internalization of satisfactory nurturing relationships creates an unbearable situation which can be experienced in different ways. Rather than feeling frustration (deprivation), which requires mental representations of at least partially satisfactory experiences, these patients describe an inner feeling of "disruptive emptiness." They are aware of their inability to be satisfied but may express this indirectly. For instance, some borderline patients describe an uncertainty as to whether they are alive or dead. The capacity to receive satisfaction and the sense of aliveness are related.

Most clinicians have "unreasonable" patients sometime during their careers, often when they are still residents or beginning practitioners. These patients constantly seem to intrude into the clinicians' lives, calling them on the telephone at all hours, and presenting them with endless emergencies and loud pleas for help. More often than not, there is no substance to their pressing despair and appeals. Therapists wind up feeling uncertain as how to begin to respond to these tremendously needy and demanding patients. Furthermore, such patients test therapists' tolerance to the utmost, creating mounting exasperation. These patients are "unreasonable" in that their needs are not only insatiable but incomprehensible. They need their therapists' immediate attention and constant presence.

Instinctual satisfaction and the endopsychic registration of satisfactory experiences lead to the acquisition of psychic structure that includes the establishment and further structuralization of needs.

Borderline patients' needs are imperfectly developed inasmuch as they suffer primarily from privation. Since they have little internalization of gratifying nurture, which includes all caretaking activities, basic needs such as discretely felt impulses do not become established and undergo emotional development. Some borderline patients complain of not knowing what they feel. They cannot distinguish inner sensations. Many of these patients literally do not know whether they are hungry, thirsty, have sexual feelings, or need to defecate or urinate. Instead of being aware of the inner source of their perceptions, they simply experience a general, vague sensation of discomfort. Thus, their demands represent an attempt to achieve responses that might help them define their needs. *To the outside world, this is puzzling because most of us are accustomed to the sequence of the need creating the response, rather than the response creating the need.* From our frame of reference, this sequence strikes us as "unreasonable," but for borderline patients fixated at early psychopathological levels of privation, it is eminently reasonable.

As infants, these severely disturbed patients experienced an unreasonable and unpredictable world. It was unreasonable in part, because it was unpredictable. This world was not ordered and organized around their earliest needs, which were under the dominance of circadian rhythms. In a sense, these infants did not know what to expect and consequently never developed the security necessary to contain feelings which then became painfully disruptive. For example, what should have been pleasurable excitement of anticipated gratification became chaotic agitation instead.

From one viewpoint, "unreasonable" patients are involved in a reconstructive process, although therapists may find it difficult to keep that in mind. First, these patients are trying to re-create an environment similar to their infantile environment, to *repeat* in the present the unreasonable ambience that surrounded them in infancy. However, as Freud (1920) pointed out, the repetition compulsion attempts to turn a passively experienced trauma into an active repetition in the service of mastery. "Unreasonable" patients intrude "unreasonableness" into the environment to prevent feeling assaulted by an unpredictable world. Thus, they feel less helpless and vulnerable as they attempt to gain psychic equilibrium. However, these attempts at mastery may not be apparent to recipients of patients' demands, who may perceive in patients' frenetic behavior a lack of any adaptive organization.

The demand that the therapist be constantly available can be examined further. Besides being determined by patients' inability to hold a mental representation without external reinforcement, it also represents an attempt to maintain continuity and to make the external world predictable. This is a reparative activity.

The patient who reacted violently when I took trips had never known continuity. Her early life was characterized by a series of abrupt events with no bridge or transition from one experience to another. As long as she could perceive herself as constantly with me, she would not lose my mental representation because I would always be there to reinforce it—there would be no discontinuity. In an inconstant world, events are experienced as a series of impacts. It is a confusing and unpredictable world. In many instances, "unreasonable" patients are trying to construct a predictable world.

A supervisee reported a patient who made his living by gambling and had amassed an immense fortune. He had had an extremely traumatic infancy that he remembered as being completely unpredictable. He described his parents as unpredictable hypocrites who would approach him in a kind, giving fashion and then give him a beating. He recalled several occasions when he was spanked after he had gone to bed and fallen asleep. He also stressed that frequently when he asked for something, he was violently rebuffed while at other times, when he least expected it, he would be lavished with gifts. However, there was no consistency to this pattern. He was not always given the opposite of what he wanted; on occasion, his parents would satisfy his requests. However, he never knew when this would occur.

In school, he was frequently attacked by other students but trained himself to be a good fighter. His teachers believed that he provoked them rather than being a helpless victim of circumstances. In view of the school's attitude and the number of scrapes he got into, he was labeled a sociopath and thought of himself in such terms.

The patient emphasized his extreme vigilance. He frequently spoke of one of his favorite films, a Pink Panther movie in which

Peter Sellers, as Inspector Clouseau, instructs his servant to attack him when he least expects it. The patient mentioned two particularly comical surprise attacks: in one, the detective opens the refrigerator door and the servant springs out at him, and in the other, the detective is attacked while he is in bed with a beautiful blonde.

The patient's profession suited him admirably. Gambling represented the infantile environment, an exciting and unpredictable world full of risks. He had been able to make an unpredictable world a predictable one. He had taken all of the excitement out of gambling and had minimized the risks. He had practically a photographic memory and was a good mathematician. He thoroughly understood the theory of probability and knew what the odds of winning were for every game. He played very few games—only dice, poker, and blackjack. As he described it, gambling was not fun, but rather, hard and extremely profitable work. He did not play regularly because he lived in Chicago and had to make periodic trips to Las Vegas to earn his living. He was wealthy but continued to gamble because something within "drove" him to do so, something which he perceived as a need to restore his self-esteem and to feel "replenished and safe."

"Unreasonable" patients' attempts to repeat and cope with their unpredictable infantile environment make them difficult to treat, as their adaptations are disruptive to the analytic setting. They are generally disruptive in the external world as well, where they may be angrily rejected. We may make certain adaptations in the analytic setting to allow analysis with these patients to proceed. However, first we have to understand how their particular psychopathology distorts the developmental process and inevitably creates some specific transference-countertransference interactions.

PRIVATION AND THE
PSYCHOTIC TRANSFERENCE

As has been repeatedly stressed, borderline patients suffer primarily from ego defects rather than intrapsychic conflicts, Kernberg (1976) discusses their structural problems in the context of separation-individuation and traces their difficulties to traumatic early object relationships. In view of many of the subtle but serious dilemmas that occur in the therapeutic interaction, I believe that we should explore much earlier relationships and levels of psychic development. Inasmuch as regression in treatment recapitulates primitive ego states to some degree, these interactions can be best studied in a therapeutic context, by a case example.

The patient, a 30-year-old married woman, had been bedridden for several months previous to our first appointment. She lay in bed all day, moaning and reproaching herself for her ineptness. She literally tore her hair as she wailed and lamented. Many drugs had been prescribed for her: antianxiety agents, tranquilizers, tricyclic antidepressants, and M.A.O. inhibitors. She was addicted to the degree that she felt she would "fall apart" without them.

When I first saw her, I knew nothing about the circumstances of her decompensation and was able to piece them together only after several years of treatment. Briefly, an aunt who literally had been directing the patient's life remarried and left the city, leaving her to rely on her own resources. The patient's almost total dependency on this aunt had been far from obvious and those close to her did not recognize how meaningful and life sustaining that relationship had been for her. She started treatment in a noisy, stormy fashion, pleading with me to help her, to save her. However, there was no substance to her questions and demands. Even if I had been inclined to respond, I would not have known how. The helplessness of this type of patient, which causes the analyst to feel helpless as well, is based on a lack of memory traces of satisfactory nurturing experiences—in a word, privation.

This patient revealed that her mother had had a postpartum psychosis that led to long-term hospitalization immediately after the patient's birth. She had been raised by a series of cruel or indifferent maids and never had seen her mother. Her father was seldom home and unconcerned about her welfare.

Probably she had been somewhat autistic during childhood. She had been unable to remain in school and had been sent to a residential treatment center. She had total amnesia about her life prior to early adolescence. Others told her that she had not talked until she was seven years old and that she had totally withdrawn from her surroundings, not relating to adults or peers. Her widowed aunt had entered the picture when the patient was hospitalized for severe anorexia nervosa. She had taken her niece out of the hospital, installed her in her house, and become her vigilant caretaker.

The sequence of this patients' life events was to some measure repeated in her analysis with me. For example, while being cared for by maids, she reportedly had been uncontrollable. As an infant, she had cried all the time and could not be soothed. Each maid had remained only a short time. After infancy, the patient had become somewhat autistic. During the first period of treatment, the patient cried and screamed inconsolably, recapitulating the noisiness of infancy. This was followed by a period with autistic features.

In early sessions, she thrashed around on the couch and frequently made sudden jerky movements that resembled convulsions. Like the "unreasonable patients" described earlier, she demanded to be filled up, complaining that she felt empty, that she had a void that never could be filled. In view of the depth of her regression, her drug addiction, and her primitive, chaotic behavior, I began thinking in terms of privation, the lack of a coherently organized nurturing matrix.

As the mother's nurturing and soothing are optimally adapted to the child's needs, the child develops a sense of continuity organized around a nurturing matrix. The infant's bodily processes vary in intensity according to rhythmical automatized patterns known as circadian rhythms. The mother smoothly relates to the child at certain peaks in this cycle, responding to metabolic needs by furnishing nurture and organizing tension by soothing. Thus, there is a harmonious blending between the various phases of the biological cycle which leads to a sense of continuity, the development of a time sequence, and the establishment of a nurturing matrix.

The nurturing matrix is first experienced internally as an organizing force that prevents the child's anticipatory excitement, as it is produced by emergent needs, from becoming disruptive agitation. This excitement later is felt as pleasurable.

These processes occur prior to the stage of symbiosis, where they are further elaborated. As I have described elsewhere (Giovacchini 1979), the presymbiotic organizing and containing nurturing matrix and the symbiotic transitional situation and object (Winnicott 1953) are both part of a hierarchical developmental sequence that is important for our understanding of specific clinical situations and problems.

This patient's thrashing and jerky movements at the beginning of treatment made me think she lacked psychic as well as physical coordination. The various parts of her mind did not seem to be arranged as a cohesive whole; rather, there seemed to be little connection between primitive and more advanced levels of her personality. The fact that she experienced her feelings as concrete physical impacts accounted for her bizarre physical movements on the couch.

For the moment, I want to make a clinical digression in order to describe another patient whose movements on the couch were even more bizarre and dramatic, although in his case we were able relatively easily to explain what was happening.

A middle-aged stockbroker would unexpectedly make violent movements and shout while on the couch. He would be calmly talking and then suddenly grimace, twist his body and scream as if he were in great pain. Often he would bring his arms in front of his face as if he were warding off a blow or he would grunt and wince as he felt its painful impact.

I questioned him as to whether he felt that someone or some external force were attacking him. He acknowledged that it seemed that way but he believed that the impacts he felt were coming from within himself. The event began with a feeling which, as he was in the process of putting it into words, would "explode" and he experienced it as a concrete blow. If he grunted and wrestled with it he could shape it into words but then it would be inert and lifeless. When it "exploded" the feeling never acquired a verbal form and consequently could not be communicated except in a concrete motoric fashion.

There is much evidence from this patient's past which indicates that because of severe infantile traumas consisting of both abandonment and confrontation with parental violent feelings, he developed ego areas of precocious functioning (Bergman and Escalona 1949, Boyer 1956). However, there was no smooth connection between the primitive relatively unstructured parts of his personality and those that had been prematurely structuralized.

Another patient who unexpectedly would make violent movements and shout while on the couch imagined that he had a machine that would instantaneously tranform feelings into concrete actions. He believed that his feelings would break the machine by creating uncontrollable actions. As he talked, I had a fantasy of two electrodes; potential electric energy built up in one until it created a spark strong enough to jump to the other electrode. I asked him if this were an appropriate metaphor and he stated that it was practically identical to the way he envisioned his reactions. He compared himself to a Van der Graaf generator in which an electrical charge would increase in intensity until it jumped the gap as a spark.

This metaphor was apt for the first patient as well; both patients showed a discontinuity between various levels of the psychic apparatus. The nurturing matrix, which organizes and contains primitive excitement, undergoes a hierarchical structuralization leading to continuity with more highly integrated and cohesive psychic levels. For these patients, feelings produced at a visceral level were (Freud 1915) immediately transported into words without any intermediary modulation. The effect for both my patients was disruptive. Rather than smoothly traversing the psychic apparatus from physiological to structured psychic levels, feelings built up in intensity at lower levels and then, in a quantum jump, burst into areas that should have been dominated by the secondary process.

These patients, in some ways, remind me of the few manic-depressive patients I have interviewed, although there are many differences. The manic-depressive, in the manic phase, appears to be operating on raw energy. It seems as if his actions and thoughts are governed by unbound energy. Similar to the gap which is traversed by a spark, higher and lower levels of the psyche give the impression of being directly connected without any modulating bridge between them. Perhaps lithium furnishes such modulation, but according to some patients it "deadens feelings" rather than simply toning them down and making them manageable but still pleasurable.

Returning to the case example, my patient continued to complain and make vociferous but vague demands to which I could not respond. The context of her verbalizations seemed as amorphous and unfocused as her behavior in the outside world and on my couch. I gradually gathered the impression that my inability to provide her with the help for which she clamored was the result of her manifesting an ego state that reflected privation. She could not structuralize and communicate her need to be helped in a way that was comprehensible. To answer relevantly one has to understand the question. This patient did not even know the question, let alone the answer that would constitute a proper response. She did not have memory traces of gratifying experiences that would enable her to turn to the outside world for structured help.

In spite of many months of constant agitation, she kept all of her appointments and indicated that she was eager to come. If for some reason I had to cancel an appointment or change the time, she became even more upset. My comments were confined to her need to expose the vulnerable sides of herself to me, to get in touch with painful areas of her personality. I felt that this was not much of a contribution in view of her overwhelming and catastrophic tension, but she gained some calm as the months went by. Once she was able to make a remark indicating that I could be a soothing influence.

Her dreams confirmed that she was able, in a minimal way, to be soothed by me, but being soothed also had its traumatic aspects. For example, she dreamed of being in a large baronial hall. Hundreds of people were milling around as a sumptuous buffet dinner was served. In the southern corner of the room, a small chamber orchestra played very pleasant music. She found the music peaceful and as she listened to it she felt tranquil. At the same time, she was seized by ravenous hunger, which rapidly escalated to a terror that she was on the verge of starvation. She rushed to the buffet table but was dismayed to find only low-calorie dishes that would furnish little, if any, nutrition. She became very upset and described feeling an agitation identical to that that she had experienced in practically all of our sessions. She then focused upon the music, whose location represented my chair in the consultation room, and felt soothed. However, alongside the soothing experience, she still had gnawing inner pains which she associated to the fear of starving to death, of never being able to find a situation in which she would feel secure about being fed. She stated that these paradoxical feelings generated in the dream were now with her constantly. This dream was followed by other similar ones which could be considered sequels.

The patient had another type of dream that reflected her agitation over her belief that she was incapable of being nurtured. She felt "as if things were falling apart inside of me" and these parts included me. She could not remember much of the imagery of the dream; rather, she was more aware of all-encompassing anger and agitation. She felt further frightened that she would destroy me. When she was able to have a distinct picture of me, she was afraid that she would hurt me and, on several occasions, pictured me walking around with a bent back, as if I were a cripple. However, she was still glad that I was alive. After such a dream, she would request more sessions, usually to reassure herself that I had not been destroyed by her wrath and agitation.

The image of me with a bent back had its foundation in reality, because on two occasions I had had temporary but visible back problems. Nevertheless, it was extremely important that I survive the primitive levels of her psyche. The patient eventually felt reassured that she would not be able to damage me. She continued to find my presence soothing but still saw herself as starving to death.

Although the patient's stormy agitation was gradually replaced by a calm outward demeanor, she literally seemed to be withering away, as she got thinner and thinner. Furthermore, the peaceful demeanor she displayed was not particularly comfortable. This could be expectd in view of her privation, but even the soothing she mentioned, increasingly resembled apathy. I thought there were moments when she showed some enthusiasm about her treatment, but I also sensed that she was withdrawing from me.

For approximately a year, she continued in an apathetic, withdrawn fashion. She acted, and described feeling, numb. She still believed it was important to keep her appointments with me, but nothing really mattered. Rather than being depressed, she displayed a blunting of affect. She felt neither pleasure nor pain. She required very little to exist and did not experience much in the way of needs. For example, she was never aware of hunger and ate just enough to prevent starvation. Sexually, she was completely inactive.

I sensed that she would neither understand nor integrate my interpretations. She seemed totally passive and nonreceptive. Although she talked freely, it appeared as if she were talking in her sleep. My only comments were about my recognition that she felt soothed but was unable to learn from me. She frequently replied that she was incapable of taking within herself whatever I might be able to give her. I thought about her dreams earlier in the analysis when she was afraid that she would destroy me, as she had internalized my imago, but she insisted that she no longer felt that way. Now, she did not feel agitated inside and therefore could not outwardly explode and harm me. On the contrary, she felt calm; on the couch she felt like a baby being lulled to sleep in a cradle. She saw me gently rocking the cradle.

Still, in spite of her tranquil state, I felt that she was withdrawing from me and demonstrating a basic ego defect. I was reminded of that period of her childhood when she was described as autistic. She appeared to be repeating the sequence from infancy to childhood. It seemed as if she had effected some kind of inner reconciliation. She said that she would never know what it meant to be gratified, but she would settle for everything being peaceful, as it was now.

However, I felt frustrated because I could not be more active. I wanted to give her some interpretation that she could "digest" and use for psychic growth. She continued emphasizing that I could not fill her emptiness. I had nothing tangible I could possibly supply. In fact, she considered me to be ethereal, that is, without substance. She had the following fantasy. She was walking on a barren stretch of land on the moon. Finally, she reached the foot of a hill facing a cave. A hollow, mysterious voice within the cave called her name. She walked into the cave and tried to touch the owner of the voice who she believed was God. However, she could hardly see him since he was only a transparent mass of ectoplasm. He extended his hand to give her a loaf of bread but she could not grasp it because it was not solid; it was just an apparition. The fantasy was with her practically all the time but it did not cause her to feel depressed. She was resigned to her fate and just felt numb.

I pointed out to her how sad she made me feel by putting me in a position in which I could not help her. I could not symbolically nourish her. She was surprised that I was sad. She acknowledged that I was failing her, but for me to care about my failure was a new experience for her.

Gradually, after slightly more than a year, she began to show some feelings of comfort during our sessions. She revealed to me that previously she vomited every time she ate, but now she was beginning to hold food down. I noted that she had gained a little weight and was showing some interest in eating. Apparently, she had become less helpless in the outside world and had joined a friend in opening a small boutique. She had affectionate feelings toward me and stated that for the first time in her life she knew what it meant to be gratified. She claimed that our relationship provided her with nurture, and that I was genuinely interested in her without any ulterior motives. Even the aunt who had rescued her as an adolescent had self-serving reasons for acting as she had. The fact that she had abandoned the patient by remarrying also showed that she could not be trusted.

The patient had not undergone a marked improvement, but rather, a marginal one, maintained by the vigorous support of friends such as her business associate. With me, she was no longer agitated, numb, or withdrawn. She appeared relatively comfortable with her dependency on me. She looked forward to our sessions, which seemed to give her "organization." She commented that if she were inwardly disturbed when she arrived for an appointment, our relationship caused her to feel calm. She no longer complained of gnawing, painful, disruptive emptiness. She felt I was able to give her something around which she could synthesize and control chaotic feelings. Nevertheless, this was all very tenuous and she still felt an inner void. It was not completely empty as it had been, but she was not free of the pain of emptiness. She was now more aware of her feelings and could experience some pleasure, but with it there was much pain.

The peaceful calm she experienced in analysis lasted several months. Then her attitude toward herself and others, especially her business partner, changed from dependency and trust to anger and suspicion. She became preoccupied with the innumerable details of daily life with an intensity that, at times, struck me as paranoid. She would attach herself to causes with an ardor that was out of proportion in view of her goals. For example, the school her children attended had dropped soccer from its athletic program, presumably because not enough students were interested in it. The patient conducted an energetic campaign to have it reinstated because she felt it was extremely important for the students to be acquainted with this sport. Not only did she believe that soccer was an excellent physical activity, but since it was not a typically American game, students should be conversant with a sport that was played enthusiastically in other parts of the world. She felt that the school had taken a reactionary isolationist position in dropping soccer from its schedule. She wrote a letter to the editor of the neighborhood newspaper, tried to get signatures on a petition, protested to the principal and managed to have the school board set up a meeting to discuss the issue. She even bought T-shirts with soccer slogans printed on them. In spite of her efforts, she could not get anyone involved and her cause died of attrition.

Following that episode, there were many similar causes she championed, all without success. She also felt that some of her suppliers were cheating her and she came to distrust her partner, on whom she had been very dependent. The situation worsened and, after threatening litigation, she angrily left the business. She told me all of her grievances, hoping for a sympathetic ear.

She complained constantly during her sessions. She found life increasingly difficult and talked incessantly about her inner pain. She began voicing her dissatisfaction with me because I was not helping her. Her tone was different than it had been at the beginning of treatment when she was clamoring for help. She showed none of the helpless agitation that had dominated the clinical picture then. Instead, she was angry and was becoming more adept at expressing her feelings. Her rage finally was openly expressed toward me.

One day she announced in an emphatic voice that this was going to be her last session. At first, I was caught off guard, not knowing what was going on. She told me she was leaving me to see another therapist and join a group. Apparently she was going to see this therapist both individually and in group therapy. I felt some anger, which intensified as she continued talking. She started reviling me. I had been absolutely useless. I was selfish, insensitive, a chauvinistic misogynist, stupid and incompetent. I had been especially remiss toward her because I had not foreseen how badly her partner would treat her. Though in previous months she had expressed some negative feelings, the suddenness and intensity of her attack took me by surprise. I realized that she was blaming me for everything bad that had ever happened to her. I tried to console myself by trying to understand her reactions as transference, but I found my anger mounting.

The patient, although she lacked insight, was aware of my anger and she confronted me with it. At the same time, she kept attacking me for not having dissuaded her from going into business with her partner. I should have foreseen what would happen. I reached a saturation point and expressed my feelings. I told her in an angry voice that I would not accept her accusations. I could understand her need to view me in such a destructive fashion, but I would not accept the responsibility for all the pain and misery she had suffered throughout her life. I denied that I had been insensitive to her needs.

She seemingly ignored what I said and rebuked me further for having failed. I remembered how much anger her children and husband could feel toward her. I found myself identifying with them as my rage struggled to the surface. I ended the session by shouting that I did not want to put up with her provocativeness any longer and I probably called her paranoid. She was frightened and practically ran out of my office.

In retrospect, it is difficult to portray the intensity of our feelings during that particular session. I had been seeing her almost every day for practically five years. Most of the time she had seemed grateful to be in treatment. She had credited it with saving her life. Her sudden and furious hatred was a stunning experience for me. However, as I examined the course of her treatment, I could see that her hostile feelings had been emerging for some time prior to their eruption.

I tried to rationalize my loss of temper as having therapeutic benefit. I thought of it as something analogous to a transference interpretation. The patient would note that I could accept her projections only to a certain degree. My nonanalytic response would represent reality, a response to the irrationality of her allegations. She could then separate me into two components, the analyst who accepted her projections and the nonanalyst-reality component that did not. My being provoked also meant that I would not allow myself to be destroyed by her hatred by helplessly and passively accepting it. I would fight back and survive her. She would also know that she was capable of having an impact on me. These explanations made me feel better, but, for the most part, turned out to be incorrect. I was half expecting her to return to treatment, but she did not until a year and a half later.

Although this patient did not manifest any florid delusions, she clearly developed a psychotic transference. She was absolutely convinced that I was the cause of all her difficulties, even those originating in early childhood. Her feelings were not due to a delusion, but rather, to her total inability to view her feelings as stemming from conflicts or ego defects within herself; it is this inability that made me label her reactions as psychotic transference even though, as I will soon discuss, from one viewpoint her accusations were valid.

THE PSYCHOTIC TRANSFERENCE: REALITY AND EXTERNALIZATION

The delusional core of the psychotic transference may be subtle and difficult to detect. Similar to the patient discussed here, a middle-aged man severely criticized me for not having stopped him from having an extramarital affair. He was so angry with me because of this, that he finally discontinued treatment.

In reality nothing tangible was upset by his affair, or fling—a better description since he had had only one sexual experience, and with a woman whose sexual orientation was primarily lesbian.

Other than myself, no one else knew about this liaison; his friends and wife suspected nothing. However, he believed he would be scorned and ridiculed.

To some extent, I could see his viewpoint: for a respectable member of a conservative firm, living in an affluent suburb, and belonging to a prestigious country club, to have an affair with a lesbian would have a certain amount of shock value. However, in view of the fact that there was so little probability of being discovered, his anguish was somewhat puzzling. Still, he persisted in reproaching me and himself since this was not proper behavior for a man of his position and status.

After more time in analysis, I began to understand why he compulsively clung to the damaging consequence of his "affair." He spent much time in his analysis talking of his illustrious background. Apparently, in his family tree there were several illustrious, charismatic persons who made momentous contributions to western civilization. He considered himself heir of this privileged, gifted breed destined for great achievements that would change the course of mankind. He believed that he possessed special abilities such as predicting the future, but he discussed these in the context of extrasensory perception and astrology. This sounded grandiose, but not necessarily delusional, and he presented all of this material in a subdued low-keyed fashion.

However, as his reactions in the transference demonstrated, he was delusional. Basically, he believed he was the messiah who would someday reveal himself and redeem the world. If it were ever known that he had an affair with a "perverse" woman, his detractors would use this episode to attack his divinity. That was why it was so vitally important that I should have also been omnipotent and should have stopped him from this transgression. Put in this fashion, the delusional qualities of his orientation are obvious. However, this was hidden core material which was cloaked in a superficial logic, making what he said plausible and believable.

With each patient, I faced a psychotic transference but as I have stated, the first patient could support her beliefs by what had happened to her during treatment. Recall that after the first noisy phase of treatment, one in which she relived the disruptive consequences of privation, the patient recapitulated the autism of child-hood. She withdrew and felt neither pleasure nor pain. Her life was colorless and she just lived from day to day, not distinguishing one experience from another. At best her adjustment was schizoid (Giovacchini 1979) and time uneventfully flowed on without any particular awareness on her part. In fact, she had only a minimal time sense because she had so little capacity for sensory experience; everything was monotonously the same.

In spite of her withdrawal, the treatment succeeded in estab-lishing some elements of a holding environment. As her dreams indicated, she began to feel some gratification from our relation-ship. Life was beginning to have some meaning; it was no longer as grey as it had been. Her mental life had established a rudimentary time sequence punctuated by successive periods of minimal satisfac-tion.

Being able to perceive some pleasure made her aware of her own miserable emptiness and loneliness. The recognition that there were experiences and relationships that could be meaningful and enhancing made her lament all the more the innumerable abandon-ments and rejections that she experienced during the sensitive and formative years of childhood. She was seized by a poignant aware-ness of what she had missed and now could never recapture. She commented that her sense of loneliness was greatest in a crowd, that she felt torn apart when she saw other people loving and enjoying each other. She was even able to remember traumatic events from childhood that had been totally submerged in amnesia before she started treatment.

To repeat, she experienced some pleasure and much pain. Her anger mounted and she could work up considerable rage toward her mother for leaving her and toward all the inept and uncaring members of her family. However, she did not remain in the past very long. She started directing her rage toward me, revealing that something new was happening to her. She was acutely conscious of pain for the first time. In spite of the severity of past disturbances, she never had suffered pain in the way she now described. Her pain took the concrete, specific form of spasms in her epigastrium or the pounding blows of a headache. Previously she had noted "diffuse waves of agitation" or a numbness that approached deadness. She also claimed that she did not know what anger was. She was bewildered and confused when she saw others becoming angry. In fact, she was bewildered by other people's feelings in general since she could not reproduce them in herself. Now she experienced rage to an overwhelming degree and, for the most part, it was directed toward me.

She bemoaned that she had "been asleep all of her rotten life." Now that she was no longer anesthetized, she could understand how "rotten" her life really had been. She was no longer anesthetized, but she was not "awake" either, because I was not helping her move toward "living." She tenaciously clung to her grievances about her partner, a person whom she claimed lied and cheated, someone I should have warned her against. It seemed to me that her partner kindled her anger in the outside world which she then discharged on me. During the comparatively short periods of time when she was not consumed by her rage, she stated that there was no connection between what she wanted and her inner self. She regretted that I was unable to give her something that would bridge that gap.

In any case, she left me abruptly and went to see another therapist. Eighteen months later she called me and timidly asked for an appointment. She was careful to state that she would like to see me "if she may." I was immensely curious to know what had happened to her during the last year and a half and to understand better what had been going on in our relationship. I had stopped believing that my angry reaction had had any therapeutic benefit whatsoever.

The patient immediately reclined on the couch and began by telling me that she had missed her analysis. Then, somewhat to my surprise, she started angrily reviling me for having failed her, again referring to my inability to protect her from her business partner and blaming me for all the pain she had experienced throughout her life. She was still in business with the same partner; nothing had changed fundamentally.

After she left me, she began seeing a psychiatrist who gave her lithium and antidepressant drugs. The latter did nothing for her, but the lithium calmed her. During her analysis with me, she had stopped taking drugs. Apparently she had been almost uncontrollably manic for several months after she left me.

I was most impressed when she stated that she had missed her analysis. She related to me much in the way she had during our last session, but it was somewhat toned down. I sensed that it was important that I survive her anger instead of becoming angry myself. Somehow she convinced me that it was vital that I supply her with a setting in which she could express anger.

She insisted that I had failed her and that I was the cause of her pain. I recalled how her mother had failed her by totally abandoning her. What she now felt could be the repetition compulsion recapitulated in the transference. I also began to understand how her psychotic transference had some foundation in the reality of our relationship. Prior to treatment, she had not experienced pain in an organized manner. Her agitation and numbness were primitive, amorphous feelings rather than anger. As her ability to feel pain was a result of the analysis, she could justifiably, in a sense, "blame" the analysis for this achievement.

With these thoughts in mind, I was able to relax and acknowledge that, insofar as I had represented the analysis, I had failed her. She was grateful for my admission, but demanded that I apologize for my incompetence, which I would not do. However, she was somewhat mollified when I stated that I could not have acted otherwise as her analyst. I further admitted that I had been responsible for her pain, but added that I considered this an achievement. She agreed and confirmed my belief that she had to use the analysis to work out her anger. I did not interpret the similarity of her feelings about me and the failing caretakers of the past, as I believed this would have made no sense to her. She would have seen it as an attempt to escape her anger by concentrating on the past.

In subsequent sessions she initiated discussion about how her early environment had failed her. There was an important difference between the past and present which demonstrated that the repetition compulsion did not represent an exact repetition of the past. During infancy, she had been unable to feel or express her rage, as she had been too frightened and vulnerable to direct it toward her parents. She believed that her mother already had been destroyed. Even today, she wonders how responsible she had been for the maternal breakdown. Again, there was a core of reality because her mother had suffered a postpartum psychosis; if the patient had not been born, presumably her mother would not have been destroyed. Consequently, any rage or other destructive feelings could not emerge in her weak and helpless infancy.

Since I had first introduced the patient to pain and the analysis had created a setting in which she could express it, I became the logical target of her anger. True, during the session in which she had terminated, I had lost control and could have been viewed as either dangerously destructive or already destroyed, like her childhood caretakers. She had been frightened, but only momentarily. She had faith that both of us would survive the episode and even derived some pleasure at being able to affect me to such a degree. This situation was markedly different from that of the vulnerable infant. Through the repetition compulsion, she was trying to master the helplessness she had felt as an infant by expressing the anger that she had been unable to deal with at that time.

Viewing her behavior in such an adaptive and constructive manner made it much easier for me to deal with my countertransference feelings. Still, from time to time, she was able to irritate me; this took the form of my feeling impelled to argue with her. This usually occurred when she reviled me for not having protected her from her business partner. However, generally, I was able to maintain my therapeutic perspective by recognizing that this element of her psychotic transference represented a repetition of the failure of an early environment that should have protected her from external disruptions rather than abandoning her. The situation became even more bearable when I realized that sometimes I was being reproached for not having said something that I had, in fact, said. She would lecture me by stating, "well, you should have said such and such" and I would be astonished because she was repeating my words and expressions verbatim. When this happened, I would lose my inclination to protest that I had not been derelict because this would have been defensive and would have meant that I had wanted her to stop criticizing me, which to some extent was true. Rather, I marveled that she had been able to make some elements of our interaction her own, that she had integrated them as part of herself and lost sight of the external source.

It was more difficult for me to deal with her distortions of what I had said, which had a paranoid quality about them. For instance, she complained that I had been insensitive about her business because I had pointed out that she had not really needed the money, that she had been taking the situation with her business partner much too seriously. This meant that I had not realized how meaningful this venture into the business world had been for her, how she had been trying to establish independence and self-respect. She then inferred that I had considered her venture into the business world an empty-headed frivolity. In fact, I had seen it as a significant achievement. I simply had regretted that she had converted something that should have been pleasurable—since she had been free of financial pressures—into a miserable experience. I refrained from justifying my intentions because I believed it would have been technically incorrect. Anything I said would have been a defensive attempt to exonerate myself, whereas she needed to see me as blameworthy.

As I continued surviving her anger which simply means maintaining analytic calm, she recalled that once I had been able to soothe her and that there had been times when she had felt "good" about me. As she attacked me, her life in the outside world became more pleasant, reflecting some degree of organization. Eventually, the good outweighed the bad in her treatment, and the transference developed in other more conventional nonpsychotic directions.

In the final stages of this patient's treatment, she temporarily regressed back to the ego state that had preceded the development of the psychotic transference. However, the regression did not exactly recapitulate the previous ego state. In any regression, the psyche carries later acquisitions back to earlier levels. In this instance, she took her anger back with her. It was no longer focused exclusively on me. Instead, it was generalized and free floating and lacked a target. She wanted me to soothe her and her children to mother her. Her preoccupation with outside events such as the business ceased.

Gradually the anger subsided and she began feeling generally comfortable and calm. However, her behavior became quite infantile. She slept most of the day and expected her family to look after her, which they did. The children, interestingly, did not mind catering to their mother's infantile needs. The husband, on the other hand, resented her and her treatment intensely; she eventually divorced him. She stopped going to work; instead, she ate and slept most of the time. However, she was not withdrawn or numb as she had been previously. Nor was she autistic.

This regression eventually turned out to be a positive experience. Unlike her childhood and the withdrawn phase earlier in treatment, she now allowed herself gratification. It was primitive gratification, but she was able to receive it in the context of being soothed. This represented the establishment of a minimal nurturing matrix, or foundation for emotional development. Thus her regression was reconstructive. She could progress from a basis of gratification as she was no longer in a state of privation. Her treatment with me lasted eight years, with occasional periodic returns of several months subsequent to each termination.

I would like to make some conceptual inferences and generalizations from this clinical material. I will outline what I believe to be a fairly common sequence culminating in a psychotic transference of varying intensity in schizoid and borderline patients. In some instances, the psychotic transference may not be at all disruptive.

The egos of these needy, agitated patients have very few endopsychic registrations of gratifying experiences (i.e., maternal nurturing and soothing). As discussed earlier, such patients may be "unreasonable." They may go through a withdrawn, numb phase such as my patient did, recapitulating the autism of her childhood. Whatever the sequential patterns of patients suffering from primitive mental states, the common denominator characterizing their transference will be their repetition of the traumatic failures of childhood in treatment. (There are exceptions to this general rule: some patients with a psychotic transference attribute magical omnipotent qualities to the analyst. This is, however, the other side of the coin and is just as disruptive to the goal of achieving further psychic structuralization as the overtly negative transference.)

Perhaps it seems extreme to imply that all patients suffering from primitive mental states will develop psychotic transferences. This is a matter of degree and depends on how real feelings toward their therapists seem to them. Inasmuch as these patients have poorly established ego boundaries and imperfectly perceived time sequences, their frames of reference become easily confused. Such patients do not clearly distinguish between the past and the present.

The transference can be separated into two components. First, patients project feelings, impulses, and parts of the self into the analyst. Then they react to the transference relationship with the help of infantile defenses and adaptations. In order to do so, they have to create an ambience that will support these defenses. Elsewhere, I (1975, 1979) have called the creation of this ambience "externalization," which I have contrasted with projection. This ambience serves as a "backdrop" for projection.

In general, patients attempt to create an atmosphere similar to their infantile environment. For example, let us suppose a topnotch sergeant was reared in a violent household where his parents constantly quarrelled and physically attacked each other and their children. From early infancy on, the sergeant learned to adapt to violence. As an adult in the army, he adjusted well to battle; in fact, he thrived in a dangerous environment where most people would be paralyzed with fear. On the other hand, during peacetime, this sergeant might emotionally decompensate. In the army during the war, he had found a milieu similar to the violent environment of infancy with which he had learned to cope. Thus, if the infantile environment is not too different from current reality, the person's adaptive techniques will function in a smooth, reality-attuned fashion.

In treatment, patients reproduce the world of their infancy. One patient, a highly successful industrialist, had been reared in the ghetto. His parents seemed to thrive on violence. As a child, he received frequent beatings from both his parents and his older siblings. He learned how to fight and gained prominence as a gang leader. He carried his "fighter" identity into the jungle of modern finance. In analysis, he assigned many roles to me, from the loving mother he had longed for to the hostile competitor whom he had always managed to engage in battle. These were fairly conventional projections. In addition, his manner of relating to me bore the ghetto stamp: his coarse, argumentative, provocative speech in treatment stood in marked contrast to his usual well-bred, modulated, educated style. He behaved as if he had a chip on his shoulder and was challenging me to knock it off. I could feel the ghetto ambience pervading the consultation room. His injection of this ambience was similar to projection but, inasmuch as it involved the milieu in which projection occurred, I preferred to call it externalization.

From a technical viewpoint, analysts make themselves available for patients' projections. They do not require any special techniques to accomplish this; they simply maintain the analytic setting. However, the analytic setting clashes with patients' attempts to externalize their infantile milieu. As patients learn to distinguish the analytic ambience from the infantile ambience, they cannot maintain their projections with any firm conviction. Instead, they analyze them by means of the working-through process. The crucial point is that insofar as the analytic setting differs from everything else patients have experienced in their psychic development, it causes the infantile ambience to stand out in sharp contrast. When patients cannot distinguish between the two environments, then we are faced with a psychotic transference. Again, it must be remembered that this is a matter of degree. To some measure, all patients want to submerge the analytic setting in the world of infancy. The extent to which patients succeed in doing so determines how psychotic the transference is. The firm establishment of the past in the analytic present also indelibly fixes the patients' projections; thus patients view their analysts—at least functionally—as the caretakers who failed them.

Thus, the psychotic transference is the outcome of patients' confused frames of reference. Patients' externalizations destroy the analytic setting. I have often wondered whether the psychotic transference is an inevitable occurrence in the treatment of severely disturbed patients or whether it is the result of a technical error produced by adverse countertransference feelings. With respect to the patient who held me responsible for all the bad things that had happened to her, it seemed that reliving the failing infantile environment and experiencing the previously unexpressed infantile rage were inevitable consequences of analysis. However, this patient firmly believed that I was the *actual* culprit—that is, she did not have enough self-observing ego to distinguish between the past and the present.

The self-observing ego is an important attribute of the analytic setting. My patient apparently had succeeded in destroying this element of the analytic milieu, replacing it entirely with the infantile setting. I wondered if I had somehow participated by responding to her in a manner reminiscent of her depriving early world. I know that there were moments when I resented her agitated demands. It is quite possible that I was nonempathic and created an empty, ungratifying environment for her.

I would like to comment on the reason for my distinction between externalization and projection. I believe that there is an advantage in thinking in terms of two components of the projective process because during primitive phases of development, the infant relates in two frames of reference. These frames of reference have been described by various names. Winnicott (1960b) refers to the holding environment as the background for the feeding experience. I have discussed recently the dichotomy of soothing and nurture (Boyer and Giovacchini 1980).

SOOTHING AND NURTURE

The maternal holding elements of the infantile environment produce a setting that calms the infant and allows him to be optimally nurtured. I believe that the soothing background of the infantile environment is externalized during treatment while the foreground nurturing relationship constitutes the basis for projection. The fact that both soothing and nurture have been experienced as traumatic will be reflected in the treatment relationship. Patients will attempt to replace the holding, soothing elements of the analytic setting with their disruptive but familiar infantile environment. Similarly, projections are based upon the early nurturing relationship. The analyst may be viewed as giving and loving or, based upon patients' psychopathology, as cruel, greedy, inconstant, abandoning, withholding, and in other painful ways or with other painful traits. There are many variations, both normal and psychopathological, in patients' perceptions of the soothing and nurturing experiences. The patient presented in the previous section indicated graphically in a dream that she had some capacity to be soothed but a very limited ability to be nurtured.

Those whose ego states are still relatively unstructured may confuse soothing and nurture; I have called this state *primal confusion* (Boyer and Giovacchini 1980). For example, adolescents may feel soothed in surroundings that most adults would find excruciatingly painful and disruptive. They may seek peace and solace in smoke-filled, noisy discotheques; peace and quiet, or even soft melodic music may make them feel agitated and miserable.

As emotional development proceeds to the acquisition of more structured ego states, soothing and nurture become increasingly blended. For example, adults extend their dining experience beyond the food to include the surroundings as well. Thus, restaurant reviews describe the ambience as well as the food.

During regression, patients once again separate the soothing and nurturing components into the mother's holding and feeding functions. This regression may exhibit itself in dramatic or subtle fashion and may lead to special technical dilemmas. The following case example clearly illustrates how one patient used two therapists in his regressive separation of soothing and nurturing.

A young scientist in his twenties came to see me for consultation. He presented me with the problem of choosing between two therapists, although this turned out not to be the real dilemma. He had been seeing a well-known psychoanalyst for several years, but his sessions were becoming more and more disruptive for both patient and therapist. He bitterly attacked the therapist for being insensitive and withholding his feelings. About a year before our meeting, the patient had found another therapist who he saw when his first therapist was on vacation. Since then, he had continued seeing both of them.

The contrast between the sessions with each therapist was striking. With his first therapist, he lamented that he regressed deeply and disruptively. He conjectured that his analyst could not stand it and accused him of not having an "observing ego" or of not having "formed a working alliance." Regardless of what actually had happened between the two of them, this was how the patient perceived their interaction. He reported being told that he was nonanalyzable because he had a character defect. With the second therapist, the situation was quite different. He could regress there. At first, he stated that perhaps he did not regress as deeply with the second therapist. Then he reflected that maybe he did, but because this therapist could accept his regression as having something of value, he, the patient, was more comfortable in his regression.

He then went on to describe further how painful his sessions had been for his first therapist and himself. On several occasions, they had gone well over the allotted time. According to the patient, during one session, he had been so disturbed that the therapist had kept him in his consultation room for four hours and then had driven the patient home as he had felt that the patient was too agitated to go home alone.

I smiled after he furnished these descriptions and almost simultaneously we asked each other what I was supposed to "arbitrate." Did he want my support to enable him to leave the first therapist for the more comfortable setting provided by the second therapist? I did not think so and, after thinking it over for a moment, neither did he. Together we realized that he was getting something out of each relationship and really wanted my approval to continue both relationships as long as necessary. I was forming the uneasy feeling that he might also be seeking a third therapist.

He relaxed, seemingly reversing his initial position, and spoke in affectionate terms of his first analyst. He stated that for years he had been nurtured by him and, in spite of the present turmoil, still felt he was being nurtured and wanted to continue with him. I conjectured that the nurturing experience had been traumatic, but that he had had adequate soothing, most likely from his father or another family member. However, I only mentioned my suspicion of traumatic nurturing to him, which he confirmed.

His mother apparently used to excite him when she fed him and then do nothing to calm him. Being left in this state of excitement was painful; he experienced it as being "dropped." He emphasized that at present he was getting what he needed from both therapists. He did not consider what was happening with his first therapist therapy. He saw it more as an actual life experience, a kind of acting out, or acting in, which helped him to repeat an infantile experience. The second therapist soothed the agitation caused by his interactions with the first therapist, enabling these interactions to be analyzed.

Leaving aside the issue of whether this patient should have been "permitted" to see two therapists—the supposition being that feelings have to be worked out in the transference with one therapist—I did not consider it within my power to disagree with the patient's decision to continue with both therapists. The therapists had agreed to this arrangement: the second therapist had accepted the arrangement comfortably and the first somewhat more reluctantly. The issue relevant to the present discussion is the interplay of early soothing and nurturing mechanisms which leads to psychopathological manifestations and may emerge in the transference, as it represents the repetition of infantile relationships and traumas.

There is much evidence to support the patient's assertion that he did not have an analytic relationship with the first therapist. The therapist himself stated that the patient could not be analyzed because he did not have a self-observing ego. In the context of their relationship, that was probably true. In view of the actions of the first analyst as reported by the patient, it seemed likely that the therapist himself lacked a self-observing ego. He reportedly had become angry and shouted at the patient and had given him a four-hour session that had been so upsetting that he had had to drive the patient home. However, in spite of all this turmoil, the patient still felt "nurtured" by this relationship. In his own words, he felt both "replenished" and uncomfortably agitated after each session.

The patient viewed the first treatment situation with the first therapist as a segment of his reality rather than therapy. He considered his therapist a person of actual, rather than symbolic, significance for him. They seemed to be involved with each other at the content level. The therapist had entered the patient's life and they had established a relationship that was tumultuous but satisfying for the patient. It represented a repetition of the past but it was not analytic material because neither had the proper observational perspective to analyze it.

I conjectured that the second therapist was operating in an analytic frame of reference. The patient could be soothed by him. This relationship provided a holding environment that served as a background for the analytic interaction. This background, which defines the analytic setting, is a prerequisite for analysis. Unless the relationship can provide some degree of soothing, there cannot be sufficient self-observing ego to permit analysis.

From material I acquired after this consultation, I learned that the patient felt that he had absorbed the first therapist's agitation. That analyst apparently could become quite anxious and irritated during sessions. The patient revealed that his mother was a very excitable person who had stimulated him while feeding him. He had felt so much inner pain after each meal that he had been diagnosed as having colic. He recalled that his mother had become content and calm as he had become agitated, presumably because he had absorbed her agitation. This interaction was being repeated with his first therapist. Instead of the mother providing both soothing and nurturing, apparently she had nurtured her son while he had soothed her.

This brings to mind another patient who dreamed she was having sexual relations with her mother. She felt that her mother was "filling her up," which was pleasant and exciting. The mother also was excited and the patient was able to bring her to orgasm. After she had an orgasm, the mother was no longer interested in her daughter, who did not obtain relief. The patient awakened in a state of painful agitation.

Perhaps the reversal of roles regarding soothing might help explain why the young scientist could not be soothed by his first therapist. He was repeating the early maternal relationship. Although he initially was able to establish a fairly tranquil analytic relationship with the therapist, once the regressive process was set in motion, he became disrupted and needed another therapist to contain his painful inner feelings.

Undoubtedly, disturbing countertransference feelings were also involved. However, I suspect that something intrinsic in this patient's character structure also contributed to the unmanageability of the analytic context. The similarity between what had happened in infancy (I received further confirmatory material later) and what was happening in treatment almost suggested a psychotic transference. I wondered how much continuity there was between various levels of his psyche. If different levels of the psyche were not "well connected" with each other, they could only be dealt with in different relationships; such a fragmentation of the psyche occurred with my housewife patient, who had a psychotic transference.

This fragmentation of the psyche is different from dissociation and splitting, mechanisms which frequently have been identified as the psychic processes of the borderline patient. Splitting takes place on one psychic level: an internal object is split into good and bad components and then is handled by projection or is otherwise dissociated from the main psychic current. In contrast, I have been discussing relationships between different psychic levels. There is no splitting. Rather, I have been describing a structural defect manifested by a relative lack of a bridging continuity between primitive amorphous and better-structured, later acquired psychic levels in contrast to a dissociation of an internal object which represents only one structure.

Returning to the young scientist, I commented toward the end of the session that with his first therapist he was repeating his infantile past and with his second therapist he was trying to work through this material. He then told me the following dream from the previous night. He was lying on a couch. Next to him, his first therapist lay on another couch. Seated behind them were his second therapist and myself. We were discussing the patient, who was calm and pleased. Then his first therapist turned around and tried to talk to us. The patient became furious and shouted at him to lie down and not interfere. He awakened feeling angry at his first therapist.

Obviously, I could not deal with this dream in an exhaustive analytic fashion as this young man was not my patient. Still, in view of the striking manifest content, it was possible to make some speculations. Both he and his first therapist were in the reclining position of analytic patients. They were on the same level literally and with regard to manifest content. Clearly, he did not see his first therapist as an analyst, but as a person who operated at his own infantile level. Relative to each other, neither had a self-observing function or a working alliance.

His second therapist, by contrast, was placed in the position of an analyst who was not personally involved with him and who tried to understand him from a professional viewpoint. The second therapist had asked me to supervise him shortly before my consultation with the patient. We had not yet met, but the patient knew that we had arranged to do so. He felt secure that we would be making formulations about him. In the dream, when the first therapist tried to break into the analytic frame of reference of the second therapist and myself, the patient became furious. Each of us had his place. When someone tried to move to another level, the patient became angry and disrupted.

This young man eventually made a borderline adjustment, although there were times when he was unable to function. While his therapeutic experiences were unusual, they were the outcome of specific ego defects commonly found in borderline patients. At the early developmental levels that I have chosen to discuss, he did not have a well-integrated nurturing experience. As an infant, he could not receive soothing and nurture from the same person. This led to serious difficulties later in life which had their effects on his ability to relate in the external world and made it impossible for him to sustain an intimate relationship. These inabilities can also be explained on the basis of problems at higher levels of the personality, but the patient's primitive antecedents were prominent. I wish to focus on the relationship of the borderline patient's early developmental stages to his later discontinuity of personality and defensive adaptations.

"DEADNESS" AS LIFE SUSTAINING

The state of relative privation is experienced as painfully disruptive agitation. By definition, total privation, would result in a total absence of endopsychic registration of gratifying experiences in the infant. This would probably result in marasmus and death. Partial privation implies faulty infantile gratification. As the case of the housewife demonstrated, some infants are better soothed than nurtured; others, such as the infants in the orphanage that Spitz (1945) described, are better nurtured than soothed.

I have noted that several patients who have revealed impoverished maternal care and difficulties in early soothing experiences refer to themselves as being "dead." They have a very limited sense of aliveness. This was true of my housewife patient who developed a sense of deadness during her treatment. Her autistic childhood phase was probably also a manifestation of deadness.

The explanation of such a feeling as deadness leads to the question of the development of the sense of aliveness. In a satisfactory caretaking maternal relationship, the child's inner tensions (produced by the child's internal needs) are converted into pleasurable excitement as the underlying needs are met. Excitement is contained as the child is fed and soothed. Needs become sources of anticipated pleasure. The interactions that are required for the sustenance of life are gratifying. To be fed, to grow, and develop— that is, the process of living—is exciting and the child reacts to new experiences with curiosity and eagerness rather than dread and despair.

My patient who felt "dead" experienced her needs as painful because of early life events. This was recapitulated during analysis, when she was faced with the unbearable situation that to live is painful. This is a common situation with depressed, suicidal patients.

The severly disturbed patients I have been describing, however, have not reached the degree of psychic organization that we ordinarily attribute to depression. Rather than dealing with oral ambivalence, these patients are primarily conflicted about their inner needs, which may be only dimly and imperfectly perceived. The patient's inability to organize internal percepts sufficiently may make them "explosively painful." It may be that some patients who show a typical depressed syndrome prove to have underlying structural defects similar to those that I am discussing. Certainly, the state of intractability, misery, and torment so many depressed patients manifest is comparable to the disorganization of patients suffering from primitive mental states.

I am reminded of a patient described by Flarsheim (1975), a young girl in her early twenties who suffered from depression and anorexia nervosa. Certain aspects of her infancy are especially pertinent to the thesis I want to develop. She apparently was a fussy baby who constantly shrieked as if she were in pain. The mother hired a nurse who bragged she could convert any baby into one who would "give no trouble."

Her method was simple and effective. She related to the child in an intense fashion. Whenever the child was needy, the nurse would respond immediately, but not to the specific need. For example, if the baby's diaper were soiled and she cried in discomfort, the nurse would feed her rather than change the diaper. If she were hungry, then perhaps she would change the diaper or rock her in a soothing fashion instead of feeding her. When the infant tried to suck her thumb, the nurse put metal gloves on her hands to make sucking impossible.

The nurse was true to her word. By the time the patient was 6 months old, she was an extremely compliant baby. She no longer fussed. Therefore, no one had to pay any attention to her because she behaved as a person without needs. She was a "dead baby," but she did not annoy anyone.

This demeanor of deadness became prominent again during her adolescence, when she was brought to analysis because she was starving herself to death. Among other things, anorexia meant that she had no needs. It represented an extreme rejection of any

dependency whatsoever. She denied that her body had any requirements.

A person's sense of aliveness is the outcome of a variety of
sensory experiences. It consists of an awareness of vital inner
forces, a conscious perception of structuralizing and life-sustaining
processes. The perception of one's own needs, the building up of
anticipatory excitement, and the ensuing satisfaction and reestab-
lishment of a homeostatic balance all contribute to a cohesive sense
of wholeness that stabilizes into the conviction that one's existence
is secure.

Flarsheim's patient must have felt pain along with her needs
since she was vigorously responded to to fulfill a need but not the
need she was experiencing at the moment. This was also true of
my patient—anticipatory excitement became abruptly transformed
into painful agitation. Even the solace of being able to soothe
herself by thumbsucking was not available to her as her hands
were covered by some medieval device.

If one's inner needs, which define one's sense of aliveness,
become disruptive, one simply concludes that to be alive is unbear-
ably painful. My housewife patient defended herself by feeling
"dead."

The anorexic patient did not acknowledge her body as a live
body because a live body has to be fed and her body did not need
food. My housewife patient, in turn, denied there was an external
world in which one could live when she withdrew into her autistic
shell. This sense of "deadness" has adaptive and defensive ramifications.

Often patients who feel "dead" establish "dead" object relationships in a merger with a parent, lover, or spouse. The fusion is
based upon the premise that excitement has to be kept at a
minimum and feelings have to be deadened. In these relationships,
there is no spontaneity, vitality, or joy. Relationships have to
remain futile, hopeless, and nonproductive because hope and
achievement are associated with aliveness. Much of modern literature is devoted to describing "dead" people in "dead" relationships.
It recognizes, however, how such relationships are required to
sustain life.

Patients with a need for "deadness" will attempt to create similar mergers with their analysts. In some analyses, this can lead to countertransference problems severe enough to create a treatment impasse. In such impasses, both patient and analyst feel quite comfortable; as long as nothing happens to change the situation, the fusion continues. Neither participant feels discomfort, but the therapeutic relationship is dull, colorless, and unproductive. Analysts may be lulled into a false sense of security that treatment is going well simply because it is not upsetting anyone. When analysts also find certain aspects of aliveness painful, then they collude with such patients to strengthen the fusion. At best, such interminable therapy enables patients to function in the external world. However, the therapeutic relationship has no foundation built on the gratification of needs and emergence of the sense of aliveness, as the latter would threaten to disrupt the merger.

In such treatment relationships, certain defenses may develop in an attempt to deny the existence of a merger. This often leads to the construction of what Winnicott (1960a) calls the "false self" for both analyst and patient. I believe this issue can be discussed best in the context of narcissistic defenses.

THE FALSE SELF AND PSYCHIC DISCONTINUITY

When "deadness" is used as a defense against the pain of feeling alive, analyst and patient may merge in a symbiotic fusion, thereby maintaining a delicate balance. In their "deadness" they can cling to life and create the impression of aliveness. However, this aliveness is based on the construction of a false self in both patient and analyst.

The patient has formed a self-representation that is not an upward extension of an hierarchically arranged sequence of increasingly structured needs and modalities that gratify these needs. Once the upper layer of the personality achieves some stability, it becomes the false self. Winnicott (1960a) stated that the false self was directed toward, and was a product of compliance with, the outer world; it had little connection with the person's inner core.

In Winnicott's view, the false self was a defensive construction against the impingements of the outer world. In this context, the false self can be conceptualized as a further structuralization of the stimulus barrier, or Freud's *Reizschutz* (1920), which is a protective shield against external stimuli.

In discussing "deadness" as a defensive reaction to early disruptive internal stimuli, it must be remembered that these stimuli originate in biological needs and are not intrinsically disruptive. It is the response of the outer world that causes them to be painful rather than pleasurable. A false self is born which acts as a shell against internal feelings and any external situations that stimulate these feelings.

This protective false self may be a narcissistic superstructure whose defensive function accomplishes two purposes: (1) the denial of underlying feelings of helplessness and vulnerability, and (2) the appearance of aliveness to cover the feeling of "deadness." The two purposes are intertwined. The attempt to maintain a semblance of aliveness often results in a stance of arrogance and abrasiveness, as well as an apparent involvement with persons and causes which is, at best, only a pseudoinvolvement.

In the analytic relationship, the analyst may relate to the patient's false self as they merge with each other. This may appear to be intense analytic involvement; the patient may be completely dedicated to analysis and devoted to the analyst, viewing their relationship as life saving. From one viewpoint it is, as it provides the patient with a modicum of comfort. However, analytically speaking, there is no progressive development. The relationship is in a state of stagnation.

In such a relationship, the analyst only goes through the motions of analyzing the patient and thus is acting as a pseudoanalyst. The analyst may appear to be very actively interpreting, but the interpretations relate to the false self rather than the inner core, and thus strengthen the merger. This may be an example of "interpreting upwards" (Boyer and Giovacchini 1980).

The analyst's unwitting reinforcement of the patient's false self may be the result of supporting the patient's narcissistic defenses.

Both analyst and patient believe they are engaged in productive analysis. The patient's self-esteem is strengthened as he or she acquires ego integration through the analysis and the analyst's professional ego ideal is elevated insofar as a difficult patient appears to be making progress. Unfortunately, there is no substance to these enhancing self-evaluations.

Some patients may sense that the analyst's formulations have very little connection to disturbances at primitive levels. Basically, they cannot integrate interpretations because the latter have no gratifying potential; that is, they cannot reach the level of privation. At the level of the false self, the interpretations can only be experienced as assaultive impingements or intrusions. However, the patients' need for the merger causes them to react with a false self-compliance, thereby further consolidating the establishment of the false self.

Patients also seek situations in the outer world that will support the false self by helping them secure their narcissistic defenses. In this form of externalization, patients become involved with a seemingly meaningful environment that has no substance—that is, one based on shallow and superficial ideals that appear to be profound and meaningful. On the surface, these patients appear to value creativity, but they cannot experience creative urges within themselves. Their outlook is purely intellectual. In fact, they are intolerant of truly creative activity and reject the innovative. This is understandable because they lack the connection between the primitive and the better-structured levels of the psyche which is the sine qua non of creativity.

As stated, they can become involved in intellectual endeavors, but only at the level of the false self. This is pseudocreativity. They can rework already established ideas, introduce new terms without contributing any new substance, and undertake compilations and classifications of already established concepts. Basically, there is no true dedication or interest in the ideas themselves.

If the treatment of such patients is to be effective, the analytic ambience must not unwittingly provide the same supports for the false self that the patient has managed to find in the external world. As we have seen in the case examples, treatment may cause the patient to feel pain and may lead to the formation of a psychotic transference.

My housewife patient felt considerable pain, but this was related to the fact that she had begun to feel some gratification. The analysis had succeeded in creating a holding environment for her. Her first words when she returned to treatment were, "I missed my analysis." Although a violent tirade followed, I felt more accepting of her anger than I ever had before because I could distinguish a benign background behind her dominant rage. It was as if I were witnessing destructiveness supported by a foundation of tenderness and affection.

The gratification she felt was connected to the primitive, infantile parts of her personality. This gave her the potential for emotional growth and the establishment of a nurturing matrix. The satisfaction she experienced at primitive levels "made up for" early privation and even though this occurred in a traumatic painful way, this was, nevertheless, a reconstructive experience.

How does an analyst get in touch with these early levels and establish a holding environment, rather than encourage a merger that has apparent vitality but is really based on a disconnected false self? As with all other elements of psychoanalytic technique, there is no specific answer. The analyst has to respond intuitively to the patient's infantile desperation. At times, I failed my housewife patient by absorbing her ego defects. I could feel as empty as the patient believed me to be. I found it difficult to hold a mental representation of her when I was not in her immediate presence.

Probably the most important element in our relationship was the acceptance of her need to bring the primitive elements of her psyche into the treatment setting. Interpretations containing structured content such as complex feelings and reactions toward projected infantile imagos would have taken us away from her primitive level of privation and thus would have represented an attempt to construct a false self. This patient had very little of a false self superstructure, so there was very little chance that my "interpreting upwards" would fixate her psychopathology.

At the beginning of her treatment, I was able to make connections between sequences of emotional states she was showing me and phases of her childhood development (primarily her move from a stormy demanding phase to an autistic one). I also interpreted her behavior in the treatment setting as a repetition of her early experiences of privation, in that she had to view me as not being able to gratify her. Eventually, this understanding became gratifying and she entered into the psychotic transference I have described.

TECHNICAL DEVIATIONS

Does the treatment of primitively fixated patients require parameters? Elsewhere (Giovacchini 1972) I have discussed how close examination of certain interactions that appear to be deviations from analysis (in that they do not seem to be transference interpretations) shows that they are, in fact, equivalent to transference interpretations. The technical deviations in the four case examples that follow are *analytic* activities designed to preserve or establish the treatment setting. Returning to Winnicott (1960b), they are basically attempts to construct or maintain the holding environment.

Case 1

A young analyst whom I supervised was highly motivated to treat patients and was willing to go to extraordinary lengths to keep patients in treatment.

He told me of a particularly trying young woman who was an extreme example of the "unreasonable" patient. Briefly, she phoned him as many as 20 times a day and would not leave his office at the end of the hour. On one occasion, he had to carry her out; she took revenge by scraping his name off the door with a penknife. The analyst was consumed with rage but wanted to continue treating her. He thought of hospitalization, but the patient adamantly refused to comply with such a suggestion.

Finally, he thought of a solution. Instead of seeing her in his office, he would see her early in the morning at a corner table in the restaurant in his building. When the session was over, he would leave. He saw this as an unorthodox procedure for which he needed my approval. I encouraged him because clearly the only other alternative was to dismiss her as a patient.

The therapist found that he could relax with her in the restaurant and the material unfolded as might be expected. Even the telephone calls became manageable. After several months, she had some dreams indicating that she was ready to return to his office. She did and for six months the end of the hour was no problem. Then she regressed and they had to return to the restaurant, but only for two weeks.

Case 2

A patient of mine presented me with a wooden statuette of a naked woman during the first week of treatment. It was about eighteen inches high and somewhat grotesque, but with some artistic merit; it resembled a Giacometti sculpture. I accepted the statuette, as I felt that if I did not, there would be no treatment.

Later, I learned, as I had suspected, that the statuette stood for her self-representation, which she needed me to have in my perceptual sphere when she was not with me. This patient was incapable of maintaining a mental representation of me without my actual presence and she had attributed the same defect to me. Later in treatment, when she had gained sufficient psychic structure to internalize me, she took the statuette back. From the beginning of treatment, she had to have a setting in which her presence would not be lost. The statuette established a place for her, the holding environment she had never had during infancy. Her slogan regarding her childhood was "out of sight, out of mind." She had come to feel that her existence was tenuous because no one recognized or gratified her needs. She sought to remedy this situation with the statuette.

Our relationship proceeded on an analytic basis. The statuette stood in its place as an unobtrusive piece of furniture until the patient took it back. However, without it, I doubt that it would have been possible to establish an analytic relationship.

Case 3

Another patient, a 19-year-old college student,[1] had all the symptoms Erikson (1959) described as characteristic of the identity diffusion syndrome. Initially, he was withdrawn and taciturn and responded mainly in monosyllables. After several weeks, he felt comfortable enough to talk about some routine and pedestrian situations. Unlike my reaction to the questions of the lawyer patient described earlier, I found myself eager to respond. I felt excited by his questions and answered them in considerable detail.

Even when not asking questions, the patient would get me to discuss uninteresting events with enthusiasm. For example, there was a change in the schedule of the train he took to come to my office. Actually, the change improved the schedule. However, he presented this change as if it were going to present a problem for our appointment. We both discussed this event with an intensity that blew it up to the proportions of a global catastrophe. Although our interchange would have seemed bizarre to an outsider, it was necessary in order to establish a therapeutic relationship and progress in the direction of acquiring psychic structure. The excitement that we both felt at the beginning of therapy created a holding environment and represented a mode of relating that helped to structure the patient's needs (as in asking questions) so that they had the potential of being gratified.

Case 4

The final example relates to the termination of treatment. The therapist had to terminate treatment because he was moving to another city. The patient, a middle-aged single woman, asked the therapist to give her a photograph of himself. He hesitated be-

---

[1] I have discussed the interesting and stormy course of this schizoid young man's treatment elsewhere (Giovacchini 1979).

cause no one had ever made such a request before. He was inclined to believe that to give her a picture would cause her to remain nonproductively dependent on him. The patient's subsequent material indicated otherwise.

Since the patient found it difficult to hold a mental representation of her therapist between sessions, transition periods were especially difficult for her. She could not smoothly move from one frame of reference into another. She did not have a unity and cohesiveness of psychic structure; there was a lack of continuity among various psychic levels. Thus she found it painful to shift from the treatment setting to the nontreatment environment. Such patients often feel dizzy when getting up from the couch. She also anticipated how painful it would be to live in a world without her therapist. The photograph of the therapist would help her maintain a cohesive integration by mitigating the impact of his leaving; it would represent the synthesizing qualities of the therapeutic process.

The therapist finally agreed to give her his photograph. The patient felt soothed and seemed to accept the impending separation with equanimity.

With all four patients, the technical deviations had a cohesive effect; they gave the therapeutic relationship direction and growth and thereby helped the patients to acquire some psychic synthesis. They provided a secondary-process base that prevented primary-process material from becoming overwhelmingly chaotic. In the case of the adolescent patient, the developmental process was set in motion. I do not believe that any of these technical deviations are deviations from analysis. Interpretation within the transference context is still the principal analytic method, but there is an attempt to achieve more than the resolution of intrapsychic conflict. Through their acquisition of insight and new modes of relating, primitively fixated patients acquire psychic structure. These patients have been traumatized at early psychic levels and have known little gratification or understanding. The analytic relationship attempts to provide them with gratification through understanding.

SUMMARY

The population of borderline and other primitively fixated patients has received increasing attention in the past several decades. Recently, the treatment of such patients has moved from an exclusive focus on psychopathology to one that includes the therapeutic interaction in a psychoanalytic frame of reference.

This chapter focuses on a particular subgroup of patients whose psychopathology is defined by their ego defects, a subgroup I call the "unreasonable" patients. These patients have ego segments characterized by privation, a term Winnicott (1963) coined to mean the absence of an internalized matrix of previous gratifications. Since the infantile environments of these patients were withholding and unpredictable, they experience the world as "unreasonable." Therefore, in treatment, they assert their right to be "unreasonable."

In this chapter, I present various clinical examples, giving particular attention to a patient who developed a psychotic transference. I use the term somewhat in the same fashion Grotstein does in his chapter as something that can be worked with analytically, although it may be extremely difficult at times. This patient made me responsible for all the pain she had experienced during her life, a "delusional" belief that had some basis of reality. As treatment enabled her to experience some gratification, it also enabled her to feel the pain of deprivation. She achieved a capacity for minimal pleasure and maximum pain. Since the analysis was responsible for these achievements, she could blame it for her misery. The treatment was different from her infantile past in that in therapy she could have angry reactions, which were potentially reconstructive. With such patients, analysts may find themselves in the throes of disruptive countertransference reactions.

The early maternal relationship has two components: the nurturing one, which meets metabolic requirements for growth, and the soothing one, which becomes the foundation for the establishment of a holding environment. I give further clinical examples demonstrating disturbances of these early interactions. These traumatic disturbances lead to discontinuity of psychic levels, rather than a smooth hierarchical structural progression from primitive to advanced ego states. Patients characteristically cope with this discontinuity with special adaptations, such as narcissistic defenses and mergers based on sharing a feeling of "deadness."

The aim of treatment for borderline patients goes beyond the resolution of intrapsychic conflict to the acquisition of psychic structure. The achievement of this goal may require technical adaptations that go beyond interpretations within the transference context. Still, such adaptations are designed to establish a holding environment that is an intrinsic aspect of the psychoanalytic setting. I give specific examples of interactions in which patients used the analytic setting as a cohesive force to develop new psychic structures. The latter structures lead to the ability to form and hold mental representations and to construct endopsychic registrations of gratifying experiences. In other words, analysis enables these patients to use potentially helpful experiences in the outer world for the first time. The analytic setting is a paradigm for such experiences.

REFERENCES

Bergman, P. and Escalona, S. (1949). Unusual sensitivities in very young children. *The Psychoanalytic Study of the Child* 3-4: 333–352.

Boyer, L. B. (1956). On maternal overstimulation and ego defects. *The Psychoanalytic Study of the Child* 11: 236–256.

—— and Giovacchini, P. (1967). *Psychoanalytic Treatment of Schizophrenic and Characterological Disorders.* New York: Science House.

—— (1980). *Psychoanalytic Treatment of Borderline, Schizophrenic and Characterological Disorders.* New York: Aronson.

Erikson, E. H. (1959). *Identity and the Life Cycle.* New York: International Universities Press.

Flarsheim, A. (1975). The therapist's collusion with the patient's wish for suicide. In *Tactics and Techniques in Psychoanalytic Treatment: Countertransference Issues,* vol. 2, ed. P. Giovacchini, A. Flarsheim, and L. B. Boyer, pp. 155–196. New York: Aronson.

Freud, S. (1911-1915). Papers on technique. *Standard Edition* 12: 89-170. London: Hogarth Press, 1958.

—— (1914a). On narcissism: An introduction. *Standard Edition* 14: 67-102. London: Hogarth Press, 1957.

—— (1914b). Remembering, repeating, and working through. *Standard Edition* 12: 145-156. London: Hogarth Press, 1958.

—— (1915). Instincts and their vicissitudes. *Standard Edition* 14: 103-140. London: Hogarth Press, 1957.

—— (1920). Beyond the pleasure principle. *Standard Edition* 18: 3-66. London: Hogarth Press, 1955.

—— (1937). Analysis terminable and interminable. *Standard Edition* 23: 216-254. London: Hogarth Press, 1964.

Giovacchini, P. (1972). Interpretation and definition of the analytic setting. In *Tactics and Techniques in Psychoanalytic Therapy*, pp. 291-307. New York: Aronson.

—— (1975). *Psychoanalysis of Character Disorders*. New York: Aronson.

—— (1979). *Treatment of Primitive Mental States*. New York: Aronson.

Kernberg, O. (1976). *Object Relations Theory and Clinical Psychoanalysis*. New York: Aronson.

Kohut, H. (1971). *The Analysis of the Self*. New York: International Universities Press.

Mahler, M. S., Pine, F., and Bergman, A. (1975) *The Psychological Birth of the Human Infant*. New York: Basic Books.

Masterson, J. and Rinsley, D. (1975). The borderline syndrome. *Internat. J. Psycho-Anal.* 56: 163-177.

Schafer, R. (1976). *A New Language for Psychoanalysis*. New Haven: Yale University Press.

Searles, H. (1978). Psychoanalytic therapy with the borderline adult. In *New Perspectives in the Treatment of the Borderline Adult*, ed. J. Masterson, pp. 41-66. New York: Brunner/Mazel.

Spitz, R. (1945). Hospitalism. *The Psychoanalytic Study of the Child* 1: 53-75.

Stone, L. (1954). The widening scope of psychoanalysis. *J. Amer. Psychoanal. Assn.*: 562-594.

Winnicott, D. W. (1953). Transitional objects and transitional phenomena. In *Collected Papers: Through Paediatrics to Psychoanalysis*, pp. 229-242. New York: Basic Books, 1975.

—— (1956). Primary maternal preoccupation. In *Collected Papers: Through Paediatrics to Psychoanalysis*, pp. 300-306. New York: Basic Books, 1975.

———— (1960a). Ego distortion in terms of true and false self. In *The Maturational Processes and the Facilitating Environment*, pp. 140–152. New York: International Universities Press, 1965.

———— (1960b). The theory of the parent-infant relationship. In *The Maturational Processes and the Facilitating Environment*, pp. 37–56. New York: International Universities Press, 1965.

———— (1963). The mentally ill in your case load. In *The Maturational Processes and the Facilitating Environment*, pp. 217–230. New York: International Universities Press, 1965.

Wong, N. and Rinsley, D. (1980). The inner void: Overview. In *A Continuing Education Service from Smith, Kline and French.*

2

ANALYTIC EXPERIENCES IN WORK WITH REGRESSED PATIENTS

L. Bryce Boyer

For almost thirty years, I have used psychoanalysis with few parameters in the treatment of patients whose character structures placed them in or near the psychotic end of the continuum of psychopathological disorders. This treatment was done almost exclusively on an outpatient basis. Early in my work with such patients, I (1961) concluded that unresolved countertransference problems constitute a major obstacle to the successful outcome of their treatment. During the past twenty years, I have also come to believe that the therapist's emotional responses to the patient's productions may be used to enhance therapy.

Freud showed an ongoing concern with impediments to analytic success. Although he wrote a few papers that dealt with external obstacles, his principal preoccupation was the forces within the

---

This chapter is a synthesis and expansion of previously published papers (Boyer 1978a, 1978b) and presentations made at the twelfth Latin American Psychoanalytic Congress, Mexico City, February 1978; at 1979 meetings of the San Diego, San Francisco, and Southern California Psychoanalytic Societies; and at the Fifth Melitta Sperling Memorial Address in New York, 1979. I am especially grateful for the sapient discussions offered by Drs. Edward C. Adams, Gordon Bermak, Luis A. Chiozza, Allan Compton, Jack Gaines, Merton Gill, Peter L. Giovacchini, Samuel Hoch, Milton Lozoff, Lloyd C. Patterson, David Rosenfeld, Harold F. Searles, and Sanford Shapiro, elements of which have been incorporated here.

patient which militate against a favorable outcome. One such force was the "adhesive" (A. Freud 1969), or "sticky," libido. In general analysts have continued to focus on the contributions of patients' character structure to psychoanalytic treatment problems.

In 1910, Freud cited countertransference as a treatment impediment, but he never devoted a specific study to the phenomenon. He considered countertransference to be roughly the obverse of transference, in that it consisted of the repetition in the therapeutic relationship of the analyst's irrational, previously acquired attitudes. Freud assumed that countertransference was the result of the therapist having been inadequately analyzed. Prior to Hann-Kende's 1933 suggestion that the emotional responses of the therapist could be used as facilitators of the analytic process, psychoanalysts uniformly viewed countertransference in a pejorative light (Ferenczi 1919, Gruhle 1915, Stern 1924). After Hann-Kende, the next therapist to recommend the use of counter-transference as an analytic tool was Little (1951).

There is a large literature pertaining to countertransference reactions in the analyses of patients with neurotic transferences, including a number of reviews (Glover 1955, Orr 1954, Reich 1960). The most comprehensive recent review is that of Langs (1976), although it is restricted to writings that have appeared in English. During the past quarter of a century, increasing attention has been paid to the role of countertransference in the treatment of regressed patients, both as an impediment to and as a facilitator of the therapeutic process (Adler 1975, Arbiser 1978, Arieti 1955, Bion 1955, 1957, Epstein and Feiner 1979, Fromm-Reichmann 1950, Giovacchini et al. 1975a, Hill 1955, Kernberg 1974, Kusnet-zoff and Maldovsky 1977, Maltzberger and Buie 1974, Marcondes 1966, Milner 1969, Modell 1963, 1975, Nadelson 1977, Prado Galvão 1966, Robbins 1976, Searles 1965, E. Shapiro et al. 1977, Sperling 1967, Szalita-Pemow 1955, Volkan 1973, 1976, 1978, Wilson 1970, Zetzel 1971). Therapists who use analytic treatment for regressed patients note that their countertransference responses with these patients differ considerably from those experienced with neurotic patients.

Analysts have long been concerned with the means by which the psychological attributes of one person are assumed by another; many have written about the influence of patients' introjection of analysts' attributes on the transference relationship (Fairbairn 1952, Freud 1915a, Giovacchini 1975a, Guntrip 1961, Hartmann 1939, Loewald 1960, 1979, Schafer 1968). Fenichel (1945) was the first to note that analysts' countertransferences are largely determined by their introjections of patients' attributes, which may be communicated verbally or nonverbally; subsequent authors have corroborated Fenichel's observation (Federn 1952, Fliess 1953, Weigert 1954).

PRIMITIVE DEFENSE MECHANISMS OF REGRESSED PATIENTS

The intimate relationships of borderline and other regressed patients are characterized by the use of two closely related primitive defense mechanisms—namely, splitting and projective identification (E. Shapiro 1978). Many analysts believe that the regressed patients' tendency to use defenses that involve projection, combined with the introjective aspects of countertransference with such patients, results in countertransferential involvement different in kind and intensity from that commonly experienced in work with neurotic patients.

Splitting

Melanie Klein (1946) hypothesized that in the first months of life the infant has an omnipotent fantasy that unwanted parts of the personality or internal objects can be split, projected into an external object, and controlled. Kernberg (1975, 1976) found that an underlying pattern of sharply polarized relationships is "activated" in the transference of borderline patients and that the polarization is determined by the defensive maneuver of "splitting." That is, the love and hatred associated with internalized, relationships are split to avoid the anxiety that would result if they were experienced simultaneously. Patients defend themselves against anxiety by projecting the split-off unwanted personality aspect onto the therapist in the transference relationship.

With the successful negotiation of the rapprochement subphase of separation-individuation, the child develops the capacity for ambivalence and object constancy (Fraiberg 1969, Mahler et al. 1975, Settlage 1979). Although Giovacchini (Boyer and Giovacchini 1980, chapter 9) believes the psychopathology of borderline patients may be rooted in earlier periods of development, most observers think that it lies in patients' failure to traverse the rapproachement subphase successfully (Carter and Rinsley 1977, Mahler 1972, Masterson 1972, 1976, E. Shapiro et al. 1975, Zinner and E. Shapiro 1975).

Various authors have questioned the validity of characterizing splitting as a primary defense mechanism of regressed patients (Gunderson and Singer 1975, Heimann 1966, Mack 1975, Pruyser 1975, Robbins 1976). Nevertheless, therapists seem to agree that such patients are unable to integrate and modify their impulses and affects, which results in their alternately viewing their therapists as omnipotent and omniscient, and as helpless and ignorant. These patients experience scant dependency on their therapists in the sense of love and concern, but instead, undergo sudden shifts from total need to total devaluation. Therapists who do not expect such treatment by and reactions from regressed patients, or who are dependent on patients' approval for their sense of well-being, are expecially susceptible to anxiety-provoking, adverse countertransference reactions.

Projective Identification

The validity, necessity, and utility of the concept of projective identification, the second primitive defense mechanism characteristic of regressed patients, are sometimes questioned by those therapists who do not consider psychoanalysis the treatment of choice for such patients.

The type of material projected by regressed patients is determined by the immature nature of their mental operations, including
the selectively deficient modulation of their drives. Many therapists
(Fromm-Reichmann 1952, 1958, Hartmann 1953, Klein 1946,
Lidz and Lidz 1952, H. A. Rosenfeld 1952b, Winnicott 1960) have
noted the central position of conflicts related to the presence of
primitive, untamed aggression in borderline psychotic, and other
deeply regressed patients. The vicissitudes of the expression of
primitive aggression result in therapists' experiencing eeriness,
anxiety, and confusion, sometimes in empathy with patients' experience. Bermak (1979) remarked that "the projective identification type of countertransference occurs characteristically in treating
regressed patients . . . I have noticed that the feeling of being
affected profoundly and of having a sense of no longer being in
contact and of having departed from my well-established analytic
ego stance occurs particularly with patients who have borderline
features." His comment reflects the subjective experience of an
analyst confronted with the pressure of the patient's coercive and
seductive primitive projections.

Goldberg's position (1979, p. 347) that "in work with psychotic
patients transference and countertransference should not be regarded as separate entities" gives the flavor of the experience of
the analyst of the regressed patients. An evergrowing number
of analysts (Bion 1956, Carpinacci et al. 1963, Cesio 1963, 1973, Giovacchini 1975b, Grinberg 1957, 1958, 1962, Kernberg 1975, 1976,
Langer 1957, Novick and Kelly 1970, Paz et al. 1975, 1976a,
1976b, D. Rosenfeld and Mordo 1973, H. A. Rosenfeld 1952a,
1954, Searles 1963, Siquier de Failla 1963, Zinner and R. Shapiro
1972) turn to the concept of projective identification to understand
their countertransference responses to such patients and to use
these responses as facilitators of the analytic process.

Projective identification may be considered an early form of the
mechanism of projection (Kernberg 1975). It frequently has been
associated with both splitting and transitional relatedness (Modell
1968, 1975). Uncomfortable aspects of the personality, be they
elements of impulse, self-image, or superego, are dissociated and

projected onto another person, with whom the projecting person then identifies. According to Schafer (Ogden 1978), the projecting person feels "at one with" the person into whom he fantasizes he has projected an aspect of himself. Klein (1955) noted that once the split part of the personality has been projected onto another person, it is lost to the subject and an alteration of the object-perception process ensues. Projective identification may involve a nonhuman subject. Anna Freud (1967) wrote of a girl who projected her feelings of loss and sadness onto a cap that she had left at a campsite; she then could grieve, ostensibly for the deserted cap.

In the treatment situation, projective identification creates bewildering situations as patients attempt to evoke feelings and behavior on the part of their therapists that conform to the projection and the therapists consciously or unconsciously accept the projected attributes as parts of themselves (Grinberg 1963, 1976, Malin and Grotstein 1966). Such evocation is particularly characteristic of regressed patients. Many authors have written of the subtlety and effectiveness of such patients' attempts to accomplish this goal and the resulting countertransferential complications.

Patients who use projective identification as a defense are selectively inattentive to the real aspects of their therapists that may invalidate the projection (Brodey 1965). After imbuing their therapists with disclaimed and projected attributes, these patients consciously perceive the therapists to be unlike themselves, but they maintain an unconscious relationship with them in which the projected aspects can be experienced vicariously (Zinner and E. Shapiro 1975). The projective aspects of projective identification and projection per se differ in that, in the former, a greater degree of contact is maintained with the part of the personality that has been externalized. Those who use projective identification as a defense are somewhat aware that they are seeking to rid themselves of a property of themselves; in addition, they try to develop relationships with their therapists via the projection, to involve them as collusive partners who conform to the patients' perceptions of them. From the standpoint of countertransference, difficulties arise when therapists unwittingly become such collusive partners.

Racker (1968) wrote of concordant and complementary counter-transference identifications. In concordant countertransference identification, analysts identify with the corresponding part of patients' psychic apparatus: e.g., ego with ego and superego with superego. Under the influence of concordant countertransference identification, analysts experience as their own the central emotion being experienced by patients; they can behave empathically. In complementary countertransference identification, analysts identify with the internalized transference objects of patients; they have introjected patients' projections unconsciously. These projections stimulate unresolved unconscious conflicts in analysts, causing them to repeat earlier life experiences. Analysts then experience the emotions ascribed to them by patients as transference objects, while patients relive emotions experienced in the past with parental figures. For example, if an analyst identifies with a superego formation connected with a stern, forbidding father figure, he will seek aggressively to control the patient and an impasse may result. Racker (1953) has also discussed what he calls "indirect counter-transference," that is, therapists' emotional reactions to third persons involved in the treatment program and the latter's adverse effects.

Grinberg (1979) holds that in complementary countertrans-ference identification, analysts always react in ways that correspond to their own conflicts. At times, the analyst takes onto himself a reaction or a feeling that comes from the patient. He calls this phenomenon "projective counteridentification," describes how it may lead to treatment impediments, and cites interpretive steps from his own and Segal's case material (1956) to illustrate how the impediments can be removed once the therapist becomes aware of the problem.

An important but rarely discussed facet of projective identifi-cation in the therapeutic situation is the reintrojection by patients of that which they projected. Ordinarily, the projection involves patients' hostility, which they perceive to be exceedingly dangerous. Many regressed patients are particularly interested in how thera-pists handle their own aggression. These patients often are un-usually sensitive to hostility in their therapists and are masters at provoking it. Over time, as patients observe that their therapists' own hostility and/or that which they believe was projected into them have harmed neither the therapists nor themselves, they come to view hostility as less dangerous. Of course, acquiring the capacity to make such an observation depends on complex interactions in the developing transference and real relationship (Loewald 1960). Patients' observation that hostility will not destroy them or their therapists, combined with a taming of patients' aggression as a result of successful therapy, allows them to reintroject their modified—or, in the words of a patient, "detoxified"— hostility and integrate it into their evolving personalities. Milton Lozoff (personal communication 1979) has suggested that patients' improved ability to handle their aggression may be due in part to their identification with analysts' management of *their own* aggression.

In the fifth year of her successful analysis, a severely obsessive-compulsive woman who had had periodic, transient psychotic regressions over many years both in and out of therapy made the following statement:

> I always treasured my anger as a child, but I kept it secret because I was afraid my thoughts, let alone my words, had killed my aunt, made my mother hate me, and my father leave me. I've always been afraid my angry feelings would kill you and the first time you went away, I spent the days and nights on my knees on street corners praying to God that He would protect you from my anger and keep you alive. I know now that for years I've tried to hurt you with my thoughts, words, and actions, although I thought for a long time it was you who were trying to hurt me with yours. Now I know my anger is not dangerous like I thought before.

However, it is not only hostility that may be viewed as magically dangerous by the regressed patient. Giovacchini (1975a), Klein (1946), Searles (1958), and I have had patients who deemed their love to be destructive. During treatment, these patients had the omnipotent fantasy that they projected their love into their therapists for safekeeping, with the idea that they would reintroject it when they no longer considered it so potentially harmful. Bion (1956), among others, has written of regressed patients' projection of their "sanity," or the nonpsychotic portion of their personality, into the therapist.

I first became aware of the patient's use of the therapist as a repository before I underwent psychoanalytic training. At that time, I was a psychiatrist in the army. A man in a straitjacket was brought to the hospital where I worked. He had been catatonically excited for some weeks. Because I received several hundred new patients along with him, I was initially too busy to give any of them more than cursory attention. I told him that I could not talk with him at length. I asked him to record the experiences he wanted to communicate to me, as I wouldn't be able to see him for a few days. He received no medication and only routine ward care until I saw him a week later. By then, he appeared to have recovered completely. When I invited him into my office, he presented me with two thick notebooks filled with his handwritten account of his aggression-laden hallucinatory and delusional experiences, among others. No apparent regression transpired during the ensuing month; then I asked him why he had recovered. He was surprised and said it was because he had given me his crazy ideas in the notebooks. He had watched me carefully and was amazed that his writings had not visibly affected me.

Some ten years later, I received a letter from him stating that he had remained well; he expressed concern about my mental health. This patient seemed to have used the written word, and then his therapist, as the repository for his mental aberrations.

THE "STICKY" LIBIDO

Let us turn to the notion that a "sticky" libido in and of itself may be responsible for an unresolvable psychoanalytic impasse. Early in my clinical experience, the analyses of two female patients with severe characterological disorders were terminated because triadic relationship interpretations of their highly eroticized transference reactions were ineffective. I was all too willing to believe that the onus should be placed on the so-called adhesive libido. However, nagging uneasiness and troublesome dreams led me to conclude that countertransference involvement had been responsible for the therapeutic failures. Self-analysis was contaminated by too many scotomas; therefore I reentered formal analysis, during which I discovered that the seductive way these women had presented their conflicts, and the nature of the conflicts themselves, had stirred up unconscious problems of my own. Through Racker's complementary countertransference identification (1968), or the counterreaction Chediak (1979) described as "the analyst's transference to the patient," I had identified these patients with an important person of my past.

I came to understand that hidden behind my patients' view of me as a genitally withholding father surrogate was their projection onto me of bad self-objects and maternal part objects. My impatience over their failure to accept my misdirected interpretations had supported their view that I was sadistically frustrating. Following my own reanalysis, one of them returned to me and was successfully treated.

INTERPRETATION OF
DYADIC RELATIONSHIPS IN
THE TRANSFERENCE

Partly as a result of my experiences with these two women patients, early in my work with regressed patients I learned to respond only to certain aspects of transference reactions that had oedipal coloring and appeared early in treatment. After some years, I learned that therapeutic impasses commonly followed triadic relationship interpretations of such material. However, focusing on the material's aggressive aspects within the context of dyadic relations avoided such stalemates (Boyer 1966). Such an approach is consonant with the current developmental conceptualization of the nature of therapeutic action in psychoanalysis (Settlage 1979). The clinical experiences of Atkins (1967, the Ornsteins (1975), H. A. Rosenfeld (1966), Sperling (1967), Volkan

(1978, 1979), and Wilson (1970), among others, corroborate my findings. These clinicians agree that following the mending of the splits and fragmentations of regressed patients' identity via modern representations of their earlier dyadic relationships, analysis with such patients is scarcely different from that with neurotic patients, who typically use pre-oedipal rather than oedipal material in the service of defense. Only after the dyadic material has been repeated and worked through can investigation of the oedipal transference be fruitful. A clinical example follows.

At one time a young woman came to see me, complaining of genital anesthesia. I was overjoyed at having found what I initially thought was a classical case of hysteria. Soon, however, I had to revise my judgment; after she had been on the couch for a few days, she misunderstood an adventitious noise to mean that I was openly masturbating behind her and she complacently started to rub her own pubis, stating that as a child she had manipulated her genitalia while surreptitiously watching her father masturbate. What appeared to be a floridly erotic oedipal transference ensued for a very short time. I viewed it as a pseudo-oedipal resistance, which turned out to be correct. Her treatment proceeded unusually smoothly for some three years, during which time her projection onto me of bad self-objects and maternal part objects was analyzed.

A year before I was to take a sabbatical to do other work, I informed this patient of my impending absence. Dr. D.'s consultation room adjoined my own and he then became a fantasized father surrogate for the patient. A few months before I was to depart, she said she wanted to continue her analysis with him after I left. She continued to use me primarily as a maternal surrogate throughout our work together. Her treatment with Dr. D. lasted a year and dealt solely with classical oedipal problems, which Dr. D. considered typical of analyses of hysterical neurotic patients. This woman has shown no regression in the twenty-odd years since her termination.

During her analysis with me, which lasted nearly three years, the patient valiantly sought to get me to behave as her mother had behaved during the patient's early childhood. In her studies of psychotic children and their mothers, Sperling (1974) found that mothers unconsciously induced psychosis in their children. Wilson (personal communication 1979), who noted that his regressed patients often strove assiduously to get him to repeat the roles and behaviors of their mothers, suggested that success in treatment depends on our analyzing such efforts by patients, rather than identifying with and repeating their mothers' actions.

ANALYTIC TOLERANCE OF REGRESSIVE BEHAVIOR

Clearly, analysts' capacity to remain objective and empathic is of paramount importance in the treatment of all patients, but such an equilibrium is especially difficult to maintain with regressed patients whose communications are more strongly influenced by the primary process. Kernberg (1975, 1978) has advocated that when one undertakes the treatment of borderline patients, it may be advisable to set formal limits on these patients' behavior and to obtain their permission to be hospitalized should their regression in the analysis lead to behavior that makes it difficult for the analyst to remain objective.

Analysts' tolerance of patients' behavior varies widely. In part, this is due to the nature of their training. Psychoanalysis is being used for an ever-widening scope of disturbances, as a result of (1) the vast expansion of child analysis and longitudinal studies of infants, children, and the mother-child dyad, (2) the increased emphasis on the analysis of the ego, (3) therapeutic revisions based on changed theoretical concepts (e.g., the overshadowing of the topographical by the structural hypothesis, with a consequent etiological shift toward viewing psychopathology as the outcome of both developmental deficiencies and conflict), and (4) the growing sophistication of developmental and object-relations theory.

Despite these developments, many training institutes still teach candidates that psychoanalysis should be offered solely to patients with transference neuroses and that other patients should receive supportive therapy or diluted versions of psychoanalytic psychotherapy which largely exclude interpretation of the transference.

Since the inception of psychoanalysis as a treatment modality, there has been a gross discrepancy between this traditional view and the actual practice of psychoanalysis (Boyer and Giovacchini 1980, chapters 2 and 3). Freud analyzed numerous patients who clearly suffered from severe characterological disorders, borderline conditions, and even psychoses (Binswanger 1956, Reichard 1956). Parenthetically, there seems to be no question that failures in the treatment of some of Freud's seriously disturbed patients resulted from countertransference impediments (Giovacchini and Boyer 1975).

As a result of this traditional training, some candidates and young psychoanalysts either forego offering analysis to many patients for whom it is optimally suitable or offer it to them with great guilt and anxiety. The state of both their knowledge and their own emotions interferes with the treatment process. Some observers point to another serious deficiency in traditional psychoanalytic education: supervisors who fail to help candidates see that "a countertransference response is often an indication of some need within the patient and can be a guide to a deeper understanding of both the patient and the therapist" (S. Shapiro 1979).

One message included in the traditional training of candidates is that regression to early pregenital states in the transference situation is an indication to abandon psychoanalysis as the treatment of choice. Yet it has been recognized that oscillations between regression and progression are a necessary aspect of psychological development (A. Freud 1965). Regression and ego disorganization are crucial steps in the progressive consolidation of the personality (Loewald 1960). The periods of consolidation around the time of the emergence of the Oedipus complex and toward the end of adolescence often follow phases of regression, at times to the level of dyadic relationships, and ego disorganization. Such regressions are to be expected in insight-oriented treatment of the patient population we have been discussing.

Regression generally constitutes a return to early failure or success (Winnicott 1954). Regression may represent (1) a failure or defect in current modes of mastery, (2) a reactivation of earlier modes of adaptation generally associated with ties to libidinally gratifying objects, or (3) an attempt to master a previous failure using techniques that may be inconsistent with current modes of mastery (A. Freud 1936, Freud 1926a, Schur 1953). Such an attempt may be in the service of progression.

The development of transference in analysis may bring about new and deeper regressive tendencies that may seriously threaten the therapeutic (Zetzel 1956), or working alliance (Greenson 1965). Some analysts see regressive tendencies as undesirable analytic obstacles that must be eliminated. Others see them as defensive moves against the "dangers" of the analytic situation (Calder 1958, Holzman and Ekstein 1959) that may be used to master early trauma and perhaps even to "unblock" arrested maturation and development (Alexander 1956, Bettelheim 1967, Giovacchini 1979a, Khan 1960). Kris (1950) viewed psychoanalytic treatment as a creative experience in which the patient's ego has an opportunity to use regression in the service of the analytic work and the patient's maturation.

There is a growing minority view that patients should not be denied psychoanalytic treatment on the basis of a phenomenological diagnosis of severe characterological disorder or psychosis. Instead, according to this view, analyzability should be determined on the basis of a therapeutic diagnosis (Winnicott 1954), that is, a statement concerning patients' capacity to use treatment. The therapeutic diagnosis depends primarily on two factors. First, patients must be able to sustain themselves between therapy hours and to get to and from their appointments. They may require assistance from family members and, in extreme instances, adjunctive casework management, to accomplish this (Flarsheim 1972). Second, patients' behavior in therapy hours must be tolerable to their analysts. Analysts' thresholds of discomfort will vary with their idiosyncratic personal interests and sensitivities, their prior experience with regressed patients, the ego state and psychopathology of the patient involved, and their unconscious reactions to the patient's behavior and verbal productions (Hoedemaker 1967). Giovacchini (1979b, p. 236) has stressed the importance of the last factor: "The judgment whether a patient is treatable . . . depends more upon the analyst's psychic integration than the patient's psychopathology."

Analysts respond differently even to fairly ordinary behavior. Patients' silence, which has been discussed from the standpoint of resistance, transference, and countertransference, is a case in point (Bergler 1938, Levy 1958, Loomie 1961, Waldhorn 1979). Racker (1957) stressed that at times patients' words and ideas may serve as needed gratification or "nutriment" for the analyst. Zeligs (1960) wrote of the analyst's retributive hostility engendered by patients' silence. Erikson (personal communication 1948) was so intolerant of silent patients that he gave up treating them. Searles (1961) wrote of analysts' incapacity to tolerate the intimacy of silence; he suggested that their interpretations sometimes serve the defensive function of breaking what patients perceive to be a needed silence, during which time they can fantasize being in a state of symbiotic union with their therapists.

Flarsheim (1972) once analyzed a psychotic man who was frequently mute. Indeed, one of his silences lasted for three months. Flarsheim felt the man needed to experience in a controlled and safe environment his regressed, magical means of control over parental images through silence, as a manifestation of withholding. Flarsheim's therapeutic philosophy contributed to his comfort during the patient's silences, but he also read and wrote to control his retributive hostility. Eventually, the patient's silences became a means of communicating how he wanted to be treated, rather than being merely a magical device to control. Flarsheim's tolerance of his regression had contributed to his development of a more integrated ego.

Some analysts take a pessimistic view of any psychosomatic regression, despite the work of many clinicians (Alexander and French 1950, Bruch 1973, Chiozza 1976, 1978, 1979, Garma 1978, Schneer 1963, Sperling 1974, 1978, Thöma 1967, Wilson 1968) who have illustrated so graphically the meanings, uses, and analyzability of psychosomatic disorders. Others see the occurrence of such regressions during the treatment of some patients as a necessary step in the development of trust and the capacity for dependency on which the therapeutic alliance relies. Atkins (1967) stressed that the quality of that alliance reflects to a considerable extent patients' actual relationships with early caretakers; when their capacity for dependency is threatened by fears and distrust, the latter must become a primary focus of analytic work and interpretation.

Fortified with this therapeutic philosophy, Atkins was able to tolerate the extremely regressive behavior of one patient over a period of several years. When he invited this patient to relax his censorship of thoughts and feelings and to communicate through free associations, the patient mumbled, at times incoherently. Relaxation gradually extended to his sphincters. During asthmatic attacks, he produced copious amounts of sputum and vomit; he also passed urine and feces and ejaculated without erection or conscious feelings or fantasies. Atkins (1967, p. 593) wrote, "During deeply regressed times in the transference he felt himself to be actually his mother, not simply like her." In the third year of analysis, his regression reached its deepest phase and was finally experienced solely as a physiological experience. Despite the severity of the patient's disturbance, it was possible to maintain what Atkins called the "ordinary analytic situation" and to analyze the regressive experience, which was understood to be a reliving of a disturbed mother-child relationship. The regressions during the remainder of the analysis were like the transient ones commonly seen in a transference neurosis.

Case Example: Regression in a Borderline Patient

A married woman in her twenties, fit the modern criteria for borderline personality disorder (Gunderson and Kolb 1978, Gunderson and Singer 1975, Kernberg 1975, Perry and Klerman 1980, Spitzer et al. 1979) very well. When she was permitted to live out her regression, which was limited to the analytic situation, it led to a reliving experience that seemingly made possible the release of innate maturational capacities.

The patient suffered a catatonoid withdrawal when she left home to attend college (Boyer 1971). To some degree, she knew she needed to establish contact with a substitute for her mother, whom she consciously scorned and hated. But her unconscious fear of overt homosexuality made her avoid females. She kept herself relatively intact psychologically by making a mother surrogate of a young man with whom she had her first dates. A virgin, she refused intercourse the first time they went out because she was unconsciously afraid that his phallus would grow to the size of a baby and rip her apart. On their second date, she quite willingly consented to fellatio, a practice which was their customary sexual activity for some weeks. While sucking on his penis, she entered into blissful trances that included fantasies of nursing on the fantasized phallus-nipple of her mother. Eventually, the young man demanded intercourse and she became pregnant.

They married and she left school while her husband continued his studies. She briefly believed that their two children resulted from parthenogenesis. Partly because she was jealous of her husband's attention to the children, she became sadomasochistically provocative and inordinately demanding of his time and attention. She often slept in the bathtub, sometimes in continuously running hot water. As would be expected, she unconsciously equated that experience with a return to the fantasized bliss of intrauterine life. She barely disguised her pleasure when her husband responded to her defiant sleeping in the bathtub by beating her and subsequently raping her, using either her vagina or her mouth. Eventually he left the family, although they remained legally married. After his departure she became confused and paranoid and entered analysis.

Soon after she found that her analyst was able to understand some of her diffuse, primary-process dominated productions and was apparently unafraid of her leechlike aggression, she began to improve in her everyday life. She was able to get her first paying job and to become self-supporting; she could then divorce her husband. Her life outside of the consultation room became better organized, but during her therapy hours she became increasingly dreamy and her verbal productions became increasingly bizarre. Then, for about six months, she lay on the couch fantasizing that she was performing fellatio on me every day, believing at times that she was actually sucking on my penis. She was worried about draining my bodily contents and depriving me of power and substance in her efforts to fuse with me or take me totally inside her. There was no doubt that the penis, which never was erect in the continuing fantasies that were unaccompanied by sexual excitement, often represented an amalgam of both her parents, but predominantly her mother. Searles (1975) believes that through such fantasies patients re-establish an imagined symbiotic state within the transference.

During that six-month period, I just waited; I was comfortable with my periodic fantasies of merging with her and my transitory oceanic feelings while she engaged in what for her was a singularly gratifying experience, one which she unsolicitedly said she must live through in order to emerge from "some stunted stage of infantile development." She was psychologically unsophisticated and had read no analytic literature. Had I chosen, no doubt I could have focused on the aggressive and defensive aspects of her behavior and shortened her regressive episode. However, as I considered the modified reliving and abreactive experience to be in the service of her psychological development, I did not interfere.

Subsequent to the regressive period, her genitalia became cathected and for the first time she could feel sexual excitement that was not associated or confused with excretory functions. She later matured to a state in which I served as a clear whole object father surrogate. After partial analysis of what had then become an oedipal transference neurosis, she left treatment and remarried. Five years later, she returned for analysis of a neurotic problem. There had been no subsequent psychotic regression, although a brief one occurred during her second analysis. My philosophical orientation contributed to my tolerance of this patients' regressed behavior and enabled me to avoid adverse countertransference reactions.

The following vignettes illustrate how treatment impasses with severely regressed patients can be turned into therapeutic enhancers by using the countertransference experience productively.

Case Example: Regression in a Patient with a Severe Impulse Disorder

Fifty-three years old when first seen, Mrs. X. was a twice-divorced, friendless white file clerk who lived alone and was almost totally impulse dominated (Boyer 1977). Under continuous psychiatric treatment of many different kinds for emotional aloofness, impulsivity, and chronic alcoholism for almost twenty years, she had been hospitalized frequently for weeks to months at a time, and usually had been diagnosed as schizophrenic. She had been jailed many times and while in the "drunk tank" had masturbated openly, smeared feces and menstrual effluvia, and screamed endlessly. She had lived dangerously, provoking sexual assault by black gangs in ghettos on various occasions. When she came for treatment, she literally believed that she had never had angry impulses and that any behavior which might have been interpreted as such had been motivated by altruism. Her principal stated reason for seeking psychoanalysis was that she had been told by the therapist of her psychotic son that her interactions with him contributed to the continuation of his disturbance; she eagerly had sought a form of treatment that she knew would be very painful in the service of helping him to improve. She had sought psychoanalysis from highly reputable practitioners several times previously, but none had accepted her for such treatment.

Mrs. X. was the child of a self-centered, vain, impulsive, and hypochondriacal mother and a depressed, exhibitionistic, profligate father who committed suicide during her adulthood. His chronic alcoholism had led to the loss of the fortune inherited from his and his wife's families. In her preschool years, Mrs. X. had read and done arithmetic precociously, but after the first year of school, she became barely literate and lost her mathematical abilities. Her failure to pass any examination in all her school years after the first grade did not disturb her parents, whose goal for their four daughters, of whom she was the second, was that they use their grace and beauty to acquire rich husbands, preferably doctors, who would support the family lavishly. During an early session she stated that she thought she had had a secret liaison during her grammer school years with a swarthy chauffeur who wore black gloves.

She had had a severe obsessive-compulsive neurosis with strong altruistic features from the age of seven or eight till twelve, when she was sent to a girls' finishing school where she felt loved by an adored classmate. At sixteen, she felt deserted by her idol and withdrew to such a degree that she functioned essentially as a robot for almost six years. She had no boyfriends, although she was quite beautiful, and she behaved mechanically at social functions, including her own debut. When she was twenty-one, her older sister seemed to have "hooked" a rich medical student from an elite social level. Mrs. X. was galvanized into action, apparently by her need to be the family savior, and got the man to marry her instead.

Her sexual passivity and frigidity infuriated her self-centered and unfeeling husband, who had many affairs that he flaunted before her in a manner reminiscent of her father. While her husband attended school in another city, she lived with his parents. Her father-in-law, a retired minister, ascribed her passivity to possession by demons, which he sought to exorcise by giving her enemas while she was naked in the bathtub, an action endorsed by her husband and her parents. She was unaware of either anger or sexual excitement, but had fantasies of seducing her father-in-law and destroying him by public exposure and ridicule. Following her husband's graduation, he entered the army and they moved to a distant area. He was soon sent overseas. As a result of her shyness and passivity, she was almost constantly alone. She began to drink in solitude and had drunken autoerotic and vengeful fantasies that were repressed when she sobered up. She bore three children, none of whom she believed to be her own for varying periods after their births. She feared touching them, and a succession of nursemaids were hired to take care of them and her. She began to frequent bars where she picked up men and had short-lived affairs.

Her third child was an autistic, feces-smearing, exceedingly hyperactive boy who was hospitalized when he was two or three years old. He rarely acknowledged her existence. Her husband divorced her and henceforth had only rare contact with her or the children. She limited her sexual partners to black men, repressing the actual sexual experiences. On the occasional weekends that her son was with her during the next few years, she brought men home with her and submitted to fellatio and sodomy before him, subjecting him to primal scene traumas that repeated her own early experiences, which she had repressed. She also repressed the behavior to which she exposed her son, learning of her actions only through her nursemaids. After her daughters were taken away from her, her behavior became increasingly irrational, resulting in her being hospitalized and jailed.

During one of her hospitalizations, Mrs. X. met a man who was a chronic alcoholic. They began to live together and eventually got married. As she had uncritically idealized her mother and later her schoolmate, she now idealized him. As would be expected, she uncritically despised certain authority figures, projecting the "bad mother" onto them as she had done earlier with her father. Her new husband was so like her physically that she often wore his clothes. At times they drank together and spent days in bed, performing polymorphous perverse sexual activities to the point of exhaustion while lying in their own excreta. She often experienced bliss, consciously believing they had achieved a symbiotic physical union. They lived on welfare and grudging charity from her relations. A psychiatrist suggested that she would have more self-value if she became employed. She managed to complete a course in practical nursing and had some success in state hospitals, caring for psychotic and senile patients with empathic tenderness. She was fired repeatedly because of drunkenness.

Eventually her husband left her, an action she could not comprehend since she believed that he depended on their fantasized physical and psychological continuity as she did, and because she supported him financially. A few years before beginning treatment with me, she had obtained a job as a file clerk in a place where her inefficiency and instability were tolerated. Her low-cost therapy was financed by an allotment from a deceased family friend.

Following an early session to which she came drunk, seeking through bizarre behavior to test my anxiety tolerance, to seduce me, and to establish a symbiotic union through sexual actions, Mrs. X. decided not to come to the office intoxicated. Soon thereafter, she spontaneously vowed to cease going to bars and picking up men or, as she expressed it, "to be a good girl." Nevertheless, during the first four or five months of treatment, on most weekends she drank wine or beer at home and often woke up in the company of some man whom she could not recall having met. She had no memory of their activities. After a time, she was able to recall the intervening step of going to bars to pick up men. I understood her behavior to have the unconscious, symbolic, communicative role of informing me of the meanings of past activities (Ekstein 1976). She was confused by and rejected my initial transference interpretation that I was a surrogate father figure; eventually I comprehended that my transference role was that of an idealized, phallic, surrogate maternal figure.

On Mondays, she often presented dreams or fantasies in which a young animal or child was tortured or unjustly punished. I assumed they were connected to her weekend activities and silently hypothesized that these activities constituted an identification with what she had perceived to be aggression toward her when as a child she had been exposed to parental sexual behavior and had felt tortured or unjustly punished. I knew I would have to wait a very long time to validate my hypothesis. However, retrospectively I believe I had begun effectively to ignore her as an adult and to perceive her only as a kind of puppet. Treatment stagnated and she began to get drunk and pick up men during the week. I felt increasingly incompetent, helpless, and annoyed with her. I now doubted her claim that she had forgotten the actual sexual activities with the various men; she could not have been unaware of my accusing anger.

During one session, after I silently called her a liar, I became sleepy (McLaughlin 1975). While dozing, I pictured myself as a young child whose contradictory wishes to be good and bad controlled me without my will. With a start, I became alert and thought that it must have been necessary for her to subject me to her emotional experience and that my own emotional needs were being satisfied by an empathic response. I briefly recalled Searles's oft-repeated statement that work with severely regressed patients requires *mutual* emotional growth. I then consciously put myself in her place and supposed that she was experiencing similar helplessness in the face of contradictory wishes. I further assumed that she experienced my repeated questions as accusations, that my past actions had supported her externalized self-punitive need, and that she had expected a reward for her vow to be a "good girl," but felt that she had received none.

When I voiced my assumptions, she acknowledged their validity and recognized her disappointment over my previous lack of awareness of what she had been experiencing. She said she must have been trying to put parts of herself into me and thus get rid of them. Soon thereafter, for the first time during her analysis, she recalled a specific detail of her actions in a bar. She had been disappointed when a man refused her advances, saying she was "too old a pussy" for him. She then dreamed that a boy put kerosene on a kitten's tail and lit it; the kitten ran away terrified, although it wanted to claw and bite its tormenter. In association to the dream, she recalled an early interview in which I had refused her sexual advances. She had responded by trying to claw my face and kick my genitals (my "tail"), which she had sought to put "on fire."

After the foregoing material was discussed, Mrs. X. stopped going to bars and became aware of her anger toward the men she picked up, although the sexual interactions remained repressed. It was a large step forward for her to become aware that she *had* anger and angry wishes that could not be rationalized as stemming from altruistic motives. However, she was not yet aware that her various disappointments with me screened angry feelings toward me. Her projection onto me of the forgiven, uncritically idealized good-mother object remained intact.

When I began treating Mrs. X., I informed her that after six months, I would be leaving for a period of several weeks. Periodically during the six months, she recalled vividly that when she had been a child, her mother customarily had gone to Europe alone on the Grand Tour. The patient had been bitterly disappointed and lonely at such times, and had feared that her mother would die or would not return because she did not want her children and despised her husband. Mrs. X. also had believed that mother had left her because of Mrs. X.'s secret malfeasances with the chauffeur and envy of those sisters who got more of mother's attention than she did through their temper tantrums and other disturbing behavior. Mrs. X. had assumed the role of family martyr in part to assuage her guilt. When I left, I felt secure that her separation anxiety had been dealt with adequately.

Upon my return, I was completely surprised to learn that im-

mediately after I had departed she had attempted to commit
suicide by taking sedatives she had saved from previous therapy
and that her effort had been thwarted quite accidentally. Her
suicide attempt had been determined by several unconscious motivations. As a child, she had believed that her parents had a limited
quantity of love to distribute among their daughters. She had
blamed the emotional upsets of her sisters on her existence, which
had diminished the supply of parental love. She had often contem-
plated altruistic suicide for their welfare. She had also equated her
mother's absence with death and had thought that she could re-
establish symbiotic union with her mother when she died. But a new
element gradually emerged from repression.

We now learned that during her preschool years, the patient's
maternal grandfather had been a consistent love object for her; he
had held her on his lap, read and told her fairy tales, and admired her
reading and mathematical precocity. He had died during her first
school year, but she had not been allowed to view his corpse and unconsciously had retained the belief that he was still alive. He had
once promised her a white elephant and she had taken him literally.
From the Kipling stories he had read to her, she knew that white
elephants might be found in India. In later life, she became seriously
involved in Eastern religions, unconsciously believing that they
would lead her to the white elephant and reunite her with her grandfather. She also retained the idea that if she were to die, she could
join him in heaven and reestablish the gratifying relationship she
had experienced before. Two additional motives for her attempted
suicide were discovered. First, since childhood she had believed
that her death would make it possible for her sisters to obtain
more love from their parents to whom she ascribed finite love—
too little in quantity to be shared by four daughters. Her altruistic
thought helped her deny her death wish toward her sisters. Now
she believed that her death would enable me to give better care to
my other patients, her surrogate sister figures. And second, she
unconsciously hoped her suicide would destroy me professionally,
to avenge herself for my presumed favoritism for other patients.
Even though she talked about her anger toward me, she spoke
intellectually; her anger was not experienced consciously. We found
that the loss of her capacity to learn, that is, to read and to do

mathematics, was based in part on her attempt to deny the knowledge that her grandfather had died.

After much of this material had been worked through, another therapeutic impasse occurred as a result of my unconscious response to disturbing material of which she sought to rid herself by placing it in me. It will be recalled that during her son's home visits as a small boy, he had seen her drunken sexual behavior with men. Sometimes, when she was unconsciously angry with me, she would return to her shameful memories of being confronted by the nursemaids with those actions. For a few weeks, her interviews were dominated by this issue. I did not know why she was angry with me and felt further frustrated because I could not understand why she expressed that repressed anger with seemingly endless repetitions of material that seemed to lead nowhere. I gradually noted that when she began her ruminative iterations, I responded with irritation and sleepiness. She reverted to picking up men in bars and our rapport all but disappeared. For the first time I regretted having accepted her in analysis and wondered why I had done so.

I found myself fantasizing during one hour, but later could not remember my fantasies. Over the years, I have come to the conclusion that the fantasies I have during sessions are often my empathic responses to what patients are trying to tell me or have me experience. Accordingly, I thought that I had forgotten my fantasy because I had needed to defend myself from internal conflicts that our relationship was reawakening. That night, I had a dream that reminded me of my own past. Through my own analysis, I had learned that I had become an analyst with the unconscious motivation of curing an important love object of my childhood who had suffered from a regressive personality disorder. Analysis of my dream made me aware that another reason for my becoming an analyst was that I had sought to protect a younger sib from the effect of that adult's personality disorder. I knew then that I had accepted Mrs. X. in therapy not only to help her but to help her psychotic son as well.

I then became aware that underlying my conscious identification of her with the disturbed love object of my past lay an unconscious identification of her abused son with my sib and myself as children.

I was expressing my anger by withdrawal and refusal to recognize her, as her autistic son had done during the first several years of his life. Such knowledge permitted me to regain my objectivity. Finally, I could interpret her wish to provoke my abuse and punishment for her treatment of her son and me. She responded by remembering dreams and hypnopompic fantasies in which she was forced to watch women being raped anally and having huge phalluses shoved into their mouths. This led to the recovery of memories of what had transpired between her and the black-gloved, swarthy chauffeur. She had equated him with a kind black waiter who had once comforted her; following her grandfather's death, she had sat on the chauffeur's lap, seeking to make him a surrogate grandfather figure. However, after initially telling her fairy tales, he had held her head and forced his phallus into her mouth. After this, the themes of her interactions with the chauffeur and her behavior before her own son all but disappeared in the analysis. About three years after the recovery of this memory, when these themes reappeared, they could be interpreted as attempts to master—by action—her theretofore repressed terror and feelings of dissolution when she had watched parental sexual activities.

Case Examples: Regression in
Schizophrenic Patients

The final clinical example illustrates how clinical experience and increasing knowledge have enabled me to turn threatened impasses into analytic facilitators. It seems to me that what transpired in this instance can be understood best through use of the concept of projective identification, with its intrapsychic and interpersonal aspects.

In "The Unconscious," Freud (1915b, p. 199) wrote, "in schizophrenia words are subjected to the same process as that which makes the dream-images out of dream-thoughts." He was referring to the well-known fact that regression sometimes involves the loss of one's capacity to use words as symbols. I have twice observed patients who in the course of interviews underwent regressions during which they used not only words but syllables as concrete objects. Curiously, each of them bisected the same word, table, into the syllables "tay" and "bul."

When I was an anxious new practitioner, a young man who seemed to me to be suffering from an obsessive-compulsive neurosis requested treatment. The first two vis-à-vis interviews proceeded in a routine manner. When he came the third time, he was anxious and after a short period he hesitantly reported a dream, the manifest content of which involved his having been attacked homosexually. He began to slap a small table which abutted the arm of the chair in which he sat. As he did so, he said the word table. Soon his eyes had a glazed appearance and he seemed bewildered. I became frightened and could only think of seeking to help him regain contact with reality. He paid no attention to my calling him by his name nor to my reassurances. Instead, he looked past me as though he were talking to someone behind me and asked if the object he was slapping *were* a table. He then repeatedly yelled the word table but soon repetitively shouted "tay" and "bul." I hospitalized him and he was eventually treated by electroconvulsive therapy, with transient improvement.

Many years later, the father of 17-year-old Robert sought analysis for his son as a last resort (Boyer 1976). Robert had undergone an acute schizophrenic regression two years before and had been treated first with electroconvulsive therapy and then with supportive therapy and antipsychotic drugs, but had shown continuing hebephrenic deterioration. His therapist had become ill and had had to interrupt his practice.

Our first four interviews were spaced over a period of some months. Robert was skeptical about changing therapists. During the first interview, I understood some of his incoherent utterances to express symbolically a fear that if he were to leave his hospitalized therapist, that man might die. However, I limited my interpretations to suggesting that Robert's silliness, incoherence, and vagueness were efforts to disguise information that he feared I might use against him. He became briefly lucid and was relieved and intrigued.

In our second meeting, I said I thought he was using hallucinations in the service of secondary gain. He was delighted that I

considered the functions and content of his hallucinations interesting data for investigation and said he wanted to become a
psychologist like me.

During the third session, I asked if he was afraid that his anger
at his therapist had made that man ill. Again, he was relieved.
Following that session, he asked his father whether anger was ever
justified and was forcefully told that it was not.

The fourth time we met, I indicated that he feared not only
intense, hostile feelings but deeply experienced positive ones as
well. He then asked me to take him into analysis. I told him I
would be willing to undertake such therapy on an experimental
basis when time became available, but only if his parents agreed.
Accordingly, I met with them. I learned that his schizoid mother
had been a virgin until her marriage at thirty-six and that she
considered sexual relations disgustingly intrusive. His father was a
severe obsessive compulsive who controlled his aggression in large
part by using reaction formations. Although the parents' communications to me were guarded, I surmised that Robert's mother
was a domineering and grossly exhibitionistic woman who unwittingly stimulated her sons sexually but thwarted their efforts to be
physically affectionate with her once they reached puberty.

Our fifth interview followed two events: (1) Robert had taken a
two-week driving trip with his twin brother and (2) Robert had
moved out of the family home for the first time, to live in a college
dormitory in a nearby city. Only the first of these events was
known to me at the time. In the interview, Robert sat stiffly on the
edge of his chair and was suspicious and apprehensive, in contrast
to his previous shy but friendly behavior. I assumed that he was
projecting hostility and silently recalled his disappointment and
regression when his father told him that angry feelings were
taboo.

As mentioned earlier, along with Heimann (1950), Racker
(1957), and others, I have come to assign increasing importance to
the roles of projective identification and counteridentification in
the interactions between patients, especially regressed patients,
and their therapists. Accordingly, when I think or fantasize about
some person who is important to the patient, I wonder whether

I may be responding to the patient's need to have me, or fear that I will, assume some role or attribute of that person. With Robert, I suspected the presence of an acute transference psychosis, conjecturing that he might have become unable to distinguish me from his father. I asked him whether he might be thinking of his father. He nodded in agreement, relaxed, and settled back into the chair. After he had looked at me for a minute or so, he focused on the upper part of my face for some time. I was reminded both of the similar behavior of a previous schizophrenic patient and of the watchful behavior of a nursing baby (Boyer 1956). I silently wondered whether he would begin to confuse me with his mother and become fearful of fantasized fusion.

Robert began to rub the wooden arms of his chair rhythmically. I had the sensation that my own arms were being caressed and recalled that wood often symbolizes women in dreams and folklore. I asked whether he was thinking of his mother. He quickly nodded in agreement and then became frightened again. I found myself feeling confused and fearful. Reflection after the interview led me to think that I had empathized with his regression (which may have gone back to the undifferentiated phase of early infancy [Katan 1979]) to such a degree that I had feared loss of my own ego boundaries. During the interview, my uneasiness continued; my worry that he would confuse me with his mother and become lost in me as her surrogate intensifed, but I remained silent and watchful.

He suddenly began to hit the desk with his palms and asked me if it was a table. Then he began to say the word "table" every time he slapped the desk. He seemed to enter a dissociated state; I felt I had lost contact with him. He became progressively more frightened and repetitively shouted the word "table," although he had ceased slapping the desk. I felt better after I remembered that the table often symbolizes the mother in dreams and folklore. Freud's dictum about the schizophrenic's use of words came to my mind. Then it occurred to me that Robert had ceased using the word table as a symbol. Now he was only concerned with the word as an object. Soon he was repetitively saying "tay-bul, tay-bul" and then "tay-tay-tay, bul-bul-bul."

Again, I found myself feeling unreal and I turned to the use of active thinking and recall in the service of regaining my personal sense of integrity. I remembered that before children can speak words, they become actively interested in their vocal utterances as discrete phenomena and that when they learn to speak, they like to play with the sound qualities of their newly acquired words.

I considered the possibility that Robert's regression was being used in the service of defense and that he had begun to use word fragmentation as a primitive representation of body or world destruction. That is, perhaps he had lost his sense of personal identity in an imagined fusion with his mother or me, as a representation of her. Concurrently, I felt somewhat fragmented, but I calmed myself with the knowledge that I could test the validity of my thoughts by questions and interpretations. I remembered that Robert had told me that when he returned from trips and tried to hug his mother, she pushed him away. I recalled both her frustrating exhibitionism and her uneasiness around the boys after they reached puberty, and wondered whether she had projected incestuous wishes onto them and feared overt sexual advances by them.

By this time, I had formulated what seemed to be a rational approach to determining the validity of my assumptions. I asked Robert whether he had missed his mother while on vacation with his brother. He immediately regained his personal integrity and contact with me, nodded in agreement, and cried. After a time he said, "She pushed me away," referring to the mother's response to the boys' return. He then began to speak of his loneliness in the coeducational dormitory.

On the preceding Saturday, he had been frightened by observing interactions between male and female students that indicated to him that they were going to have sexual relations. He had thought that one girl had wanted to have sex with him but he had heard God's voice say, "Thou shall not commit adultery." (Both of his parents, but particularly his mother, demanded premarital sexual abstinence of their sons.) He had tried unsuccessfully to get super-ego support from a faculty member and then had driven home, where his parents had greeted him with seeming displeasure. When he had tried to hug his mother, she had been unresponsive.

He had been unable to tell his parents why he had to come home, feeling the need for some demonstration of affection before he could confide in them. Later, when his mother had been undressing in her bedroom with the door open, he had approached her, seeking an understanding word or caress. She had reacted with terror, screaming for his father and claiming that Robert wanted to rape her. His father then had reproached him furiously for disturbing his mother and had accused him of incestuous desires.

By the end of the interview, Robert was calm, shy, and friendly and eagerly sought reassurance that our next appointment would be held at its regularly scheduled time.

In subsequent interviews, we retraced the events of this dramatic session in detail and confirmed the accuracy of my various conjectures. Concurrently, it was possible to review in detail the onset of his overt psychosis at the age of fifteen and to understand that all the essential elements that had led to that regression had been recapitulated prior to the interview when he had made concrete objects of words and syllables.

Robert subsequently entered psychoanalysis, which continued for about three years. He improved greatly until he became aware of the fact that his mother was becoming more and more paranoid and disorganized as he improved. He then decided to stop treatment so that his younger brothers might have some semblance of a normal home life. Unfortunately, after he stopped treatment, Robert lost many of his therapeutic gains and became a marginally functioning schizoid character. In addition, all three of his brothers were hospitalized at various times for schizophrenia.

SUMMARY

This chapter discusses a number of issues pertaining to the analytic treatment of regressed patients; these issues are illustrated by case material. Foremost among them is the importance of countertransference for the outcome of therapy.

Analysts' responses to regressed patients are often quite different from those experienced with neurotic patients. Such responses are better understood and therefore more manageable when one bears in mind that regressed patients, especially borderline patients, typically use projective identification as a primitive defense mechanism with both intrapsychic and interpersonal aspects. A synthesis of analytic ideas pertaining to projective identification is presented, with special emphasis on the role of the reintrojection of patients' projections onto analysts, following the modification of these projections in the treatment process.

REFERENCES

Adler, G. (1975). The usefulness of the "borderline concept" in psychotherapy. In *Borderline States in Psychiatry*, ed. J. E. Mack. New York: Grune and Stratton.

Alexander, F. (1956). Two forms of regression and their therapeutic implications. *Psychonal. Q.* 25:178–196.

—— and French, T., eds. (1950). *Psychosomatic Medicine*. New York: Norton.

Arbiser, A. (1978). Patología de la contratransferencia en los tratamientos interminables. *Revista de Psicoanálisis* 34:753–765.

Arieti, S. (1955). *Interpretation of Schizophrenia*. New York: Brunner.

Atkins, N. B. (1967). Comments on severe psychotic regressions in analysis. *J. Amer. Psychoanal. Assn.* 15:584–604.

Bergler, E. (1938). On a resistance situation: The patient is silent. *Psychoanal. Rev.* 25:170–186.

Bermak, G. E. (1979). Discussion of this chapter at the San Francisco Psychoanalytic Society and Institute, September.

Bettelheim, B. (1967). Regression as progress. In *The Empty Fortress*, pp. 290–298. New York: The Free Press.

Binswanger, H. (1956). Freud's Psychosentherapie. *Psyche* 10:357–366.

Bion, W. R. (1955). Language and the schizophrenic. In *New Directions in Psycho-Analysis*, ed. M. Klein, P. Heimann, and R. E. Money-Kyrle, pp. 220–230. London: Hogarth Press.

—— (1956). Development of schizophrenic thought. *Internat. J. Psycho-Anal.* 37:344–346.

—— (1957). Differentiation of the psychotic from the nonpsychotic personalities. *Internat. J. Psycho-Anal.* 38:266–275.

Boyer, L. B. (1956). On maternal overstimulation and ego defects. *The Psychoanalytic Study of the Child* 11:236–256.

—— (1961). Provisional evaluation of psycho-analysis with few parameters in the treatment of schizophrenia. *Internat. J. Psycho-Anal.* 42:389–403.

—— (1966). Office treatment of schizophrenic patients by psychoanalysis. *Psychoanalytic Forum* 1:337–365.

—— (1971). Psychoanalytic technique in the treatment of certain characterological and schizophrenic disorders, with follow-up. In *Psychotherapies: A Comparative Casebook*, ed. S. J. Morse and R. I. Watson, pp. 71–89. New York: Holt, Rinehart, and Winston, 1977.

—— (1976). Meanings of a bizarre suicidal attempt by an adolescent. *Adolescent Psychiatry* 4:371–381.

—— (1977). Working with a borderline patient. *Psychoanal. Q.* 46: 386–424.

—— (1978a). Countertransference experiences with severely regressed patients. In *Countertransference: The Therapist's Contribution to the Therapeutic Situation* ed. L. Epstein and A. H. Feiner, pp. 533–574. New York: Aronson, 1979.

—— (1978b). Countertransference experiences while working with severely regressed patients. In *Psicoanálisis Actual: Caracter, Transferencia y Contratransferencia, Fantasiá, y Realidad*, ed. F. Cesarman. Mexico City: Asociación Psicoanalitica Mexicana.

—— and Giovacchini, P. L. (1967). *Psychoanalytic Treatment of Schizophrenic and Characterological Disorders*. New York: Science House.

—— (1980). *Psychoanalytic Treatment of Schizophrenic, Borderline and Characterological Disorders*, 2nd rev. ed. New York: Aronson.

Brodey, W. M. (1965). On the dynamics of narcissism: I. Externalization and early ego development. *The Psychoanalytic Study of the Child* 20:165–193.

Bruch, H. (1973). *Eating Disorders: Obesity, Anorexia Nervosa and the Person Within*. New York: Basic Books.

Calder, K. T. (1958). Panel report: Technical aspects of regression during psychoanalysis. *J. Amer. Psychoanal. Assn.* 6:552–559.

Carpinacci, J. A., Liberman, D., and Schlossberg, N. (1963). Perturbaciones en la comunicación y neurosis de contratransferencia. *Revista de Psicoanálisis* 20:63–69.

Carter, L. and Rinsley, D. B. (1977). Vicissitudes of "empathy" in a borderline patient. *Internat. Rev. Psychoanal.* 4:317–326.

Cesio, F. R. (1963). La comunicación extraverbal en psicoanálisis: Transferencia, contratransferencia, e interpretación. *Revista de Psicoanálisis* 20:124–127.

———— (1973). Los fundamentales de la contratransferencia: El yo ideal y las identificaciones directas. *Revista de Psicoanálisis* 30:5–16.

Chediak, C. (1979). Counterreactions and countertransference. *Internat. J. Psycho-Anal.* 60:117–130.

Chiozza, L. A. (1976). *Cuerpo, Afecto, y Lenguaje: Psicoanálisis y Enfermedad Psicosomática.* Buenos Aires: Editorial Paidós.

———— (ed.) (1978a). *Ideas para una Concepción Psicoanalítica del Cancer.* Buenos Aires: Editorial Paidós.

———— (1979). *La Interpretación Psicoanalítica en la Enfermedad Somática en la Teoría y en la Práctica Clínica.* Buenos Aires: Universidad de Salvador.

Ekstein, R. (1976). General treatment philosophy of acting out. In *Acting Out*, ed. L. E. Abt and S. L. Weissman, pp. 162–171. New York: Aronson.

Epstein, L. and Feiner, A. H. (1979). *Countertransference: The Therapist's Contribution to the Therapeutic Situation.* New York: Aronson.

Fairbairn, W.R.D. (1952). *An Object Relations Theory of the Personality.* New York: Basic Books.

Federn, P. (1952). *Ego Psychology and the Psychoses.* New York: Basic Books.

Fenichel, O. (1945). *The Psychoanalytic Theory of Neurosis.* New York: Norton.

Ferenczi, S. (1919). On the technique of psycho-analysis. IV. The control of the countertransference. In *Further Contributions to the Theory and Technique of Psycho-Analysis*, pp. 186–189. London: Hogarth Press.

Flarsheim, A. (1972). Treatability. In *Tactics and Techniques in Psychoanalysis*, ed. P. L. Giovacchini, pp. 113–131. New York: Science House.

Fliess, W. (1953). Counter-transference and counter-identification. *J. Amer. Psychoanal. Assn.* 1:268–284.

Fraiberg, S. (1969). Libidinal object constancy and mental representation. *The Psychoanalytic Study of the Child* 24:9–47.

Freud, A. (1936). *The Ego and the Mechanisms of Defense.* New York: International Universities Press.

———— (1965). *Normality and Abnormality in Childhood.* New York: International Universities Press.

———— (1967). About losing and being lost. *The Psychoanalytic Study of the Child* 22:9–19.

—— (1969). *Difficulties in the Path of Psychoanalysis.* New York: International Universities Press.

Freud, S. (1910). The future prospects of psychoanalytic theory. *Standard Edition* 11:139–157. London: Hogarth Press, 1957.

—— (1915a). Mourning and melancholia. *Standard Edition* 14:237–260. London: Hogarth Press, 1957.

—— (1915b). The unconscious. *Standard Edition* 14:156–216. London: Hogarth Press, 1957.

—— (1926). Inhibitions, Symptoms and Anxiety. *Standard Edition* 20:77–179. London: Hogarth Press, 1959.

Fromm-Reichmann, F. (1950). *Principles of Intensive Psychotherapy.* Chicago: University of Chicago Press.

—— (1952). Some aspects of psychoanalytic psychotherapy with schizophrenics. In *Psychotherapy with Schizophrenics,* ed. E. B. Brody and F. C. Redlich, pp. 89–111. New York: International Universities Press.

—— (1958). Basic problems in the psychotherapy of schizophrenia. *Psychiatry* 21:1–6.

Garma, Á. (1978). El Psicoanálisis: Teoría, Clínica y Técnica, 3rd ed. Buenos Aires: Editorial Paidós.

Giovacchini, P. L. (1975a). *Psychoanalysis of Character Disorders.* New York: Aronson.

—— (1975b). Self-projections in the narcissistic transference. *Internat. J. Psychoanal. Psychother.* 4: 142–166.

—— (1979a). *Treatment of Primitive Mental States.* New York: Aronson.

—— (1979b). Countertransference with primitive mental states. In *Countertransference: The Therapist's Contribution to the Therapeutic Situation,* ed. L. Epstein and A. H. Feiner, pp. 235–265. New York: Aronson.

—— and Boyer, L. B. (1975). The psychoanalytic impasse. *Internat. J. Psychoanal. Psychother.* 4: 25–47.

—— Flarsheim, A., and Boyer, L. B., eds. (1975). *Tactics and Techniques in Psychoanalytic Therapy. II. Countertransference.* New York: Aronson.

Glover, E. (1955). *The Technique of Psychoanalysis.* New York: International Universities Press.

Goldberg, L. (1979). Remarks on transference-countertransference in psychotic states. *Internat. J. Psycho-Anal.* 60:347–356.

Greenson, R. R. (1965). The working alliance and the transference neurosis. *Psychoanal. Q.* 34:155–181.

Grinberg, L. (1957). Perturbaciones en la interpretación por la contraidentificación proyectiva. *Revista de Psicoanálisis* 14:23–28.

——— (1958). Aspectos mágicos en la transferencia y la contratransferencia. *Revista de Psicoanálisis* 15:15–26.

——— (1962). On a specific aspect of countertransference due to the patient's projective identification. *Internat. J. Psycho-Anal.* 43:436–440.

——— (1963). Psicopatología de la identificación proyectiva y de la contratransferencia. *Revista de Psicoanálisis* 20:112–123.

——— (1976). *Teoría de la Identificación.* Buenos Aires: Editorial Paidós.

——— (1979). Countertransference and projective counteridentification. *Contemporary Psychoanal.* 15:226–247.

Gruhle, H. W. (1915). Selbstschilderung und Einfühlung; zugleich ein Versuch der Analyse des Falles Bantung. *Zeitschrift für die Gesamte Neurologie und Psychiatrie* 28:148–231.

Gunderson, J. G. and Kolb, J. E. (1978). Discriminating features of borderline patients. *Amer. J. Psychiatry* 135:792–796.

——— and Singer, M. T. (1975). Defining borderline patients. *Amer. J. Psychiatry* 132:1–10.

Guntrip, H. (1961). *Personality Structure and Human Interaction.* New York: International Universities Press.

Hann-Kende, F. (1933). On the role of transference and countertransference in psychoanalysis. In *Psychoanalysis and the Occult*, ed. G. Devereux, pp. 158–167. New York: International Universities Press, 1953.

Hartmann, H. (1939). *Ego Psychology and the Problem of Adaptation.* New York: International Universities Press, 1958.

——— (1953). Contribution to the metapsychology of schizophrenia. *The Psychoanalytic Study of the Child* 8:177–198.

Heimann, P. (1950). On countertransference. *Internat. J. Psycho-Anal.* 31:81–84.

——— (1966). Discussion of "Structural derivatives of object relationships" by Otto F. Kernberg. *Internat. J. Psycho-Anal.* 47:254–260.

Hill, L. B. (1955). *Psychoanaltyic Intervention in Schizophrenia.* Chicago: University of Chicago Press.

Hoedemaker, E. D. (1967). The psychotic identification in schizophrenia: The technical problem. In *Psychoanalytic Treatment of Schizophrenic and Characterological Disorders*, ed. L. B. Boyer and P. L. Giovacchini, pp. 189–207. New York: Science House.

Holzman, P. S. and Ekstein, R. (1959). Repetition functions of transitory regressive thinking. *Psychoanal. Q.* 28:228–235.

Katan, M. (1979). Further exploration of the schizophrenic regression to the undifferentiated state: A study of the "assessment of the unconscious." *Internat. J. Psycho-Anal.* 60:145–176.

Kernberg, O. F. (1974). Further contributions to the treatment of the narcissistic personality. *Internat. J. Psycho-Anal.* 55:215–240.

——— (1975). *Borderline Conditions and Pathological Narcissism.* New York: Aronson.

——— (1976). *Object Relations Theory and Clinical Psychoanalysis.* New York: Aronson.

——— (1978). Contrasting approaches to the psychotherapy of borderline conditions. In *New Perspectives on Psychotherapy of the Borderline Adult,* ed. J. F. Masterson, pp. 75–104. New York: Brunner/Mazel.

Khan, M.M.R. (1960). Regression and integration in the analytic setting. *Internat. J. Psycho-Anal.* 41:130–146.

Klein, M. (1946). Notes on some schizoid mechanisms. *Internat. J. Psycho-Anal.* 27:99–110.

——— (1955). On identification. In *New Directions in Psychoanalysis,* ed. M. Klein, P. Heimann, and R. E. Money-Kyrle, pp. 309–345. London: Tavistock.

Kris, E. (1950). Notes on the development and on some current problems of psychoanalytic child psychology. In *The Selected Papers of Ernst Kris,* pp. 54–79. New Haven and London: Yale University Press.

Kusnetzoff, J. C. and Maldovsky, D. (1977). Aportes al estudio de una paciente borderline de base esquizóide: Análisis componencial y consideración de los "lugares psíquicos." *Revista de Psicoanálisis* 34:803–842.

Langer, M. (1957). La interpretación basada en la vivencia contratransferencial de conexión o desconexión con el analizado. *Revista de Psicoanálisis* 14:31–38.

Langs, R. (1976). *The Therapeutic Interaction. II. A Critical Overview and Synthesis,* pp. 273–329. New York: Aronson.

Levy, K. F. (1958). Silence in the analytic situation. *Internat. J. Psycho-Anal.* 39:50–58.

Lidz, R. W. and Lidz, T. (1952). Therapeutic considerations arising from the intense symbiotic needs of schizophrenic patients. In *Psychotherapy with Schizophrenia,* ed. E. B. Brody and F. S. Redlich, pp. 168–178. New York: International Universities Press.

Little, M. (1951). Counter-transference and the patient's response to it. *Internat. J. Psycho-Anal.* 32:32–40.

Loewald, H. (1960). On the therapeutic action of psychoanalysis. *Internat. J. Psycho-Anal.* 41:16–33.

——— (1979). Reflections on the psychoanalytic process and its therapeutic potential. *The Psychoanalytic Study of the Child* 34:155–167.

Loomie, L. S. (1961). Some ego considerations in the silent patient. *J. Amer. Psychoanal. Assn.* 9:56–78.

Mack, J. E., ed. (1975). *Borderline States in Psychiatry.* New York: Grune and Stratton.

Mahler, M. S. (1972). A study of the separation-individuation process and its possible application to borderline phenomena in the psychoanalytic situation. *The Psychoanalytic Study of the Child* 26:403–424.

——, Pine, F., and Bergman, A. (1975). *The Psychological Birth of the Human Infant.* New York: Basic Books.

Malin, A. and Grotstein, J. S. (1966). Projective identification in the psychotherapeutic process. *Internat. J. Psycho-Anal.* 47:26–31.

Maltzberger, J. T. and Buie, D. H. (1974). Countertransference hate in the treatment of suicidal patients. *Archives of General Psychiatry* 30:625–633.

Marcondes, D. (1966). A regressão na contratransferencia. *Revista Brasileira de Psicanálise* 2:11–21.

Masterson, J. F. (1972). *Treatment of the Borderline Adolescent: A Developmental Approach.* New York: Wiley.

—— (1976). *Psychotherapy of the Borderline Adult: A Developmental Approach.* New York: Brunner/Mazel.

McLaughlin, J. T. (1975). The sleepy analyst: Some observations on states of consciousness in the analyst at work. *J. Amer. Psychoanal. Assn.* 23:363–382.

Milner, M. (1969). *The Hands of the Living God: An Account of Psychoanalytic Treatment.* New York: International Universities Press.

Modell, A. H. (1963). Primitive object relationships and the predisposition to schizophrenia. *Internat. J. Psycho-Anal.* 44:282–291.

—— (1968). *Object Love and Reality.* New York: International Universities Press.

—— (1975). A narcissistic defense against affects and the illusion of self sufficiency. *Internat. J. Psycho-Anal.* 56:275–282.

Nadelson, T. (1977). Borderline rage and the therapist's response. *Archives General Psychiatry* 134:748–751.

Novick, J. and Kelly, K. (1970). Projection and internalization. *The Psychoanalytic Study of the Child* 25:69–95.

Ogden, T. H. (1978). A developmental view of identifications resulting from maternal impingements. *Internat. J. Psychoanal. Psychother.* 7:486–506.

Ornstein, A. and Ornstein, P. (1975). On the interpretive process in schizophrenia. *Internat. J. Psychoanal. Psychother.* 4:219–271.

Orr, D. W. (1954). Transference and countertransference: A historical survey. *J. Amer. Psychoanal. Assn.* 2:621–670.

Paz, C. A., Pelento, M. L., and Olmos de Paz, T. (1975). *Estructuras y/o Estados Fronterizos en Niños Adolescentes y Adultos. I. Historia y Conceptualizatión.* Buenos Aires: Editorial Nueva Visión.

—— (1976a). *Estructuras y/o Estados Fronterizos en Niños y Adultos. II. Casuística y Consideraciones Teóricas.* Buenos Aires: Editorial Nueva Visión.

—— (1976b). *Estructuras y/o Estados Fronterizos en Niños y Adultos. III. Investigación y Terapéutica.* Buenos Aires: Editorial Nueva Visión.

Perry, J. C. and Klerman, G. L., (1980). Clinical aspects of the borderline personality disorder. *Amer. J. Psychiatry* 137:165–173.

Prado Galvão, L. de A. (1966). Contratransferencia frente a regressão. *Revista Brasileira de Psicanálise* 2:22–34.

Pruyser, P. W. (1975). What splits in "splitting?" *Bull. Menninger Clinic* 39:1–46.

Racker, E. (1953). A contribution to the problem of countertransference. *Internat. J. Psycho-Anal.* 34:313–324.

—— (1957). The meanings and uses of countertransference. *Psychoanal. Q.* 26:303–357.

—— (1959). Countertransference and interpretation. *J. Amer. Psychoanal. Assn.* 6:215–311.

—— (1968). *Transference and Countertransference.* New York: International Universities Press.

Reich, A. (1960). Further remarks and countertransference. *Internat. J. Psycho-Anal.* 41:389–395.

Reichard, S. (1956). A Re-examination of *Studies in Hysteria. Psychoanal. Q.* 25:155–177.

Robbins, M. B. (1976). Borderline personality organization: The need for a new theory. *J. Amer. Psychoanal. Assn.* 24:831–853.

Rosenfeld, D., and Mordo, E. (1973). Fusión, confusión, simbiosis, e identificación proyectiva. *Revista de Psicoanálisis* 30:413–423.

Rosenfeld, H. A. (1952a). Transference-phenomena and transference analysis in an acute catatonic woman. *Internat. J. Psycho-Anal.* 33:457–464.

—— (1952b). Notes on the psycho-analysis of the super-ego conflict of an acute catatonic schizophrenic patient. *Internat. J. Psycho-Anal.* 33:111–131.

—— (1954). Consideration regarding the psycho-analytic approach to acute and chronic schizophrenia. *Internat. J. Psycho-Anal.* 35:135–140.

—— (1966). Discussion of "Office treatment of schizophrenia" by L. B. Boyer. *Psychoanalytic Forum* 1:351–353.

Schafer, R. (1968). *Aspects of Internalization.* New York: International Universities Press.

Schneer, H. I., ed. (1963). *The Asthmatic Child.* New York: Harper and Row.

Schur, M. (1953). The ego in anxiety. In *Drives, Affects, Behavior,* ed. R. M. Loewenstein, pp. 67–103. New York: International Universities Press.

Searles, H. F. (1958). Positive feelings in the relationship between the schizophrenic and his mother. In *Collected Papers on Schizophrenia and Related Subjects,* pp. 216–253. New York: International Universities Press, 1965.

—— (1961). Phases of patient-therapist interaction in the psychotherapy of schizophrenia. In *Collected Papers on Schizophrenia and Related Subjects,* pp. 521–559.

—— (1963). Transference psychosis in the psychotherapy of chronic schizophrenia. In *Collected Papers on Schizophrenia and Related Subjects,* pp. 654–716.

—— (1965). Feelings of guilt in the psychoanalyst. *Psychiatry* 29:319–323.

—— (1975). The patient as therapist to his analyst. In *Tactics and Techniques in Psychoanalytic Therapy. II. Countertransference,* ed. P. L. Giovacchini, A. Flarsheim, and L. B. Boyer, pp. 95–151. New York: Aronson.

Segal, H. (1956). Depression in the schizophrenic. *Internat. J. Psycho-Anal.* 37:339–343.

Settlage, C. F. (1979). Clinical implications of advances in developmental theory. Presented at the 31st International Psycho-Analytical Congress, New York, August.

Shapiro, E. R. (1978). The psychodynamics and developmental psychology of the borderline patient: A review of the literature. *Amer. J. Psychiatry* 135:1305–1315.

——, Shapiro, R. L., and Zinner, J. (1977). The borderline ego and the working alliance: Indications for family and individual treatment in adolescence. *Internat. J. Psycho-Anal.* 58:77–87.

——, Zinner, J., Shapiro, R. L., and Berkowitz, D. A. (1975). The influence of family experience on borderline personality development. *Internat. Rev. Psycho-Anal.* 2:399–411.

Shapiro, S. (1979). Discussion of this chapter. Presented at the San Diego

Psychoanalytic Association Symposium on the Borderline Syndrome, January.

Siquier de Failla, M. (1963). Transferencia y contratransferencia en el proceso psicoanalítico. *Revista de Psicoanálisis* 23:450–470.

Sperling, M. (1967). Transference neurosis in patients with psychosomatic disorders. *Psychoanal. Q.* 36:342–355.

—— (1974). *The Major Neuroses and Behavioral Disorders in Children.* New York: Aronson.

—— (1978). *Psychosomatic Disorders in Childhood.* New York: Aronson.

Spitzer, R. L., Endicott, J., and Gibbon, M. (1979). Crossing the border into borderline personality and borderline schizophrenia. *Archives General Psychiatry* 36:17–24.

Stern, A. (1924). On the countertransference in psychoanalysis. *Psychoanal. Rev.* 11:165–174.

Szalita-Pemow, A. B. (1955). The "intuitive process" and its relation to work with schizophrenics. *J. Amer. Psychoanal. Assn.* 3:7–18.

Thöma, H. (1967). *Anorexia Nervosa.* New York: International Universities Press.

Volkan, V. (1973). Transitional fantasies in the analysis of a narcissistic personality. *J. Amer. Psychoanal. Assn.* 21:351–376.

—— (1976). *Primitive Internalized Object Relations: A Clinical Study of Schizophrenic, Borderline, and Narcissistic Patients.* New York: International Universities Press.

—— (1978). The night of the living dead. Paper presented before the meeting of the American Psychoanalytic Association, New York, December.

—— (1979). The "glass bubble" of the narcissistic patient. In *Advances in Psychotherapy of the Borderline Patient*, ed. J. LeBoit and A. Capponi. New York: Aronson.

Waldhorn, H. F. (1979). Panel report. The silent patient. *J. Amer. Psycho-Anal. Assn.* 7:548–560.

Weigert, E. (1954). Counter-transference and self-analysis. *Internat. J. Psycho-Anal.* 35:242–246.

Wilson, C. P. (1968). Psychosomatic asthma and acting out: A case of bronchial asthma that developed *de novo* in the terminal phase of analysis. *Internat. J. Psycho-Anal.* 49:330–335.

—— (1970). Theoretical and clinical considerations in the early phase of analysis of patients suffering from severe psychosomatic symptoms. *Bull. Philadelphia Assn. Psychoanal.* 20:71–74.

Winnicott, D. W. (1954). Metapsychological and clinical aspects of re-

gression within the psycho-analytic setup. *Internat. J. Psycho-Anal.* 41:407–412.

—— (1960). Countertransference. *Brit. J. Med. Psychol.* 33:17–21.

Zeligs, M. A. (1960). The role of silence in transference, countertransference and the psychoanalytic process. *Internat. J. Psycho-Anal.* 41: 407–412.

Zetzel, E. R. (1956). Current concepts of psychoanalysis. *Internat. J. Psycho-Anal.* 37:369–376.

—— (1971). A developmental approach to the borderline patient. *Amer. J. Psychiat.* 128:867–871.

Zinner, J. and Shapiro, E. R. (1975). Splitting in families of borderline adolescents. In *Borderline States in Psychiatry.* ed. J. E. Mack. New York: Grune and Stratton.

Zinner, J. and Shapiro, R. E. (1972). Projective identification as a mode of perception and behavior in families of adolescents. *Internat. J. Psycho-Anal.* 53:523–530.

3

REGRESSION: SOME GENERAL CONSIDERATIONS

Hans W. Loewald

Editor's Notes

Many of the other chapters in this book implicitly incorporate Dr. Loewald's ideas in their understanding of the therapeutic relationship. As in his past works, in this essay Hans Loewald elaborates on various aspects of the therapeutic process, focusing upon regression and acting out in severely disturbed patients. Dr. Loewald believes that although acting out may prevent emotional development, regression has a structuralizing potential. In analysis, through interpretation, the primitive parts of the psyche that emerge during a regressive experience acquire structure and meaning through a process called validation.

Dr. Loewald stresses that analysts must be at a psychic level corresponding to that of their patients when offering an interpretation. Otherwise the therapist's ego state will be the outcome of a false self. As analysts interact with patients at relatively primitive psychic levels, higher levels of the therapist's psyche are simultaneously invoked, bringing the earlier states into a broader context. As Dr. Loewald succinctly states: "Islands of experience and states of mind lose their isolation. This often entails a loss in intensity and a gain in lucidity and consistency of experience, conveying a sense of safety."

These observations and conclusions seek to explain some elements of the treatment process as they lead to the acquisition of higher psychic structures. They could also refer to the resolution of intrapsychic conflict but, for the most part, I am impressed how neatly they serve the purpose of constructing a therapeutic rationale for patients suffering from structural psychopathology and ego defects.

In patients with severe structural psychopathology, traumatic infantile relationships have been split off from the main psychic current, thereby continuing to exert their pathological effects on both the patients' inner mental equilibrium and external adaptations. These early "islands" of trauma also influence the general course of emotional development, and the kinds of psychic structures that evolve. Many clinicians believe that there is an innate developmental drive propelling the psyche progressively to structuralize much in the same way the soma follows a prescribed direction of maturation if it is provided with proper conditions. In the patient population discussed here, the constriction, arrest, and distortion of this drive by severe traumas in infancy have produced a variety of characterological malformations.

If one had to choose the feature that is most characteristic of structural defective patients, it would be rigidity. Because these patients have lacunae in their executive system, they have very little flexibility in their adaptations to the outer world. They may construct defenses that permit them to relate to only a small segment of the external world. Or they may transform reality so that it will be consonant with their modalities of relating. At best, they create compensated states, psychotic compensations, which are characterized by extreme degrees of rigidity. Those with characterological disorders such as schizoid characters and borderline states have difficulty maintaining psychic equilibrium and frequently decompensate. This state of disorganization often brings these patients into treatment.

Regression is an important theme with severely disturbed patients. In the outer world regression is often the cause for patients to seek therapy and in treatment it is the vehicle for their acquisition of higher levels of psychic integration. In the therapeutic process, which can be disruptive if it is uncontrolled, some adaptations are temporarily lost. Patients feel vulnerable and need the support of an organizing, safe experience. Analysts must respond to patients' vulnerability. At the same time, patients lose some of their rigidity and thus have greater potential to relate flexibly to the inner and outer world. It is a unique quality of analytic regression that flexibility and vulnerability go hand in hand. Regression can even provide security if it occurs in the holding environment of the analytic setting. Dr. Loewald spells out how this occurs.

He also calls our attention to some pertinent ideas first formulated by the great neurologist, Hughlings Jackson. Contrary to what we might expect, Hughlings Jackson stated that lower levels of the central nervous system are better organized than higher levels. By this, he meant that they are automatized and relatively indestructible; the autonomous nature of the higher levels makes them more vulnerable. Jackson distinguishes between organization as a *state* and organization as an *activity*. Higher levels function in an organized fashion but inasmuch as their basic structure is not organized in that they are autonomous rather than automatized, they are vulnerable rather than indestructible. Freud comes to mind as he emphasized the vulnerability of the ego as it had to face both a powerful id and superego. However, Freud also stressed that the ego was able to appease these powerful psychic agencies, especially the id, as well as reconcile them to the outer world. These formulations are relevant to our understanding of the analytic process as regressive shifts bring different levels of the psychic apparatus into the foreground.

Thus, in one sense the ego may be weak but it is,

nevertheless, able to carry out synthesizing and organizing activities. The paradigm of "where id was, there shall ego be" highlights that what is powerful and destructive in the id becomes vulnerable, weak, and organized in the ego area. Obviously weakness is not the right word but id elements once they have reached the ego lose their power to be disruptive.

Dr. Loewald asserts that interpretation of lower levels of the psyche—that is, bringing them into consciousness—revives them, validates them, and gives them "immediacy and intensity of living." From this we can infer that those parts of the psyche that are repressed or split off from the general ego organization are, in a sense, dead. Structurally defective patients supply us with considerable data that support this formulation. For example, many complain of an all-pervasive sense of "deadness." They go through the motions of living but they do not feel truly alive. I believe that this can be explained in part by the fact that they do not have access to various parts of their psyches. The latter are walled off and inaccessible.

The psychoanalytic process facilitates the recovery of these hidden and damaged psychic elements and transforms them into adaptations that increase patients' range of ego functioning and enhance their autonomy. By becoming incorporated into higher areas of the psyche, they acquire an organization that gives them a unique individuality that they never had previously. They add a new dimension to the self-representation and thus further consolidate the sense of identity.

Dr. Loewald makes the interesting point that in the initial phases of analysis, it is unnecessary to distinguish between the unconscious of the patient and that of the therapist. He conjectures that the unconscious does not differ much among people. When we deal with the lower, more primitive areas of the psyche, we encounter less structure. These levels are relatively amorphous. As analysts get in touch with the unstructured, more primitive parts of their own mind, they have the opportunity to relate intuitively to patients because the differences in mental orientations become minimized. This is another example of what we might call the progressive factors of regression.

The beginning phases of analysis are characterized by a regression in the patient and a parallel process in the therapist. Rather than being disruptive, this regression leads to a sense of security for both patient and therapist. At these early levels, vulnerabilities, if they do not disappear, at least diminish considerably. This creates a holding environment that can support the re-experience of infantile traumas and vulnerabilities at ego levels. The analyst introduces new perspectives that enable the patient to resolve fears, acquire a sense of aliveness, and add new dimensions to his or her personality.

In this chapter, Dr. Loewald explores how the regressive process leads to the creation of higher levels of integration and new psychic structures for the patient as well as the analyst.

P. L. G.

Paul Valéry, in his Oxford lecture on "Poetry and Abstract Thought" (1939), introducing his subject, writes: "For my part I have the strange and dangerous habit, in every subject, of wanting to begin at the beginning (that is, at my own beginning), which entails beginning again, going back over the whole road, just as though many others had not already mapped and traveled it." Thus, he speaks of repeating a beginning and going back over the whole road. These are aspects of regression, not those most obviously relevant to our clinical and therapeutic concerns, but aspects that to my mind are central to a proper consideration of regression. Freud, in his own very different way, indulged in the same "strange and dangerous habit," evolving through it the science and art of psychoanalysis and helping patients to use such a method in the service of their own mental well-being. Whoever has what we call an *original* thought or insight does—within a narrow orbit—something similar: such a thought comes more directly from its origin in one's own experience; or thinking goes back to and then forward again from that experience, instead of relying on ready-made thoughts.

Concluding these introductory remarks by way of a cautionary tale, I quote again from Valéry's lecture. Speaking of the "strange property of our verbal material" he writes:

> Each and every word that enables us to leap so rapidly across the chasm of thought, and to follow the prompting of an idea that constructs its own expression, appears to me like one of those light planks which one throws across a ditch or a mountain crevasse and which will bear a man crossing it rapidly. But he must pass without weighing on it, without stopping—above all, he must not take it into his head to dance on the slender plank to test its resistance! Otherwise the fragile bridge tips or breaks immediately, and all is hurled into the depths. Consult your own experience; and you will find that we understand each other, and ourselves, only thanks to our *rapid passage over words*. We must not lay stress upon them, or we shall see the clearest discourse dissolve into enigmas and more or less learned illusions.

Words and concepts (such as regression and the rest) reveal themselves as flimsy or enigmatic or ambiguous, if they are not merely used as shortcuts and as currency in the exchange of thoughts but are given weight and consideration in their own right. The passage quoted also warns us that any discourse like the one presented here, using words and concepts in its progression, is composed of such dubious bridges of thought. No undue weight should be given to any one bridge. It is the context, and what is bridged, that give them meaning.

If we think of regression as clinicians and therapists, patients' regressive tendencies and behavior are dangerous: they bring them into discord or collision with themselves and their environment; and patients might get stuck back there, not find the paths that lead forward again. Regressive behavior is strange as it deviates from normal, accepted, familiar behavior and ways of thinking and feeling.

Regression implies a standard of norm from which one deviates, and deviates in a backward direction. If we call behavior regressive, we stamp it, in terms of development, as going below a norm that had been reached (or should have been reached), and not above or beyond that norm. It is also implied that such deviations hark back to an earlier developmental stage, resuming or repeating it.

In psychoanalysis, we speak of regression predominantly in developmental terms, considering those mental processes and behaviors regressive that do not conform to what we see as a more advanced and desirable, although never fully attained, mode of organizing reality and thought. In this developmental sense, regression is also understood as a *means* for better approximating that rational standard mode by resuming development at a stage where it had begun to go astray or had stopped in significant areas. In analysis, in order to facilitate this instrumental function of regression, we analyze defenses interfering with that resumption, those that impede the regressive movement itself (impede the unfolding of a transference neurosis), and those defenses that stand in the way of renewed progression. There is a connection between this instrumental aspect of regression and Valéry's "beginning again, going back over the whole road" in an effort to arrive at an original treatment of a subject of discourse. Obviously, Ernst Kris's (1952), "regression in the service of the ego" also belongs here.

Regression, then, would be pathological as compared to a standard mental plateau, as well as therapeutic in view of its being a potential step toward more normal development. The "therapeutic" gain, in analysis and creative work or comparable contexts, need not, however, be simply a return to a plateau of normality. It may constitute an improvement on it (this applies in particular to training analyses) insofar as it involves a richer and rational understanding of the steps taken in organizing the plateau: normality now may become an insightful process and achievement, instead of being a more or less unthinking, unelucidated state.

Much that was unconscious becomes conscious; and the psycho-analytically elucidated psychic life is richer and presumably more productive than previously. Thus, psychoanalysis represents an advance in civilization and human potential.

Regression may make a healthier resumption of development possible, but it does not make it inevitable. The patient in analysis, with his defenses in disarray, may get caught up in the tumult of his regressed state, or may indulge in the apparent freedom and pleasure of an earlier state relatively unencumbered by the constraints and exigencies of present-day life. Unless regression can be controlled, limited in depth and extent by what we think of as an ego sufficiently unaffected by regression, the regressive transference neurosis becomes a precarious venture. Perhaps we should say that it is not regression per se which is therapeutic, but the resumption of progressive development made possible by regression to an earlier stage or to a "fixation point."

With these qualifications, the relationship between regression as pathological and regression as therapeutic vehicle seems clear enough. The transference neurosis—and I include here for our purpose that transference illness which develops in the psychoanalytic treatment of narcissistic disorders—is a prime example of regression in these two aspects. It is an illness, brought into the open, controlled, flowering, and, as such, a main vehicle of therapy. It is now generally agreed and stressed that the transference neurosis and its resolution are not something that comes about only by virtue of the patient's inherent momentum and the analyst's nonreactive neutrality, important as a rightly understood neutrality is. But the flowering and course of the transference neurosis are codetermined by the analyst's adequately conveyed responsiveness. I distinguish here between reacting and responding, meaning by 'reacting' some kind of seductive or defensive countermove, and by 'responding' a move that is empathic. The latter includes analytic neutrality: empathy, as I understand it, does not take sides with one side of the patient, although it may speak to one side, to one particular regressive mode of functioning, one particular impulse, mood, belief, or affect, at a given time. In principle, in their overall attitude, analysts side with patients as whole persons, including what analysts perceive as patients' potential, and including those aspects of the personality which are not caught up in regression.

These views are consonant with present understanding of the role of object relations in development and in the constitution of an individual self. Progression and regression do not take place in a vacuum. The patients' environment and object relations codetermine at every phase of development the general course in one direction or the other. The analytic process itself is that kind of development-process. The traditional psychoanalytic view on regression took the constitutive function of object relations into limited account by acknowledging the importance of frustration and overindulgence in the establishment of fixation points.

THE ELUCIDATION AND RESTORATIVE FUNCTION OF REGRESSION

I have spoken of regression represented by the transference neurosis. We must now add that in the transference neurosis, regression becomes *manifest*. If we go deeper, we cannot say that patients enter treatment and then begin to regress. The illness or maladjustment for which they seek treatment is for us a sign of regression, or of their unsuccessful struggle with regressive impulses and tendencies, counteracted by regressive defenses. In the transference neurosis, patients overtly regress to earlier stages of instinctual and ego development, to oedipal and pre-oedipal modes of relatedness to the analyst. Regression, in the psychoanalytic situation, becomes oriented to the analyst, thus entering a new force-field. In this process, regression becomes manifest. This is partially due to the loosening and/or excessive tightening of defenses that come about in the development of the transference neurosis. Symptoms, character pathology, and maladjustment are disguised or compromise expressions of patients' regressive functioning. This gradually becomes manifest and conscious in the course of the psychoanalytic process and the analyst's interpretations of its various features as they get elucidated in their connections with patients' past and current life. As the transference neurosis is interpreted, prominently in regard to the mutual relations between past and present, it throws light on the sources of patients' "real life" illness. Regression may become less compelling as insight is achieved in the vivid re-experience, with a difference, of the past in the present; return to and further development of higher functioning are facilitated.

Yet, it is not merely the elucidation of regressive functioning that operates as a curative factor in the analytic process. Of equal weight, and inextricably interwoven with it, is the *restorative* function and value of regression. To put it more aptly: the elucidation of regressive functioning fulfills only part of its task if it merely highlights regression's pathological aspects. Bringing to light the regressive levels of patients' mental life does not simply make them available for introspection, accessible to patients' cognitive rational processes. It allows them to be genuinely re-experienced and self-validated, in their own right, by virtue of the analyst's recognizing and validating responses that help to free the developmental thrust of those earlier levels as they are less encumbered by inhibiting defenses. I am not speaking of defenses against the "discharge" of impulses and feelings in action, but of defenses against that inner transformative development of impulses by which they can become integral elements of the total ego organization. Regression to oedipal forms of object relations, for example, is mainly determined by repression that does not permit further integration and organization of these levels by internalization and sublimation. We know from problems of acting out during analysis that unrestrained impulse-action may and often does inhibit their higher development. Our intent in limiting acting out is not to promote repression but to create or foster conditions for that internal development. Analytic neutrality and objectivity, rightly understood and implemented, comprise an attitude that recognizes, respects, and responds to the newly available developmental thrust in the direction of more encompassing and differentiated inner organization. In this connection, Freud used the word "coherent" ego. The modern psychoanalytic concept of self is related to that ego concept.

The opposition of recollecting and repeating is to be resolved in the rapprochement and re-differentiation of affective/cognitive functioning promoted by the psychoanalytic method. Analytic interventions and noninterventions have both cognitive and experiential significance for patients. These two sides often come together only in the course of time in analysis. That is one reason why continuity over a long time-span is important. Although, in comparison to patients, analysts have a clearer view on matters, are emotionally freer, and have a greater range in areas relevant to the treatment, they, too, must have continuity and expanse of time in their work. All of us are time-bound.

Regression to earlier and deeper levels and modes of experience has a restorative function. This is an essential factor in the regressive transference in analysis, be it the classical transference neurosis or the narcissistic "self/object" transference.

VALIDATION OF EXPERIENCE THROUGH REGRESSION

Furthermore, we must acknowledge that human life is not to be seen only as a sequence of developmental steps from the cradle to the grave. We must not be transfixed by the idea of development, not be blinded by it to our fuller experience of life. That tells us of moments and stretches of time which exist for themselves as they are lived in awareness. Among them are many during which we are "regressed," returning to modes and intensities of object relations, feelings, perceptions, sensations, and thought of a simpler, less differentiated cast, closer to those experienced in childhood. In analysis, they are given a chance to return from the repressed unconscious—not only in order to find more advanced expression and integration in a developmental sense, but for their own sake; through them we regain access to the fresh immediacy and intensity of living. There is a rawness here that may be blissful and/or full of pain. Many patients, inside and outside the analysis and prior to it, experience it all too vividly and painfully if their defenses are weakened or break down and they are left alone with such an experience. In analytic treatment, it is possible for patients to have these vulnerable levels of experience validated by the therapist—whatever forms such recognizing validation may have to take with different patients and at different moments during treatment. As is true in infancy and childhood, mirroring recognition is essential in making experience viable. It takes various forms at different life stages, even if it be only a developed superego's internal validation.

Without validation human experience either does not come together or breaks down, fragments, and becomes unbearable; psychic development is arrested or interfered with. In speaking of fixation points to which regression returns, we must keep in mind that they are stages when in one way or another given instinctual and ego levels were still validated by environmental responses. But validation, as stated before, is not merely to be seen in the perspective of development toward higher stages. It affirms and confirms the dignity, reality, and truth of an experience and of its particular mode. It is, one might say, the reality test of inner experience, of psychic reality. If a regressive experience is then brought into connection with an equivalent or corresponding one of higher mental complexity, both of them gain in meaning.

THERAPEUTIC ELEMENTS OF
INTERPRETATION OF REGRESSION

Several elements, then, may be distinguished as being therapeutic in interpretations of patients' regressive functioning. Without claiming completeness for this list, I believe the following to be essential: (1) Interpretations acknowledge, if only implicitly at times, the significance of patients' regressive feeling state, fantasy, thought, or action as a manifestation of a genuine experience having its own weight, claim, and title—and this despite its incongruity with self-acknowledged and accepted contents and forms of patients' mental life, and despite its incompatibility with the accepted normal organization of external reality, object relations, etc. (2) It is the analyst who validates the regressive experience; patients are not left alone with it. The analyst's recognizing response, if genuine, cannot but flow from his or her own regressive levels of experience. If spurious, the analyst's response may be assimilated to what has been called the false self. (3) The analyst's interpretation, typically in verbal form, connects—on the basis of the patient's verbal and nonverbal material—one group of impulses, fantasies, memories, etc., with others that are perceived to be related. In this way, an interpretation may change a patient's experience to a more complex or higher form of psychic organization, by integrating it within a broader context of meaning (within the context of the coherent ego, to use Freud's words). Islands of experience and states of mind lose their isolation. This often entails a loss in intensity and a gain in lucidity and consistency of experience, conveying a sense of safety. (4) Related to this change of level of psychic organization by verbal interpretation is the analyst's usually more articulate and often more abstract language that echoes and explicates patients' productions. By "more abstract" I mean here the progression from a statement that a patient is crying, to saying that he feels hurt or angry or sad, or mourns; up to the rarely appropriate event of interpreting in terms of the language of psychoanalytic theory. In parentheses: this last form of interpretation is as a rule inappropriate, not because the theory or the language of psychoanalysis is wrong or inadequate, but because the theoretical level of discourse, its degree of abstraction, is too far removed from patients' nontheoretical levels of discourse to have an impact or to be understood. This remoteness of theoretical abstraction, however, is not in itself evidence of the theory's incorrectness or uselessness.

ORGANIZATION AND ORGANIZATIONAL LEVELS

What follows is a digression on organization and organizational levels. Hughlings Jackson, the neurologist, to my knowledge was the first one to introduce the concept of regression (though not the term itself) into the discussion of the organization of the nervous system, by speaking of its evolution and dissolution. He asserted

(1897, p. 437) that evolution (progression) to higher levels of organization, such as the cortical level, does not spell more, but less, organization on that higher level. By this he meant that, whereas lower levels of nervous system functioning operate relatively automatically and are in this sense more definitively and tightly organized, the highest levels are still in the process of organization, in the spontaneous, unpredictable flux of organizing activity. On a higher level, organization would be less perfect or complete than on lower levels and less stable inasmuch as the higher-level organizing processes have not yet arrived at a relative end-state, as lower levels have. The ambiguity of the word "organization" is involved here: "organization" signifies an observed state or structure as well as organizing activity. On high levels, organizing activity and comprehensiveness are increased as compared with low levels, but a low level has a more perfect status qua observed structure or state; in the latter sense, subcortical levels of functioning, for instance, are better organized and more resistant to disorganization than are cortical levels. On higher levels, organization is resumed as nonautomatic, more encompassing *activity*. Such a view, it seems to me, fits with Freud's notion of the "indestructibility" of the id and the relative instability of ego and superego considered as "observed" structures. Lower organizational levels—regressive relative to corresponding higher levels—are stable and function more automatically.

Let me illustrate a different perspective on organizational levels by an analogy, taking into account *interpretation* as organizing activity. A musical composition, such as a symphony, once composed as organized creation, is a definitive structure. It becomes a text to be interpreted by the conductor and his orchestra. The enduring structure of the text (encoded in the written or printed notation of it) is reenacted, reorganized in the orchestral rendition. In a good performance, the original composition, available as an organization qua finished product, becomes again that living organism, as it were, which it had been in the active process of its composition, but now under the reorganizing influence of the conductor. The actual rendition is an interpretation of the text, a reorganization. The good performance, while faithfully adhering to the text, is not a mere reiterating restatement of its elements, but revives the text by recreating and articulating its "meanings," —not all of them necessarily having been apparent to or intended by the composer. It is through the vivid understanding of those who interpret it that a text regains life. The text has a dormant life that is awakened and thus reorganized in the interpretation. Every interpretation is determined by the organization of the "text," i.e., of the available prior organizational level, which is relatively fixed, and the reorganizing activity of the interpreter.

This also applies to live understanding of the spoken word in listening, and to the "interpretation" of a written text such as a book or paper. It would be fruitful to pursue these analogies by applying them to analytic interpretations, but this would lead us too far afield. My main purpose has been to call attention to the two different senses in which organization is used, namely, as signifying a state and as signifying an activity. Thus, considered as state, a lower level of organization is more organized than a higher level; considered as activity, a higher level of organization implies more manifest and more comprehensive, organizing activity than the lower level. The musical analogy points out that a more recent, or actual, level of organizing activity does not make the prior level less valid and does not abandon it, but rather, reorganizes it, and, in so doing, revives and "interprets" it.

Organizing activity on a higher level may result in its becoming relatively fixed, a "steady state." As such, it then acquires a more perfectly organized *state*, like the lower previous level. Nevertheless, any higher organizational level is a more open process as compared to the relatively greater closure and automaticity of a lower level. In regression, a given high-level organizational state, being more open, less automatic, and therefore more prone to disorganization, is temporarily relinquished, making the lower level more accessible. That more stabilized and automatic level thereby is activated and gains the potential of being drawn out of its automaticity and into further organizing activity by which it may become reorganized differently. This reorganization constitutes the new higher level. We may picture in this way the therapeutic potential of regression. If this reorganization occurs, organization now is more complex as well as more alive and less stable on this new level. Thinking in terms of ego organization and ego development, regression thus may lead to ego reorganization in a progressive direction that is less set and more open to future. I mention in passing that the degree of automaticity (of the steadiness of the state) of a given organizational level seems to be in part determined by the existence—the pressure, as it were—of a next higher level; due to the functioning of the higher level, the lower one is more resistant to disorganization.

INTERPRETATION AND
THE ANALYST'S REGRESSION

I return to the analyst's interpretations of regressive functioning. The patient's regressive levels of experience, once given a chance to reenter fresh organizing activity by the therapist's recognizing-interpretative activities, may cease to repeat themselves in the same mode. I conceive of such recognition as being on a continuum: from concrete bodily expression of communicative interaction—as may be called for, not in psychoanalysis, but in the treatment of small children or deeply regressed adults—to forms of play; "symbolic realization" (Sechehaye 1947); verbal restatements; clarifications; and psychoanalytic interpretations. Seen from the angle of interpretation, to embrace or kiss someone in distress or pain is a primitive, concrete form of interpretation, inasmuch as such action conveys tolerable context and meaning to the experience. Seen from the angle of recognizing presence, an analytic interpretation is a form or expression of validating recognition on a high, sublimated organizational level. Such interpretative expression in articulate rational language can be convincing if two conditions are fulfilled: (a) patients' ego organization is far enough advanced to encompass, under the propitious conditions of the analytic situation, experiences that had been kept excluded from the ego's organizing activity (as is the case in repression); (b) therapists' rational form of interpretation remains for them rooted in and fed by corresponding, more archaic forms of experience. In other words; analysts must really *know* what they are saying rather than just using words and concepts they have learned more or less by rote or employing an automatized facility with acrobatics of mental mechanisms and dynamics; that is, analysts reorganize their own regressive experiences in the process of interpreting.

With this last observation, I turn once more to the subject of therapists' regression. It is clear that, in order to be attuned to where patients are at a given moment in their mental functioning, therapists must be able to regress, temporarily, to that level ("trial identification"). What I have said, however, goes further in that it makes explicit that this trial identification with patients involves therapists' identification with their own regressive level of experience as well, that the former does not occur without the latter. This temporary, circumscribed, self-regressive internal movement on the part of analysts allows for the organizing activity of a genuine interpretation. An analytic interpretation starts, as it were, at the regressive level shared by patient and analyst and from there proceeds to reorganize that experience level within a more complex and more comprehensive context, i.e., on a higher level. The regressive experience is not thereby gotten rid of, excluded, or undone, but is encompassed in the novel organizing activity and organizational level as a dynamic element. An important part of working through is the interplay by which regressive and progressive levels of experience enliven and illuminate each other.

To illustrate some of these points, I briefly discuss an episode from an analysis of which I have spoken elsewhere with a different emphasis. A patient unaccountably delayed completion of his dissertation and chided himself for not living up to his responsibility. In the course of several consecutive hours dominated by this issue, and on the basis of previous analytic work, his insistent stress on responsibility made it apparent to me that his delay was importantly related to an unconscious attempt to evade responsibility for a crime. The delay was, other motivations apart, a defense against murderous impulses and corresponding guilt directed at his father and myself as oedipal father. My interpretations brought the regressive oedipal basis for his behavior to the fore. This allowed him, in the validating atmosphere of the analytic situation, to recognize and accept once more the truth and strength of these impulses and defenses against them, as well as further to encompass and thus attenuate them within the wider and richer context of his present conscious life. It was part of a working-through process insofar as conflicts over patricidal issues had been interpreted and worked on before. The current realistic problem, the delay of his dissertation, was a particular manifestation that allowed and required further and more concentrated work with these conflicts. A full interpretation, in my experience often extending over some hours or weeks, validates the authenticity of the regressive impulse and defense, and integrates them on a more advanced level of mental functioning.

Concerning the analyst's regression, self-observation and reflection tell me that, in the example given, the connection between the delay and patricidal impulses, and particularly the meaning (unintended by the patient) of responsibility for a crime, occurred to me by way of my own associations. These arose as the patient's material and the transference issues involved stimulated memories of earlier, more primitive expressions of my own oedipal conflicts. In part by virtue of these transference-countertransference undercurrents, regressive fantasies and memories were activated in me, resonating with the patient's unconscious motivations, and initiating in me processes of reorganizing activity which, if communicated to the patient, he might make his own. Specifically, I remembered my attempt, in early adolescence, to write a play dealing with the crime and guilt of killing a father-figure (it should be noted that conceptualizing what I remembered as "dealing with the crime and guilt of killing a father-figure," already represents a reorganization or interpretation of the content of the memory in terms of my present understanding of my motivations for trying to write that play). What I told the patient was not my memory but the reorganizing interpretation I achieved. At such a point, I sometimes find it impossible and unnecessary, in an initial phase, to distinguish clearly between the patient's material and my own (the unconscious does not differ that much between one person and the next). During the subsequent internal steps, the amendments and specifications may be made which do justice to the particularities of the two participants in the analysis.

To draw a conclusion from this last statement: on regressive levels of mental functioning self-object differentiation itself regresses, dedifferentiating. This is true for patients and the analysts. Analysts, however, are able to move with considerable freedom and overall control and mastery within the orbit of different levels, with the highest level of integration being dominant.

This return with patients to regressive levels enables analysts to reactivate internal communications between various psychic levels in themselves. Nevertheless, due to the attraction of regressive levels, of the "indestructible unconscious," analysts' inner controls and equilibrium are strained by this explicit return to them, in that their own defenses tend to be activated.

REGRESSION IN "THE INTERPRETATION OF DREAMS"

Speaking of the internal communications between various psychic levels leads me to a brief discussion of Freud's first published exposition of regression in the seventh chapter of "The Interpretation of Dreams." As will be recalled, he formulates the concept there in the framework of his "topographic" model comprising the system Pcpt./Cs. and the "mnemic systems" including Ucs. and Pcs. Insofar as this model is described—not without significant qualifications—in spatial terms and illustrated by visual spatial representations (1900, pp. 537, 538, 541), it is called topographical. There are progressions and regressions, to and fro, between the systems. In essence, progressive movement proceeds from the sensory end, via sequential mnemic systems, to the motor end, as in a reflex arc. But the development of mnemic systems and Cs., that is, of the "psychic apparatus," has rendered the inner workings of that apparatus so complex and intricate that the term "reflex arc" no longer applies. Internal resistance (censorship) develops between the systems, interfering with progression from one to the next or with regression from the next to the previous one. These resistances ("countercathexes") interfere with communication between the systems and make it less immediate. Hallucinations and iconic representations in dreams, which substitute for what in normal, waking, rational mental life would be ideas and trains of thought, are examples of regression to mnemic systems lower in the hierarchy (or further back in the model) as well as earlier in development. In this process, resistances between systems, as far as retrograde movement is concerned, weaken or give way.

Freud, accordingly, speaks of *topographic* regression (within the topography of the psychic apparatus) and of *temporal* regression (in terms of ontogeny). He speaks of *formal* regression insofar as hallucinations and images are more primitive representatives of ideas and logical relations (1900, p. 548). He describes formal regression when he says: "In regression, the fabric (*das Gefüge*) of the dream-thoughts is resolved into its raw material" (p. 543). These three kinds of regression are at bottom one and the same, since what is further back toward the starting point in the spatial model occurs earlier in development and is simpler in its form of representation.[1]

Freud's original exposition of regression deals specifically with the adult structuring of the mind as revealed through dreams which adumbrate internal communications. Considering regression from the standpoint of internal communication within a continuum of irrational and rational modes and contents of mentation, a continuum of structures or systems, has the advantage that here the organization and functioning of the adult mind is in view. We are thus able to appreciate that regression per se is not pathological, but rather, a phase in the motions and transformations of psychic life.

With patients whom we describe as regressed, the flux and rhythm, the balance of phases, and the communications between rational and irrational phases are disordered in a regressive direction. We try to understand what in the history and current situation of the individual may have determined or contributed to the predominance of regression and regressive states. But we will be ill-equipped to be of help to the patient if we see regression as nothing but the return to an alien, archaic, infantile stage of

[1]Some of the material discussed here (i.e., the three kinds of regression and genetic considerations) did not appear in the first edition of "The Interpretation of Dreams," but was added in 1914 and 1919.

development which we, the therapists, have long since left behind. I am not saying that there is nothing infantile or archiac here. My point is that infantile-archaic stages find psychic permanence in the structuring of the mind, whether we are regressed patients or healthy, mature adults; and that the relative freedom, balance, and mastery of communications between the structures of the mind are the essential factors.

SUMMARY AND CONCLUDING REMARKS

In my concluding remarks, I return to certain thoughts touched upon at the end of my paper on "The Waning of the Oedipus Complex" (1979). The psychoanalytic concept of regression implies deviation in a retrograde direction from a norm or standard of behavior and mentation. Roughly speaking, this norm is rational thought and action, guided by secondary process, the reality principle, and reality testing. While Freud insisted that the irrational unconscious—and that means, from the standpoint of that norm, regressive mentation—is the true psychic reality, he was at the same time firmly committed to the rationality of conscious life as normative. I think most or all of us are caught in that dilemma, analysts probably more so than others. In a broad sense of rationality, which includes the problems of determinism and the rational order of the universe, all of modern science, and especially theoretical physics, struggles with such a dilemma. There is Einstein's famous remark, "God does not play dice"—which he made while struggling with the irrational implications of quantum theory. In direct contrast, years before Nietzsche (who was strongly influenced by the theory of evolution) spoke of "the most unexpected and breathtaking throws in the game of dice played by Heraclitus' 'great child,' be he called Zeus or Chance" (1887, 2nd essay, section 16), in reference to the evolution from animal life to the development of a human soul, a psyche. (It is no accident that he cites the philosopher Heracleitus, who preceded Socrates, Plato, and Aristotle, the founders of Western rational philosophy). A more or less intentional return to or resumption of irrational, archaic modes of

imagination, thought, and sensibility, for good and ill, is a characteristic ingredient of twentieth-century Western civilization. This is
true in sociopolitical life, modern art and literature, certain currents
of modern philosophy, research interests of cultural anthropology,
comparative psychology, and psychoanalysis itself.

In the individual, "regression in the service of the ego," to my
mind, is not simply a means for increased ability to make the
irrational rational, for extending the range of rationality. Rather, it
frees the ego from excessive domination or rationality and increases
the dimensions and the range, not of rationality, but of our ego as
an organization encompassing the irrational. What is repressed—
whether this be "sexuality" or "aggression" or other rejected realms
of human experience—and has the power to invade the ego in the
form of symptoms and troublesome character traits (return of the
repressed) is excluded from the "coherent ego" (Freud 1923, p. 17;
in German: *das zusammenhängende Ich*). The coherent organization of the ego (e.g., its synthesis and integration) is endangered by
regression, although such regression may ultimately be "in the
service of the ego." Creative work often is fraught with anxiety
brought about by this threat. In work with more deeply regressed
patients, our hard-won integration is threatened, leading only too
easily to interfering countertransference reactions.

Something similar happens in our modern society, as different
elements struggle for or against certain trends of overt behavior,
mores, ways of thinking, and feeling. These trends are manifest in
changing, looser, sexual mores and behavior, in the greater prominence of and permissiveness toward aggression, in the more pro-
nounced and more readily gratified need for intense or ecstatic and
unfamiliar sensory and emotional experiences, as epitomized in
the drug-culture, as well as in the flourishing of primitive religious
cults and communes. It is no coincidence that the word "repression" is used in a social sense in referring to the battle-cry for law
and order and its implementation (including "censorship," a term
that Freud took over from political life)—law and order in the
sense of a strictly rational, well-defended organization of society
whereby irrational, immoral, "regressive," elements are suppressed
or excluded from it, cast into outer darkness like the repressed id.

The more thoughtful members of society realize that in the long run, society as a whole is better served by the coming together and mutual interaction and influence of regressive and nonregressive elements. As is true with the individual, however, a limited amount of repression appears to be inevitable.[2]

It is imperative that, as analysts and therapists, we consider that the standards and norms by which we judge patients' functioning to be regressive are shifting and in flux, no longer as certain and un-questioned in our own mental make-up as they were for Freud; we are not always aware of this flux. Nowadays, regression in a global sense often tends to become a virtue in and of itself, as release and liberation from an overheated rationality, for therapist and patient. If it be deviation from a norm, that norm itself has become dubious; deviating from it may seem "progressive" rather than the reverse. Significant elements of our sociocultural milieu are in the throes of fluctuating, wobbly norms of conduct. Both individual members of society and groups are contributing to and affected by that milieu. Under such circumstances, as Heinz Lichtenstein has pointed out (1974, pp. 325–327), it becomes difficult to continue thinking, with Hartmann, in terms of an average expectable envi-ronment (1939 passim; Hartmann, however, had a more sophisti-cated view of these matters than he sometimes is given credit for) or, with Anna Freud (1976), in terms of average expectable "mental equipment." What is expectable, in the two senses of "to be anticipated" and "to be achieved as being expected from you," is no longer clear and unmistakable. What is, or ought to be, the average, is in doubt. This also applies to the role of the family and the problems of modern child rearing.

All this must make us question whether regression is indeed "regressive" in all respects and under all circumstances. At the very

[2]Repression in the psychoanalytic sense is a term for an unconscious process. Social-political repression is partly consciously intended and partly out of aware-ness. The German term for psychoanalytic repression, *Verdrängung,* is not used in the other sense in which the English term is used. Only the German term *Zensur* (censorship) has acquired both meanings. It is interesting to note that the general, nontechnical meaning of the verb *verdrängen* may be rendered by the English "to crush" or "displace" (in the sense of "crowd out").

least, we must revise our generally critical attitude toward regression which considers it tolerable or useful only as a passing phase in creative work and in developmental steps or as tool or vehicle in the treatment process. All the same, we cannot doubt that regression, in the interest of a life that is manageable for the individual, for his or her life in society, and for society itself, needs checks and balances and controls. But so do rationality and those forms of mentation and behavior which an older generation saw as unquestionably more advanced and mature. Deviations from a norm of rationality may at times be progressive. Although they tend to be seen as regressive, they may, like mutations, constitute or prepare novel, original forms and modes of experience and of the human mind.

REFERENCES

Freud, A. (1976). Changes in psychoanalytic practice and experience. *Internat. J. Psycho-Anal.* 57:257–260.

Freud, S. (1900). The interpretation of dreams. *Standard Edition* 5.

———— (1923). The ego and the id. *Standard Edition* 19.

Hartmann, H. (1939). *Ego Psychology and the Problem of Adaptation.* New York: International Universities Press, 1958.

Jackson, J. Hughlings (1897). Relations of different divisions of the central nervous system to one another and to parts of the body. In *Selected Writings of Jackson J. Hughlings,* vol. 2, pp. 422–443. London: Hodder and Stoughton Ltd., 1932.

Kris, E. (1952). *Psychoanalytic Explorations in Art.* New York: International Universities Press.

Lichtenstein, H. (1974). Reality perception, psychic structure, and the generation gap. In *The Dilemma of Human Identity*, pp. 323–344. New York: Aronson, 1977.

Loewald, H. W. (1979). The waning of the Oedipus complex. *J. Amer. Psychoanal. Assn.* 21:751–775.

Nietzche, F. (1887). *The Genealogy of Morals.* Garden City, N.Y.: Doubleday, 1956.

Sechehaye, M. A. (1947). *La Réalisation Symbolique.* Berne: Hans Huber.

Valéry, P. (1939). Poetry and abstract thought. In *The Art of Poetry,* pp. 52–81. New York: Random House, 1961.

4

SOME ASPECTS OF SEPARATION AND LOSS IN PSYCHOANALYTIC THERAPY WITH BORDERLINE PATIENTS

Harold F. Searles

Editor's Notes

This chapter reflects Dr. Searles's typical style in its blend of rich clinical experiences, penetrating self-scrutiny, subtle understanding, and lively exposition. The latter indicates to me that even though Dr. Searles is dealing with the most primitive, alienated levels of the psyche, he still retains the ability to convert misery and tragedy into an interesting topic for analytic enquiry without losing his sense of humor. Still, he is in no way frivolous because he is always painfully aware of the seriousness and gravity of the phenomena he chooses to study.

Borderline patients are often terrified. They move through life at a frenetic pace and openly display their vulnerability and helplessness. Dr. Searles instinctively relates to the adaptive significance of such feelings and behavior; he does not view them merely as the products of ego disintegration.

Ever clinging to the principle of psychic determinism, he sees a purpose in such reactions. His clinical experience has taught him that terror is easier for patients to bear than "deadness." The generation of an affect—even such a painful affect as terror—fills in an existential void. Dr. Searles believes that many borderline patients have internalized a dead parent who, even when alive, was perceived as "dead." Patients then have to defend themselves against this unbearable feeling of "deadness." Surface agitation and disturbed behavior may be manifestations of this defense. As we probe into the primitive, amorphous psyches of patients crippled by psychopathology, we frequently form the impression that they are not truly alive. Some of these patients do not seem to have attained the degree of vibrancy that defines life. A feeling of "deadness" is pervasive. To be able to move upward toward life by structuralizing a feeling, even a disruptive feeling, represents an immense accomplishment.

The backgrounds of these patients have been unbelievably traumatic. We feel their alienation; for many of us, the world of their infancy seems to belong on another planet. They have suffered such abuse and neglect that even having a need becomes catastrophically painful. These patients demonstrate the fundamental paradox of equating life with death. Their inner core functions on the premise that suicide is a way of life.

With this orientation, it is not surprising that borderline patients have never achieved the capacity to mourn, as Dr. Searles stresses in this chapter. He aptly points out that in order to mourn someone, that person must have had an active and significant presence for the would-be mourner. Put most simply, if the deceased person was never "there," to begin with, he cannot be missed. If the psyche has not formed a mental representation of what should have been a significant external object, then the loss of that object will not be felt. There is no corresponding psychic loss.

Dr. Searles also emphasizes that these patients cannot remember segments of their childhood, which manifests itself in treatment as amnesia. He postulates that this amnesia acts as a defense against murderous rage. In addition, it is the outcome of a structural conflict: the object relations of these patients are characterized by fusion. In the fused state, the external world and persons in it are indistinct. Persons are not differentiated from each other or from the self. Since these patients did not achieve self-object differentiation in childhood, that developmental period was not indelibly imprinted in the psyche. Furthermore, the sequence of past, present, and future was only poorly established. Not only do these patients perceive the past dimly and discontinuously, but they also have very little concept of the future. This factor contributes to patients' all-pervasive feeling of hopelessness. There is nothing to look forward to, because they do not know how to look forward.

There are many vital clinical issues in this chapter. Especially interesting are those ideas about grieving that emphasize the concept of symbiotic fusion. Here Dr. Searles introduces a fresh and unexpected viewpoint. Grief is a reaction to separation. If the separation is from symbiotic fusion, then it can be liberating, especially if the symbiosis is traumatic and constrictive, as it invariably is with severely disturbed patients. Dr. Searles believes that this type of separation is not accompanied by grief.

I want to carry these thoughts just a little further. Rather than thinking in terms of their pathological symbiosis, we can conceptualize patients with primitive mental states as never having been able to achieve symbiosis. Fusion is perceived as terrifyingly destructive. The unified and synthesized view of the world that is achieved after resolution of symbiosis is not attained by these patients. Their world is fragmented and appears to be viewed in terms of part objects that are only minimally able to meet their needs. Never having had a comfortable dependent relationship, these needy patients are unable to be dependent. They have never been valued so they do not know how to value. Since there is nothing to gain, there can be nothing to lose, nothing to grieve. An important part of the therapeutic task is to enable patients to experience a comfortable symbiosis for the first time with the therapist. Because of early trauma this may be very difficult to accomplish. The repetition compulsion impels patients to be self-destructive but the analytic setting can let them repeat infantile constellations in a reconstructive fashion. Analysts may represent early failures but they can also deal with them as projected expectations that are not necessarily inevitable or permanent.

Dr. Searles discusses his own reactions to patients' rage and the many ways this rage can be expressed. He knows that anger also has adaptive significance; if we, as therapists, can survive it we will have furnished patients with a valuable experience. Dr. Searles apparently has survived many angry attacks and he shares some of these encounters with us.

For example, he discusses patients who have the uncanny ability to open up our most painful psychic wounds and make us feel miserable and outraged, as well as useless, helpless, and vulnerable. He believes that these patients primarily relate to people on a part-object basis and tend to confuse one person with another. Their view of the world is kaleidoscopic, a mélange of hatred and fear directed at themselves and everyone around them. It is not surprising that they bring this orientation into the consultation room.

I recall patients who presented themselves in a confused and seemingly agitated fashion. They constantly felt frightened and angry but there was no focus to their feelings. They could not attach these disruptive affects to a situation; they had no psychic content. In time, these feelings were directed toward me; I became the cause of their misery and the target of their anger.

Such patients function at primitive psychic levels. Their diffuse and fragmented feelings are not integrated with other psychic activities. The treatment setting provides cohesion while analysts serve as anchors that help organize patients' feelings. Therapists may have to endure considerable psychic pain but they are rendering a valuable service, in that they are establishing causal sequences. Patients now have someone to "blame" for their feelings and, eventually, through the vehicle of transference, they can attach these feelings to the archaic and primal relationships where they were created. Previously, these patients did not have sufficient psychic structure to relate their reactions to their sources.

An affect has a certain degree of structure that can serve as an integrating force. Some states of primitive agitation owe their disruptive effects to the psyche's amorphous disorganization. The production of an affect can be a synthesizing experience. For example, some patients are either always anxious or always angry. In the former case, patients may generate anxiety to protect themselves from a more basic fear of dissolution, the terror of existential annihilation. I am particularly reminded of an identical twin who had no sense of personal aliveness but who could reassure herself that she was alive by feeling anxious. Experiencing a painful feeling was better than not feeling anything at all. Both self-torturing depressive patients and chronically but diffusively angry patients also exemplify the synthesizing capacity of affects. Once we reach the inner core of the psyche, we are confronted with areas of terror that encompass both fears of existential annihilation and the terrible pain associated with living. Anger and self-demeaning preoccupations serve to organize the inner terror of these patients, which is the outcome of their struggle with pain of living, on the one hand, and the dread of suicide, on the other.

With characteristic frankness, Dr. Searles discusses how patients awaken areas within himself that in some ways parallel the psychic levels dominating the transference interaction. He can feel intuitively connected to patients in either an empathic or a disturbed fashion. The latter may cause him to despair and feel

useless, but this is counteracted by the understanding
he derives from the interaction. Knowing that we can
be useful to patients even when we feel quite useless
helps us to maintain ourselves and to keep functioning
with hope in an exceedingly difficult relationship. Dr.
Searles articulates this situation well and we can all
profit from his years of experience, his struggles, and
his insights.   *P. L. G.*

For various reasons, borderline individuals have inordinate difficulty in integrating the experiences of separation and loss which
are inherent in human living generally, and in the course of
psychoanalytic therapy more specifically. But more than that, the
borderline personality organization itself renders separation and
loss ever present dangers. If we accept the finding of Mahler
(1968) that borderline patients' personality structure is developmentally traceable to difficulties in the phase of separation and
individuation, we see that their tenuously established individual
ego continually faces the threat of regression into symbiosis, with
the consequent total loss of individuality. Sometimes their fear of
such symbiotic fusion will impel them into such severe autism
(that is, psychosis) that they lose all human relatedness.

With such patients, analysts typically end each session in a
manner that minimizes both upset to the patients and the feeling
of loss that the analysts themselves often experience. When analysts
have to tell such patients that they will be away for a day or a week,
they tend to do so in a calm, matter-of-fact manner consciously
designed to minimize patients' separation anxiety. In this way,
patients clearly perceive that analysts feel no loss whatsoever at
the prospect of the impending separation. One could surmise, that
patients perceive little, if any, evidence that analysts will miss them
or think of them during the impending separation.

My own work and that of my supervisees and colleagues indicate
that this kind of analytic stance tends to represent an appreciable
repression of feelings of separation anxiety and loss on the analyst's
part. Thus, patients who manifest persistent difficulty in gaining
access to such feelings may well be identifying with their analysts'

defensiveness. Analysts tend to project such feelings onto patients and to look unconsciously to the latter to recognize and express such feelings for them.

At the beginning of a Monday session, a woman who had been in analysis with me for several years started speaking of "My attachment to you—it's horrendous. You know why Mondays are so blah for me?" I inquired, "Why?" and she replied, "At the beginning of the weekend you go away and leave, and then it's as though when you come back on Monday I've forgotten you—I've dismissed you. I *have* to, because it's too painful (to do otherwise)."

I sensed that she had identified with an aspect of me when she said, "I've forgotten you—I've dismissed you," which sounded as if she were doing to me what she felt I had done to her. This in itself was nothing new or surprising. But then when she added, "I have to, because it's too painful (to do otherwise)," it sounded as if she unconsciously fantasied that I had to dismiss and forget her, for otherwise it would be too painful for me. I immediately sensed that there was an element of truth in her unconscious perception of my defensive dismissal of my dependency on her.

INTROJECTION OF ATTRIBUTES OF THE ANALYST

With patients who persistently become involved in self-destructive acting out between sessions (especially during my prolonged absences), I find, time and again, that such behavior is partly based on their introjection of some of my own internal psychological contents. Much self-destructive behavior by patients during my absence proves to be directed, unconsciously, against their introjected image of me. Typically, such behavior seems to be maddeningly ego-syntonic for patients, who report it in a spirit of vindictive relish, as though they have injured me rather than themselves.

In a 1980 paper, I discussed some of the difficulties involved in borderline patients' development of an internalized image of the therapist. Indeed, such patients still may not have an enduring internalized image of the analyst. But, much more often, these patients have introjected various aspects of analysts' largely unconscious personality attributes and have manifested these identifications between sessions; however, the identifications are so disguised that analysts often do not recognize them as such for prolonged periods of time. These identifications consist of actual attributes of analysts, rather than distorted perceptions of patients in the grip of powerful transference-reactions, and they are highly unpalatable to analysts' conscious sense of identity. The more ill the patient, the more he or she tends to identify immediately with the analyst's sickest, least fully conscious introjects.

Many writers, including myself (1965), have written about the Bad Mothers of schizophrenic or borderline patients. I have gradually learned that such villainizing of these mothers (1) underestimates the importance of the patients' identifications with the Bad Mother components of their mothers; (2) results in patients blaming themselves for the emergence of the Bad Mother, with attendant guilt, grief, and rage; and (3) glosses over analysts' own ever present Bad Mother components. As I have seen these elements more clearly, my earlier view—that schizophrenic and borderline patients are more or less crippled by traumatic events of infancy or early childhood—has shifted profoundly. While I still believe there is some truth in that view, I have found over and over that borderline patients' psychopathology is continually fed and maintained through the unconscious complicity of persons, including the analyst, in the patients' current life.

To put it simply, psychotic (or borderline psychotic) patients succeed in evoking psychotic (but largely unconscious) responses from other persons. They form increments of folie à deux with many people in their daily life, such that their psychosis, or borderline psychosis, receives a great deal of verification from their external reality. For example, in 1972, I detailed the extent to which a chronic schizophrenic's delusional experience during sessions was founded on real components in my personality that I tended to maintain out of my awareness because they were alien to my own sense of identity.

EMOTIONAL SHALLOWNESS OF
BORDERLINE PATIENTS

I have found that very often borderline patients have deep-seated feelings of guilt and grief at having failed to enable their mothers to be alive and responsive to them. The inability of these patients to feel fully alive and to experience the gamut of human emotions is due in large part to their identification with a schizoid or chronically depressed aspect of their mothers. They have tried to rescue their mothers from this crippledness, but have succeeded only briefly and infrequently.

Borderline patients' inability to experience a full range of human emotions at the beginning of treatment has been reported by many therapists. These patients often show a proclivity for complexity in their lives as an unconscious defense against the realization of the emotional shallowness of their interpersonal relationships. They are reminiscent of chronic schizophrenic patients, who commonly present a lofty supercilious demeanor that says, in effect, that it is impossible for lowly others to grasp the complexity of their world. This demeanor is one of the major factors that keeps alive the general prejudice against schizophrenic patients.

In 1949, when I first began to work at Chestnut Lodge, I treated a chronically paranoid-schizophrenic young man who had made an extremely serious suicide attempt during one of his two previous admissions. He perceived me and others as "ciphers." It became evident that he was projecting onto me his subjective emptiness, deadness, and emotional impoverishment. But what made this so difficult to deal with was the way the patient attuned himself to my weakest areas, the ones that most warranted the designation of cipher. Society as a whole tends to hate schizophrenic patients because they are attuned with such hawklike accuracy to the felt deficiencies of society.

To return to borderline patients, often they are invested not only in the complexity of their lives but also in the gratifications of subjective omniscience. Time and again, there is an implied "I told you so. I foresaw this and tried to prepare you for it" message from such patients, as their only identifiable emotional response to an event that would create diverse and intense feelings for a person with the usual range of human emotions.

For example, one borderline woman began a session by saying, "Feel like I'm in a whirl of activity, like being on a merry-go-round. Going out every evening. The clinic (where she worked as a nurse) is frantically busy." In the next few minutes, she spoke of many, many activities, largely professional but also social. I noted: "It is predominantly impossible to know what the patient's feeling tone is about all this." That is, this patient showed no identifiable emotional response to the frenetic life she described.

Some borderline patients are able to experience a few emotional bands, as it were, on the spectrum of human feelings. For example, one woman said,

> I don't feel sadness; sadness isn't something I feel. . . . I under-
> stand devastation and . . . rage and . . . terror, but I don't
> know the milder forms [she had referred to sadness as being a
> mild form of devastation]. When I feel irritated or annoyed, I
> don't really feel those feelings; what I feel is rage. I can either
> feel complete devastation or nothing. I don't have those in-
> between states, they just never had a chance to develop. The
> others were too strong. So it's either those strong states or
> nothing, and most of the time it's been nothing.

In a session six months later, this same woman said, "At work, it seems to me that I just *live in terror* of being asked to do something that's not in my power to do." The words she emphasized were said in a tone that conveyed that she *really lived* only when she was *in terror*. Upon hearing her say this, I was reminded of chronic schizophrenic patients I had interviewed who felt that terror or panic was preferable to their customary boredom; one such patient had genuinely agreed with my suggestion that he felt alive only when he believed he might be murdered.

Relatively early in her analysis, another borderline patient remembered having been scared innumerable times throughout her childhood by her older sister. She reported these memories in her usual affectively enigmatic tone. Gradually it became clear that any hatred she felt toward her sister was balanced, if not outweighed, by appreciation for the relief her sister had afforded her from the chronic boredom that had permeated the patient's life.

During a phase of her analysis, one borderline woman's only felt emotion was that of being "shocked and stunned." I found evidence that this reaction involved an identification with her mother's only accessible emotion, and it helped me understand the origin of a certain daredevil quality of this patient. She had learned, in childhood, that through various daredevil activities she could evoke an emotional response from her mother—a "shocked and stunned" response. I have seen essentially the same phenomenon in a chronic schizophrenic woman with whom I have worked for many years. When the patient was a child, her mother's only consistently evocable emotional response was a shocked, deeply insulted reaction; otherwise, the mother dwelt in her own world of fantasies and was inaccessible to the patient. It is surely no coincidence that the patient developed a really remarkable capacity for being shocked and insulted in her subsequent interpersonal relationships.

THE INABILITY TO GRIEVE AND BORDERLINE STATES

The borderline individual's inability, without therapy, to accomplish grief work is both one of the major diagnostic criteria for the borderline state and one of the major foci of therapy. The Mitscherlichs' volume, *The Inability to Mourn* (1976), and Volkan's *Primitive Internalized Object Relations* (1976) and *Linking Objects and Linking Phenomena* (1981) are relevant to this general topic; however, the following observations and conclusions are solely my own.

Borderline patients' inability to grieve is one of the most difficult areas for them to mask in daily life. For example, the death of a parent highlights their inability to have the same feelings that other people have. It usually requires much work before patients are able to reveal their difficulties in the realm of genuine emotionality; before they can say, as one man said after some years of analysis, "I don't feel sorrow. I've never felt sorrow."

Patients' Amnesia

In my experience, one reliable criterion for the presence of borderline psychopathology is patients' manifestation—usually in the initial history-taking interview—of a striking loss of memory of childhood events. Typically, there will be stretches of years, somewhere between the ages of, say, three and eighteen, for which patients will have few, if any, memories. I do not mean that they will have amnesia for that whole fifteen-year span of time. Rather, within that time span there will be stretches of one or more years for which they have essentially no memory. This stands in striking contrast to neurotic patients' intact memory of childhood experiences at the outset of treatment.

Even after years of work with borderline patients, one still has only a relatively fragmented and clouded picture of the chronological events of their childhood and adolescence, and of the personalities of other family members. The more powerfully maintained patients' amnesia is, the more powerfully they are unconsciously reliving their childhood in the transference relationship. But analysts often feel greatly hampered in identifying the nature of the transference and locating it in its proper era in patients' developmental history because they have received so little consciously recalled history from patients to serve as a framework. Instead, to a great extent, the transference-derived information must itself serve as the framework.

At the most difficult times in my work with borderline patients, I am unable, for weeks or even months at a time, to locate what is happening between patients and myself either in their developmental history or mine. As a beginning psychoanalyst, I believed that work with a patient should *not* remind me very much of something from my own childhood; if it did, it indicated the need for further personal analysis. But now, many years later, I find it very helpful when the stressful and confusing interactions with borderline patients are reminiscent of scenes and events of my childhood. Such associations add another dimension to the analysis: I can then perceive what is happening in treatment both as part of a pattern of a patient's life and as part of a pattern of my own life. In those stressful instances in which one cannot locate disturbing interactions in a patient's past or one's own past, I think it erroneous to assume that more personal analysis will solve everything. Rather, I believe that what the analyst is experiencing has a counterpart in the experience of one or both parents of the patient.

The parents of these amnesic borderline patients largely tried to forget their own past when rearing their children, rather than using it in any well-integrated, freely remembered and reminisced about fashion as a guide or context for relating to them. Typically, such parents have so much unintegrated hatred and unworked-through grief, disappointment, hurt, and so on from their own childhoods that they cannot relegate their past to the past; instead, they unconsciously relive it with their children, whom they treat as transference objects.

To repeat, I suggest that when analysts cannot see meaningful historical antecedents to stressful treatment interactions, they are provided with glimpses into the inner life of patients' parents.

Patients' amnesia serves as an unconscious defense against all types of negatively toned emotions—guilt, fear, sadness, grief, and so on. It serves as a defense against murderous feelings; these patients seem to have "murdered" large periods of their own pasts unconsciously. The recall of what actually transpired during these periods revives murderous feelings of formidable intensity toward parents, siblings, and others. In this sense, patients' amnesia serves to "protect" the parents' lives.

Similarly, amnesia may serve as a defense against suicide. A patient recalled in treatment that two areas of his remembered past belonged in a certain chronological sequence, whereas they had been discrete and unrelated in his previous memory of them. I had pointed out this seemingly simple fact to him. For several days afterward, I had reason to fear that he would commit suicide. His unconscious maintenance of these areas as chronologically non-sequential had protected him from intense guilt. Furthermore, as my interpretation was not primarily a transference interpretation, he had reason to feel abandoned by me, which made it even more difficult for him to deal with previously unmanageable areas of his past. That experience served as another reminder of how essential it is to make transference interpretations and to explore patients' amnesia in terms of their difficulties in reconstructing the developing history of the therapy.

It is often strikingly difficult for borderline patients, and sometimes their therapists as well, to remember reasonably fully and in sequence the events that have occurred over the months or years of treatment. When patients fail to see connections between a current session and earlier ones, I find it of interest to notice at what point they say something that reminds me of previous sessions. More often than not, I share this observation with them; generally they are quite receptive.

A patient once said, "There's something mixed up about my chronology (i.e., the chronology of his recollections of his past). . . . I'm starting to think I must have been a good deal older for the second surgical operation—eleven or twelve." During earlier years of analysis, he had recalled the second of two operations as having been performed when he was seven years of age—a memory distortion of some five years. However, I did not notice this memory distortion at the time. Regarding another patient, who experienced relatively little continuity from one session to the next, I wrote, "It was not until thirty-seven minutes along in a very verbally interactive session that something of the preceding session came back to my memory."

Patients' amnesia also may take the following form. They recall and describe most of the family members relatively well, with the exception of one family member whom they scarcely ever mention. I have learned that this is a reliable indication that the omitted family member was quite significant in patients' upbringing. Patients may be so fused with that family member that the latter has very little existence as a separate object.

For example, a patient referred to "my brother." He had told me at the outset of the treatment that he had *two* older brothers, but "my brother" always referred to the eldest brother, who was an idealized father-figure for the patient. Only after years of treatment did it become clear he was very much fused with the other brother, whom he regarded with intense ambivalance. During our many largely silent sessions, I had represented this brother in the transference. Similarly, this helped explain why the patient, when speaking of his marriage, would usually say "I," rather than "we." In marrying his wife he had unconsciously married his next older brother as well. Many of the difficulties with "I" in the context of the marriage actually belonged to this transference brother-wife. Thus, when he would speak of financial worries that both he and his wife faced in their marriage, he would say only what "I" felt about them, and would often leave me wondering what his wife's feelings were. I came to realize that he was as fused with her as he was with his next older brother, and with me as the latter's transference representative.

Patients' Vengefulness

Vengefulness is an important aspect of the borderline personality, although it is hardly a specific criterion of the borderline state. As I have already indicated, borderline patients' areas of amnesia serve as an unconscious defense against murderous vindictiveness, among other emotions. Those who are not yet mature enough to forgive must forget instead. In my paper "The Psychodynamics of Vengefulness" (1956), I emphasized the defensive functions of vengefulness, particularly in regard to repressed grief and separation anxiety. Many borderline patients show a tenacious, rageful determination to "go back and show 'em!"—to go back, that is, to some particular earlier place and time to prove themselves to "them" (parents, other family members, schoolmates, or whomever). They feel that these significant others failed to appreciate them and misjudged them in the past.

Analysts can readily find evidence that through this vengeful determination, patients defend themselves against feelings of grief and separation anxiety vis-à-vis those earlier persons and settings. But it is also useful for analysts to see that patients' vindictiveness represents an attempt to overcome an underlying sense of discontinuity in their personal identity. That is, patients cannot fully accept their recently acquired personality aspects; thus, their burning determination to go back to that earlier time and place to which they are so emotionally fixated is an attempt to establish a stronger continuity of identity. Patients want to force "them" to accept those new attributes of themselves that, to a significant degree, they have not yet integrated into their overall personality functioning.

One borderline man said, "I have no more resemblance to myself twenty years ago than I have to you—just a completely different person—no sense of continuity. My present life began four years ago when I married Edith. A few little things remain (from his earlier life); I rediscover a little thread; recently I found myself rocking and realized that I had done that for years as a child."

Horowitz et al. (1980) describe states of pathological grief in terms of the re-emergence of self-images and role relationship models that had been held in check by the existence of the deceased person. Once the relationship with that person has been lost, patients become immersed in a review of their repertoire of self-images and role relationship models. In contrast to the review made by relatively healthy bereaved persons, for those with borderline disturbances, it becomes unusually intense and interminable. Excessive controls may prevent review of activated role relationship models so that mourning is never completed.

As patients' amnesia begins to lift, a flood of previously forgotten memories may be remembered for a few seconds, only to be covered again by the amnesia. Patients feel unable to recapture them and report them to the analyst. This phenomenon lends itself to sadistic tantalizing and sexual teasing of the analyst (an aspect of their interaction which I shall describe later), but at a level which may be genuinely unconscious for many months or even years.

The Psychological Absence of a Parent

It is impossible for patients to grieve the death of a parent with whom they had only a fleeting relationship. This does not lead to particular difficulties when the parent was physically absent nearly all the time. However, I am concerned with the far more frequent —and much more difficult—cases where the parent was physically present but psychologically absent. Parents are psychologically absent for a variety of reasons. Some are recurrently frankly psychotic. Many have "as if" personalities (Deutsch 1942) or other varieties of borderline psychopathology. To use ordinary rather than psychiatric parlance, one cannot go through an average-normal, healthy process of grieving the death of a parent who was almost always emotionally remote.

Some patients have borderline or schizoid parents whose ego functioning is so poorly integrated and who have so many uninte-grated feelings of loss from their own past, that they can rarely fully relate to their spouses and children. In treatment, their children—our patients—do not allow us to form a picture of their childhood family situation.

Borderline patients display nonrelatedness in treatment to the extent that they have identified with the remote parent. For example, in one woman's reaction at the beginning of a session, I could see a glimpse of how removed her mother had usually been. She was exceptionally startled when I opened the door to the waiting room to indicate that she should come in. In the opening moments of the session after she had assumed the couch, she said, "feel like my mind is somewhere else this evening—not sure where." This woman's deceased mother had been like this much of the time. When asked about her mother, another woman replied, "The first thing about my mother is that she's dead." Although this was literally true, I and several psychiatric residents present at the interview sensed that the patient had perceived her mother to be "dead," even when she was still living. Yet another example is a borderline man whom I analyzed. When I asked him whether he had ever confided in his much elder sister anything of the concern he was presently exploring, his reaction of profound shock helped me to realize that his sister had been psychologically dead for him during his childhood. I also realized that many of our more mori-bund sessions had to do with his relating to me in the transference as the "dead" sister.

Finally, there was the patient whose father had died when he was fifteen. This man described a recent telephone conversation in which he had calmed his anxious elder brother, adding, "I think that's what my father would have done had he lived." This man continued to idealize his dead father for years in his analysis, despite the fact that his father had been largely unavailable emotionally. When the patient made the brief statement I have quoted, although he said it without any discernible conscious anger or contempt toward his father, his tone conveyed the unconscious meaning, "I think that's what my father would have done had he *ever* lived." This patient was chronically vulnerable to feelings of fearful uncertainty about whether he himself existed, and this doubt proved to be based largely upon his being assailed, unconsciously, by his identifications with a father who never fully existed for him in terms of interpersonal relatedness.

The Chronically Teasing Parent

In this connection, the chronically teasing variety of parent merits at least brief mention. An appreciable percentage of borderline patients "tease" their analysts for years, never fully committing themselves to the treatment and thus preventing the analysts from functioning fully in their role. These patients report dreams, complete with abundant associations, and generally do all that "good" patients do in analysis, but in such a teasing fashion that their analysts almost, but never quite, acquire the necessary material for making a transference interpretation.

I have developed increasing compassion for these patients who torture me insofar as I have discovered that their sadistically teasing behavior is largely based upon identification with a dead, and usually ungrieved, mother or father whose parenting never went beyond "teasing." For instance, the father may have teasingly led his child to hope that one day he really would become a father to him—and then never have fulfilled that promise. By the same token, in the transference relationship, patients (who from the analysts' viewpoint are teasing) find a basis (and not only through projection) for feeling similarly tantalized by the hope that analysts will one day, at long last, come forth and commit themselves fully to being analysts to the patients.

Typically, the borderline patient was unconsciously perceived by the parent as the personification of the parent's own unintegrated past. Such a "transgenerational" transference to the child indicated that the loss of the parent's parent was never worked through. Thus, a mother who was unable to work through the loss of her own mother would tend to form a mother transference (the child's maternal grandmother) to her child. The more ill the adult borderline patient is, the more justified we are in assuming, until proven otherwise, that this type of interaction occurred in early childhood. This pattern is even more striking and begins at an earlier age with chronic psychotic patients.

Probably there is no more basic determinant of borderline patients' vengeful desire to "go back and show 'em!" than their need both to make their parents accept them as their children rather than their parents, and to achieve this at an internal level within themselves, in terms of introjects and identifications involved in their personal identity.

Parents who manifest "transgenerational" transference have never achieved full individuation. Thus they form a symbiotic transference with their children as a means of perpetuating the childhood symbiosis they had with their own parents. Children of such parents do not feel that they are living their own lives.

When such children become borderline adults and enter psychotherapy, they typically coerce analysts into feeling that they bear the primary responsibility for the direction of the patients' life. For example, these patients lay their career failures at the door of their analysts, inducing the guilty conviction that their failure to thrive is due to the analysts' malevolent orientation toward them. At times, one cannot help genuinely hating such patients. Much of these patients' "self"-injurious acting out is based on their introject of the hated parent-figure/analyst whom they assume is unwilling and unable to let them have their own autonomous existence. It is this hated, internalized parent-figure/analyst whom patients attempt to injure by their "self"-injurious acting out.

Splitting: A Major Defense Mechanism

Splitting has been described by Giovacchini (1975), Kernberg (1975), Masterson (1976), and others as one of the major defense mechanisms characteristic of borderline patients. I shall limit myself here to two points that I believe have not been covered previously.

To the extent that patients are still invested in an infantile-omnipotent orientation, they tend to experience grief not as a natural part of human living and dying, but rather, as something that "omnipotent" beings are attempting to inflict upon them. Work with such patients teaches us to what a striking degree this was true in their childhood. This becomes readily apparent as we become the receiving end of those split affects and transference-images that derive from patients' childhood experience with a parent whose ego-functioning involved considerable splitting.

Specifically, we learn that patients will sadistically hold the threat of leaving over our heads. Splitting plays a major role in this threat, in that patients experience the liberating and other positive aspects of the prospective separation while they project onto us any feelings of reluctance, loss, and grief associated with the separation.

For a number of years, a woman in analysis dwelled almost exclusively upon daily life events before she started giving me glimpses of her shockingly deprived childhood, which had been largely shrouded in amnesia. These memories were so appalling to me that at first I felt it had been primarily my own inner limitations that had prevented her from conveying them before. But I realized, as we went on, that these memories were available to her only when our relationship was strong enough to stand their emergence from their long dissociation. During one session, as she remembered her impoverished childhood, she said, "You didn't know it was so terribly poor, did you? The more I think about it, I guess it was." Her long-maintained denial of the traumas and extraordinary deprivation of her childhood was now being eroded through because of our analytic work.

Still, for many months, memories of her childhood emerged only infrequently, in vivid fragments a few months apart. My belief is that, during her childhood, she could not stand seeing the reality of her life continuously and fully, just as I could not stand seeing it later, in her analysis.

The patient could not grieve the loss of such a childhood situation because the situation was so bad that she, and probably the other family "participants" as well, could not remain fully in it. Instead, the reality of the situation was shrouded in a cocoon of denial which persisted during the early years of our work together.

The principle that I have just stated, namely, that in order to grieve the loss of a situation, one has to have been in that situation fully, occurred to me several years ago when I was considering the optimal timing of any patient's discharge from a psychiatric sanitarium. For patients to leave a sanitarium constructively, they must first have been in the sanitarium, psychologically as well as physically. Patients who never emotionally accept being in such a setting will be minimally prepared to integrate the inevitable unconscious feelings of loss that moving out will bring. Their inability to mourn the loss of the sanitarium will lead them to act out in ways that are designed, unconsciously, to have them return to the sanitarium.

The sporadic, fragmentary, and subjectively unpredictable nature of amnesic patients' memories of disturbing events and situations in their earlier years has a counterpart in analysts' own largely unconscious tendency to maintain amnesia for particularly shocking revelations from patients earlier in their work. For example, one of my supervisees was told of father-daughter incest, and another was told of a mother's murder of her infant daughter; both managed to forget these shocking disclosures for relatively long periods of time. That is, the therapists would be shocked anew when the patients spoke of these occurrences, as if they were hearing them for the first time.

I want to mention what I consider to be a subtle form of splitting found in some borderline patients. When a patient says "I missed you" at the beginning of the first session following an interruption in our scheduled meetings, I sometimes get a fantasy of a disappointed sniper. The reader might assume that this is merely further evidence of a paranoid stance in my relationships with fellow human beings. Surely such patients, who are struggling both to prove to themselves that they are predominantly loving and to maintain their more hostile attitudes in a state of dissociation, would have their analysts think themselves basically paranoid for having such a fantasy.

But I have had a sufficient wealth of experience with feelings of indubitably genuine missing and being missed, in both professional and personal relationships, that I can regard as reliable analytic data my fantasy of the patient being a disappointed sniper. Sooner or later I report this fantasy to the patient and find that, although it is inevitably somewhat jolting and wounding to the patient at first, it enhances our collaborative work. We cannot help borderline patients achieve genuine, rather than "as if," emotional relatedness unless they can deal with spurious emotionality as such. One woman patient who had been hampered for years in her conscious efforts toward loving relatedness with people by this split-off, disappointed-sniper area of her ego, said, "I was thinking yesterday, 'I miss you like crazy. But then I also thought, 'I miss you like poison.'"

I believe, but cannot prove, that there is an important factor in such patients' dissociated, disappointed-sniper self-image that I have postulated here which goes beyond the fact that their loving impulses are still opposed by unintegrated murderous hostility toward their analysts. This factor consists of patients' unconscious belief that grieving itself is innately murderous to the one whose absence one is grieving. That is, I surmise that, at an unconscious level, these patients are dominated by a primitiveness of thought that holds that grief is at least as much the cause as the result of a beloved person's death. I have little doubt that cultural anthropology could provide many examples of this kind of thinking among primitive peoples. I have seen clear-cut evidence of it in my work with a chronic schizophrenic woman whose long psychosis began shortly after her mother's death, which the patient could not accept as a reality. Significantly, this woman, who felt a loving,

God-like responsibility for all her good objects (including her mother), never was able to weep openly and had long been troubled by that inability. She was convinced that if one really loved one's mother, the mother would never die.

With another borderline patient, I felt so irrelevant and useless during many of our sessions that I surmised that he was wondering how I could bear to end the session and leave it at that. Indeed, this patient often seemed to hint that he did feel that way. I have found it helpful to see the important role that the patient's sadism plays in the events that require me to end the session in this context. With other patients, I am conscious of sadistically abrupt, and unnecessarily total, withdrawal of feelings before they leave the room. In many other instances, I have noticed that patients' free associations in the closing minutes of the session contain a sadistic-depreciatory thrust toward me. On the other hand, this can be seen as an unconscious sadistic defense against any genuine feelings of loss at the end of the session on the part of both patient and analyst. That is, in addition to minimizing their own loss, patients may be protecting analysts from feeling more loss than relief at their imminent end-of-session separation.

SHARING GRATIFICATIONS AND LOSS OF ILLNESS

We analysts tend to feel guilty at finding any gratification in patients' psychopathology, particularly if that psychopathology is very severe. We fear that we are morbidly fascinated with illness and secretly prefer it to health. But my experience as an analyst and supervisor has shown me that it is necessary for analysts to share patients' gratifications inherent in their illness sufficiently so that they can experience the patients' heretofore unintegrated (largely because of their interpersonal isolation) feelings of loss in gradually giving up their illness. To put it another way, patients must be helped to experience to the full the gratifications of their illness through their analysts' awareness and acceptance of such gratifications. The patients' grief work in the process of giving up the illness and all that it has represented to them for so many years can be a genuinely shared experience with their analysts. I do not see how any grief work can be successful unless it is shared with someone. Typically, psychiatric and psychoanalytic teaching have inculcated the belief that therapists should help patients "get over" the illness without the patients or anyone else—least of all the therapists—becoming aware of the positive meanings of the illness.

Concerning the working through of the loss of one's illness, my paper "Transitional Phenomena and Therapeutic Symbiosis" (1976, p. 146) is relevant. I suggest that in effective psychoanalytic therapy there is a phase in which "the patient's symptoms have become . . . transitional objects for both patient and analyst simultaneously." This observation gives a glimpse of how deeply mutual the shared grief work is in patients' relinquishment of their illness.

After one and a half years of once-a-week therapy (the patient could not finance more frequent sessions), a borderline man described some aspects of his parental family life which I found fascinating because of their schizophrenogenic aspects. Later in this session, I wondered how much analysts have to pay for such gratification with the fear that their patients will commit suicide. His so-enthralling description occupied about two to five minutes of a session largely devoted, as were most of his sessions, to current daily life events.

The following day a supervisee whom I saw once a week gave me a detailed description of a session with a borderline patient in which both patient and therapist felt an ambivalent symbiotic fusion. We recognized the guilt engendering aspect of such symbiotic intimacy. Then I told him that I wondered how much we must expect to have to pay, in terms of anxiety and other painful feelings, for the gratifications we derive from our work with borderline patients. I told him my impression that we have to atone for our conscious guilt. He immediately felt this idea to be valid. He had worked for many years with severe borderline and schizophrenic patients, predominantly in a hospital setting.

Such guilt functions mainly as an unconscious defense against analysts' feelings of loss as patients improve and primitive, symbiotic modes of relating are largely relinquished. Such feelings of loss on the analysts' part are connected with the earliest feelings of loss in their own life. They must "pay," eventually, for the intense gratifications they have derived from their transference- and countertransference-based participation in patients' parental family symbiosis. Analysts experience the loss of that symbiosis with patients.

One of the most stressful aspects of work with borderline patients is the premature termination of treatment. When this occurs, rather than experiencing healthy grief, analysts may feel only relief. Such patients represent the acid test of whether analysts can feel anything. Analysts can adapt to a rare treatment outcome of this sort, but if a considerable percentage of their patients have borderline disorders, such outcomes will not be rare. The cumulative effect of such experiences progressively undermines analysts' confidence in their ability to feel loving feelings and to be capable of grieving. Keep in mind that I am referring to those relatively frequent instances in which borderline patients break off treatment in a setting of predominantly negative transference, convinced of their analysts' malevolence and showing no sign whatever of any feelings of loss despite many months or years of considerable emotional involvement.

THE SAVAGE MOCKERY OF
BORDERLINE PATIENTS: A DEFENSE
AGAINST FUSION

Many borderline patients defend themselves against their fear of fusion by mocking, derisive, ironic, scornful "typing," or classification, of others in terms of one part aspect of each person. Patients in whom this defense is prominent possess a devasting ability to "write off" persons around them with epigrammatic, satirical characterizations, leaving them as "fixed" as flies in amber or freaks in a wax museum. Such patients have proved so formidable to me that I have been slow to realize that this is a major defense against their underlying tendency to confuse all persons with one another, that is, their inability to differentiate among them.

I find time and again that they will react to some part aspect of me—a facial expression, a gesture, an intonation, an article of clothing, or whatever—as comprising a complete personification of me at the level of my most socially uncomfortable, hopelessly inadequate, schizoid self. Typically, such patients react to part aspects at the fringe of our conscious sense of identity which we struggle to disavow. If they were reaching parts of ourselves far removed from our awareness, then presumably we could readily dismiss these slings and arrows.

This defense of borderline patients is all the more difficult to deal with technically because it is predominantly unconscious; at a conscious level, they are largely unaware of emitting such a steady barrage of roundabout needlings of their analysts, and they are far from feeling that they have the analyst at their mercy. A female patient with whom I have worked for more than two years typically makes dozens of skillfully derisive characterizations of my various oddities, but nearly always displaces them onto various persons in her daily life. My attempts to invite her collaborations in exploring these tantalizing, disparate components of negative transference and finding something coherent and meaningful in them only serve to make her feel rejected and discouraged at my taking everything personally. The treatment proceeds more smoothly when I can hold my tongue and view these many indirect barbs as defenses against her longings to identify fully and fuse with me. At times, I have had the especially helpful insight that when she is superficially most vicious in her mocking characterizations of her husband, at a deeper level of awareness, she is desperately grasping at straws (derisively perceived part aspects) to keep from drowning in undifferentiatedness, that is, her fusion with me.

When analysts attempt to interpret some aspect, inevitably only a part aspect, of borderline patients' functioning, they react as if they were trying to distance themselves and ridicule their patients. More often than not the patients are correct. Analysts indeed do a great deal of premature interpreting as an unconscious defense against their underlying fears of their longings to fuse with patients.

Another woman who manifests many typical "as if" features has been in analysis for several years, but only relatively recently have I found it feasible to make interpretations consistently. Heretofore, she subjected each of my interpretations, or other comments of any sort, to such savage and persistent mockery that she essentially destroyed them. She reduced them to the same undifferentiatedness that she felt with herself. On many occasions earlier in our work, I felt an impulse to make transference interpretations but nearly always restrained myself for one of two reasons: (1) the transference data in her communications were too tantalizingly incoherent or superficial to warrant my interpreting them yet; or (2) I shrank from committing myself to sharing the acid bath, as it were, in which she was keeping herself immersed—shrank from exposing myself to her acidly destructive mockery to such a degree.

In retrospect, I was most useful in serving silently as a holding environment until her transference hatred changed into a predominantly positive feeling tone between us during the sessions. My earlier reported concepts concerning therapeutic symbiosis (1965, 1979) stood me in good stead during those years of my work with her. It is probable that she was correct in sensing that my interpretations deserved her savage destruction, for I now believe that they were more unconscious defenses than acts of constructive interpersonal relatedness toward her; they were mainly obstacles to the development of the therapeutically necessary nonverbal symbiosis between us.

SUMMARY

Borderline patients' personality organization renders the danger of separation and loss ever present. Such patients are continually faced with the threat of loss, either of their tenuously established individual identity, through fusion with the other person, or of their fragile interpersonal relatedness, through uncontrollable flight into autism of psychotic degree.

Analysts typically tend to repress or dissociate and project into these patients the primitive personality components that the latter arouse in them. Much "self"-destructive acting out and venting of aggression by patients is directed at their introject of the "sickest," most primitive components of analysts' ego-functioning.

Borderline patients have deep-seated feelings of primary responsibility for curing the "Bad Mother," primitively hateful components of their analysts. To a significant degree, analysts, like everyone else, possess such components; but, in addition, patients project onto analysts their own powerful but unconscious identifications with comparable components in maternal figures from their childhood.

The inability of these patients to grieve effectively is but one facet of their inability to experience the full range of human emotions and is defended against by fantasied omnipotence and omniscience.

One reliable criterion of the borderline state is the striking loss of memory for large areas of childhood. I discuss some of the determinants of this amnesia. It is best dealt with in the transference context, in terms of the developing history of the course of treatment itself. I briefly discuss some typical countertransference difficulties in this connection.

This amnesia is a defense against grief, separation anxiety, and hostility of a murderous or suicidal degree; it bespeaks a discontinuity in borderline patients' sense of identity and a poor integration of fragments from disparate developmental eras.

The interpersonal basis, present and past, of the etiology of patients' difficulties with grieving are mentioned. I discuss the point that these patients often cannot fully grieve the death of a parent because the parent was never "there" for them psychologically.

In such cases, the parent's own inadequate grieving of the loss of his or her own parent led the parent to establish a "transgenerational" transference with the patient, relating to the latter as the reincarnation of the deceased grandparent. This is another important etiological factor in borderline patients' typical personality functioning, including their difficulties in grieving.

The role of defensive splitting in these patients' pathological grieving is discussed, with particular emphasis upon the interconnections between grief and sadism.

Borderline patients can eventually relinquish their illness only if their analysts have come to know and cherish, to a significant degree, the gratifications of that illness, such that the loss-of-illness experience can be a mutual, shared one. Along the way, the development of the necessary degree of therapeutic symbiosis is resisted by both participants in various typical behaviors that I briefly discuss.

REFERENCES

Deutsch, H. (1942). Some forms of emotional disturbance and their relationship to schizophrenia. *Psychoanal. Q.* 11: 301–321.

Giovacchini, P. (1975). *Psychoanalysis of Character Disorders.* New York: Aronson.

Horowitz, M. J. et al. (1980). Pathological grief and the activation of latent self-images. *Amer. J. Psychiatry* 137: 1157–1162.

Kernberg, O. (1975). *Borderline Conditions and Pathological Narcissism.* New York: Aronson.

Mahler, M. S. (1968). *On Human Symbiosis and the Vicissitudes of Individuation. I: Infantile Psychosis.* New York: International Universities Press.

Masterson, J. (1976). *Psychotherapy of the Borderline Adult: A Developmental Approach.* New York: Brunner/Mazel.

Mitscherlich, A. and Mitscherlich, M. (1975). *The Inability to Mourn.* New York: Grove Press. Originally published in German as *Die Unfahigheit zu Trauern, Grundlager Kollecktiven Verhaltens.* Munich: Piper and Verlag, 1967.

Searles, H. F. (1956). The psychodynamics of vengefulness. *Psychiatry* 19: 31–39. Reprinted in *Collected Papers on Schizophrenia and Related Subjects*, pp. 177–191. London: Hogarth Press and New York: International Universities Press.

––––– (1965). *Collected Papers on Schizophrenia and Related Subjects.* London: Hogarth Press and New York: International Universities Press.

––––– (1972). The function of the patient's realistic perceptions of the analyst in delusional transference. *Brit. J. Med. Psychol.* 45: 1–18. Reprinted in *Countertransference and Related Subjects—Selected Papers*, by H. F. Searles, pp. 196–227. New York: International Universities Press, 1979.

—— (1976). Transitional phenomena and therapeutic symbiosis. *Internat. J. Psychoanal. Psychother.* 5: 145–204. Reprinted in *Counter-transference and Related Subjects—Selected Papers*, by H. F. Searles, pp. 503–576. New York: International Universities Press, 1979.

—— (1979). *Countertransference and Related Subjects—Selected Papers*. New York: International Universities Press.

—— (1980). Psychoanalytic therapy with borderline patients: The development, in the patient, of an internalized image of the therapist. Presented as the Fifth O. Spurgeon English Honor Lecture at Temple University School of Medicine, Philadelphia, April 25.

Volkan, V. D. (1976). *Primitive Internalized Object Relations: A Clinical Study of Schizophrenia, Borderline, and Narcissistic Patients*. New York: International Universities Press.

—— (1981). *Linking Objects and Linking Phenomena*. New York: International Universities Press.

5

DISCUSSION OF HAROLD F. SEARLES'S CHAPTER

John A. Lindon

As we have come to expect from Harold Searles, his chapter is so rich and stimulating that a discussant, especially if he is as great an admirer of Dr. Searles as I am, runs the risk of giving a discussion twice as long as the original chapter. To avoid this, I will focus on some areas in which we differ, suggesting other formulations that I think may be appropriate, and I will elaborate on those areas that I think are particularly valuable with further clinical data.

First, I will briefly discuss two areas where we differ.

Although Dr. Searles feels the borderline patient's personality structure is developmentally traceable to difficulties in the phase of separation and individuation, I believe there can be smaller, intermittent, repeated deficiencies beginning as early as the first few weeks of life; videotaped research studies of mother-infant interactions support this observation.

Another area where we differ is the ego-syntonicity of acting-out behavior. Dr. Searles describes patients who "persistently become involved in self-destructive acting out between sessions," especially during the analyst's prolonged absence; such behavior "seems to be maddeningly ego-syntonic for patients" because they take such sadistic relish in injuring the internalized analyst by mechanisms described by Freud in "Mourning and Melancholia." My observations have led me to a different conclusion, namely, that such seemingly self-destructive acting out is *in fact* ego-syntonic because it is the sensible choice for patients whose only alternative is to feel dead. Experiencing pain, danger, and physical injuries in order to feel alive is preferable to experiencing disintegration and "deadness."

"DEADNESS" IN BORDERLINE PATIENTS

Dr. Searles states that "some borderline patients are able to experience a few emotional bands, as it were, on the spectrum of human emotions." His chapter focuses on the inability of these patients to feel separation and loss. He quotes a patient as saying: "I don't feel sadness; sadness isn't something I feel. . . . I understand devastation and . . . rage and . . . terror; but I don't know the milder forms (she had referred to sadness as being a mild form of devastation). When I feel irritated or annoyed, I don't really feel those feelings; what I feel is rage. I can either feel complete devastation or nothing."

I think this particular clinical example beautifully illuminates why this patient's emotional spectrum is so narrow. She cannot feel those other feelings she mentions because she must protect herself; she experiences her self as being so fragile that it can be destroyed as easily as a house of cards. Therefore it is sensible for her to avoid feeling annoyed, irritated, sad, or almost anything else, and this creates a very narrow spectrum of feelings.

The question then is, Why does she understand devastation and rage and terror? Such patients experience devastation repeatedly. It does not require a high reading on the Richter scale to shatter and completely devastate a patient whose self is as fragile as a house of cards. As this patient said, the alternative to complete devastation is to feel nothing.

It is no wonder then that such patients engage in courses of action that seem "crazy" and "self-destructive" to us; we view their behavior pejoratively because we look at it from *our* vantage point, i.e., that of the "objective onlooker," rather than trying to put ourselves in their shoes.

I found myself at an almost complete impasse with one of my patients because of my unconscious resistance to experiencing the world from his viewpoint. My patient, a businessman whose work required that he go to New York about once a month, would tell me about his lovely, solitary strolls through Central Park late at night. I felt very upset because he was frequently robbed and beaten, as might be expected.

For a long time, I understood this only as self-destructive acting-out behavior. Such an interpretation got us nowhere. It was only when I began to understand that the dangers of his actually being mugged, robbed, beaten up, or even killed (as almost happened three times) were all far lesser evils than the alternative of feeling pervasive "deadness." Subjecting himself to danger was his way of feeling some aliveness.

AMNESIA IN BORDERLINE PATIENTS

Particularly valuable is Dr. Searles's statement that "one reliable criterion for the presence of borderline psychopathology is patients' manifestation—usually in the initial history-taking interview—of a striking loss of memory of childhood events. Typically, there will be stretches of years . . . for which patients will have few, if any, memories." The most striking example of such amnesia that I ever observed occurred in a physician with whom I worked for nine years. Not only during the initial history-taking interview, but at no time during the period in which I saw him intensely, did he ever recover a single memory prior to his entering medical school at the age of twenty-four! Needless to say, I did not consider this a completed analysis. (Although, in retrospect, I believe that I served a container function for him by being there consistently, seeing him six or seven days a week, sometimes two sessions a day.) This man was in danger of committing murder as well as suicide. His wife's analyst and I were both desperately alarmed. We did not know who would murder whom and then commit suicide, but for the first six years or so of his analysis, we were both convinced that it was a very serious risk. I think I served as a self-object that helped the patient achieve sufficient stabilization to get a divorce and remarry, and to function adequately as a physician.

Dr. Searles states that "the parents of these amnesic borderline patients largely tried to forget their past when rearing their children. . . . Typically such parents have so much unintegrated hatred and unworked-through grief, disappointment, hurt, and so on from their own childhoods that they cannot consciously put their past in the past; instead, they unconsciously relive it with their children, whom they treat as transference objects." Dr. Searles describes the "transgenerational" transference in which the parent treats the patient as a transference mother or father.

I had the opportunity to observe this in two generations. Many years ago, I treated a borderline man who had total amnesia for large periods of his childhood. I was able to see how he treated his needy children as if they were his own needy parents. I did not accomplish much with this man. Almost twenty years later, his son, who had even severer borderline psychopathology than the father, came for treatment. It seems to me he verified Searles's belief that "patients' amnesia . . . serves as a defense against murderous feelings. . . . The recall of what actually transpired during these periods revives murderous feelings of formidable intensity." In order to get away from the danger of his rage toward his father, the son joined the army and was supposed to be stationed in Europe. When he was sent to Vietnam instead and went on search-and-destroy missions, he unconsciously sensed that he risked total psychotic disintegration unless he was transferred elsewhere, which he was. The search-and-destroy missions stimulated his murderous feelings of wanting to mow down his family. Parenthetically, he was fearless about himself being wounded or killed.

Especially helpful is Searles's description of his own development after he recognized the meaning of his feeling "unable, for weeks or even months at a time, to locate what is happening between patients and myself either in their developmental history or mine." He came to believe that "what the analyst is experiencing has a counterpart in the experience of one or both parents of the patient." He contrasts this to healthier parents who need not forget their pasts but instead can use memories of their own childhood in a "well-integrated, freely remembered and reminisced about fashion as a guide or context for relating" to their children. Reading Dr. Searles's chapter helped me retrospectively to understand long periods of time when I felt totally lost with patients.

Another point that is particularly valuable is Dr. Searles's reminder of "how essential it is to make *transference* interpretations and to explore patients' amnesia in terms of their difficulties in reconstructing the developing history of the therapy." In essence, Dr. Searles is saying that the transference and the analytic relationship can serve the container function that was absent from patients' childhoods.

Dr. Searles describes a patient who "was chronically vulnerable to feelings of fearful uncertainty about whether he himself existed." I think such symptoms are characteristic of borderline patients, although they may be heavily defended against and may not emerge until much work has been done. With one patient who was intellectually aware of his feelings of nonexistence, I was initially puzzled since his parenting did not seem to have been that deficient. It was only when he casually mentioned going off with his wife and leaving his infant son alone in the house that I learned that his parents had done this to him habitually when he was an infant. Independent sources confirmed that his youthful parents would leave him alone for several hours at a time from the age of two or three months on while they went off to the movies.

As we approached this material, the patient recovered memories of standing up in his crib, screaming out in terror for someone to respond, and getting no response. While discussing these memories, he experienced overwhelming terror that he had no substance, that he literally would evaporate on the couch and disappear into the air conditioning vent, never to be seen or heard of again. Frequently, while going through such periods of terror, he would seriously contemplate suicide with the idea that if he killed himself, it would prove that he had existed. An obituary is proof of existence.

In this regard, we must admire George Orwell's insightfulness. In his novel *1984*, the greatest weapon against the citizens of the all-powerful totalitarian state was not the threat of death, but the threat of obliteration—that is, all records of the person ever having existed would be obliterated and every published reference to that person would be deleted; even the newspapers listing that person's birth would be reprinted, artificially aged, and put back into the archives.

Along these same lines, another patient who had been almost housebound and paralyzed by indefinable terrors recognized a change in himself when one day he deliberately looked over the edge of a tall building and reported, "I didn't feel any terror. I thought, 'so what if I would fall, the worst that would be is I would be lying there on the pavement dead.'" We understood that his terror was not connected with death, but with obliteration and nonexistence.

Among Dr. Searles's talents is his ability to condense profound and complex insights, as evidenced by his statement about amnesia: "he who has not yet become mature enough to forgive must forget, as a poor substitute for forgiving." I especially like what he wrote about supervision and how deeply integrative it can be for both participants. He emphasizes the *mutual* therapeutic (or antitherapeutic) value of any human interaction that is at all intense and prolonged. This is especially relevant to our work with borderline patients, where part of the attraction of working with them is the continual working through of the unresolved bits of borderline psychopathology in our own personalities.

THE ANALYST'S WORKING-THROUGH PROCESS

Another valuable theme is the analyst's working-through process. In exquisite detail, Dr. Searles describes the working through required of the analyst as the patient improves and the analyst loses much of the unconscious gratification derived from relating to the patient at a primitive symbiotic level. Clearly, if such working through does not occur, the analyst's unconscious needs retard the patient's growth.

This also occurs with inpatients. I vividly recall working on a female ward as a young psychiatrist more than thirty years ago. I decided to try to work with the most violent, grossly psychotic young patient there. She was my size and was much stronger than I was. She would tear doors off their hinges, and it took five massive, male attendants to subdue her. Dr. X., the staff psychiatrist in charge of the female building, said that she was impossible to work with, hopelessly insane, and had smashed almost three hundred windows, slashing her wrists and arms on the sharp edges in suicide attempts. Incidentally, Dr. X. kept an accurate count of the suicide attempts.

I thought it a unique opportunity to work with a patient such as I would very likely never see again in my professional life, and, carefully rearranging the room so I could make a quick getaway if she became violent, I cautiously started psychoanalytic psychotherapy with her. To my amazement, within a month or so I felt comfortable working with her, and eight months later this former wild woman who had spent over half of the past three years in restraints was leaving the hospital on weekend passes and beginning to explore using her GI Bill to go to college and acquire a profession.

Dr. X. waited until I left town for a ten-day vacation. While I was gone, she managed to get through the bureaucracy at lightning speed, bring this patient before the necessary boards, and have a lobotomy performed on her. Subsequently, it was learned that various psychometric tests used in part to justify the lobotomy had been misinterpreted, that in fact the tests had revealed a marked change. She no longer showed a psychotic pattern, but rather, a hysterical neurotic one.

Another gem from Dr. Searles is his description of analysts' healthy grief over the loss of these patients as they improve. He emphasizes how analysts try to repress separation anxiety and loss, as well as their own dependent needs upon the patient. I can personally testify to the validity of this, having learned it the hard way. Some years ago, because of external circumstances—but also in part because I was denying how much patients meant to me—I terminated two long-term patients in the same month. I expected to miss them, but was startled at the intensity of my mourning reaction; the painful working through required several months.

I believe Dr. Searles is doing us all a service by emphasizing this point. I think we all tend to deny the depth of feeling and the amount of intense, intimate give and take in our work with analytic patients. It reminds me of a joke about the 5-year-old son of a psychoanalyst and the boy's school teacher.

Teacher: "What do you want to be when you grow up?"
The boy: "A patient."

We tend to deny that we have more intense, intimate relationships with patients than with family members or close friends. Of course, they are different, but nevertheless do any therapists put in the same daily effort of listening, trying to understand, and trying to put aside their own needs with a family member, no matter how much they love that person, as they routinely do with patients—especially borderline patients?

Finally, Dr. Searles reports his impression that there is a great deal of premature interpreting and points out that "some aspect, inevitably only a part aspect, of patients' functioning" is interpreted. He discusses patients' adverse reactions to this. My impression is that when we interpret only part of patients' functioning we are not recognizing them as whole people. For example, a patient was seriously contemplating whether he would be better off if he were dead, which he came very close to being because of wild drug abuse, and he specifically asked; "Why, what difference would it make, what would you miss if I killed myself?" The patient, who was a gifted surgeon by profession and a gifted artist by avocation, experienced his professional and artistic skills as parts of himself that hostilely clashed within him. I believe that my ability to recognize this and say "I would miss the person who never got to live" led to a marked reduction of his dangerous drug use.

6

DIRECT PRESENTATION OF REALITY IN AREAS OF DELUSION

Margaret I. Little

Editor's Notes

The contributors to this volume constitute a large spectrum ranging from young people with innovative ideas to pioneers who have determined the direction of clinical psychoanalysis. Dr. Little is a pioneer who has worked with severely disturbed patients for many years and has generously shared her experiences and technical maneuvers with her colleagues throughout the world. She was one of the first to dare to reveal her countertransference feelings when the existence of countertransference was still considered a sign of a serious flaw in the analyst's character. She emphasized how countertransference responses are a necessary part of psychoanalytic treatment, especially with primitively fixated patients.

Dr. Little has shown us how to tune in to patients to promote understanding and achieve higher levels of psychic integration. She is a member of the group of British analysts led by Donald Winnicott who work with patients fixated at very primitive levels, including many who are frankly psychotic.

In this chapter, Dr. Little focuses on technical issues. She refers to an undifferentiated psychic state where the differentiation between the psyche and

soma is just beginning. Patients may present this
state during therapeutic regression or it may be their
predominant ego state both in treatment and in the
external world. I have referred to this type of organization as an amorphous psychic state that represents
the very beginning of mentation. Clearly, Dr. Little is
describing a presymbiotic state. She first wrote of this
early level over twenty years ago.

She believes that analysts have to relate to these
patients differently than they would to patients with
greater psychic differentiation. Analysts have to help
these patients experience reality, often in a somatic
fashion. The latter is a body experience that is equivalent to an interpretation. The author illustrates her
points with specific clinical examples.

Basically, these patients reproduce a basic infantile
constellation in the transference regression. Dr. Little
feels merged with patients in a state of "basic unity,"
but her fundamental attitudes and feelings toward
them are different from those of the patients' archaic
objects. This is not an intentional corrective experience but nevertheless it is corrective because the
analyst introduces *analytic* reality, that is, reality based
on unambivalent and objective understanding. This
analytic reality is the spontaneous outcome of the
analytic relationship and follows the tendency toward
merger and separation that is characteristic of the undifferentiated state Dr. Little's patients present.

In several examples, the author describes how she
literally touched patients to join their reality. In one
session, a patient hallucinated his mother holding his
arm back when he wanted to throw a crumpled ball
of paper at a jug across the room. This apparently
was a repetition of innumerable childhood traumas
when the mother held his arm so that he could not
put objects in his mouth, including food and the
nipple. Dr. Little touched his arm and the patient was
able to distinguish the slight pressure she applied
from the hallucinated sensation of his mother's restraining force. The somatic reality the therapist supplied caused the delusion to disappear and the patient

then could express his rage successfully, in "play," by hitting the jug with the crumpled paper.

As a general technique, touching patients has to be seriously questioned. Dr. Little does it gently, without the impact of a sudden confrontation with a strange and alien reality. She is trying to blend her better-organized reality with the patient's primitive orientation. In the above instance, she touched the patient because he seemed to be operating almost exclusively at the somatic level. We can ask ourselves whether we have to introduce a touching parameter to be able to treat such fragile patients. It seems to work well for the author and it worked for her mentor, Dr. Winnicott, but can we generalize from their experiences? These are difficult questions and at this stage in our development there are no final answers.

Still, in treating such patients we are often impelled to relate to our patients in ways that go beyond traditional boundaries. I know that at first I felt guilty for what I believed to be breaches of the psychoanalytic relationship. I still feel uneasy about exchanges with my patients that do not seem to be based exclusively upon transference interpretations. However, many of these interactions are based upon transference elements, as patients bring the infantile environment into the consultation room and the analyst responds to and perhaps participates in some aspect of the repetition compulsion. This sometimes occurs spontaneously and is experienced as countertransference, a subject that Dr. Little has thoroughly explored.

These patients teach us about the origin of the psyche. According to Dr. Little and other clinicians, the child develops an awareness of the self and the immediate surrounding world through movement.[1] If the child's movements are responded to correctly, the psyche progresses by developing further integrative

---

[1] In Chapter 12, Dr. Fields also emphasizes the importance of somatic change in the achievement of perceptual awareness.

capacities. Dr. Little believes that memory traces of bodily experiences are the first to be established and are progressively linked to later experiences. To my mind, this linkage represents the passage from a prementational to a mentational state.

In psychoanalytic treatment, the analyst has the opportunity to study patients who have, in part, failed to become aware of the world in sophisticated psychological terms. Instead, they are concrete and somatically oriented. Often these patients express their distress primarily in somatic terms. I recall patients who squirmed, screamed, and sobbed in an animal-like fashion. At times, they writhed, and violently and spasmodically wrenched their bodies as if they were having convulsions. It is impossible to understand this bizarre explosiveness from a mentational perspective; such behavior cannot be understood in terms of organized feelings and affects and cannot be associated with traumas. At best, we learn that these are diffuse states of terror that are responses to patients' first glimpse of a dimly recognizable, dangerous world. The task of analysis is to integrate these primitive eruptions with percepts and experiences. By structuring these episodes in a psychological context, the treatment is giving meaning to reactions that initially antedated meaning.

Dr. Little amplifies normal and psychopathologically distorted emotional development beginning with these very early phases. Her concept of "basic unity," or an undifferentiated ego state, that can lead to healthy integration, empathy, and a sense of belonging, on the one hand, or to a terrifying delusion of sameness which degenerates into the terror of nonexistence, on the other, is indispensable for our understanding of primitive mental states.

Dr. Little has been working with primitively fixated patients for many years. With the passage of time, her work has become increasingly relevant.

P. L. G.

UNDIFFERENTIATEDNESS IN SEVERE
BORDERLINE STATES

In other papers I have described patients in whom areas of primary total undifferentiatedness ("basic unity") have persisted into adult life as a delusion—borderline psychotics; and how in analytic work with them they are unable, in those areas, to use the sophisticated processes of deductive thinking, drawing correct inference, symbolization, or metaphor.

This comes from the undifferentiatedness itself, as here, the symbol and the thing symbolized are absolutely one, as are the deduction, its source, and its consequences.

For this same reason, these patients are not able to test reality in many areas; they have first to *find* it. They are engaged upon processes of differentiation and integration, and not upon such things as projection and introjection, identification and repression, all of which presuppose a separateness of subject and object. This is where the psychotic annihilation anxiety lies, as separateness and merging are *both* apprehended as identical, inevitable, and annihilating. The simultaneous conflicting aims are to maintain and to destroy both identity with and total separateness from the therapist, identity and separateness between subject and object, thought, and feeling. It is a complicated and all-pervasive state indeed where such undifferentiatedness obtains.

Reality, then, has to be presented to these people without the need for deduction, inference, or symbol, that is, via the actual and concrete; the mode of presentation will be specific both to the individual patient and to the immediate context. Once the reality has reached patients' awareness, their nonpsychotic part, which has had to be suspended temporarily, can come into play, and whatever capacity for deduction they have can then be used. But this has to be secondary to the finding of the reality.

Most of the realities that need to be presented belong to a very early level—the level where differentiation between psyche and soma is beginning and long before verbalization is possible. Linking with words becomes possible only later, but is then essential.

This is the level of the undifferentiated state, where body experience is of first importance; on this level, experience that can have meaning for the patient has, in fact, exactly the same kind of effect as a correct and well-timed interpretation has in the analysis of a psychoneurotic, as I hope to show through clinical material.

Case Examples

In analysis, body movement is limited to some extent by the use of the couch, and in psychoneurotics the tendency to verbalize is increased. But borderline psychotics cannot always verbalize and often have to move first. When any patient lies down, regression occurs automatically to whatever level contains the predominant anxiety at that time; in borderline patients, it is most often to their psychotic level. The movements, although made with a fully grown body, are essentially those of an infant: an infant whose movements have been so inhibited or made so meaningless that they have remained ineffective. When an effective movement is found, it can be linked with speech. Sometimes if a particular body experience is not found, the analysis jams up completely, and further progress cannot happen.

Charles had great difficulty in keeping his analysis going at all. He missed every Monday's session, and in many weeks at least one other. When he did come, he was often unable to say anything. After months of this, the analysis was really threatened with breakdown.

One day he found that he wanted to throw something at a certain jug on my mantelshelf. Any attempt to understand why, or to imagine doing so, was useless—he did not know why, or what was stopping him talking about it, but *something* was. At last I gave him a ball of crumpled newspaper, which he threw over and over again, missing wildly every time. He became quite desperate; something was stopping him from aiming properly. He went to throw again, and when his arm was raised he suddenly said angrily, "Don't *do* that." I asked, "What happened?" "You pulled my arm," he said. He threw the ball again and hit the jug squarely.

Then he remembered his mother doing this—he had felt her pull; now he had hallucinated it. This linked with experiences of being stopped from putting things into his mouth, and of keeping it firmly shut to prevent something being pushed in or taken out, and from there to interruptions of breast feeding and memories of being forced to take medicine.

His mother seems to have organized confusion, artificially bringing conflict from outside; two texts hung on the wall: one read, "Don't worry, it will never happen," and the other, "Cheer up, the best is yet to come."

She confused him about his identity, My *nice* little boy wouldn't do that. This can't be Charles," and "*You* don't want that, do you?" He had never been able to establish the identity of his own body, and many body memories had never been assimilated.

I put my hand where he had felt the pull, and he found that he could distinguish between the real contact and the hallucination, and between me and his mother. She might quite well have touched him and denied it, or suddenly distracted his attention and confused him about what had happened. He saw her doing this kind of thing now with her grandchildren. In fact, he had been seeing it for some time with them, but only now could he deduce that she must have done it with him.

The same kind of release can come when a reality of another kind is found.

Henry had been for a holiday with his brother a few years older, a special one that he had looked forward to for a long time, to a place where he knew I had not been. He had imagined going there with me in my car. It had involved missing a few sessions.

I had shown him beforehand that there was a risk of his having an accident, because of his anger with me for not taking him on my holidays, and his expectation of retaliation. He had had car accidents before, in this kind of context. We had then been working over memories of earlier outings with his brother, from which he had come home sopping wet, cut, and bruised. I spoke too of the unconscious hate between the brothers.

When he came back he was very offhand and noncommittal about the holiday. It had been "all right," he said rather grudgingly, and then he lapsed into one of his long silences, looking deeply unhappy.

I waited and then said, "You know, I'm very glad you enjoyed the holiday so much." He opened his eyes, stared at me, and said, "Good lord! That had exactly the same effect as an interpretation." His mother had grumbled at the wetness and the cuts; she had tried to stop him from going with his brother ("You don't want to, you won't enjoy it"), and he had had to hide his excitement and enjoyment. This had been one of the factors causing the accidents, but talking about it beforehand and relating it to the transference had only been an intellectualization, whereas my telling him directly what I felt at that moment had had real meaning for him.

After this, he remembered being taken out by his older sister (who until then had come into the analysis as no more than a name), and being upset out of his pram. This was recalled with acute fear, giddiness, and headache. I related it to the sensations experienced during and just after birth—the original massive "upset"—and also to later excretory "accidents," exciting, and enjoyable, but punished severely by spanking.

What I want to convey is the way in which a piece of reality presented so, inescapably and unmistakably, not only breaks up delusion but helps to bring about differentiation which has hitherto been prevented. As the experience becomes usable, misapprehensions and wrong deductions can be sorted out by using words.

In his commentary on Jensen's *Gradiva* ("Delusions and Dreams"), Freud (1906) points out that to attempt to convince someone of the falsity of his delusional ideas is useless; it only arouses hostility. It is necessary to accept their truth *for him,* to enter into the delusion, and then break it up from inside by a direct presentation of what is real.

The analyst's entry into the delusion (without, of course, being deluded too, or accepting the truth of the delusion as actual) is an important element in finding the form of presentation best suited to the particular patient at any given moment.

For a fortnight Alice had been in an unshifting resistance, had held an unbroken silence, and had been unmoving. Today she lay twisting and writhing on the couch. Suddenly she said, "I feel trapped; I can't move, I'm caught by the leg." She went on wriggling and turning, in a frenzy, but holding one leg out stiffly toward me. I waited and then put my hand lightly on her ankle. She gave one flip with her foot, which I allowed to push my hand away. I said, "I was the trap."

She then began to talk freely; she told me how in childhood she had seen a rabbit with its leg caught in a trap and how her dog pounced on it and killed it—how very dead it had looked, motionless and silent. From there she went to primal scene material and memories of finding bloodstained clothes after her sister's birth when she was two years old. An older boy cousin caught and tormented her, and there had been some sex play with him which had been both exciting and frightening.

When I put my hand on her ankle I took over being the trap (on the delusional level) so that she no longer had to be both trap and rabbit. That liberated the energy of the part of her that was being the trap (the mouth) and so let the "rabbit" part be strong enough to break free and move and speak.

In the nonpsychotic part of her, Alice was fully aware that her leg was *not* caught in a trap, that my hand did not really restrict her movement at all, and that I knew this, too. But in her psychotic area, there was absolute belief that I *was* a trap that was holding her, that I was the cousin who had held her forcibly, the mother who had often restrained her, and also the drive of the birth forces. But since I could move, and she and I were one, then she could move too, and *in moving* she became aware of being separate from me. There was a delusion of being caught in a trap that meant destruction and annihilation, and to move meant to be annihilated. There was delusion of being identical with me. Only when I accepted the reality for her of the delusional ideas and their *psychic* reality for us both, could she recognize their *factual* unreality.

To have said anything like, "You feel yourself caught and you think I am the trap, as you thought you were the rabbit" would have been quite useless to the psychotic part of her, which was not joined up with the nonpsychotic part. Only showing her on the level of body sensation that she could move safely could break up the delusion and bring about the necessary fusion of psyche and soma, and of her psychotic and nonpsychotic parts.

An alternating rhythm develops of merging psychically with patients, imaginatively becoming one with them, and then separating out again, which enables them in turn to find oneness with me and to separate themselves out again from there.

I know that this sounds like projective and introjective identification, but the word *identification* already implies separateness between subject and object. I am trying to make clear a rhythmic process of differentiation out of a homogenous mass, followed by a reattachment or assimilation back to it, a process which is repeated many times and can later be varied. It is the forerunner of projective and introjective identification.

The importance of such movements lies in the fact that memory is primarily body memory and that movement plays a great part in bringing about differentiation and discovery of realities about both self and the environment. Movements that are met in the right way can be psychically elaborated; they are assimilated and join up with other experiences, becoming something to be repeated, something creative, and a starting place for new movements and new experiences. Most important of all, perhaps, they become assertions of the self and a starting point for developing relationships.

If an infant puts out a hand and meets the mother's hand, or breast or face, he ultimately discovers, through many repetitions of the experience, something about the existence, nature, and activity of a part of his environment and his relation to it. He comes to know that he has a hand, that it moves, and something happens. If he only meets hard cot bars, a slap, or the smothering of the mother's body in a restraining "absorption" (as described by Bonnard 1958), the experience will mean something quite different, and unavoidable repetitions of it will not help him in his differentiation/integration processes, nor in his sorting out of reality from delusion, or inner from outer reality. What should be there only as fantasy becomes reality for him and cannot then be subjected to the ordinary processes of projection and introjection. Ego organization may be seriously impaired in this way.

Martin had infantile eczema, which persisted throughout his childhood, and his hands were always bandaged. His mother avoided all body contact as far as she could and brought him up according to the Truby King method. She told him that it hurt *her* when he cried, and he had not understood that he cried when something hurt *him*.

He would lie on the couch with his head almost in my lap and hold my hand, which he would explore with his own, and smell, saying "soap," "onions," etcetera, according to what he found. In a frenzy, he would move his hand so as to get his wrist held by me, and then make punching and lunging movements. I let go, being pushed away. His fear of hitting me was so great that he hit the wall on his other side. I pointed out that he was hurting himself—that he didn't seem to know the difference between me and the wall—if he thumped the couch he would hurt neither of us, but would be hitting something of me—my couch—which could be an imaginative extension of my body, as the wall was. I took his hand and brought it first to touch my face, and then to touch the couch, which he thumped and thumped, till he was satisfied.

Next time he was angry, he pushed my hand away with a minimal movement that I had shown him to be effective (he needed to be shown this in order to discover that he could be effective). He made an unrehearsed movement suddenly and hit my face about as hard as a baby might, and I showed him the importance of this for differentiation and reality appreciation. He found great relief from this and joined it up with his difficulty in passing a driving test, an accident he had had in which a man died (where the police had had to determine whether he had been responsible or not), and my having spoken of a car as a lethal weapon. He hardly even knew that he had hands, let alone what they were doing or might do. Then he could find, too, that although I minded things hurting him, that didn't mean that his crying hurt me.

Lack of experiences which most people take for granted, and indeed hardly believe could be missing from any childhood (such as the free kicking of a naked baby or crying oneself to sleep), and the presence of other experiences (such as being left tightly rolled in a shawl with the feeding bottle propped up on a pillow, all limb movement being prevented) reinforce the lack of basic unity or its premature interruption, and so prevent differentiation and the assimilation of experience.

Finding these new experiences and reliving the memories of the old ones in the new setting of the analysis restores the unity, though the immediate effect of disturbing the delusion is that of shock. Relief, restoration, and change come later.

Hilda arrived early for her session in an obviously excited state. She lay down while I was still drinking my midmorning coffee.

"Will you give me some of your coffee?" she asked; I drank some more and then handed her the mug. She held it between her hands for a few moments, then gazed at me in amazement, drank the coffee quickly, and handed back the mug. "What did you think I would do with it?" she said, and I replied that I had not known, but had half expected that she might throw it in my face. She said she had thought she would pour it over her own head, "But when I felt the lovely shape of the mug in my hands, and the warmth, and smelled the coffee, I found I just wanted to drink it." The excitement was discharged, and we went on to something else.

Hilda's infancy and childhood had been so traumatic that in order to survive she had had to hide her feelings both from other people and from herself. She had also had to imagine pleasurable happenings, but disaster followed whenever she tried to bring them about. Different standards prevailed in her childhood home between grown-ups and children. She had thought of my coffee as belonging to the world of the grown-ups and expected to get a rebuff, or something from the "nursery" world, from me. She would show her revolt as she always had done, by pouring the coffee on her head. But she found my spontaneous response different, and this changed her feelings altogether, and her behavior. She could then join sensation and emotion together and link both with words, through my movement and her own, without disaster.

EXPRESSION OF THE ANALYST'S FEELINGS

Occasionally the full force of feeling turns up in direct impact, and to restrain its expression then could only put the brakes on the whole movement of the analysis. These moments are important for both partners, and they are often remembered as outstanding. The whole course of one patient's analysis was altered when I showed her my feeling about her intense grief for the loss of her mother. It was the point at which I entered into her delusion, though I did not recognize this at the time. And I once shouted at this patient, in a fury. She had often *heard* what I said as shouting, but this time she heard the difference, and it mattered. A turning point for another patient came when I moved my chair from behind the head of the couch so as to sit facing him, where he could see me. He had expected to be looking at me all the time (and that I would be looking at him), but found that after the first few minutes, he only looked occasionally, when he needed to for some specific reason.

Apart from direct expression of the analyst's feelings, talking about them in a simple, straightforward way, what they are now, or what they were at a particular time often helps someone who, because words or actions are seen only in the light of a set of delusional ideas, cannot deduce what another person is thinking or feeling. The truth can only be found if it is presented "straight."

In speaking of letting my feelings show, or expressing them, I do not mean only positive feelings such as love, friendliness, or appreciation. I mean the whole range of feelings that turns up, from laughter to tears and from love to hate. What matters is that they are *real*. Nor do I mean that any and every feeling is disclosed as and when it is there, only that it has its place, and that in that place it is right and valuable. Far more often its use and expression are indirect, even when the feeling itself is fully conscious. This does not mean that an analyst's feeling is stronger or better than another person's, only that it is important that whatever is there should be freely available for use, whether in direct or indirect expression.

This calls for a straightforwardness in the analyst that matches what we ask of our patients, and that is surely desirable in all our dealings, though in our ordinary lives and with less ill patients, reticences and reserves are no obstacle and can be taken for granted. If, as sometimes happens, we cannot avoid being less than truthful—to safeguard someone else, or even for self-protection—

it is essential to recognize both the fact and the reason for it; otherwise we make difficulties for ourselves as well as for others.

It is surprising how little detail a patient will want. "How do you know these things about being ill?" I have been asked, and I have answered, "By having been ill myself and gotten well." Only the question, "Were you as ill as I am?" and the answer, "Yes" or "No," were needed beyond this.

Talking to patients about their illness and prognosis, the meaning of "breakdown," and the issue of suicide calls for the same directness. They need to be told the truth as far as the analyst knows it, even though somewhere they already know it themselves.

If a patient were to kill himself, what would the analyst feel? His right to do so must be admitted, but only a clear statement that the analyst *would* care, would feel grief and loss, can convey the fact that the analyst takes the question seriously and feels the responsibility, but would neither die nor kill himself if it were to happen. And the ultimate responsibility must be shown to rest with the patient. If a patient *really* does want to kill himself, the analyst cannot prevent it and it will be final. (To a small child, dying means merely going away and coming back when wanted, so the finality of suicide must be stated.) All this is true and fitting, and it allows of both oneness and separateness between the two.

But it is also an assertion of the analyst as a real person, allowing patients their reality, too. Nothing can be lost through such an assertion, even if it is exploited by patients many times and in many ways. In my experience, it brings so much clear gain, in recognition of truth that stands.

In the end, of course, patients have to find that my feelings, words, or movements are of no use to them as a substitute for their own, and it is this that finally breaks up the delusion of our being identical. Patients discover that while we may feel the same way about some things, we feel quite differently about others, and that although we share many happenings, our experiencing of them is not the same. But these can only come about through my first accepting fully the truth *for* the patients of their delusion of identity with me and then showing its objective untruth, but also its truth, *in inner psychic reality for us both.*

This principle of oneness of patient and analyst cannot be shown unless it is honestly accepted, though it is there to some extent in every analysis. The two are *in fact* part of one another's lives over a long stretch of time and are deeply engaged in the analysis in which they have both common and mutual interest. Patients may experience this as something so close that it obliterates any boundary between them and the analyst—a parallel to the body closeness of the patients' faces and the cushion when, lying on the couch, they cannot perceive where their faces end and the cushion begins.

REALITY AND DELUSION

In the analysis of areas of delusion, then, reality is presented in a very direct way, on the same level as that of the delusion—a primitive, preverbal, preambivalent, preobject-relation, body-experiencing level. The disturbance of the delusion is experienced as a painful shock because one of the patients' "catastrophe" points has been reached, but the outcome is relief when the cathexis shifts from the delusion to the reality. The delusion loses its here-and-now immediacy and may remain as a memory or may be forgotten. The altered modes of perception result in altered ways of thinking and behavior. Energy that has hitherto been used in unending struggles against destructiveness and despair comes free for creative purposes; the ego begins to function in a more coordinated way; it becomes accessible to verbal interpretation, so that ordinary analytic technique is appropriate and can be used.

Delusion can still turn up in times of stress, for it is not done away with in any area that remains psychotic—there it remains unchanged. The difference is that it has become possible for patients themselves to recognize that a state of frenzy, disproportionate feeling, or inappropriate behavior must relate to delusion if ordinary reflection cannot change it; they can then seek it out and understand it as their analysts have done before. They become able to find the movement that will bring them out of their frenzy, or the relevant memory, and to trust to the basic unity within themselves.

I have said elsewhere that these delusional ideas not only come from the factual reality of the oneness of mother and fetus before birth, but also that they have a positive value. It seems to me that the idea of fundamental oneness, or "basic unity," is in fact the basis of not only stability in the individual and society but also such things as family life, home, and any sense of belonging. All transference phenomena, symbolization, and empathy are rooted in it. The implications are enormous and, once the idea is grasped, it can throw light on may things hitherto not understood.

SUMMARY

Such episodes as those I have described usually come after long and careful work. Trust in the analyst has had to be built up through experience of his or her reliability and general predictability. A good deal of repetition is often needed in the working through.

What I am chiefly talking about is dealing with patients' "catastrophe areas" (Galatzer-Levy 1978) or "catastrophe points," where sudden changes come about when the analyst's constant pressure ceases to have a consistent effect and *reverses* the patients' reaction. Aggressive impulses can change to flight, expressions of hate to expressions of love, and vice versa.

In my view, this experience is not "corrective." The original damage cannot be undone, but providing other experiences to put alongside the earlier ones enables patients to bring their more mature, nondelusional self into action.

But patients are individuals in a setting, and consistent pressure in the outside world, where they are faced with a reality hitherto unacknowledged, can bring about sudden change in exactly the same way. This can be dangerous, precipitating a psychotic episode, which the analyst should be ready to meet if it comes.

The variables are almost infinite, and so are the potentialities for change; but both must be *real,* not matters of fantasy, and a very large degree of stability in the analytic situation is essential, as the "uncertainty principle" is also involved. One can neither measure nor accurately predict the changes, for even in observing them one alters both the changes themselves and the events that follow by one's own unconscious reactions.

This brings in the matter of analysts' integrity. Their responsibility for both good and bad changes resulting from their work is that of researchers to their material. It means that analysts working in catastrophe areas or areas of delusion must be willing to know and use similar areas in themselves; otherwise their countertransference will create further difficulties for both patients and themselves.

I will end with two quotations from Rudyard Kipling's *Captains Courageous* (1908).

"When Disko [the skipper of a Cape Cod trawler] thought of cod he thought as a cod."

When I am analyzing a borderline psychotic patient, I have to think not only *like* a borderline psychotic but *as* a borderline psychotic, i.e., using my own psychotic areas.

"Dan did things automatically . . . as he made his dory a part of his own will and body, but he could not communicate his knowledge to Harvey."

One's technique becomes a part of oneself, but it is difficult to communicate it to others. Every analyst has to find things for himself and develop his own individual ways of working.

REFERENCES

Bonnard, A. (1958). Pre-body ego types of (pathological) mental functioning. *J. Amer. Psychoanal. Assn.* 6:581–611.

Freud, S. (1906). Delusions and dreams in Jensen's *Gradiva. Standard Edition*, 9:3–97.

Galatzer-Levy, R. M. (1978). Qualitative change from quantitative change: mathematical catastrophe theory in relation to psychoanalysis. *J. Amer. Psychoanal. Assn.* 26:921–935.

Kipling, R. (1908). *Captains Courageous.* London: Macmillan.

7

OBJECT RELATIONS THEORY AND PSYCHOTHERAPY WITH PARTICULAR REFERENCE TO THE SELF-DISORDERED PATIENT

Donald B. Rinsley

Editor's Notes

Dr. Rinsley has a flair for bringing together large, seemingly disparate clinical and theoretical areas into a cohesive whole that highlights their interrelationships and historical continuity. The introductory part of this chapter, although comparatively brief, provides us with a condensed history of object-relations theory that should be helpful to all of us who feel a need for some stabilizing anchor around which we can organize our ideas and experiences.

Concerning borderline patients, Dr. Rinsley shares the belief of Masterson, Searles, and other clinicians that disturbances of the separation-individuation phase, as postulated by Mahler, are especially important for the production of characterological psychopathology. He stresses the etiological significance of this developmental phase for borderline patients. Undoubtedly these patients have tremendous problems in defining their boundaries.

When dealing with psychopathology, the task of determining etiological sequences is especially difficult. Freud constantly struggled with the problem of the choice of neurosis and the problem becomes even more complicated when dealing with structural defects. A maternal relationship that, in some ways, will be traumatic to the course of emotional development will exert its deleterious effects *from the very beginning*. Borderline patients' mothers have very little intuitive awareness of their children's needs and, to a large extent, are unable to acknowledge them as persons in their own right. These mothers find it inordinately difficult to nurture or soothe their children adequately, creating a traumatic situation that will determine the course of emotional development and psychic growth.

The effects of early deprivation will be felt at all developmental levels and will lead to defective resolutions and maldevelopment. Structural psychopathology rooted in such deprivation represents the essence of character disorders. Dr. Rinsley writes specifically about the borderline personality, but much of what he discusses could apply to all patients suffering from ego defects. He uses the term "borderline" in a descriptive sense to refer to patients hovering on the edge of psychosis, patients who can move in and out of psychoses. Although there has been considerable controversy about nosologic classification, neither Dr. Rinsley nor any of the contributors to this volume dwell on diagnostic distinctions in developing their ideas about specific treatment issues.

I want to elaborate on this point for a moment. I acknowledge the usefulness of diagnostic distinctions for statistical and research purposes, but for the psychoanalyst engaged in regressed transference-countertransference interactions, diagnosis may be of limited value. In my view, far too much time is spent debating what constitutes the borderline condition. Theoretically, it would be interesting to describe a continuum of structural disturbances alongside a developmental timetable. Some clinicians, including myself, have outlined such schemas, which have been useful as conceptual organizers. Still, as Dr. Rinsley well recognizes, our conceptual understanding has to be combined with subjective responses as the transference relationship unfolds.

Dr. Rinsley has noted that many so-called borderline patients frequently, if not characteristically, employ splitting defenses as they deal with internal objects. The types of internal objects are determined by the significant persons in the infantile environment. Severely disturbed patients have had complex and unique archaic object relationships.

I would add that these early ties are significant factors in determining emotional maldevelopment long before they can be conceived of as object relations. Caretaking and soothing activities are incorporated into the psyche and help create structural configurations that permit the ego to internalize further aspects of the external world. Conversely, when nurturing and soothing are perceived as traumatic, various ego systems will be deleteriously affected so that later, when object relationships should be established, there will be problems in perceiving whole objects and in achieving object constancy. Dr. Rinsley discusses how some patients cannot maintain an internal image of an external object without the actual presence of that object. He recognizes the large role this defect plays in the formation of serious psychopathology.

An ego that cannot hold mental representations will demonstrate other defects as well. It may be only precariously and tenuously organized. It also may be extremely rigid, with very little capacity to extend its perceptual range beyond a viselike attachment to the external world. Dr. Rinsley describes some patients who are so concretely minded that they have little, if any, ability to get in touch with their feelings and fantasies. In fact, they do not seem to have the capacity to fantasy; in analysis, they cannot conceptualize what free association means. This poses difficult, but not necessarily insurmountable, problems in therapy.

We are faced with other problems when these patients cannot maintain their defensive rigidity. Their controls become deficient and they tend to act out rather than free associate. In such cases, Dr. Rinsley finds it necessary to institute controls so that treatment can proceed. In a sense, he is attempting to supply a regulatory structure that the patient never had or lost during regression.

Clearly, an important aspect of the therapeutic process is the formation of new psychic structures. Whether this is to be achieved through customary analytic techniques (i.e., transference-countertransference insights), or through some modification of the external world that compensates for patients' deficiencies is a question that requires considerable exploration.

P. L. G.

The so-called British school of psychoanalytic object-relations theory may be said to have emerged from the writings of two theorist-clinicians, Melanie Klein and W. Ronald D. Fairbairn. However, its foundation lies firmly embedded in classical psychoanalytic metapsychology, particularly Freud's differentiation of instinctual aim and instinctual object (1905, 1915). Based on his seminal "Project" (1895), Freud originally conceptualized instinct theory in terms of what latter-day psychologists would term "drive reduction"; instinctual aim was accordingly viewed as minimizing the "quantity" of nervous excitation (Freud's somewhat enigmatic "Q"), of "working toward a yield of pleasure" and minimizing unpleasure in accordance with the demands of the pleasure principle (Freud 1911). But pristine psychoanalytic drive-reduction theory could not account for such divers phenomena as the perseverative nature of children's play, the so-called traumatic neuroses of war, the characteristics of those individuals "wrecked by success" (Freud 1916), the phenomenon of masochism and, of course, the basis and nature of therapeutic transference; these phenomena led Freud (1920) "beyond the pleasure principle," as he postulated the operation of an even more fundamental characteristic of the psychic apparatus—the repetition compulsion.

In formulating the concept of the *object* as the instrumentality by and through which the *aim* of an instinct (drive) is achieved, Freud became, in effect, the first object-relations theorist. That his particular biological, Helmholtzian bent caused him to emphasize instinctual aim over instinctual object is certainly not surprising. Nor is it surprising that, in reversing Freud's instinctual emphasis and asserting the primacy of object over aim, object-relations theorists should attempt to eschew Freud's biological under-pinnings, thereby creating a personology devoid of neurology (Guntrip 1961, 1968, 1971, Rinsley 1979).

The classical psychoanalytic emphasis on aim over object relates in part to the particular nature of the close-knit Victorian family (Woodward and Mark 1978), whose disturbed members were the first analysands, and in part to the fact that psychoanalytic theory and technique originally evolved from the retrospective analysis of adult cases. In contrast to today's so-called liberated family structure and child-rearing practice, the fin de siècle European ménage, with its relatively clear-cut age, gender, and generational distinc-tions, functioned on the basis of the inhibition, renunciation, and displacement of instinctual needs, whose strict control was a pre-requisite for the growing child's progressive socialization (Freud 1930). The early psychoanalytic emphasis on the Oedipus complex and its associated triadic-sexual issues as etiologic for the infantile neurosis and later neuroses evolved from observing the familial hothouse atmosphere, which was governed by guilt over unex-pressed instinctual urges. Emergent from such repressive circum-stances, the adults whom Freud and his colleagues psychoanalyzed displayed psychopathology that was originally viewed in terms of unrequited and "repressed" libidinal (sexual) needs and regressive, desexualized efforts at mastery (anal defenses) of these needs. As a result, the depth and pervasiveness of many of these early patients' illnesses were underestimated, as the famous cases of Anna O, Dora, the Wolf Man, and the Rat Man amply illustrate.

As Freud's "Project" (1895) established psychoanalysis essen-tially as a drive-reduction theory, it likewise established it as a self-as-process theory, as contrasted with a self-as-object theory (Rinsley 1962, 1979). Basic to the self-as-process view is the notion of endopsychic structures, notably with ego, as impersonal *systems* or *mechanisms* remote from or devoid of direct, intimate, subjective apprehension and experience. Perhaps the most comprehensive statement concerning human personality as a congeries of mechanisms or systems found expression in the so-called American school of ego psychology, epitomized in the writings of Heinz Hartmann (1964) and his associates, who viewed their approach as capable of forging scientific links with nonanalytic "academic" psychology.[1] American ego psychologists spoke of a *conflict-free ego sphere,* of *ego apparatus,* of *primary* and *secondary autonomy,* and of *neutralized* and *unneutralized drive energies* in an essentially impersonal fashion. Its classical adherents were wont to emphasize the importance of strictly observed, noninterventive analytic technique (Arlow and Brenner 1964, Boyer and Giovacchini 1967).

The origins and development of much of contemporary object-relations theory may be traced to the writings of a small number of highly original investigators beginning with Melanie Klein who, despite admitted theoretical shortcomings (Glover 1945), drew exceedingly close to the inner worlds of her young patients. Federn (1952), who studied perception and attempted to analyze schizophrenics, viewed the ego as no mere abstraction, but rather, as directly accessible to experience. Sullivan (1953, 1962) wrote of "fantastic personifications." And Edith Jacobson's contributions to the metapsychology of (endopsychic) representations (1954a,b,c, 1957, 1964, 1971) further opened the door to a view of human personality that was at considerable variance with the impersonal systems, or self-as-process, view. Interestingly, the academic psychologists called this approach "self as object." In its latter-day form, it comprises an amalgam of the "pure gold" of psychoanalysis and what Eissler (1953, 1958) has termed "parameters," that is,

---

[1]A comprehensive statement of the psychoanalytic systems concept of the human personality is represented in the 1963 work, *The Vital Balance,* by Menninger et al.

disciplined departures from the strict application of the basic rule (including the rule of abstinence), which is almost impossible for children, borderline patients, and psychotics to observe. Indeed, as the results of the Menninger Foundation Psychotherapy Research Project indicate (Kernberg 1972), and as Kernberg has affirmed (1975), the borderline patient responds best to therapeutic technique that judiciously combines both support and exploration (uncovering). Support parameters thus help strengthen the patient's ego for the work of analysis. In Simmel's original concept of the psychoanalytic sanitarium (1929), he expresses the importance of support parameters for the psychoanalytic treatment of patients who are unable to withstand the rigors of outpatient treatment (Rinsley 1963).[2] Federn's support parameters took the form of introducing a female (= maternal) colleague into the analyses of schizophrenics. Winnicott's concept of the "good enough" mother and environment (1950–1955, 1960) and Modell's concept of the holding environment (1968, 1975, Khan 1963) are basic to it although their work with such patients has been primarily extramural.

Freud's formulation of the concept of the repetition compulsion to account for clinical phenomena that were inexplicable in terms of drive reduction represented a profound insight. His understanding of it was ultimately based on the death instinct, which was itself explicable in terms of innate human aggression. Of course, the concept of the repetition compulsion, of the overdetermined tendency to recapitulate, and hence to re-experience, past events, especially those of a traumatic nature, represents an effort to understand the present in terms of the past while retaining the notion of the primacy of instinctual aim over instinctual object. Whether expressed in autoplastic or alloplastic symptoms

[2]It should be noted that Kernberg's (1980a) view of the use of support parameters is closely akin to Simmel's in that he sometimes relies on the wider social, including hospital, environment for their application and eschews support maneuvers within therapeutic hours. Boyer and Giovacchini (Boyer 1976, Boyer and Giovacchini 1967, Giovacchini 1975), and Volkan (1976) among others, work with regressed patients in the outpatient setting and rely almost exclusively on interpretations.

or behavior, the repetition compulsion represents an effort to master trauma, to bind its associated dysphoria, and to work it through; it represents an attempt to heal a narcissistic wound or, in other words, to *mourn*. And what is thus mourned? The answer, so eloquently expressed in "Mourning and Melancholia" (Freud 1917), is *object loss*.

When Melanie Klein and Ronald Fairbairn tell us that object assumes primacy over aim, they tell us that it is the object relationship that counts, rather than the mere reduction of instinctual tension or the "yield of pleasure" for which the ego works (Freud 1911). In object-relations terms, the repetition compulsion recapitulates *relationships;* thus the phenomena that originally puzzled Freud become understandable in terms of the need to recapture or re-experience relationships rather than merely to feel good.[3]

When Giovacchini (1979) writes that he doubts he has ever seen a neurotic individual in analysis or treatment, he reminds us that our psychotherapeutic practices appear to be preponderantly, if not exclusively, devoted to patients whose developmental fixations are of pre-oedipal nature. If the phrases *narcissistic wound (trauma)* and *object loss* thus refer to pre-oedipal events and experiences, then we must ask what those events and experiences are. Again, if oedipal-triadic determinants of later psychopathology are indeed pathogenic epiphenomena engrafted, as it were, on prior traumas, then what constitutes the latter and how do they come to be expressed in later symptomatology? And finally, how can object-relations theory help us understand them?

Our psychotic, borderline, and narcissistic patients seem to be telling us that something happened, or did not happen, in their early infancy that induced what Balint (1968) has termed a *basic fault;* this basic fault has rendered them confused, feeling both impotent and grandiose, and prone to regressive perceptual, cognitive, and affective decomposition or fragmentation. They are fear-

---

[3]Thus the masochist, who seeks the experience of pain, counterphobically courts discomfort because it in effect guarantees that some form of relationship is possible, that one has not been abandoned and will indeed survive, albeit uncomfortably (Berliner 1958).

ful that their aggressive and libidinal-affiliative instinctual urges will destroy them or others, or at least will preclude relationships, leaving them bereft, rejected, and abandoned. For them, oedipal-incestuous rivalries constitute symptomatic luxuries when self-survival is the fundamental issue. They are, indeed, enigmas to themselves and others. The higher-level narcissists (narcissistic personalities) emerge either as inveterate miser- and injustice-collecting masochists or else as detached, loveless tyrants whose families and associates exist for their greater glory as they go on to ever-greater achievements at the frightful expense of those who attempt to care for them (Bursten 1978). Recent clinical investigation indicates that these patients have a common endopsychic structure that places them in the diagnostic-developmental continuum or spectrum known as *disorders of the self* (Kohut 1971, 1977, Ornstein 1974, Rinsley 1980a, 1981).

To understand this endopyschic structure, it is necessary to consider the nature of the primal trauma that underlies it. When this is done, then two early infantile phenomena come immediately to mind, viz., the young infant's primitive "all good"–"all bad" perceptual and responsive organization and his enormous vulnerability to those pervasively disruptive, mass-reflexive "affecto-motor storms" that ultimately can only be put to rest through the ministrations of a "good enough" mothering figure (Winnicott 1960).

In accordance with the pleasure principle, the infant will "take in" (accept) a "good" food item, such as a dilute sugar solution placed on his tongue, and will "spit out" (reject) a "bad" food item, such as a dilute acetic acid solution. Acceptance of a good food item signifies its incorporation and ensuing physico-chemical assimilation accompanied by the laying down of a good (positively valent) memory trace. Likewise, rejection of a bad food item is accompanied by the laying down of a bad (negatively valent) memory trace.[4] A

It should be remembered that "good" milk may be rendered "bad" if the mother proffers it to the infant with ambivalent, disruptive, or rejecting attitudes and feelings, which may be expressed through muscular tension, inappropriate holding of the infant, and other somatic concomitants of disturbed nurturing.

preponderance of bad food items is thus seen to result in the build-up of an ever-expanding repository of negatively valent memory traces. These, in turn, fail to damp down the infant's indigenous visceral-autonomic lability, which is episodically expressed in the affecto-motor discharges, resulting in (1) an ongoing or unremitting condition of heightened irritability and tension, and (2) a repository of negative memory traces that progressively consolidate into what will later become a negative identity. These are, of course, the pathological effects of the "bad breast" or, more accurately, the bad breast part object. As Fairbairn (1954, 1963) has pointed out, this bad breast part object (what he calls the *bad* or *rejected object*) undergoes powerful introjection and subsequent splitting (what he calls the *split internalized bad object*); the results of this splitting are Fairbairn's *exciting object* (E.O.) and *rejecting object* (R.O.), which Masterson and I (1975) have termed, respectively, the *rewarding part-object-representation* or *part-object-image* and the *rejecting (withdrawing) part-object-representation* or *part-object-image*. From the side of the infant are generated two corresponding part-self-representations or part-self-images, or what Fairbairn calls the *libidinal ego* (L.E.) and the *anti-libidinal ego* (anti-L.E.); these correspond to Masterson's and my (1975) *rewarding part-self-representation* or *part-self-image* and *rejecting (withdrawing) part-self-representation* or *part-self-image*, respectively, and become associated with the rewarding and rejecting part-object-representations or part-object-images.

The *anlage* of the *good breast part object* (good object), without which the infant's survival would be impossible, likewise undergoes internalization; Fairbairn terms this the *ideal object* (I.O.). The I.O. forms an "alliance" with what he terms the *central ego* (C.E.) of the infant. There thus comes into existence a complex endopsychic structure comprising three "alliances": the "good" or "accepted" I.O.–C.E., and the "bad" or "rejected" dyadic E.O.–L.E. and R.O.–anti-L.E. The latter two are kept separate through the overdetermined operation of the splitting defense and both in turn, are, split from the I.O.–C.E. What thus began as an expression of the reflexive swallowing or spitting out of proffered food becomes imbued with symbolic-representational significance and passes over into a true defense (Rinsley 1979).[5] Unless otherwise influenced by the intervention of restitutive mothering or, lacking that, by appropriate treatment provided at a later time, there evolves in the growing child an ensuing "all good"–"all bad" world view, a symptomatic hallmark of the self-disordered (psychotic, borderline, narcissistic) individual (Ornstein 1974, Rinsley 1980a, b, 1981).

For object-relations theory to have clinical significance and application, however, it needs to be understood in a developmental context. That context is provided by classical psychosexual state theory (Abraham 1924, Fenichel 1945), carried to its highest point of development in those contributions of Margaret Mahler and her colleagues (Mahler et al. 1975) devoted to symbiosis and individuation. The interdigitation of object-relations and Mahlerian developmental phase concepts allows for a coherent, developmentally based diagnostic nosology of much greater validity than the one provided by pristine psychosexual stage theory. In addition, it provides the necessary ingredients for a rational approach to psychoanalytic treatment, particularly treatment of the major psychoses and personality (characterologic) disorders, or disorders of the self (Kohut, 1971). Indeed, it was Mahler herself (1971) who speculated that borderline phenomena were expressions of failure of separation-individuation, an insight that was to provide the impetus for Masterson's and my later publications on that subject (Masterson 1974, 1975, 1976, Masterson and Rinsley 1975, Rinsley 1978, 1979, 1980a, b).

The 1975 Masterson-Rinsley paper recognized Fairbairn's split internalized bad object as basic to the developmental arrest and ensuing symptomatology of borderline adolescents and adults. In that paper, as well as in its more detailed successors, we could confirm Mahler's speculations (1971) as we antedated the developmental arrest or fixation that underlies borderline personality disorder to the *rapprochement subphase of separation-individuation* (occurring at 16–26 months of age). Our inferences were based upon Masterson's and my analytic treatment of both inpatient and

[5]For further evaluative discussion of these "alliances," see Kernberg (1980b).

outpatient borderline ("symbiotic") adolescents and their families, my own supervisory work in the treatment of similar preadolescents and their families, and my observational study of psychotic and borderline mothers and their preschool children, carried out in the Child Development Center of the Children's Section of Topeka State Hospital between 1970 and 1975.

The endopsychic structure, analogous to Fairbairn's E.O.–L.E. and R.O.–anti-L.E. alliances, which Masterson and I (1975) originally described, is known as the *split object-relations unit* (SORU) of the borderline; it comprises two representational-affect complexes, as described earlier by Kernberg (1966). It originates in the push-pull mother-infant relationship, prominent during the rapprochement subphase of separation-individuation, in which the mother rewards the infant for dependency (hence, for inadequacy) and withdraws from or rejects him in the wake of his efforts toward growth, thereby fixating him at the phase of partial self-object differentiation. The infant's recurrent and resurgent symbiotic needs for refusion or reunion coexisting with his chronic feelings of frustration, rage, and impotency constitute what Masterson and I have termed *abandonment depression*. The structure of the SORU comprises the introjective representational precipitates of this twin theme and is basic to the internal object relations and symptomatology of the borderline personality.

It is evident that the repetitive self-injurious, self-defeating, essentially masochistic behavior of these self-disordered individuals can only be adequately understood in terms of the primacy of the pathogenic maternal object tie and not in terms of any postulated instinctual aim. When we carefully examine both the higher-level narcissistic personality and the regressed, fragmented psychotic, we discover the presence of a basically similar endopsychic structure. As Ornstein (1974) has clearly pointed out and I have elsewhere affirmed (Rinsley 1977, 1980a, 1981), the diagnostic groups of the major psychoses, the borderline disorders, and the narcissistic personalities may be aligned along a continuum based on degrees of regressive "fragmentability" of archaic internal self-objects. The persistence of self-objects bespeaks failure of self-object differentiation and desymbiotization, and the persistence of impaired object constancy (Fraiberg 1969), part-object relations, and the inability to mourn (Rinsley 1978).

APPLICATIONS TO PSYCHOTHERAPY

Fundamental to the practice and goals of psychotherapy is the generation of the therapeutic alliance. The more expeditiously this is accomplished, the more effective the treatment will be. This means, among other things, facilitating the positive transference in order to optimize the self-disordered patient's limited capacity to trust the therapist, and hence, to generate what Goldstein (1959) termed "communion" with him. As Kernberg (1975) and Boyer (1977) have aptly noted, with borderline patients the therapist must employ skillful confrontation, clarification, and, when feasible, interpretation of the negative transference. Masterson and I (Masterson 1976, Masterson and Rinsley 1975, Rinsley 1978) describe this approach in terms of relatively early confrontation and clarification of the deleterious nature of the patient's symptomatic behavior, which paves the way for developing insight into the patient's SORU. One also begins psychotherapy with all self-disordered patients with the awareness that they suffer from a relative deficiency of "good internal objects," and hence, of the libidinal energy normally associated with these objects (Federn 1952, Rinsley 1968). Finally, therapeutic approach and technique should be flexibly based on the patient's variable—and often profound—need for support parameters (v. inf.).

Emotional Lability and Unpredictability

With the possible exception of the higher-level narcissistic personality, self-disordered patients often puzzle and confuse their therapists with an array of polar-opposite and rapidly alternating and fluctuating emotions; their often kaleidoscopic "psychotic" transferences readily convey their redoubtable reliance on projective-introjective defenses, epitomized in the "two D's"—Deification and Devaluation. Their complaints of feeling "uptight," "mixed-up," "a mess," "in total confusion," and the like reflect an ongoing condition of heightened inner tension (anxiety); this condition is readily traced to the persistent affecto-motor storms of the young infant that were never adequately put to rest by a "good enough" mother, which produced a chronic state of visceral-autonomic hyperirritability in the infant. This engendered a chronic state of overalert watchfulness reflected in a persistent "scanning" function, and expressed as a seemingly uncanny ability to intuit the unconscious or unexpressed motives of others, including those of the therapist (Carter and Rinsley 1977, Krohn 1974).

One patient, a 31-year-old borderline man, often prefaced his replies to his therapist's questions with, "Ummm . . . I guess you want me to say . . ." This was most evident when he was pathologically idealizing the therapist while simultaneously viewing himself as the therapist's puppet. Repeated confrontation finally evoked the interpretable fact that, as a child, the patient had concluded that he could only repeat the words and ideas expressed by his sadistic adoptive father and that he had "no right" to those of his own.

Persistent proneness to affecto-motor turmoil finds frequent expression in these patients' problems with sphincter zone specificity, conveyed in polymorphous-perverse sexuality (Rosenfeld and Sprince 1963). Their sexual behavior, including their genital sexuality, is often in the service of more primitive pre-oedipal needs for nurturant warmth and closeness. They will "purchase" the latter at the expense of mature genital relations, sometimes by means of homosexual perversity and other primitively overdetermined sexual actions.

Another patient, a 39-year-old unmarried professional woman, could readily admit that her heterosexual promiscuity served the purpose of temporarily alleviating her chronic, intense feelings of loneliness. Not surprisingly, she was anorgastic and in fact found sexual intercourse to be disgusting, occasionally leading to nausea.

With arresting pseudoinsight she commented, "It's like vomiting up my mother . . . !"

The patient often experiences significant relief, accompanied by reinforcement of the positive transference, when the therapist conveys awareness of the patient's affecto-motor turmoil—that is—the patient's simultaneous mistrust and highly overdetermined, often frightening need for closeness. Following one such communication by the therapist, a middle-aged narcissistic patient replied, "Well . . . I guess it's any port in a storm!" [sic]

Object Inconstancy and Object Impermanency

Adler (1979, 1981) has recently re-emphasized these exceptionally important characteristics of self-disordered patients. Among psychotics and severe borderline cases, failure of evocative memory or recall finds expression in the patient's inability to generate and maintain a stable inner image of the therapist between therapeutic hours (object impermanency); viewed as a defense, it conveys the patient's need to scotomatize or negatively hallucinate the therapist. In higher-level self-disordered patients, including the more purely narcissistic personalities, evocative recall of the therapist's image remains intact, but neither the image nor the actual therapist is consistently invested ("cathected"), which is reflected in the undercurrent of mistrust and suspicion (object inconstancy) found in these patients.

The disruptive significance of object impermanency and object inconstancy in the psychotherapeutic process cannot be overestimated, as it creates numerous peculiar and disturbing varieties of acting in and acting out (Rinsley in press).

One example is a 27-year-old borderline man who told his therapist, "When you're gone I feel I hate you!" This was followed by a spate of obscene invectives directed at the therapist. When the therapist then confronted the patient's inability to imagine or visualize the therapist in the latter's absence, the patient replied, "Yeah, that's right, and I have to do a lot of things to get in trouble so you'll see me. . . ." This statement conveys the disarming pseudoinsight that such self-disordered individuals often display; it likewise conveys failure of self-object (in this case, patient-therapist) differentiation, as expressed by the patient's use of the word "see," which is representative of his projection of scoptophilic partial aims into the therapist.

Fantasy Deficiency

The self-disordered patient's deficiency both in the amount of fantasy he is able to generate and in his adaptive and creative use of that fantasy has a significant impact on his therapy. Often, if not invariably, the patient's self-depreciative use of such terms as "empty," "hopeless," "meaningless," "confused," "fake," "façade," and the like conveys a self-experience of impoverished inner content that reflects the fantasy-deficient condition. The relationship between waking fantasy ("daydreams") and nocturnal dreaming is underscored by the fact that many of these patients report deficiencies in both; thus, they are unable to use fantasy to plan and set realistic goals; nor can they use the nocturnal dream to work through unconscious conflict and integrate it with the here-and-now represented in the day residues.

Recently, Nemiah and Sifneos (Nemiah and Sifneos 1970, Sifneos 1973, 1975) have described a condition they have termed *alexithymia*, comprising a poverty or deficiency of fantasy associated with an inability to describe one's subjective feelings; this condition is common in self-disordered patients with pre-oedipally determined symptomatology (e.g., in those with psychosomatic disorders).

The fantasy deficiency of self-disordered patients is related to their impaired object permanency and object constancy. As noted, the self-depreciative terms they employ to convey this endopsychic state reflect their inability to summon up "good" mental images or representations. The fantasy deficiency is also related to developmental arrest involving pathological persistence of the transitional object and mode of experience (Modell 1968, Winnicott 1951), reflecting fixation at the level of infantile grandiosity and part-object relations.

The self-disordered patient's well-known feeling of "entitlement" reflects the pathological persistence of infantile-grandiosity (infantile-megalomania) seemingly paradoxically coexisting with pervasive feelings of impotency, worthlessness, and hopelessness. Magical expectations of cure reflect profound passive-anaclitic (symbiotic) needs that, in turn, evoke the patient's anxiety, leading to devaluation of projective identifications with the therapist and to related angry demands on the therapist.

The therapist's ability to recognize and deal sensitively with the patient's fantasy deficiency and, ultimately, with the patient's fantasies as they are elaborated in the therapeutic transference, constitutes one of the essentials of treatment. The apprehensions of self-disordered patients regarding their evolving fantasies, or their lack of fantasies, are found to center on the following: *any* fantasy per se is dangerous to one's self and to others, most notably to the therapist; having fantasies implies that one is "crazy"; fantasies are secrets that the therapist will steal or otherwise take away (the so-called primal exchange: Modell 1971); fantasies must be acted on; and masturbatory and other sexual fantasies, again in relation to the therapist, are particularly fearsome and dangerous. Experience amply demonstrates that as the patient's image of the therapist becomes evocably stabilized and reliable, that is, as the therapeutic alliance becomes strengthened, the patient's "fantasy work" proceeds apace. The major caveat has to do with the therapist's own developed capacity for such work within the counter-transference, such that both therapist and patient come to develop a genuine interest and belief in the understandability and inter-pretability of the patient's evolving and increasingly freely communicated fantasy in the therapeutic hours.

A highly intelligent 15-year-old borderline adolescent girl in full-time residential treatment (P) put it succinctly to her male therapist (T):

T: I know its hard to tell me what you think about, or daydream, or even fantasize. . . .

P: Yup . . . I'm afraid to.

T: Why is that?

P: Well, because if I tell you about those things you'll have them and I won't have them any more.

T: Uh, uh . . . if you tell me, then you'll have them and I'll have them . . . we'll both have them.

P: Yipe! I never thought of that!

Basic Fault

This phrase, as used by Balint (1968), refers to the self-disordered individual's impairment of primary and secondary narcissism and of (internal) object relations based upon defective early mother-infant bonding. In Federn's terms (1952), it refers to defective medial ego feeling or "prereflective narcissism," which lies close to the core of the self. It is experienced and conveyed in the patient's abiding feeling that in some indefinable way he is flawed, defective, imperfect, or damaged, that there has long been "something wrong" or "something missing." The phrases "not all there" and "not playing with a full deck" convey this chronic, disquieting self-perception. Metaphorically, basic fault means "I am (feel) bad." In Fairbairn's terms, it reflects ongoing sadistic assaults by the R.O.–anti-L.E. alliance (Fairbairn's primitive superego) against the L.E.; in Masterson's and my terms, it reflects the untrammeled operation of the rejecting (withdrawing) SORU part-unit (i.e., the "alliance" between the rejecting [withdrawing] part-object-image or part-object-representation and the rejecting [withdrawing] part-self-image or part-self-representation, with their associated *abandonment depression*).

The self-disordered patient attempts to "make good" this perceived self-defect, in part by means of the welter of approach-avoidance symptomatology he displays, particularly in the therapeutic transference. The higher-level narcissistic patient usually denies the perceived self-defect; he may project it onto others, viewing them as incompetent and himself as "the greatest"; or, as Bursten (1978) has noted, he may deny it by means of masochistic, injustice-collecting self-aggrandizement.

A 25-year-old divorced male graduate student said, "I never felt right about myself . . . there was always something vaguely wrong . . . missing, and I could never figure out what it was."

The "as if" features that the basic fault imparts to the symptomatology and object relationships of the self-disordered patient are succinctly encompassed in Adler's comment (1981), "Kohut describes the sense of inner incompleteness that temporarily disappears within a therapeutic relationship when the therapist performs needed functions that the patient does not possess at that moment." When this occurs, the patient temporarily "feels good" and when, at significant therapeutic junctures, it does not, he "feels bad," with ensuing reactivation of affecto-motor turmoil, and hence, of feelings of abandonment, at which times the patient will lash out at the therapist or indulge in self-defeating and self-injurious behavior in a magical attempt to "punish" the therapist and to force him to banish the "bad" feelings.

The case vignette of the 27-year-old borderline woman reported by Masterson and myself (1975, pp. 172–173) illustrates how the patient's perception of abandonment by the therapist provoked symptomatic behavior, especially as therapeutic progress reactivated her fear of losing the therapist.

Again, judicious confrontation, clarification, and, when possible, interpretation of the components of the SORU as they come to be expressed in the patient's symptomatic communications and behavior during therapeutic hours, as well as in his symptomatic behavior outside them, will expose the pathogenesis of the basic fault.

A 33-year-old borderline man with a history of alcoholism and illicit drug usage told the therapist, "Whenever I'd get feisty my mother would always shove food in my mouth . . . lots of times I didn't want it and I'd almost puke but I was afraid she'd hate me or hit me if I didn't eat when she wanted me to . . . she fed me to shut me up. . . ." After over 100 hours of therapy, the patient could say, "I can see that being 'bad' got me food so eating kept me from 'being bad' . . . that's why I used to drink or get stoned . . . to not feel bad . . ." After the therapist asked, "And what else?" the patient replied, "to keep her from leaving me. . . ."

Limits and Controls

No discussion of the psychotherapy of the self-disordered patient would be complete without reference to the patient's need for externally imposed limits or controls. A partial exception is the higher-level narcissistic personality, for whom such a need may be rather less important during the course of therapy.

My own experience with these patients, including adolescents and adults, amply underscores their need to have limits set for them relatively early. Among other things, this means that the psychotherapist should never acquiesce in, much less promote, the patient's self-injurious acting in and acting out; nor should the therapist assume a permissive or laissez-faire attitude toward symptomatic behavior that the patient invariably, if not admittedly, perceives is harmful to himself. In some cases, this limit setting assumes the form of a direct command, such as to cease all alcohol intake, drug use, or perverse sexual activities; in other cases, it is expressed as disapproval of the deleterious symptomatic act or behavior communicated in the context of acceptance both of the patient as a whole, and of the *need* that underlies the particular act or behavior.

The rule of abstinence plays a significant role in the psychoanalytic treatment of self-disordered patients, much as it does in the case of less seriously disturbed individuals, by promoting the exposure, understanding, and interpretation of the "underlying material" that the symptomatology symbolically conveys and maintains apart from the patient's conscious awareness.[6] For these patients, since absence of disagreement means agreement, therapeutic failure or needless prolongation of treatment may result when reliance is placed on "strict" analytic technique.

It is amazing how latter-day psychoanalysts and other analytically trained and sophisticated therapists "permit" their patients all varieties of acting out, including marriages, divorces, and changes in occupation and domicile location, without dealing with the

---

[6]As Eissler (1958) has reminded us, the "rule of abstinence" originally referred to the requirement that the analyst refrain from gratifying the patient's wishes and needs within analytic hours. As used here in its more extended sense, it applies to symptomatic behavior that subserves secondary gain *both within and outside therapeutic hours.*

enormous resistances they convey. In this connection, one is reminded of the aphorism attributed to Freud, to wit, that "psychoanalysis cannot compete with sex."

SOME FURTHER CONSIDERATIONS OF THERAPEUTIC TECHNIQUE

Basing his conclusions on his own experience as a psychoanalytic clinician, as well as on the findings of the Menninger Foundation Psychotherapy Research Project, Kernberg (1972, 1975) has affirmed that optimal psychotherapeutic technique with borderline patients combines both exploration (uncovering, transference interpretation) and support.[7] His diagnostic "structural interview" focuses on the use of confrontation and clarification to generate "tension" and to provoke responses that provide insight into the patient's defenses, identity conflicts, and degree of reality testing.

In a number of respects, the therapeutic technique that Masterson and I have recommended is similar. Its major focus, moreover, is on the confrontation, clarification, and interpretation of the SORU, with the aim of facilitating the patient's insight into it, as well as on promoting the development of the therapeutic alliance ("healthy object-relations unit") in the therapeutic transference. When successful, this approach uncovers the original push-pull mother-infant relationship that is etiologic for the self-disordered patient's pathological internal object relations and associated symptomatology.

Kohut's treatment of higher-level narcissistic patients (1971, 1977), whom he differentiates from borderline patients, focuses on his now well-known *grandiose self* and *idealized parental image* as they come to be expressed in the so-called mirroring transference. His concept of the *self-object* as characteristic of psychotic, borderline, and narcissistic personalities reflects their impaired self-

---

[7]To be sure, Kernberg (1980a) avoids the direct use of support parameters within the therapeutic hours; instead, he relies on them being provided "from the outside," including, for example, the hospital environment and associated activities.

object differentiation (Ornstein 1974, Rinsley 1980a, 1981), with the added understanding that the self-objects of the narcissistic personality are relatively stable, that is, resistant to regressive fragmentation, and hence, to repersonification or reanimation ("demetabolization": Kernberg 1966). My own clinical experience with narcissistic patients confirms both the relative stability of their self-objects and the etiologic importance of the SORU for their symptomatology. The relatively greater stability of the self-objects in such patients accounts for their therapeutic responsiveness to a "stricter" analytic technique than borderline and more seriously disorganized patients can tolerate.

SUMMARY

Object-relations concepts are finding increasing application in psychoanalytic and dynamic psychotherapeutic practice in the wake of the increased numbers of pre-oedipally fixated, self-disordered patients who find their way into the consulting room, psychiatric hospital, or residential treatment facility. In extending and deepening classical psychoanalytic metapsychology, object-relations theory widens the range of clinical therapeutic technique while remaining solidly within the framework of psychoanalysis, which is ultimately the most thoroughgoing theory of personality and of psychopathology that has yet been developed.

REFERENCES

Abraham, K. (1924). A short study of the development of the libido, viewed in the light of mental disorders. In *Selected Papers of Karl Abraham*, pp. 418–501. London: Hogarth Press, 1927.

Adler, G. (1979). The myth of the alliance with borderline patients. *Amer. J. Psychiat.* 136:642–645.

——— (1981). The borderline-narcissistic personality disorder continuum. *Amer. J. Psychiat.* 138:46–50.

Arlow, J. and Brenner, C. (1964). *Psychoanalytic Concepts and the Structural Theory*. New York: International Universities Press.

Balint, M. (1968). *The Basic Fault: Therapeutic Aspects of Regression*. London: Tavistock.

Berliner, B. (1958). The role of object relations in moral masochism. *Psychoanal. Quart.* 27:38–56.

Boyer, L. B. (1976). *Die Psychoanalytische Behandlung Schizophrener*. Munich: Kindler Verlag.

Boyer, L. B. (1977). Working with a borderline patient. *Psychoanal. Quart.* 46:386–424.

Boyer, L. B. and Giovacchini, P. L. (1967). *Psychoanalytic Treatment of Schizophrenic and Characterological Disorders*. New York: Science House.

Bursten, B. (1978). A diagnostic framework. *Internat. Rev. Psycho-Anal.* 5:15–31.

Carter, L. and Rinsley, D. B. (1977). Vicissitudes of "empathy" in a borderline adolescent. *Internat. Rev. Psycho-Anal.* 4:317–326.

Eissler, K. R. (1953). The effect of the structure of the ego on psychoanalytic technique. *J. Amer. Psychoanal. Assn.* 1:104–143.

——— (1958). Remarks on some variations in psychoanalytic technique. *Internat. J. Psycho-Anal.* 39:222–229.

Fairbairn, W. R. D. (1954). *An Object-Relations Theory of the Personality*. New York: Basic Books.

——— (1963). Synopsis of an object-relations theory of the personality. *Internat. J. Psycho-Anal* 44:224–225.

Federn, P. (1952). *Ego Psychology and the Psychoses*, ed. E. Weiss. New York: Basic Books.

Fenichel, O. (1945). *The Psychoanalytic Theory of Neurosis*. New York: Norton.

Fraiberg, S. (1969). Libidinal object constancy and mental representation. *The Psychoanalytic Study of the Child* 24:9–47.

Freud, S. (1895). Project for a scientific psychology. *Standard Edition* 1:283–397. London: Hogarth Press, 1966.

——— (1905). Three essays on sexuality. *Standard Edition* 7:130–243. London: Hogarth Press, 1968.

——— (1911). Formulations on the two principles of mental functioning. *Standard Edition* 12:218–226. London: Hogarth Press, 1971.

——— (1915). Instincts and their vicissitudes. *Standard Edition* 14:117–140. London: Hogarth press, 1957.

——— (1916). Some character types met with in psycho-analytic work. *Standard Edition* 14:311–333. London: Hogarth Press, 1957.

——— (1917). Mourning and melancholia. *Standard Edition* 14:243–258. London: Hogarth Press, 1957.

——— (1920). Beyond the pleasure principle. *Standard Edition* 18:7–64. London: Hogarth Press, 1955.

——— (1930). Civilization and its discontents. *Standard Edition* 21:64–145. London: Hogarth Press, 1968.

Giovacchini, P. L. (1975). *Psychoanalysis of Character Disorders.* New York: Aronson.

——— (1979). *Treatment of Primitive Mental States.* New York: Aronson.

Glover, E. (1945). Examination of the Klein system of child psychology. *The Psychoanalytic Study of the Child* 1:75–118.

Goldstein, K. (1959). The organismic approach. In *American Handbook of Psychiatry*, vol. 2, ed. S. Arieti, pp. 1333–1347. New York: Basic Books.

Grinker, R. R. et al. (1968). *The Borderline Syndrome: A Behavioral Study of Ego Functions.* New York: Basic Books.

——— and Werble, B. (1977). *The Borderline Patient.* New York: Aronson.

Guntrip, H.J.S. (1961). *Personality Structure and Human Interaction: The Developing Synthesis of Psycho-Dynamic Theory.* New York: International Universities Press.

——— (1968). *Schizoid Phenomena. Object Relations, and the Self.* New York: International Universities Press.

——— (1971). *Psychoanalytic Theory, Therapy, and the Self.* New York: Basic Books.

Hartmann, H. (1964). *Essays on Ego Psychology: Selected Problems in Psychoanalytic Theory.* New York: International Universities Press.

Jacobson, E. (1954a). Contributions to the metapsychology of psychotic identifications. *J. Amer. Psychoanal. Assn.* 2:239–262.

——— (1954b). On psychotic identifications. *Internat. J. Psycho-Anal.* 35:102–108.

——— (1954c). The self and the object world: Vicissitudes of their infantile cathexes and their influence on ideational and affective development. *The Psychoanalytic Study of the Child* 9:75–127.

——— (1957). Denial and repression. *J. Amer. Psychoanal. Assn.* 5:61–92.

——— (1964). *The Self and the Object World.* New York: International Universities Press.

——— (1971). *Depression.* New York: International Universities Press.

Kernberg, O. F. (1966). Structural derivatives of object relationships. *Internat. J. Psycho-Anal.* 47:236–253.

—— (1972). Summary and conclusions: Psychotherapy and psycho-analysis. Final report of The Menninger Foundation's Psychotherapy Research Project. *Bull. Menninger Clin.* 36:181–195.

—— (1975). *Borderline Conditions and Pathological Narcissism.* New York: Aronson.

—— (1980a). Developmental theory, structural organization, and psychoanalytic technique. In *Rapprochement: The Critical Subphase of Separation-Individuation,* ed. R. F. Lax et al., pp. 23–38. New York: Aronson.

—— (1980b). Fairbairn's theory and challenge. In *Internal World and External Reality: Object-Relations Theory Applied,* pp. 57–84. New York: Aronson.

—— (in press). The theory of psychoanalytic psychotherapy. Paper presented at the Annual Meeting of the American Psychoanalytic Association, Atlanta, Georgia, May 7, 1978.

Khan, M.M.R. (1963). The concept of cumulative trauma. *The Psychoanalytic Study of the Child* 18:286–306.

Kohut, H. (1971). *The Analysis of the Self.* New York: International Universities Press.

—— (1977). *The Restoration of the Self.* New York: International Universities Press.

Krohn, A. (1974). Borderline "empathy" and differentiation of object representations. *Internat. J. Psychoanal. Psychother.* 3:142–165.

Mahler, M. S. (1971). A study of the separation-individuation process and its possible application to borderline phenomena in the psychoanalytic situation. *The Psychoanalytic Study of the Child* 26:403–424.

——, Pine, F., and Bergman, A. (1975). *The Psychological Birth of the Human Infant: Symbiosis and Individuation.* New York: Basic Books.

Masterson, J. F. (1974). Intensive psychotherapy of the adolescent with a borderline syndrome. In *American Handbook of Psychiatry,* vol. 2, 2nd rev. ed., ed. S. Arieti et al., pp. 250–263. New York: Basic Books.

—— (1975). The splitting defense mechanism of the borderline adolescent. In *Borderline States in Psychiatry,* ed. J. E. Mack, pp. 93–101. New York: Grune and Stratton.

Masterson, J. F. (1976). *Treatment of the Borderline Adult: A Developmental Approach.* New York: Brunner/Mazel.

—— and Rinsley, D. B. (1975). The borderline syndrome: The role of the mother in the genesis and psychic structure of the borderline personality. *Internat. J. Psycho-Anal.* 56:163–177. Revised and reprinted in *Rapprochement: The Critical Subphase of Separation-*

Individuation, ed. R. F. Lax et al., pp. 299–329. New York: Aronson, 1980.

Menninger, K. A. et al. (1963). *The Vital Balance.* New York: Viking Press.

Modell, A. H. (1968). *Object Love and Reality.* New York: International Universities Press.

———— (1971). The origin of certain forms of pre-oedipal guilt and the implications for a psychoanalytic theory of affects. *Internat. J. Psycho-Anal.* 52:337–346.

———— (1975). The ego and the id: Fifty years later. *Internat. J. Psycho-Anal.* 56:57–68.

Nemiah, J. and Sifneos, P. (1970). Affect and fantasy in patients with psychosomatic disorders. In *Modern Trends in Psychosomatic Medicine*, vol. 2, ed. D. W. Hill, pp. 26–35. London: Butterworth.

Ornstein, P. H. (1974). On narcissism: Beyond the introduction. Highlights of Heinz Kohut's contributions to the psychoanalytic treatment of narcissistic personality disorders. *Annual. Psychoanal.* 2:127–149.

Rinsley, D. B. (1962). A contribution to the theory of ego and self. *Psychiat. Q.* 36:96–120.

———— (1963). Psychiatric hospital treatment, with special reference to children. *Arch. Gen. Psychiat.* 9:489–496.

———— (1968). Economic aspects of object relations. *Internat. J. Psycho-Anal.* 49:38–48.

———— (1977). An object-relations view of borderline personality. In *Borderline Personality Disorders: The Concept, the Syndrome, the Patient*, ed. P. Hartocollis, pp. 47–70. New York: International Universities Press.

———— (1978). Borderline psychopathology: A review of etiology, dynamics, and treatment. *Internat. Rev. Psycho-Anal.* 5:45–54.

———— (1979). Fairbairn's object-relations theory: A reconsideration in terms of newer knowledge. *Bull. Menninger Clin.* 43:489–514.

———— (1980a). The developmental etiology of borderline and narcissistic disorders. *Bull. Menninger Clin.* 44:127–134.

———— (1980b). Diagnosis and treatment of borderline and narcissistic children and adolescents. *Bull. Menninger Clin.* 44:147–170.

———— (1981). Dynamic and developmental issues in borderline and related "spectrum" disorders. *Psychiat. Clin. North Amer.* 4:117–132.

———— (in press). Object constancy, object permanency, and personality disorder. In *Self and Object Constancy*, ed. R. F. Lax et al. New York: Aronson.

Rosenfeld, S. K. and Sprince, M. P. (1963). An attempt to formulate the meaning of the concept "borderline." *The Psychoanalytic Study of the Child* 18:603–635.

Sifneos, P. (1973). The presence of "alexithymic" characteristics in psychosomatic patients. *Psychother. Psychosom.* 22:255–262.

——— (1975). Problems of psychotherapy of patients with alexithymic characteristics and physical disease. *Psychother. Psychosom.* 26:65–70.

Simmel, E. (1929). Psycho-analytic treatment in a sanitarium. *Internat. J. Psycho-Anal.* 10:70–89.

Sullivan, H. S. (1953). *The Interpersonal Theory of Psychiatry*, ed. H. S. Perry and M. L. Gawel. New York: Norton.

——— (1962). Schizophrenia as a human process. In *The Collected Works of Harry Stack Sullivan*, vol. 2, pp. 7–363. New York: Norton.

Volkan, V. D. (1976). *Primitive Internalized Object Relations. A Clinical Study of Schizophrenic, Borderline and Narcissistic Patients.* New York: International Universities Press.

Winnicott, D. W. (1950–55). Aggression in relation to emotional development. In *Collected Papers: Through Pediatrics to Psycho-Analysis*, pp. 204–218. New York: Basic Books, 1975.

——— (1951). Transitional objects and transitional phenomena. In *Collected Papers: Through Pediatrics to Psycho-Analysis*, pp. 229–242. New York: Basic Books, 1975.

——— (1960). Ego distortion in terms of true and false self. In *The Maturational Processes and the Facilitating Environment: Studies in the Theory of Emotional Development*, pp. 140–152. New York: International Universities Press, 1965.

Woodward, K. L. and Mark, R. (1978). The new narcissism. *Newsweek*, Jan. 30, pp. 70–72.

Part II

Severely Incapacitated and Hospitalized Patients

8

THE SCHIZOPHRENIC STATE OF NONEXPERIENCE

Thomas H. Ogden

Editor's Notes

Dr. Ogden describes his treatment of a patient regressed to the most primitive mental levels. Building
on the work of Bion and Melanie Klein, he conceives
of projective identification as a mechanism that determines the form and content of the transference-
countertransference interaction. Clinical investigations have shown that patients with severe character
disorders resulting from early fixations and ego defects characteristically rely on the mechanism of projective identification.

Dr. Ogden goes beyond previous clinical work with
such patients; he introduces us to developmental areas
that have not received much attention from psychoanalysts because they antedate the formation of the
representational world. Limiting himself to clinical
interaction and treatment issues, Dr. Ogden concentrates on the defensive use of nonrepresentational
areas. He investigates how it is used by some schizophrenic patients as a defense against total psychotic
collapse. According to Dr. Ogden, these patients
cease to function in the representational world. He
presents us with a fascinating example of a schizophrenic patient's retreat into a state of "defensive
nonexperience." In such a state, all thoughts, fantasies,
and feelings are stripped of meaning.

At this point, many analysts would throw their hands up in dismay and ask, how can anyone analyze patients whose dominant orientation is not in terms of psychological experiences, patients who are fixated at, or have regressed to, psychic states characterized by "nonlinkage" and "nonmeaning"? The projection of impulses, feelings, and self- and object-representations—that is, the essence of transference—cannot occur because all of these elements are part of the representational world and are endowed with meaning. If, as many analysts believe, the sine qua non of psychoanalytic treatment is the analysis of the transference then these very primitive patients cannot be analyzed because they are incapable of forming transferences.

This chapter serves as an outstanding argument against such a limited view. Step by step, Dr. Ogden demonstrates how his patient presented himself and how he, the analyst, "survived" the clinical phase in which the patient regressed to a state of defensive nonexperience. With patience, perseverance, and creative understanding that easily turns into intuitive compassion, the author lets us witness a "burnt-out schizophrenic" become a live person. If the patient had not had the good fortune to find an analyst such as Dr. Ogden, he most likely would have spent the remainder of his days on the back ward of a state hospital.

New ideas are often greeted with the label of abstruse theory and to some degree this is true. No new theory can have the organization and consistency within the conceptual system of what precedes it because it is new. Still, even though Dr. Ogden's theory will be strange to many readers, it gains substance and familiarity as he uses it as a basis of understanding for some very difficult moments with the patient.

All therapists would find the circumstances this patient created difficult to face without interventions. Therapists can go only so far in accommodating themselves to patients' psychopathology. In order to preserve their own sanity, analysts may be forced to impose some restrictions on manifestations of psychopathology.

The patient's offensive, malodorous condition was deeply disturbing to Dr. Ogden. When he discovered the adaptive significance of what the patient was doing, his attitude changed from irritation and annoyance to analytic interest. He was able to understand how his patient was struggling to maintain psychic equilibrium. He then could place this period of treatment in a sequence that could lead to the acquisition of higher structural levels. I might note that allowing such a sequence to develop is no easy task.

The author concluded that the patient was trying to "invade" him. The stench that he brought into the consultation room represented invasive elements within the patient, who was attempting to suffuse the therapist with them. Dr. Ogden explained this phenomenon on the basis of projective identification, a controversial formulation in light of the extremely primitive state of the patient. The reader can decide whether the therapist's formulation is satisfactory. It was satisfactory for Dr. Ogden and the treatment proceeded if not in an orderly sequence, in at least, an understandable one.

The editors of this volume believe that this crucial and decisive period of treatment depicted a mental state too primitive to make use of the relatively structured psychic mechanism of projective identification. For the patient, this phase of nonexperience may have represented a primordial merger involving amorphous levels antedating symbiotic fusion. After all, Dr. Ogden focuses upon the area of nonexperience, an area which would be located at the most primitive end of the developmental spectrum.

However, this is not to say that Dr. Ogden has misplaced the level in the structural hierarchy of his interaction with his patient during that period of treatment. Oftentimes in the treatment of severely regressed patients, the patient reacts at one level and the therapist's responses come from a higher level. This is well illustrated in Dr. Flarsheim's chapter in this volume. Dr. Ogden could have felt the patient's impact as a projection whereas the patient might have been trying to suffuse his poorly differentiated and incompletely separated external world in a global fashion. This differential between patient and analyst can become established as a foundation for psychic structuring. The distinction between projection and converting the external world into a reflection of the internal world, a much more diffuse phenomenon, might be a factor in Dr. Ogden's distinction of two types of transference.

In the past, clinicians working with such patients have been reluctant to disclose the results of their studies for fear of incurring the disapproval, if not the outright ridicule, of their colleagues. Fortunately, we have advanced from that medieval position. By revealing how he treated his patient, Dr. Ogden has enriched our clinical understanding of severely regressed states and, one hopes, has emboldened others to follow in his footsteps.

P. L. G.

Beginning with Freud, therapists and analysts have attempted to develop psychoanalytic formulations that encompass both the unique interpersonal phenomena encountered in treating schizophrenic patients and the peculiar shifts in these patients' psychological capacities ("the alterations in the ego": Freud [1937]). In the past, these attempts have tended to focus either on the content of the schizophrenic patient's conflicted thoughts and feelings (Arlow and Brenner 1969, Kubie 1967, Pao 1973), or on impairments in the schizophrenic's capacity for thought (Freeman 1970, London 1973a, b, Wexler 1971). In the present paper, clinicial phenomena encountered in the treatment of schizophrenia will be conceptualized in terms of an *interplay* between the schizophrenic patient's conflicted psychological content and his capacities to generate experience and thought.

The ability of schizophrenic patients to manage feelings within the psychological sphere of representations is frequently exhausted; when this happens, patients resort to primitive and pathological modes of defense that are outside the sphere of psychological representation. These modes are types of "actualization" of warded-off emotional content. The treatment of schizophrenic patients forms the clinical data base for an exploration of a unifying analytic formulation that addresses the way psychological representations are actualized both interpersonally and intrapersonally; this includes the way in which events in the psychological sphere of mental representations (e.g., fantasies) are played out, enacted, made actual, both in relation to other people and in relation to the patient's own mental capacities. The rationale for the content and timing of the therapist's interpretations and other processing of the clinical data will be formulated in terms of the framework of interpersonal and intrapersonal actualization.

THE CONCEPT OF ACTUALIZATION

The sphere of psychological representations is made up of thoughts, feelings, fantasies, memories, perceptions, and so forth, often in diffuse, inchoate, and archaic form. These thoughts, feelings, etc., are organized around sets of affectively charged self- and object-representations and constitute the realm of conscious and unconscious experience.

The nonrepresentational aspects of psychological life, that is, the sphere of psychological capacities, are in Freud's structural theory referred to as the id, ego, and superego functions and psychological structures. This sphere, which includes the capacity to perceive, to remember, to attach meaning to perception, to create, maintain, and process thoughts and feelings, exists independent of, but in direct relation to, the sphere of psychological representations. In fact, this sphere produces the thoughts, feelings, etc., that comprise the representational sphere.

In addition to the sphere of mental capacities and that of psychological representations, a third sphere that will be considered is that of other people existing outside of oneself. Although

other people can be given representation in a psychic representational sphere, they also continue to exist in their own right outside
of their depiction in that sphere.[1]

The sphere of psychological representations and meanings has
been treated by many analysts as the only sphere of reality to
which analytic conceptualizations ought to be applied (Benedek
1973, Ogden 1978b, Ornston 1978). As a result of its almost
exclusive emphasis on defensive shifts within the intrapsychic
sphere, analytic theory has developed very few concepts for examining the interplay between the different spheres of reality. For
instance, the concept of identification, formulated in terms of
modifications of one's self-representations in association with shifts
in one's system of motives and patterns of behavior (Schafer 1968),
addresses the intrapsychic sphere exclusively. This formulation
offers neither a framework with which to conceptualize the impact
of identification on its object nor a means of exploring how the
object's personality influences the identificatory process. The same
is true for the concept of projection, as traditionally formulated in
terms of disavowal of an aspect of oneself in association with the
attribution of the disowned qualities to an external object-
representation.

We cannot adequately understand many of the clinical phenomena encountered in the treatment of schizophrenia if our
conceptualizations deal separately with the intrapsychic sphere of
thoughts and feelings, the interpersonal sphere of relations with
other people, and the sphere of mental capacities. Instead, our
concepts must focus upon the dynamic interplay among these
spheres. A summary of the concept of projective identification may
help clarify the latter interaction.[2] This concept refers to the
interplay between the intrapsychic sphere of thoughts, feelings,
and fantasy, on the one hand, and the sphere of the other person,
on the other. The person projectively identifying (the "projector")
unconsciously fantasizes getting rid of an unwanted or endangered

[1]The relationship between the sphere of psychological representations and
one's physiological capacities (a fourth sphere of reality) is beyond the scope of
this paper.

[2]See Ogden (1979) for an extended discussion of projective identification; also
see chapters 2 and 4 of this volume.

aspect of the self by placing that self-aspect into another person in a powerfully controlling way. Moreover, the projector exerts real interpersonal pressure on the object (in fantasy, the "recipient") of the projective identification to take in the projection and behave in a manner congruent with the projective fantasy (Grinberg 1962).

When the object of a projective identification manages, "contains" (Bion 1967), and "processes" (Langs 1978) the induced thoughts and feelings in a more mature way than did the projector, the recipient's methods of handling the "ejected" thoughts and feelings become available for internalization by the projector via identification or introjection. On the other hand, if the recipient finds it necessary to resort to expulsion or annihilation of the induced feelings, the projector's identification with the recipient's rigidly defensive stance leads to further entrenchment of, or expansion of, the projector's pathology.

Projective identification must be differentiated from projection. The latter process can be described entirely in terms of shifts within the sphere of conscious and unconscious psychological representations: one's self- and object-representations are modified so that qualities formerly attribuied to a self-representation are disowned and attributed to an external object representation. In contrast, projective identification can only be described in terms of the psychology of two separate personality systems in relationship with one another. The projective fantasy of one person does not remain simply an alteration in the representational sphere of that person. In projection, the projector feels estranged from what has been attributed to the object, while in projective identification the subject unconsciously feels "at one with" (Schafer 1974, personal communication) the aspect of the self that he has, in fantasy, put "into" the other person. In projective identification, there is an effort to change the other person himself, rather than one's view of that person. This psychological-interpersonal process entails an effort to actualize the projective fantasy in the sphere of interpersonal reality.

From this view of projective identification, it is now possible to delineate further the meaning of actualization. Joseph Sandler's use of the term "actualization" is akin to my own; we both differ with Maslow (1968), for whom the term denoted a realization of one's potential. Sandler (1976a, b, Sandler and Sandler 1978) uses the term to mean "to make actual" or "to realize in action or fact." He feels that actualization is the process by which wish-fulfillment generally takes place. In particular, he believes that dreams entail hallucinatory actualization in which symbolic representations of wishes are experienced as real. In the interpersonal sphere, Sandler discusses role-actualization wherein wished-for roles found in one's unconscious object-representations are elicited from another person and in that sense made actual. My own use of the term (1980) overlaps Sandler's usage and includes the idea of realization in action or fact, but differs in that I refer specifically to the *transformation of an aspect of the representational sphere into a form that exists outside the representational sphere*. That is, an intrapsychic element such as a thought, feeling, or fantasy, either is enacted in the interpersonal sphere of real, other people, or produces changes in functioning in the nonrepresentational sphere of psychological and physiological capacities).[3] This view of actualization provides a means of unifying interactions between the representational sphere and the other spheres.

In considering whether it makes sense to speak of transformations between a representational sphere of thoughts and feelings and a nonrepresentational sphere of psychological capacities, the findings of psychosomatic medicine should be borne in mind. For example, the mutual influence of sets of thoughts and feelings, on the one hand, and the physiologic functioning of acid-secreting cells of the gastric mucosa, on the other, has been demonstrated both clinically and experimentally (Engel et al. 1956, Kehoe and Ironside 1963). Fantasies about the functioning of these cells (or

[3]One runs into difficulty if, like Sandler (1976a, b, 1978), one speaks of "psychological representations," e.g., in dreams or hallucinations, as actualizations of unconscious wishes. The fact remains that hallucinations and dream representations, however real they may feel, are still *thoughts*. I therefore limit the term "actualization" to those phenomena where events have been translated from the representational sphere into activity within a sphere outside of one's thoughts and feelings. A further distinction between Sandler's work and my own is that he does not discuss the fact that actualization of psychological representations may involve the sphere of psychological capacities.

about something "eating" or "burning" one from within) are commonly elaborated secondarily, but this is not a necessary component of the interplay between the representational and physiologic (nonrepresentational) spheres. I shall use the term "intrapersonal actualization" to refer to an analogous interplay between one's thoughts and feelings, on the one hand, and one's "nonrepresentational" psychological capacities, on the other.

One of the principal arenas in which the concept of intrapersonal actualization offers the basis for an important theoretical distinction is in the conceptual differentiation of neurotic and schizophrenic conflict (see Ogden 1980). Freud sometimes utilized a conflict model of schizophrenia (1894, 1895, 1896) and at other times leaned toward an ego defect model (1896, 1915c, 1926, 1937). My own theory of schizophrenic conflict was built on Freud's efforts to integrate his two models (1911, 1914a, 1915c, 1924a, b), as well as the contributions of Bion (1962a, 1967) and Grotstein (1977a, b). In my view (1980), any theory of schizophrenic conflict must clearly conceptualize the interplay between two levels: that of the psychological representations (including intrapsychic conflict) and that of the mental capacities (including the capacities to create and maintain psychological meanings and representations).

Neurotic-type conflict is based upon psychological operations in which conflicting sets of meanings (e.g., filial and sexual feelings experienced in relation to the same maternal object) are allowed to coexist in tension with one another. Such coexistence is possible because of defensive rearrangement of these meanings within the sphere of psychological representations. For example, filial feelings toward, and corresponding self- and object-representations of, a parent may remain conscious while sexually colored representations of the parent are rendered dynamically unconscious (e.g., by repression). This arrangement within the sphere of psychological representations does not alter the meanings involved (Freud 1915a). In neuroses, meanings are not destroyed; they are rearranged, disguised, removed from consciousness, isolated from affect, etcetera.

In contrast, schizophrenic conflict cannot be understood solely in terms of shifts and linkages of thought within the sphere of psychological representations. It must also be understood in terms of actualization that goes *beyond the sphere of psychological repre-sentations* and involves limitation of the capacity for experience and thought.

At its core, schizophrenic conflict involves a conflict between wishes to maintain a psychological state in which meanings can exist, and wishes to attack and destroy all meaning and ultimately to create a field of nonexperience (Ogden 1980). This latter set of wishes is enacted in the form of unconscious self-limitation of the capacities to create experience and to think. Nonexperience, a con-cept derived from Bion's work (1962a, 1967), refers to the failure to attach meaning to perception; it leaves one with raw sensory data that are not experienced.[4] This conflict over whether to destroy meaning or to allow its existence can be represented within the sphere of psychological representations. However, in schizophrenic conflict, the wishes to destroy meaning are actualized in the form of a real attack upon the ability to create and maintain experience and thought, resulting in an actual limitation of the capacity to attach meaning to perception, and to link thoughts to one another.

One cannot understand the nature of schizophrenic conflict if one blurs the distinction between fulfilling wishes via symbolic representation (what Sandler [1976a, b] misleadingly refers to as "symbolic actualization") and fulfilling them via enactment outside the representational sphere, such that the nonrepresentational reality of one's mental capacities becomes modified. When wishes to destroy meaning predominate, objects are perceived, but almost nothing is experienced or attributed emotional significance. That which is perceived remains undigested; the person is left with things in themselves, raw sensory data without meaning. When one's perceptions cannot be experienced, one cannot learn.

Although this state is common in schizophrenic regression, it has not been sufficiently discussed, partly because of the lack of a

[4]Freud (1920) introduced a similar model when he proposed that traumatic flooding of the psyche with stimuli is dealt with by means of "an anti-ca-thexis . . . on a grand scale, for whose benefit all the other psychical systems are impoverished so that the remaining psychical functions are paralyzed or reduced" (p. 30).

conceptual framework for it. The oft-used, pejorative term "burnt-out schizophrenic" entails a recognition, but not an understanding, of the fact that chronic schizophrenics very commonly evidence a state of psychological inertness, or what I have called "non-experience."

Recently, analysts treating very regressed patients have begun to describe related states. Giovacchini (1979, 1980) has discussed primitive, nonideational mental states as "prementational," more physiologic than psychological.[5] Green and Donnet (Donnet and Green 1973, Green 1975, 1977) observe an inert psychotic state that they refer to as a "blank psychosis"; Grotstein (1979) refers to a similar phenomenon as a state of psychotic "invisibility" or "nonbeing."

Understanding this state of nonexperience as an actualization of one pole of the schizophrenic conflict (i.e., an actualization of wishes to destroy the capacity for experience and thought) is quite different from saying that meanings have been rendered dynamically unconscious (e.g., by means of repression, splitting, denial, projection, displacement). All of the latter processes are rearrangements of meanings *within* the sphere of psychological representations and meanings; repressed meanings (thoughts and feelings) are maintained unconsciously and are experienced in derivative form (e.g., in dreams, slips, and symptoms). Actualization, on the other hand, entails interference with the very capacity to *create* and *maintain* meanings.

The differences in the technical implications of these formulations are considerable. If one imagines that a set of meanings is unconsciously maintained and understood by the patient, then one addresses oneself to the patient's resistance to becoming aware of

[5]Giovacchini (1980) views the "living vegetable"-like schizophrenic state as a reflection of early environmental failure that resulted in extensive fixation at the prementational phase of development, and later, in severe ego defects. In contrast, I view the nonexperiential state as the result of early pathogenic interactions that led to ego distortion in which ordinary defenses were exhausted and superseded by defenses that annihilated all—even sensory-level—meaning. In short, Giovacchini describes a fixation at sensory-level experience while I discuss defensive nonexperience.

these meanings. However, if one conceives of a set of meanings as not being allowed to exist, then one focuses on the patient's need to limit his or her capacity for experience and thought. In the latter case, one also must recognize that the value of verbally interpreting this need is limited until such time as sufficient symbolic representation of it has been achieved. One's notions of transference and resistance are significantly affected when attempting to incorporate concepts of interpersonal and intrapersonal actualization into clinical thought.

Case Presentation

Referral

Robert, age 22, was 19 when he was admitted to the long-term, analytically oriented hospital for treatment. He had experienced periods of hallucinations and paranoid delusions since early latency, but had managed to keep those experiences secret. He was born with a congenital degenerative disease of the retina (retinitis pigmentosa) that was not diagnosed until age 5, but which did not prevent him from reading slightly enlarged print until he was 12 years old. By age 16, he had lost most of his sight, except for perception of very large objects that were visualized as shadowy forms with almost no definition or color. Mental representation continued to be predominantly visual even after the loss of his sight. When brought to the hospital for admittance, Robert trembled continuously and his eyes were rolled back in their sockets so that only the murky white sclerae were visible. He was experiencing "visual" hallucinations of thousands of spiders surrounding him, some of which he felt entering his throat, stinging him, and suffocating him from within.

Family History

Robert was the only child of a progressively decompensating borderline schizophrenic mother and a father who became emotionally withdrawn soon after the patient's birth.[6] The patient's

[6]Extensive interviews were conducted with the patient's parents and other important figures in the patient's life. In the interest of confidentiality, it is necessary to leave unclear the specific sources of information for aspects of the history.

mother had a pattern of becoming intensely involved with a given view of herself and living out that view for extended periods of time lasting from six months to many years. She would then rapidly disengage herself from all her attachments and move on to another concept of herself in relation to a new set of people. Before marrying Robert's father, she had been married for about a year to a carnival parachute jumper; shortly after that marriage ended, she remarried a nationally known professor of theoretical physics. The second marriage ended after four years when Robert's mother became involved with the patient's father, a highly success-ful attorney. The patient's mother seemed to move quite easily from one marriage to another, in contrast to the extreme emotional distress suffered by her second husband. She seemed to immerse herself totally in each husband's life while their marriage lasted; then, when she changed partners, she abruptly shifted the terms of her own life. It was not that the previous person was actively rejected; he simply did not have a place in her new frame of reference. These frames of reference, terms, or meanings were the product of an elaborate system of internal fantasy that kept Robert's mother only marginally in touch with reality. Certain people found the patient's mother magnetically attractive at first and afterwards spoke of her bitterly, almost as if she were a witch with magically alluring powers that she used to hold them in her "spell."

The marriage to Robert's father was part of the mother's fantasy of "suburban life." They bought a home in the suburbs and owned two cars; she immersed herself in local women's activities and had a child (Robert) about a year and a half after the marriage. She continued breast feeding Robert for over a year, despite the fact that his teeth, which appeared early, cut into her nipples and gave her extreme pain and intermittent infection. Robert's father, whose withdrawal had begun following the birth, became even less avail-able and arranged to be away on business almost all of the time.

The patient's mother labored to be a "model mother" and, reportedly with phenomenal energy, devoted herself entirely to this task. In her words, she "threw herself into the baby" and attempted to anticipate his every desire. However, this was punctu-ated by periods of abrupt withdrawal when the mother became so involved in some other activity (dance classes, for instance) that she sometimes did not return home for several days, leaving 6-year-old Robert alone in the house.[7] In addition, the mother's ability to perceive the infant realistically and respond empathically to him was quite limited: his visual defect had been subtly present for at least two years before a friend of the family pointed it out to the patient's mother, and medical studies were performed when Robert was 5. As a small boy, Robert had a propensity to kiss with his mouth open in a way that left a mass of saliva on the face of the person being kissed; the patient's mother felt that this "French kiss" reflected premature, perverse sexuality. The infant's enthusiasm for a gift that the mother gave him resulted in extreme jealousy on her part and led her to view him as a "strangely materialistic child from the beginning."

The patient's first eight years were characterized by intermittent bouts of depressive withdrawal on the mother's part, during which time she would cry for most of the day. During one of these periods, she became involved in a lesbian relationship with a woman who moved into their home and remained for a year. The relationship ended abruptly when the other woman felt as if she were "drowning" and had handed over all capacity to think to Robert's mother. It was at the point of the breakup of this homosexual relationship that Robert's parents were divorced.

For the next ten years, Robert and his mother lived the lives of transients, moving from the guest room of a friend's home into a boarding house, remaining in that locale for a few months, and then moving to a similar setting in a new city or country. As mother and child shared a single room until Robert reached puberty, he was present during his mother's sexual relations with men and women.

Robert was rarely sent to school (even before the "wandering" began) and, by the time he was 18, had had only about four years of school, including tutoring. He learned to read and in latency spent much of his time alone with books in his room. As the patient's eyesight began to fail, he received no instruction in mobility, braille, or any other sort of training for the blind.

At about age 9, Robert experienced visual hallucinations and

[7]Her behavior is reminiscent of that of many Apache mothers (Boyer 1979).

delusions of spiders invading and suffocating him from inside his throat. He did not reveal these experiences to anyone and remained uniformly docile and compliant, never once inquiring into the reasons for all the moving. Beginning at about age 15, he spoke very little and, when he did speak, used single words or short phrases. Robert probably never had any sexual experience, including masturbation. His level of sexual understanding remained primitive and was dominated by a cloacal fantasy of the female anatomy.

Robert's father visited once or twice a year. When the patient was 18, the father noticed that he was subtly hostile toward his mother. Robert avoided his mother's presence and refused to eat meals with her. This led the father to believe that Robert might still be "salvageable" and he proposed having Robert come to live with him. The patient's mother was growing tired of the burden of taking care of Robert, whose rapidly worsening blindness was increasingly difficult to deny. By this time, she had become deeply involved with religious missionary work and lived with Robert in a primitive town in Greece.

Robert went to live with his father (who had not remarried) and was sent to a school for the blind. However, within a year after the move, the patient became floridly psychotic and was hospitalized. For three years, all contact between Robert and his mother ceased. Then she visited him for a few days when her missionary work caused her to return to America.

Therapy: First Clinical Phase

Robert was seen five times per week in individual psychotherapy. The initial months of treatment were marked by a steady deterioration of his mental state. Robert was initially able to give single-word replies to the therapist's questions to communicate aspects of the psychological collapse he was undergoing. Primarily, the patient felt under attack by spiders that he felt had surrounded him, infested his food, and entered his throat to sting him to death and suffocate him from within. He reported delusions of being drowned by his hospital roommate and of being blown apart by a bomb that had magically been placed inside him. His only statement regarding any member of his family was about his father, who was said to "haunt" him. During these sessions, Robert sat rigidly in his chair, trembling, with his eyes either fixed on some corner of the ceiling or entirely rolled into the upper vault of his skull.

Robert became increasingly withdrawn and mute. This was accompanied by a diminution of anxiety and a disappearance of manifest psychotic symptomatology. At times, I felt anxious about slipping into a "black hole" with the patient. For instance, I insistently asked questions about his symptoms in an effort to hold onto a disappearing thread of meaning and connectedness with him. However, verbal communication diminished and ultimately ceased, leaving me with a sense of extreme disconnectedness from the patient.

By the fourth month of therapy, the sessions had become very still and they remained so for the succeeding nine or ten months. Both my desperate attempts to hold onto the dwindling meaning and the vividness of the psychotic symptomatology were over. While I did not feel that the absence of florid psychotic symptomatology indicated progress, I no longer felt anxious about slipping into something unknown and dangerous. There was a timeless quality to the treatment that left me devoid of a sense of urgency to do anything or make anything particular happen. The notions of cure, progress, improvement, and helping the patient were not a part of my emotional vocabulary in this period of therapy.

Long hours of silence seemed neither interesting nor oppressive during these months. Over these stretches of time, I observed the other person sitting in my office. I watched the patient use his cane to cross the room, lightly touch the foot of the chair with it, pivot on one foot, drop like a dead weight into the chair, and sink into the cushion. He then would recover from his fall, adjust himself in the chair, and shift his gaze from one lightbulb to another. Finally, he would adjust the position of the cane next to his chair.

Robert, a tall, lanky adolescent with almost shoulder-length red hair, could not be identified as blind by his appearance. I wondered about the patient's relatively healthy-looking eyes. I wondered what could the patient see. How much fluctuation in visual capacity existed? The patient had dandruff and inch-long facial hair, not dense enough to constitute a beard. When it rained, he came to the office drenched and sat lifelessly in his chair in his wet, clinging clothing. I was not moved to take any action to remedy this and was aware that I felt less compassion for him than I would have felt with someone else under similar circumstances.

The patient's verbal productions were rare, lifeless, and mechanical. He answered questions and made statements using short, high stereotypic phrases that were usually repetitions of others' ideas. For instance, after the death of a senior member of the hospital staff, I asked Robert how he had taken the news. He answered with a mechanical repetition of several words that other patients had used in the community meeting just prior to the session.

Robert demonstrated almost infinite compliance. Changes in appointment time, vacations, changes in the therapy office, changes in roommates—all were absorbed without question and without observable change in his behavior or demeanor. Again, when asked about his feelings concerning any of these events, his reply merely echoed the language of the questioner or someone else (e.g., "Did you feel angry about being pushed by Fred?" "Felt angry.") The robotlike tone of his replies left me feeling that there was no genuine connection between the language used and the feeling state that the words denoted. I had no inclination to pursue such replies with further questions, as I had done in the earliest months of treatment.

The patient slept for portions of the sessions, sometimes lying back in his chair and sometimes stretched out on the floor. After ten or fifteen minutes, I would awaken him and ask him to remain awake for the rest of the session. To me, Robert did not look like an infant when he slept, as did other patients who slept during parts of their sessions. Rather, I saw Robert as not fully human, as some type of creature whose behavior was neither threatening nor endearing. When Robert came to the office in drenched clothing and shook the water from himself, it was very much like watching someone else's dog shaking water from its fur.

In contrast to my experience with other borderline and schizophrenic patients, I noted that Robert showed no evidence of perceiving, or in any way responding to, the variety of conscious and unconscious wishes and needs that I recognized or retrospectively came to recognize in myself (cf. Ogden 1976, 1978a, Searles 1975). I did not feel that Robert was withholding something; rather, I sensed that he could not know what (if anything) he was feeling and therefore had no means of responding to my emotional state.

This phase of therapy represented "the phase of nonexperience," which is characterized by a virtual absence of mental activity on the part of the patient and a corresponding absence of interpersonal meanings. The patient's total compliance and robotlike responses were modes of behavior reflecting an internal "shutdown" of attribution of meaning to perception, as well as an almost total absence of thought. This state of nonexperience is partially describable in terms of what is absent in the mental activity and behavior of the patient; but, equally important, one becomes aware of a therapeutic phase of nonexperience by what is absent in the therapist's response to the patient. I did not feel repulsed by or attracted to Robert. With others in similar circumstances, I might feel compassionate, fatherly, frustrated, and so on, but in a phase of nonexperience, the therapist merely notices and observes. I did not feel that my existence was actively denied; I was merely noticed and that was the extent of it.

I did not attempt to interpret the meaning of the patient's behavior. Rather, Robert's behavior was understood as an actual shutdown of the capacity to create experience and think. Attempts at interpretation would entail a denial on my part of the way everything in the patient's life had been rendered meaningless to him. Although a phase of nonexperience superficially resembles a state of catatonia, the countertransference in the former lacks the tension, rage, and fear experienced with a patient in catatonic withdrawal. Catatonia is a defense mustered against intensely affect-laden meanings (often omnipotent rage). Schizophrenics in a phase of nonexperience have gone beyond defensive management of meanings; they have actualized wishes to destroy meaning by limiting their capacity to attach meaning to internal and external perception.

From the perspective of the schizophrenic conflict over whether to allow meaning to exist, the phase of nonexperience is a psychological state in which there is an overwhelming ascendancy of wishes to destroy meaning. These wishes are actualized in the form of the self-limitation of mental capacities. The therapist's tolerance of the long periods of silence and the absence of discernible mental activity is not a reflection of the therapist's heroic capacity to endure pain; rather, this phase of therapy, which is marked by its peculiar lack of interpersonal pressure of any kind, requires specific psychological work on the therapist's part to prevent a defensive denial of the patient's state.

Despite the fact that I did not communicate my ideas about the patient's apparent lack of mental activity to him, the formulations I made for myself were an essential aspect of the treatment. The principal "silent interpretation" (Spotnitz 1969) of this period consisted of statements to myself about the unusual and often disconcerting impact of being with someone who had dealt with his psychological pain by completely preventing anything or anyone from having meaning for him, or to be thought about. If the patient were regressing, I would have made formulations about his opposition to awareness of meanings that continued to exist unconsciously. But this patient was not hiding something from himself; rather, he had limited his power to know and to think. Previous meanings were not denied; they remained raw data, things in themselves that had no emotional significance for him. Even meaninglessness and nonthought were not experienced by the patient; absolutely nothing was experienced.

Such silent interpretations, derived from my awareness of the countertransference, allowed me to refrain from making interpretations that would have been appropriate for a catatonic patient, but, as I maintain, countertherapeutic for a schizophrenic in a phase of nonexperience. Repeated interpretations offered in a phase of nonexperience usually represent defensive activity that prevents the therapist from being open to serving as a container for the patient's projective identifications, if and when they begin to occur.

Deep schizophrenic withdrawal has, until now, been formulated largely in terms of regression in the transference to the earliest, most undifferentiated phase of human experience (Katan 1979). Searles (1963) discusses types of transference symbiosis in which patient treats the analyst not as a person or even as a part object, but as an undifferentiated "matrix" (that is external at some level) out of which the patient's own ego may become differentiated (p. 663).

Margaret Little's discussion (1958) of the delusional transference in work with schizoid patients focuses upon the regression to an absolutely undifferentiated phase of development in which "subject and object, all feeling, thought, and movement, are experienced as the same thing. That is to say, there is only a *state of being* or of experiencing, and no sense of there being a *person*; e.g., there is only an anger, fear, love, movement" (p. 135).

Balint (1968) terms the most regressed phase of treatment the phase of "the harmonious interpenetrating mix-up" in which therapists are treated as if they were an undestructible primary substance, like air: "It is difficult to say whether the air in our guts is us or not us; and it does not even matter. We inhale the air, take out of it what we need, and after putting into it what we do not want to have, we exhale it and we do not care at all whether the air likes it or not" (p. 136).

Rosenfeld (1952) similarly described the most deeply regressed phase of treatment of chronic schizophrenia as one in which patients "confuse" themselves with the therapist. This confusion is understood to result from powerful oral incorporative fantasies operating simultaneously with fantasies of entering inside the object.

Each of these analysts has attempted to describe the transference *experience* of a psychologically undifferentiated state using different language and imagery. These formulations differ markedly from the one I am proposing, in that I believe the first clinical phase is characterized by an almost total absence of experience, including the primitive experience of "basic unity" (M. Little 1958).

Building upon the work of Bion (1959, 1962a, 1967) and Grotstein (1977a, b, Malin and Grotstein 1966) I would suggest that transference repetition of the undifferentiated phase of development only partially accounts for the phenomena of the clinical phase of nonexperience. I would understand this type of schizophrenic withdrawal in terms of a revival of a *pathological* early state of partial differentiation from the mother in which the infant's projective identifications were inadequately contained by the mother. Ordinarily, with "good enough" mothering (Winnicott 1951), the infant develops the capacity to experience and contain his own thoughts and feelings by inducing corresponding feelings in the mother, who allows these feelings to "repose" (Bion 1959) in her. When the mother is capable of "reverie" (containment of the infant's projected feeling state), a modified version of the original feeling is reinternalized and experienced by the infant in a meaningful way. In this way, the infant develops the capacity to attach meaning to perception in a way that allows raw sensory data (internal and external) to be experienced.

When the mother is unable or unwilling to be a container for the infant's projective identifications, any rudimentary meaning attached to the infant's projected feeling state is drained away by the mother's denial of the infant's feelings. For example, let us imagine that an infant who has begun to differentiate between outside and inside is in extreme discomfort because his diaper is wet and cold. He kicks and screams under the pressure of the abrasive stimulation on his skin. In the first months of life, the infant begins to organize perceptions (raw sensory data) into the rudiments of an inchoate experience, which is communicated to the mother through the quality of the infant's cry, muscle tone, body movements, facial expression, feeding and excretory activity, breathing, etcetera. In our example, the infant's kicking and screaming communicate his fear, anger, and outrage over his situation, which he expects to be immediately and magically rectified.

Let us say that the mother of this infant is struggling with her own ambivalent feelings toward the infant, including her unresolved, unconscious murderous wishes. She may accurately deduce the physical source of the infant's discomfort, but rigidly close herself off from emotional recognition of the infant's feelings of anger, fear, and outrage.[8] Thus she may change the infant's diaper efficiently but mechanically, and may fail to offer herself as a container in which the infant's primordial rage can be rendered meaningful. When this happens, the infant's anger and fear are denied and returned to him stripped of meaning. What had formerly constituted the elements of the experience of pain-induced rage and fear is reduced to a signal for the initiation of mechanical activity. In this way, the very earliest experience that the infant is able to generate is stripped of meaning.[9]

The mother's denial of the infant's projective identifications is experienced as an attack on the principal linkage between mother and infant (Bion 1967). The linkage-attacking mother is internalized and serves as the model for the schizophrenic's defensive response to unacceptable reality. What begins as a transference repetition of a schizophrenic's experience with a linkage-attacking mother becomes less and less an interpersonal transference state as the schizophrenic's attack generates a phase of nonexperience in which even the meaninglessness itself and the psychological catastrophe it represents are not experienced. The transference repetition entails progressive limitation of the capacity for experience that eventually results in a state so devoid of meaning that it is questionable whether it still can be thought of as a transference phenomenon with all of the intrapsychic and interpersonal meanings that transference signifies.

Therapy: Second Clinical Phase

For almost a year, the sessions with Robert had settled into the described routine and had become entirely predictable; there were

[8]When mothering is "good enough," this process of attribution of meaning to the infant's perceptions occurs unconsciously and unobtrusively. The mother's subsequent handling of the infant and his environment communicates her unconscious equivalent of the therapist's accurate interpretation.

[9]Winnicott (1956) refers to the mother's capacity to contain the infant's projective identifications as her ability to "feel herself into the infant's place" (p. 304). He describes the stripping of meaning as follows: "After a persistence of failure of the external object, the internal object fails to have the meaning to the infant, and then . . . the transitional object becomes meaningless, too" (1951, p. 237).

long periods of silence, the patient shifting in his chair, occasional naps on the floor of the office, and brief statements of fact without elaboration or detectable fantasy content. The patient's blindness seemed so in keeping with the level of his capacity that I no longer thought of him as blind. He had a numbing effect on me, but only in retrospect did I realize how dull we had allowed our powers of perception to become during our first year of work as a result of the almost total absence of discernible mental activity on his part.

Over a period of several months, a series of subliminally perceptible changes occurred in Robert's personal hygiene. His hair, which had grown to shoulder length, became greasier and greasier; large, oily, white flakes of dandruff collected throughout his scalp and over his forehead. The office took on a foul odor that I had been only dimly aware of previously, but which I now felt was assaultive. A powerful stench wafted after the patient as I followed him into the office at the beginning of each session. Stunned by the deterioration of the patient's personal hygiene, I wondered why I had not been alert to it previously and grew very anxious about finding a means to resolve the problem, I stared at Robert and noticed, not for the first time but in a decidedly different way, that Robert's face was coated with a thin layer of dirt and grease. I noticed flecks of food in his inch-long facial hair. His clothes were covered with stains and layers of caked-on food, some of which remained on my chair and carpet after each session. I now viewed the chairs as property of mine that was being abused by the patient. I had never felt such keen feelings of ownership of the furniture. As Robert leaned back in his chair, my muscles tightened as I watched him grind his filthy hair into the back cushion. Impelled by a great sense of urgency to correct this situation, I asked him why his hygiene had deteriorated so dramatically. He did not reply and I experienced this lack of response as defiance, whereas previously I had had no such impression when he did not respond to questions.

The patient's behavior made me feel out of control, and I wanted him to stop doing whatever it was that was bothering me. In the past, I had found some relief from similar interpersonal tension by analyzing such situations in terms of projective identification. However, at present, such attempts to understand the situation seemed overly intellectual and of limited value in helping me extricate myself from the maelstrom into which I felt myself being drawn.

I was further enraged when the patient's odor worsened and permeated the chair cushion, which emitted a stench even after he had left the office. I washed the pillow several times over the next weeks with different types of solvent, but to no avail. I became so preoccupied with the patient's odor that I found myself changing seats in restaurants and movie theaters in order to avoid people with odors that reminded me of Robert. Initially, he resisted every pressure placed upon him by the hospital staff to bathe. Finally, he consented to shower daily, but did so in such a perfunctory manner that the improvement was minimal.

I seethed as I watched him sitting in "his" chair and felt that the patient, with his ability not to think, was far better equipped for this kind of silent struggle than I was. I imagined that the patient's blindness was an additional aid in insulating him from my anger as I scrutinized his food-flecked face and grease-laden hair. During one of these sessions, a loud ambulance or police car siren passed by and the patient, not unexpectedly, said, "A siren." He then chuckled and added "They're coming to get you, to lock you up." After a long pause, he added, "You're surrounded." This was the first instance of verbalized fantasy activity since the early psychotic symptomatology. I felt momentary relief from the pressure of the interpersonal struggle and said, "You mean invaded, don't you?" The patient smiled but did not reply. Over the next year, each time he heard a siren (which was at least once a week), he would say, "They're gonna come in and get you."

With the help of the patient's verbalized fantasy material and the atmosphere of the somewhat lowered interpersonal tension, I could begin more fully to understand aspects of the nature and meaning of the interaction centering on the patient's odor. I was finally able to free myself from operating within the rigidly limited range of thoughts, feelings, and self- and object-representations that I had confined myself to for some time. Gradually, I was able to formulate more accurately the meaning of what had been transpiring between the patient and myself. As this occurred, I found that Robert's odor no longer had the same powerfully engaging and infuriating impact on me. The odor was still unpleasant, but I no longer felt the need to escape from it.

Over the next two or three months, the patient's personal hygiene improved, more because he lost interest in being filthy than because he acquired new skills. Also during this period, further fantasy material consistently reflected the centrality of the theme of invasive, suffocating attack. The early hallucinations of spiders invading and suffocating him from within his throat,[10] as well as the fears/delusions of being drowned by his roommate and "haunted" by his father, could all now be seen as vivid confirmation of the patient's consuming feeling of being invaded and suffused.

I came to view this phase of therapy as having begun with the rapid deterioration of Robert's personal hygiene to the point that his odor became a vehicle for the interpersonal actualization of an unconscious fantasy (i.e., a vehicle for projective identification). The fantasy involved the idea of ejecting into the therapist the feeling of being permeated by, and suffocatingly intertwined with, another person. I was pressured to experience myself as contaminated by and suffused with the invasive quality of the patient,

---

[10]Freud (reported by Abraham, 1922) was the first of many analysts interested in spider symbolism to draw attention to the biological fact that female spiders during sexual union frequently kill the male by forcefully fastening him in her grip and sucking his body contents until only a lifeless shell remains. In the analytic literature, the spider has been understood to symbolize the frightening, castrating, phallic mother (Abraham, 1922) and, in particular, the danger of loving and being loved by the mother in the oral phase of development (R. Little 1966, 1967, Sterba 1950). In what is to date the most comprehensive psychoanalytic study of spider symbolism, Graber (1925) states that in mythology, legends, dreams, and symptomatology, the spider symbolizes both death and sexuality, which are equated with one another. The death that the spider brings is the "death of love." In the case under discussion, the spider is understood to represent a particular facet of the danger inherent in the earliest form of relatedness to the mother, namely, the danger involved in symbiotic union. The spiders surrounding the patient and suffocatingly entering his throat represent the mother of late symbiosis, who is alluring and yet threatens to haunt and suffuse the patient (or be suffused by him) to the point that the two dissolve into one another—thus annihilating the patient as a separate entity.

symbolized by his odor. Under this pressure, I feared that my possessions (with which I had become closely identified) had been permanently and destructively infiltrated by him. Unable successfully to contain and integrate the induced feelings, I felt overwhelmed by these feelings and driven to escape from them. In Robert's mind, it was not enough for me to understand what it was *like* to be suffused. His primitive wish was for me *to be Robert, to be suffused myself.* The patient's omnipotent fantasy was to inhabit and control me and, in this way, be known by me. In addition, he hoped that I might also be able to contain a hated and destructive part of himself.

Nonverbal transference enactments in conjunction with the associated countertransference states were important sources of data for this formulation. In a predominantly nonverbal phase of therapy, it is necessary to rely heavily on such data. Interactions and communications in later, more verbally symbolic, stages of therapy provide data that can confirm or invalidate the earlier formulations. For instance, looking ahead to the third year of therapy, (fourth clinical phase), Robert experienced a circumscribed psychotic regression. By this time, he had made significant advances in self-object differentiation and in the capacity to use words to represent ideas and feelings. At that point, Robert was able to symbolize in words aspects of the state of symbiotic fusion that had been enacted interpersonally in the projective identification of his odor.

During a psychotic regression in the third year, Robert began to feel that I was "haunting" him. He experienced auditory hallucinations of my voice as intertwined and "blended" with the sound and feel of his own thoughts. At moments of greater differentiation, he felt angry at me for "haunting" him. He vomited after four sessions in which he experienced such hallucinations. As Robert regressed further, he said that he felt that his head had been chopped off ("like an atom being split") and that his "haunted head" felt as if it were haunting me. He initially reported that I was able to see only out of his eyes. Then I became indistinguishable from the split-off, haunted head. The patient's rebellion against being suffused, or haunted, was clearly symbolized in his fantasy of splitting off and projecting the haunted aspect of himself. Moreover, he fantasized that the suffused self (the haunted head) was deposited into me in a way that at first controlled him and then merged with him.

In the course of discussing these feelings and ideas with him, I commented that he had had almost identical feelings earlier in the treatment when his odor had filled the office. The patient admitted that he had felt something very similar during that period, but added that he "wasn't a person then." Now he felt more like a person but was "afraid of becoming nobody if his head is chopped off too many times and haunts too many people." Thus, Robert verbalized his fears of losing himself in the form of a fantasized ejection of his suffused self into the therapist. He also made reference to fears that he would again attempt to become nonexistent in order to escape conflicted feelings related to being suffused. At this point in the therapy, such fears could be represented in words, whereas previously such ideas could only be enacted interpersonally, in the form of projective identification (the second clinical phase), or intrapersonally, via limitation of his mental capacities (the first phase of therapy).

Therapy: Third Clinical Phase

In the middle of the second year of therapy, Robert evidenced signs of mounting anxiety that quickly developed into a stage of paralyzing fear. When asked about it, he would simply say that the cause was "being with you." Robert again arrived at his sessions trembling, with his eyes rolled back into their sockets so that only the white sclerae were visible. When I inquired further into the basis of his extreme fearfulness, he tried to answer but almost immediately became blocked. He frequently turned his head rapidly in one direction or another in what I inferred (and what was later confirmed) to be a response to visual hallucinations. These hallucinations were later called "black and white forms" and consisted of a cluster of tormenting shapes that the patient felt were separate living remnants of a shattered face.

As the blocking continued, his failed attempts at speech appeared to become more and more painful. For the first time in eighteen months, he experienced anxiety. Not only was he now able to observe and attach words to this feeling state, but he also could begin to conceive of feelings as responses to other people. I viewed this development in the context of a progression in the transference from an initial phase of defensive nonexperience, to a symbiotic phase characterized by management of feelings through projective identification, to the present capacity to experience and observe his anxiety about being with me. On the basis of this understanding of the first eighteen months of work, I gradually offered the interpretation that he had begun to allow himself to think and to experience feelings. In short, simple sentences, I stated that he thought these activities (thinking and feeling) made him vulnerable to pain from which he had formerly fled by attempting to prevent himself from experiencing anything at all. Now that he dared to have his own thoughts and feelings, he found it extremely frightening to be with another person, his therapist.

In each session in which I offered a part of this interpretation, he grew visibly calmer. His trembling steadily declined, his eyes returned to a flexible, forward gaze, his muscle tension decreased markedly, and his blocked attempts at speech ceased. I became aware of a definite quality of childlike softness about the patient which I had not noticed before. As I offered these comments and observed his responses to them, I experienced rather intense feelings of pleasurable closeness and maternal protectiveness. For the first time, I had fantasies of "curing" him. When he began to speak in a more sustained way, I imagined that his voice sounded just like mine.

During one anxious session, the patient quite unexpectedly said in a thin, muffled voice, "Your voice sounds like mine." He would not elaborate on this comment. I was surprised by the fact that Robert also seemed to be thinking about the relationship between the sound of his voice and mine. Long periods of silence followed and then, again unexpectedly, the patient asked, "Are you crazy?" (Another patient had accused me of being crazy in a community meeting that Robert had attended earlier that same day.) I replied, "So, you think I might be crazy." The patient smiled one of his rare but warm smiles and said, "Only when you talk." When asked more about my craziness, Robert said, "Your crazy talk is not as crazy as me." It became clear over the next several sessions that he took great pleasure in the idea of my being crazy in my "own special way" and that he equated the sound of my voice with a kind of craziness that had a profoundly calming effect on him.

A pattern developed over the next few weeks wherein Robert became extremely frightened between sessions and telephoned me as often as a half-dozen times a day, including weekends. He would say nothing, not even hello, but would wait for me to speak. When I finally said something, his anxiety diminished immediately. This type of interaction, which was repeated within the therapy hours as well, made it clear that Robert experienced my speech as powerfully soothing.

I told Robert that he believed I could rid him of his craziness by transporting his painful thoughts into my own mind, where I would then render them harmless by putting them into words. He immediately responded, "Well, can't you?" I laughed and said, "Perhaps you and I might sometimes wish that were so. Fortunately, or unfortunately, we each have our own thoughts and feelings that we have to live with."

Following this session, the phone calls continued but changed markedly in quality. Robert began to use the phone calls playfully, identifying himself as "Dr. Zhivago." In part, this was a humorous parody of my name, but it also represented a symbolic verbal statement of wished-for oneness with the healing aspects of a therapist. The playfulness then gave way of humorless, relentless intrusiveness as the frequency of the calls increased. I interpreted to the patient his growing awareness of, and resentment about, his separateness from me. At that point, the telephone calls stopped.

I offered verbal interpretations for the first time during this phase of therapy. The patient gave some evidence of a capacity for causative, verbally symbolized thought. "Being with you" was iden- tified by him as the source of anxiety. He attempted to use speech and symbolic thought to master his anxiety. In my initial interpre- tation, I formulated his upsurge of psychotic symptomatology as a reflection of the strain arising from his efforts to contain his experience and thought. Observation of the patient's responses to the initial interpretation, as well as analysis of the countertransference, led to the second group of interventions, which concerned his illusion of curative focal merger. (This illusion had emerged in response to the initial interpretation.)

My partial "belief" in the illusion that my mind and voice could absorb and render safe his insanity is analogous to the "good enough" mother's "belief" in the illusion of the magically comforting powers of the transitional object (Winnicott 1951). Although the mother's belief in the transitional object is genuinely felt, it is not a delusion; nor is it violently forced upon her by the infant. She believes because the infant believes, and both are on their way to no longer believing. Neither the infant's mother in the transitional object stage nor the therapist in the third clinical phase of therapy experience their respective illusions as assaults on their hold on reality; rather, these partially shared illusions are smoothly integrated into the ordinary functioning of their larger personality systems.

Therapy: Fourth Clinical Phase

As the therapy progressed, three concurrent developments were observed to be proceeding: (1) Robert's capacity to contain his thoughts and feelings expanded, which led to more frequent periods of anxiety that he was increasingly able to define and symbolize verbally; (2) Robert's reliance on projective identification as a mode of communication, form of defense, and type of interpersonal relatedness diminished; and (3) I more frequently verbalized aspects of formerly "silent" interpretations.

Toward the end of the second year of therapy, Robert evidenced a dramatic change in his behavior and psychological state. Within the space of several weeks, he talked incessantly, but not in a pressured way. He found interest and excitement in almost every detail of life, particularly in the varieties of emotion that could arise between himself and others. For the previous two years, Robert's verbalizations had been restricted almost entirely to very brief phrases or sentences, which he spoke softly, indistinctly, and with very little affect. The sound of Robert's voice in sustained speech had been unknown to me until this time. Now the patient talked almost without interruption for entire sessions at a time. I felt as if Robert were introducing himself, despite the fact that he and I had spent more than five hundred hours alone together over the previous two years. He did not talk directly about the changes that had occurred in him, but I was invited to participate in what felt like a celebration, I commented again and again on the sound of his voice, which had become a symbol of his separateness and capacity for independent thought and behavior. (In retrospect, I can see that this symbol actually developed over the entire course of the therapy.)

In his interactions with other people, Robert would determine their job, role, or position, and then insist that they behave in conformity with that definition. Braille bus routes, train schedules, and street maps became a focus of intense interest, and then a source of pride, as he became an "authority" on these matters. Emotions and judgments were given shadings, subtlety, and complexity that they had lacked previously. His capacity to learn in a school setting increased so dramatically that within several months he was able to take remedial classes five days a week at a local community college while living at a halfway house.

His continuous verbiage frequently became a drone that no longer seemed to be used to communicate ideas. Similarly, questions addressed to me very often were not intended to elicit thoughts or information; instead, the questions were rhetorical and he did not even pause long enough for me to respond.

Interactions with others were initiated primarily for the pleasure of discovering what kind of jam or fix he could create; he used the other person almost as a painter would use a set of paints to create various textures and colors. For example, Robert immersed himself in vigorous campaigning (telephone canvasing and leaflet distributing) in support of a state referendum that he neither favored nor fully understood.

I sometimes was used as one of these "sets of paints," but more often was used as an audience to whom he would present unedited, verbatim recollections of the ordinary day-to-day events that he now found so pleasurable. He seemed to feel that it would be a shame to experience these events only once. Robert recounted and demonstrated feelings of self-righteous outrage, sage cynicism,

condescending pity, etcetera, and seemed to enjoy a sense of freedom and excitement in all of this. He frequently demonstrated
arrogance in his relations with other people; this sometimes
reached the point of almost ludicrous disregard for the feelings,
rights, and property of others.

He experienced a feeling of "power" accruing from his newly
achieved level of self-definition and autonomy. For example, in the
initial school classes, he would demand that a certain topic be
covered on a given day and, if the teacher refused to comply, he
would leave the class, syaing, "If you're not going to teach me what
I need to learn, I don't have to stay and waste my time." As I
listened to accounts of this sort of behavior again and again, I
became firmly aware of the fact that for the first time Robert had it
fully within his power to flee from therapy if he so chose. It was
not unrealistic to feel that there was some risk of this occurring if
his fear of his own wishes to re-enter symbiotic dependency became too intense. However, I knew that my anxiety over the
patient's power to flee from therapy also reflected my own, as well
as the patient's reluctance to give up the illusion of mutual ownership involved in the symbiotic transference and countertransference.

Clearly, he had begun to form an object tie to me. This was
particularly evident just before breaks in therapy. He treated my
suggestion that he was disappointed and angry about my upcoming
vacation as ridiculous. Yet upon leaving the therapy hours during
this period, Robert used his cane to hit the back of a city bus as it
pulled out from the bus stop. When I vacationed, he loudly and
repeatedly proclaimed his vast relief at being free of the burden of
his daily appointments. At the same time, he openly and sadistically taunted my more poorly integrated patients (who lived in the
same halfway house) by constantly reminding them of my absence.

Some months later, Robert first reported memories of childhood
events. Emanating an intense sense of secretiveness, he would
reveal only one memory fragment in a session and then cut himself
off by stating that that was all I was going to learn about him. The
most guarded of these secrets, memories of his mother, were
consciously disguised and censored before being revealed and were

permeated by feelings of intense protectiveness from fantasized condemnation by me. Also for the first time, he began openly to acknowledge his blindness, although anxiety, fearfulness, the feeling of the unfairness of it, etcetera, were all conspicuously absent from his matter-of-fact references to his progressive loss of sight. However, his cane, which he now used to hit every telephone pole and lamp post that he passed, had by this time had its tip and handle broken while its shaft was becoming increasingly mangled.

This phase of therapy portrayed the unmistakable quality of an advance to a new level of psychological organization and interpersonal relatedness. Robert experienced a combination of the strain of erecting a form of manic defense[11] and the genuine excitement of Mahler's "practicing subphase" of separation-individuation (1972), wherein the infant becomes "intoxicated with its own faculties and with the greatness of the world."

As in previous stages, aspects of the increasingly ambivalent symbiotic transference continued alongside the accumulated gains in the achievement of differentiated object relatedness. Earlier themes of invading and being invaded by other people (or parts of self and object) now took the form of the patient's active interpersonal intrusiveness, which was enacted primarily with words in the context of more differentiated object relations. However, in this phase, the limitation of the capacity to attribute meaning to past and present experience (including painful experience) was significantly lifted. The patient felt free after years of self-imposed sensory deprivation. He seemed to rediscover feelings, especially those arising from interactions with others. He experienced immense satisfaction in delineating and clarifying the details, boundaries, and shading of self- and object-representations and the relations between them.

---

[11]The term *manic defense* refers to an unconscious effort to defensively ward off depressive feelings of loss, dependency, and vulnerability. This is achieved by means of assertions of control over and contempt for others. If the other person is felt to be controlled, then one cannot be deserted by him; if the other person is seen as despicable, then his loss does not matter (Klein 1940, Segal 1964).

Equally important was his increased capacity to experience and contain painful thoughts and feelings. His earlier mode of defense had taken the form of massive "shutdown" of the capacity to endow present and past perceptions with meaning, with the result that all perceptions existed as raw sensory data, things in themselves that were not experienced. In the stage of nonexperience, feelings and thoughts concerning my vacations, Robert's blindness, and memories of Robert's mother were not defended against by means of removal from conscious awareness (e.g., denial or repression), by being disguised as their opposites (e.g., reaction formation, idealization, or manic defense), by being attributed to another person (e.g., projection or displacement), or by other rearrangements of meaning within the sphere of psychological representation. Such defenses involve rendering the painful meanings dynamically unconscious; as Freud (1915a) pointed out, this is never an entirely successful procedure. Inevitably and inescapably, the unconscious meaning is experienced in some derivative form (e.g., in dreams, symptoms, slips, involuntary modifications of behavior, or inexplicable or overly intense feeling states). The hallmark of the phase of nonexperience resulting from limitation of the capacity to attribute meaning to present and past perceptions is the absence of such derivatives. Meanings are not disguised or removed from awareness; instead, experience is denuded of meaning and the process of generating new meanings is paralyzed. Without meanings, there can be no derivative meanings.

In contrast, in the last phase of therapy described, the fact that Robert's limitation of his capacity to attribute meaning to painful past and present perceptions had been lifted to some extent, was reflected in his prominent use of denial, displacement, projection, and isolation of affect in relation to separation from me, his blindness, and memories of his mother. Although he vehemently denied that my vacation meant anything to him save welcome relief, derivatives of his unconsciously maintained meanings (mental representations of Robert and myself colored by feelings of anger and loss) were evident in his violent attack on the departing bus and in the way he relentlessly and sadistically reminded "weaker" minded "weaker" patients of my absence. Similarly, his matter-of-ment of his blindness, along with the mangling of his cane, reflected the fact that his anger at being blind had not been denuded of meaning and continued to exist in the psychological sphere, albeit in a form in which affect was isolated from conscious thought. Moreover, Robert's hostile feelings toward his mother were no longer emptied of meaning. They were managed by means of displacement and projection (as opposed to projective identification) onto me, indicating that he could use defenses within the representational sphere effectively. I could now draw Robert's attention to these derivatives in what was becoming more of a joint effort (of two separate people) to understand the patient's present and past experience. However, his use of defensive operations within the representational sphere had not entirely supplanted his efforts to defend by destroying meaning and thought. In this regard, his droning can be viewed as representative of an unconscious effort to drain language of its symbolic and communicative value.

IMPLICATIONS FOR CLINICAL THEORY

There are important consequences of the distinctions I have made between shifts within the representational sphere and changes involving actualization beyond the sphere of psychological representation. Many psychoanalytic concepts have been defined exclusively in terms of changes within the representational sphere and, as a result, fail to include facets of the phenomena they address that lie beyond that sphere. The classical view of transference (Freud 1912, 1914b, 1915b) focuses on the modification of the patient's psychic representation of the analyst (or another person) in congruence with features of the conscious and unconscious representation of an internalized past object relationship. The patient displaces and projects feelings and ideas derived from previous significant relationships (often from childhood) onto present object-representations (Moore and Fine 1968, Rycroft

1973). Giovacchini states that "The essence of transference in psychoanalysis is the projection of the infantile, or relatively infantile, elements onto the mental representation of the therapist" (1975, p. 15). Thus, transference has been formulated in terms of the mental operations of one person, i.e., as an intrapsychic event. A person alone in a room can project (or displace) feelings derived from a previous relationship onto an imaginary person (or hallucinated image), a movie star, a political figure, a personified government agency (for example, the FBI), and so on. This conception of transference does not require that a second personality system either be affected by, or have an influence on, the process.

Fairbairn (1944, 1946) sharpened the analytic conception of what is repeated in the transference by pointing out that neither objects nor object-representations are internalized; rather, a representation of the *self in relation to the object,* and the specific affective link that characterizes their relationship, are internalized. The work of Balint (1968), Bion (1959), Boyer (1978), Giovacchini (1975),[12] Khan (1974), Klein (1946, 1955), Langs (1978), R. Little (1966), Racker (1968), Rosenfeld (1952), Sandler (1976b), Searles (1963), Winnicott (1947), and others has led to a widening of the original focus of the transference concept to include not only the idea of a shift in the psychological representation of the analyst, but also an *interpersonal enactment* of that representational shift in the form of pressure on the therapist actually to experience himself and to behave in a manner congruent with the self- and/or object-representation depicted in the internalized relationship. This is a conception of transference as a two-person phenomenon requiring the interaction of two separate personality sytems. Translated into the terms used here, these analysts believe that the transference necessarily involves interpersonal actualization.

I am proposing that the analytic formulation of transferences

[12]Despite Giovacchini's view of transference as a form of projection, operationally he uses the concept as a two-person phenomenon in which "the patient projects his rudimentary organized self *into* the analyst. When he once more incorporates it as his own, there has been a realignment of various parts of the self that permit further development" (1975, p. 32).

encountered in work with schizophrenic patients be widened still further to encompass an additional facet that is inherent in Fairbairn's contribution but has not yet been sufficiently recognized: that is, that transference may also involve *intrapersonal actualization* wherein patients modify their own psychological capacities (and not simply their self- and/or object-representations) in congruence with features of the self- and/or object-representation in the earlier object relationship. In other words, patients limit their psychological capacities in the transference in conformity with the ego state represented in the internalized object relationship. Transference is thus conceptualized in terms of three interrelated facets: (1) the projection of an internal self- and/or object-representation onto the psychic representation of the therapist (an intrapsychic event); (2) the interpersonal actualization of that fantasy such that the therapist is exposed to interpersonal pressure to conform to the unconscious projective fantasy (projective identification); and (3) patients' limitation of their own psychological capacities in congruence with the state of their ego as depicted in the internalized object relationship (an intrapersonal actualization).

From this perspective, there is also a need to broaden the psychoanalytic formulation of resistance. Resistance, which Freud (1923) saw as the manifestation of patients' opposition to becoming aware of dynamically unconscious meanings (see also LaPlanche and Pontalis 1973), has been broadened by others to include all manifestations of patients' opposition to psychological growth (Schafer 1973). In this tradition, I would suggest that resistance also encompasses patients' opposition to change in their capacity for thought and experience. Opposition to ending a limitation of psychological capacities for thought and experience is as much a manifestation of resistance as is opposition to the uncovering of the repressed. The schizophrenic not only resists awareness of meanings, but also resists creating and maintaining both conscious and unconscious meanings and representations. It is the latter form of resistance that has led many to label schizophrenic patients "ego defective" and "unanalyzable" (A. Freud 1976, Kohut 1977, London 1973a, b, Wexler 1971).

SUMMARY

I have described aspects of the first three years of the psychoanalytic treatment of a blind, schizophrenic patient. After an initial period of progressively diminishing psychotic symptomatology, the patient developed a mode of behaving and relating that was more like that of a "creature" then a person. However, nothing indicated that the patient felt like, or fantasized being, a "creature." I noted that I felt neither the compassion nor the revulsion that I ordinarily experienced during work with severely regressed schizophrenic patients.

After about a year, almost imperceptibly, the patient began to become present, to exist in a way that created discernible and sustained forms of interpersonal pressure. This diffuse pressure on me initially took the form of sensory impingements (unlabeled odors, sounds, and sights). Only gradually were we able to learn about the specific meanings of these impingements. In fact, the capacity to endow sensory data with meaning was precisely what had been absent in the first year of work. In the second year, through my "processing" of the patient's predominantly nonverbal productions, as well as the accompanying countertransference feelings, the patient gradually was able to endow his formerly diffuse, sensory-level experiential state with meaning. This unfolding meaning centered around the patient's conflicted rebellion against feelings of being symbiotically suffused or "haunted."

From the latter half of the second year through the third year of therapy, the patient progressively developed the capacity to experience and contain his own feelings and thoughts. He initially retreated from such containment through the illusion (in which I was subtly invited to participate) that we were not quite separate and that my voice could render safe his insane thoughts and feelings. Gradually, as this illusion was interpreted, the patient began to experience feelings of exhilaration and power resulting from his new conception of himself as a person with the capacity to think, feel, and act. This excitement also reflected manic defense against the feelings of loss, abandonment, and powerlessness that inevitably accompany awareness of separateness. The patient's defenses occasionally became overtaxed, leading to brief periods of psychotic regression with partial loss of self-object differentiation. These regressions offered further opportunity to rework the many incompletely resolved aspects of the previous phases of work.

The clinical phenomena described in this case report cannot be adequately formulated in terms of changes within any *one* sphere (i.e., the representational, interpersonal, or intrapersonal sphere). Rather, I have tried to develop the beginnings of a conceptual framework with which to describe, organize, and ponder the various forms of interplay among these spheres. I have discussed transformations from the representational sphere into one of the other spheres in terms of "actualization." Projective identification can then be thought of as actualization in which unconscious fantasies are made actual by evocation of congruent feelings in another person. Similarly, I have used the term "intrapersonal actualization" to describe the way schizophrenic patients not only imagine mental catastrophies but actually bring about and maintain severe limitations of their own capacities for experience and thought. The latter sometimes reaches the point of an almost complete psychological shutdown, or a state of nonexperience.

REFERENCES

Abraham, K. (1922). The spider as a dream symbol. In *Selected Papers,* pp. 326–332. London: Hogarth Press, 1927.

Arlow, J. A. and Brenner, C. (1969). The psychopathology of the psychoses: A proposed revision. *Internat. J. Psycho-Anal.* 50:5–14.

Balint, M. (1968). *The Basic Fault.* London: Tavistock.

Benedek, T. (1973). *Psychoanalytic Investigations.* New York: Quadrangle/The New York Times Book Company.

Bion, W. R. (1959). Attacks on linking. In *Second Thoughts.* New York: Aronson, 1967.

——— (1962a). *Learning from Experience.* New York: Basic Books.

——— (1962b). A theory of thinking. In *Second Thoughts.* New York: Aronson, 1967.

——— (1967). *Second Thoughts.* New York: Aronson.

Boyer, L. B. (1978). Countertransference experiences with severely regressed patients. In *Countertransference*, ed. L. Epstein and A. Feiner. New York: Aronson, 1979.

—— (1979). *Childhood and Folklore. A Psychoanalytic Study of Apache Personality.* New York: Library of Psychological Anthropology.

Donnet, J. L. and Green, A. (1973). *L'Enfant de Ca. Psychoanalyse D'un Entretien. La Psychose Blanche.* Paris: Editions Minuit.

Engel, G. L., Reichsman, F., and Segal, H. (1956). A study of an infant with a gastric fistula. I. Behavior and the rate of total hydrochloric acid secretion. In *Psychopathology: A Source Book*, ed. C. F. Reed, I. E. Alexander, and S. S. Tomkins, pp. 93–126. Cambridge: Harvard University Press, 1958.

Fairbairn, W. R. D. (1944). Endopsychic structure considered in terms of object-relationships. In *Psychoanalytic Studies of the Personality.* London: Routledge and Kegan Paul, 1952.

—— (1946). Object-relationships and dynamic structure. In *Psychoanalytic Studies of the Personality.* London: Routledge and Kegan Paul, 1952.

Freeman, T. (1970). The psychopathology of the psychoses: A reply to Arlow and Brenner. *Internat. J. Psycho-Anal.* 51:407–415.

Freud, A. (1976). Changes in psychoanalytic practice and experience. *Internat. J. Psycho-Anal.* 57:257–260.

Freud, S. (1894). The neuro-psychoses of defense. *Standard Edition* 3:45–61. London: Hogarth Press, 1962.

—— (1895). Draft H: Paranoia. In *The Origins of Psycho-Analysis*, ed. M. Bonaparte et al. New York: Basic Books, 1954.

—— (1896). Further remarks on the neuro-psychoses of defense. *Standard Edition* 3:162–185. London: Hogarth Press, 1962.

—— (1911). Psycho-analytic notes on an autobiographical account of a case of paranoia (dementia paranoides). *Standard Edition* 12:9–84. London: Hogarth Press, 1958.

—— (1912). The dynamics of transference. *Standard Edition* 12:97–108. London: Hogarth Press, 1958.

—— (1914a). On narcissism: An introduction. *Standard Edition* 14:73–104. London: Hogarth Press, 1957.

—— (1914b). Remembering, repeating, and working through. *Standard Edition* 12:145–156. London: Hogarth Press, 1958.

—— (1915a). Repression. *Standard Edition* 14:146–158. London: Hogarth Press, 1957.

—— (1915b). Observations on transference love. *Standard Edition* 12:157–171. London: Hogarth Press, 1958.

—— (1915c). The unconscious. *Standard Edition* 14:166–204. London: Hogarth Press, 1957.

—— (1920). Beyond the pleasure principle. *Standard Edition* 18:7–66. London: Hogarth Press, 1955.

—— (1923). The ego and the id. *Standard Edition* 19:12–68. London: Hogarth Press, 1961.

—— (1924a). Neurosis and psychosis. *Standard Edition* 19:149–156. London: Hogarth Press, 1961.

—— (1924b). The loss of reality in neurosis and psychosis. *Standard Edition* 19:183–190. London: Hogarth Press, 1961.

—— (1926). The question of lay analysis. *Standard Edition* 20:183–258. London: Hogarth Press, 1959.

—— (1937). Analysis terminable and interminable. *Standard Edition* 23:216–154. London: Hogarth Press, 1964.

Giovacchini, P. L. (1975). Various aspects of the analytic process. In *Tactics and Techniques of Psychoanalytic Therapy*, vol. 2, ed. P. L. Giovacchini et al. New York: Aronson.

—— (1979). *Treatment of Primitive Mental States.* New York: Aronson.

—— (1980). Primitive agitation and primal confusion. In *Psychoanalytic Treatment of Schizophrenic, Borderline, and Characterological Disorders*, ed. L. B. Boyer and P. L. Giovacchini. New York: Aronson.

Graber, G. H. (1925). Die Schwarze Spinne: Menscheitsentwicklung nach Jeremais Gotthelfs gleichnamiger Novelle, dargestellt unter besonderer berucksichtigunger Rolle der Frau. *Imago* 11:254–334. (Trans. S. Ruddy and C. Michel, unpublished.)

Green, A. (1975). The analyst, symbolization, and absence in the analytic setting (on changes in analytic practice and analytic experience). *Internat. J. Psycho-Anal.* 56:1–22.

—— (1977). The borderline concept. In *Borderline Personality Disorders*, ed. P. Hartocollis. New York: International Universities Press.

Grinberg, L. (1962). On a specific aspect of countertransference due to the patient's projective identification. *Internat. J. Psycho-Anal.* 43:436–440.

Grotstein, J. S. (1977a). The psychoanalytic concept of schizophrenia: I. The dilemma. *Internat. J. Psycho-Anal.* 58:403–425.

—— (1977b). The psychoanalytic concept of schizophrenia: II. Reconciliation. *Internat. J. Psycho-Anal.* 58:427–452.

———— (1979). Demoniacal possession, splitting, and the torment of joy. Contemp. Psychoanal. 15:407–445.

Katan, M. (1979). Further exploration of the schizophrenic regression to the undifferentiated state: A study of the "assessment of the unconscious." *Internat. J. Psycho-Anal.* 60:145–176.

Kehoe, M. and Ironside, W. (1963). Studies on the experimental evocation of depressive responses during hypnosis: II. The influence of depressive responses upon the secretion of gastric acid. *Psychosom. Med.* 25:403.

Khan, M.M.R. (1974). *The Privacy of the Self.* New York: International Universities Press.

Klein, M. C. (1940). Mourning and its relation to manic depressive states. In *Contributions to Psycho-Analysis, 1921–1945.* London: Hogarth Press.

———— (1946). Notes on some schizoid mechanisms. In *Envy and Gratitude and Other Works, 1946–1963.* New York: Delacorte Press/Seymour Laurence, 1975.

———— (1955). On identification. In *Envy and Gratitude and Other Works, 1946–1963.* New York: Delacorte Press/Seymour Laurence, 1975.

Kohut, H. (1977). *The Restoration of the Self.* New York: International Universities Press.

Kubie, L. (1967). The relation of psychotic disorganization to the neurotic process. *J. Amer. Psycho-Anal. Assn.* 15:626–640.

Langs, R. (1978). *The Listening Process.* New York: Aronson.

LaPlanche, J. and Pontalis, J. B. (1973). *The Language of Psychoanalysis.* New York: Norton.

Little, M. (1958). On delusional transference (transference psychosis). *Internat. J. Psycho-Anal.* 39:134–138.

Little, R. (1966). Oral aggression in spider legends. *Amer. Imago* 23:169–179.

———— (1967). Spider phobias. *Psychoanal. Q.* 36:51–60.

London, N. (1973a). An essay on psychoanalytic theory: Two theories of schizophrenia. I: Review and critical assessment of the development of the two theories. *Internat. J. Psycho-Anal.* 54:169–178.

———— (1973b). An essay on psychoanalytic theory. Two theories of schizophrenia. II: Discussion and restatement of the specific theory of schizophrenia. *Internat. J. Psycho-Anal.* 54:179–193.

Mahler, M. S. (1972). On the first three subphases of the separation-individuation process. *Internat. J. Psycho-Anal.* 53:333–338.

Malin, A. and Grotstein, J. (1966). Projective identification in the therapeutic process. *Internat. J. Psycho-Anal.* 47:26–31.

Maslow, A. (1968). *Toward a Psychology of Being.* New York: Van Nostrand.

Moore, B. and Fine, B., eds. (1968). *A Glossary of Psychoanalytic Terms and Concepts.* New York: American Psychoanalytic Association.

Ogden, T. H. (1976). Psychological unevenness in the academically successful student. *Internat. J. Psychoanal. Psychother.* 5:437–448.

———— (1978a). A developmental view of identifications resulting from maternal impingements. *Internat. J. Psychoanal. Psychother.* 7:486–507.

———— (1978b). A reply to Dr. Ornston's discussion of "Identifications resulting from maternal impingements" *Internat. J. Psychoanal. Psychother.* 7:528–532.

———— (1979). On projective identification. *Internat. J. Psycho-Anal.* 60:357–373.

———— (1980). On the nature of schizophrenic conflict. *Internat. J. Psycho-Anal.* 61:513–533.

Ornston, D. (1978). Projective identification and maternal impingement, *Internat. J. Psychoanal. Psychother.* 7:508–528.

Pao, P. N. (1973). Notes on Freud's theory of schizophrenia. *Internat. J. Psycho-Anal.* 54:469–476.

Racker, H. (1968). *Transference and Countertransference.* New York: International Universities Press.

Rosenfeld, H. (1952). Notes on the psycho-analysis of the superego conflict of an acute schizophrenic patient. *Internat. J. Psycho-Anal.* 33:111–131.

Rycroft, C. (1973). *A Critical Dictionary of Psycho-Analysis.* Towata, N.J.: Littlefield Adams.

Sandler, J. (1976a). Dreams, unconscious fantasies, and "identity of perception." *Internat. Rev. Psycho-Anal.* 3:43–47.

———— (1976b). Countertransference and role responsiveness. *Internat. Rev. Psycho-Anal.* 3:43–47.

———— and Sandler, A. M. (1978). On the development of object relationships and affect. *Internat. J. Psycho-Anal.* 59:285–296.

Schafer, R. (1968). *Aspects of Internalization.* New York: International Universities Press.

———— (1973). The idea of resistance. *Internat. J. Psycho-Anal.* 54:259–285.

Searles, H. (1963). Transference psychosis in the psychotherapy of schizophrenia. In *Collected Papers on Schizophrenia and Related Subjects.* New York: International Universities Press, 1965.

—— (1975). The patient as therapist to the analyst. In *Tactics and Techniques in Psychoanalytic Therapy,* vol. 2, ed. P. L. Giovacchini et al. New York: Aronson.

Segal, H. (1964). *An Introduction to the Work of Melanie Klein.* New York: Basic Books.

Spotnitz, H. (1969). *Modern Psychoanalysis of the Schizophrenic Patient.* New York: Grune and Stratton.

Sterba, R. (1950). On spiders, hanging, and oral sadism. *Amer. Imago* 7:21–28.

Wexler, M. (1971). Schizophrenia: Conflict and deficiency. *Psychoanal. Q.* 40:83–100.

Winnicott, D. W. (1947). Hate in the countertransference. In *Collected Papers: Through Paediatrics to Psycho-Analysis,* pp. 194–203. New York: Basic Books, 1975.

—— (1951). Transitional objects and transitional phenomena. In *Collected Papers: Through Paediatrics to Psycho-Analysis,* pp. 229–242. New York: Basic Books, 1975.

—— (1956). Primary maternal preoccupation. In *Collected Papers: Through Paediatrics to Psycho-Analysis,* pp. 300–305. New York: Basic Books, 1975.

9

THE ANALYSIS OF A BORDERLINE PATIENT

James S. Grotstein

Editor's Notes

Dr. Grotstein introduces us to an interesting clinical phenomenon that is fairly commonly encountered in borderline and other severely regressed patients. These patients often appear to be suffering from a nondisruptive neurosis when they enter analysis, but later in the treatment their underlying psychotic self emerges. Dr. Grotstein does not present the initial assessment of these patients as neurotic as a diagnostic error. On the contrary, he believes that once one gains sufficient familiarity with such patients, one realizes the inevitability of their undergoing deep regressions during treatment, such that the therapist will have to revise previous assessments. Over the past two decades, experiences such as these have caused many of us to reconsider our concepts about psychopathology and analyzability. The analytic method has been extended to a wide variety of patients, including those with severe character disorders and, in some cases, psychoses.

Dr. Grotstein emphasizes some very important reactions that arose as his patient underwent a psychotic regression. He discusses in detail the characterstics of his patient's psychotic and delusional transferences. He finds it useful to distinguish these, as do other clinicians who use the concepts of Melanie

Klein and Bion to shape their clinical formulations. He further believes that these patients make intense use of projective identification and splitting mechanisms.

The editors of this volume believe that Dr. Grotstein is a pioneering member of an ever-increasing cadre of psychoanalysts who have been able to extract the best parts of Kleinian theory and sensibly apply them to their understanding of primitively oriented patients. Dr. Grotstein demonstrates how splitting and projective identification determine the content and manifestations of the psychotic transference. He suggests using different types of interpretations depending upon the state of the patient's psychotic equilibrium at a given time. In this regard, he is entirely different from the "classical" Kleinian analyst. Dr. Grotstein is very cautious about what he interprets, showing acute sensitivity to the vulnerability and the lack of protective shields that characterize primitive mental states.

While the focus of this chapter is the treatment of an individual patient, other important issues are mentioned which require elaboration. For example, the author mentions that his patient had two therapists when she was in the hospital—a therapist who was responsible for her management on the ward and Dr. Grotstein who was responsible only for her analysis. In view of the patient's vulnerability and weak, blurred ego boundaries, this division of responsibilities was absolutely essential. The assignment of multiple therapists for patients who manifest varying levels of regression toward different staff members is a valuable new therapeutic maneuver in the psychoanalytically oriented treatment of hospitalized patients. Psychoanalytic treatment of hospitalized patients is an alternative to the behavior-control, psychopharmacological approach. Our experiences have convinced us that many patients can make enormous improvement without drugs and that lasting structural changes can be achieved in a milieu designed to cater to the patients', rather than the staff's, needs. For some patients—and Dr. Grotstein's patient is a case in point—the hospital represents a protective setting in which analysis can continue.

Dr. Grotstein offers us a complex—at times, abstruse—theoretical foundation for important treatment issues with borderline patients. However, his abstract formulations are always made in a clinical context that makes them explicit and "alive" as he uses them to understand the delicate and subtle transference-countertransference reactions that regularly occur in the treatment of these deeply regressed patients. Often it is helpful to think in terms of metaphor when dealing with the primitive personality layers of these patients. The metaphor can later be translated into scientific statements within a metapsychological framework. Dr. Grotstein's view of the psychotic part of his patient as a "dead twin" is a good example of such metaphoric conceptualization.

The hospital treatment of Dr. Grotstein's patient illustrates a definable pattern that might occur more frequently than we suspect. After the patient regressed to a state of psychotic disorganization, she followed a recognizable sequence from autism, to symbiotic fusion, to a view of Dr. Grotstein as someone separate from herself. This progression highlighted the essence of her psychopathology and emphasized its developmental antecedents.

Dr. Grotstein believes that patients suffering from severe structural defects have had catastrophic "experiences" in childhood which led to the development of an infantile psychosis. An understanding of patients' early development and its accompanying psychopathology can have predictive value regarding the unfolding of various ego states and their transference connections during treatment. The analyst who knows what to expect, even in a vague, imperfect way, may be able to avoid disruptive countertransference reactions and be more understanding and receptive of the patient's material and behavior.

The combination of Dr. Grotstein's conceptual therapeutic system and sensitive use of countertransference responses to understand his patients demonstrates how the intellect and intuition can join hands in the therapeutic process.

P. L. G.

The pioneering work of Bion (1957, 1977), Boyer and Giovacchini (1967), Green (1977), Kernberg (1975), Rosenfeld (1965, 1978), and others, has established the validity and appropriateness of the psychoanalytic treatment of borderline patients. In this chapter, I present a case to demonstrate some unique problems of borderline patients. This particular patient entered treatment with me in 1970, before the borderline syndrome had been as definitively outlined as it is today. I took this patient into analysis believing that she was neurotic; only later did I learn of her deeper and more pathological core.

TYPES OF TRANSFERENCES IN THE BORDERLINE PATIENT

Whereas neurotic patients in treatment tend to develop a transference neurosis as a recapitulation of their infantile neurosis, borderline patients tend to develop a transference psychosis or a delusional transference in place of, or in addition to, a transference neurosis. According to Rosenfeld (personal communication), a delusional transference is characterized by the patient's belief that the analyst is indeed a persecutor; there is no therapeutic alliance to mitigate the patient's belief of victimization. A transference psychosis, on the other hand, is a transference situation that predicates a therapeutic alliance in which the patient has delusional feelings about the therapist, but at the same time realizes that they are part of the treatment and can yield to analytic understanding. The transference psychosis implies that there is a reasonable observing ego as well as an experiencing ego, whereas the delusional transference implies that the observing ego has vanished and that there is only an experiencing ego. Rosenfeld's distinction between delusional transference and transference psychosis is useful for analytic work.

The transference psychosis recapitulates the infantile psychosis, a stage of development that occurs side by side with the earliest stage of the infantile neurosis. As Klein (1946) hinted, the infantile neurosis begins at birth and constitutes a succession of conflictual situations relevant to difficulties experienced in what Freud (1905) and Abraham (1924) called the oral, anal, phallic, and oedipal-genital stages, and what Mahler et al. (1975) refer to as the conflicts following the "hatching" phase of separation-individuation (Grotstein 1980a). The infantile neurosis also helps organize the narcissistic sense of self prior to the Oedipus complex. The infantile psychosis reflects an early breakdown in the proper functioning of the infantile neurosis followed by an infantile catastrophe. According to Bion (1957), this primitive mental catastrophe causes the infant to experience fragmentation, dissolution, and loss of self-continuity. This infantile psychotic break with reality is then supervened by a state of deficiency rather than conflict. Thereafter, according to Bion, a neurotic and a psychotic portion of the personality follow separate developmental lines, the former presumably organized by the infantile neurosis and the latter by the infantile psychosis.

Patients who develop psychotic illnesses often give histories that suggest primitive mental catastrophies in infancy. Masterson and Rinsley (1975) believe that the borderline personality emerges when the mother has been adequate only up to the hatching phase of separation-individuation (Mahler et al. 1975); as a result of her subsequent inadequacy, the child never completes the transition from symbiosis to separation and individuation. Symbiotic and parasitic attachments to objects, which are so characteristic of borderline patients, seem to confirm this supposition. However, it is also possible that the development of borderline and psychotic patients was deficient and defective from the very beginning of life, but that the difficulties did not manifest themselves until the stage of separation-individuation. Further clinical work is needed in this area.

THE USE OF PRIMITIVE MENTAL MECHANISMS

Kernberg (1975), following Rosenfeld (1965) and Bion (1957), called attention to borderline patients' polarized splitting of the personality and of objects. Borderline splitting seems to involve gross dissociations of the personality, rather than the minute splitting or splintering characteristic of frankly psychotic states.

At times, the presence of a split-off or dissociated self has to be inferred from patients' material presentation of themselves. At other times, it is clear enough to be apparent to the patients themselves. Autoscopic phenomena (seeing one's "double") may accompany partial dissociation. The relationship between the normal or neurotic personality, on the one hand, and the more primitive or psychotic personality, on the other, is a complex one with borderline patients. There is a collusive interpenetration of the two or more personalities in these patients so that they behave as if they were neurotically psychotic or psychotically neurotic (Grotstein 1979a, 1980b, 1980c; Cattell and Hoch 1959). These patients experience a great deal of both secondary gain and regression, a unique combination that characterizes their transferences and splitting mechanisms.

The gross dissociative splitting that takes place in borderline personalities may dictate a particular course of analytic treatment (Grotstein 1980d). It creates at least two distinct, polarized personalities: the neurotic and the psychotic (or some variant of the latter, such as the "dead," mutilated, or violently disruptive personality). Katan (1954) and Bion (1957) first noted and Rosenfeld (1965) confirmed this phenomenon in schizophrenic patients; Kernberg (1975) applied it to borderline patients. Ignoring such dissociation can be hazardous for patient and analyst. For example, while the neurotic personality may gain from psychoanalytic interventions and form a workable transference neurosis, the psychotic personality may be too primitive to gain from interpretations. Thus, successful analysis of the neurotic personality will increase the separation between the two personalities and create tension, which may be manifested via disruptive acting out, frankly psychotic episodes, states of depersonalization, and negative therapeutic reactions. As the preverbal nature of the more primitive personality does not allow it to gain from analytic interpretations as readily as the neurotic personality, it must first "announce" itself through actions. The psychotic personality has a frightened, envious relationship with the neurotic personality and tries to sabotage the latter's progress so that it won't be left behind by its more successful "twin." Thus, the psychoanalysis of borderline patients often progresses satisfactorily for a while as the neurotic personality is analyzed and then seems to come to a standstill, or even a deep regression, as the psychotic "twin" asserts its needs for recognition.

I use the term "twin" in the sense that Breuer and Freud (1893–1895) used the term "double conscience," by which they meant double consciousness. The term designates that preternatural experience in which a split-off aspect of the self is projected into the image of an external object and thereby alienated from the self. For the projecting patient, this alienated aspect of the self becomes a personified amalgam that includes "the other." Insofar as this projective amalgam hovers in an eerie orbit around the patient and is always attempting a re-entry into the patient's awareness, it becomes a persecutor. When these projected objects undergo re-entry into the patient's awareness (especially in psychoanalysis and psychoanalytic psychotherapy), they are uncannily experienced as twin selves. The twin conveys the experience of the strange and the familiar simultaneously, as Freud (1919) himself suggested.

Borderline patients characteristically use projective identification for many different purposes. They use it to merge with an object in a primitive (autistic or symbiotic) object relationship. They also tend to use projective identification to rid the psyche of unwanted feelings, thoughts, needs, etcetera, by hurling them into the object, where they become "confused" with the object and then return as persecutory objects. All infants and all patients utilize projective identification both as an object relationship and as a vehicle for the "transference" of mental pain from self to an object. What distinguishes the projective identification of neurotic patients from that of borderline and psychotic patients is that the former involves the splitting off and projection of unwanted feelings and thoughts (contents of the mind), whereas the latter involves the splitting off and projection of the mind itself. As a result, after the employment of projective identification, borderline and psychotic patients often experience feelings of emptiness, disorientation, confusion, claustrophobia, agoraphobia, and acrophobia. Parenthetically, both projection and projective identification involve a disidentification of the feelings of the self, followed by their translocation and reidentification in an object (whether it be an internal object, an object-representation, or an external object).

The external object of projective identification does not actually have to identify with the projection for the mechanism to work; in the patient's mind, the object's identification with the projection has already occurred. *There can be no projection without identification, and there can be no projection without an object to contain the projection.* Perhaps a better way of demonstrating this is to utilize the paradigm of the Siamese twin, which emphasizes symbiosis: that is, fusion *and* separation at the same time. *Projection cannot take place in a vacuum.* With every projection, there must be some awareness of the object with which one is identified. Projective identification can only take place where ego boundaries between the self and the object disappear so that there is a temporary merger of the self and the object (Federn 1952, Grotstein 1980d). In the next moment, splitting takes place; aspects of the self are translocated in the object, and aspects of the object are translocated in the self. A separation seems to take place. However clinical evidence has established that patients experience themselves more as a Siamese twin than as a separate person.

The technical handling of splitting and projective identification in borderline patients must be done very carefully and with great regard for patients' sensitivity. Like psychotic patients, borderline patients may believe that interpretations of their projective identifications are simply attempts by the analyst to project back into them in order to persecute them. One reason for this belief is the fact that the projections themselves have been split-off and dis-identified and are, therefore, experienced as alien. Interpretation of them so as to effect reidentification by patients runs the risk of attacking patients in a state of maximum vulnerability. Borderline patients' experience of interpretations will depend on the degree to which they can comprehend the metaphoric and symbolic nature interpretations.

THE COURSE OF ANALYTIC TREATMENT WITH BORDERLINE PATIENTS

The course of analysis with borderline patients may vary, but it typically includes certain characteristics. When the borderline patient develops a transference neurosis, it may be indistinguishable from that of the neurotic, and, if a traumatic situation does not intervene, therapist and patient may be none the wiser. When there is an abrupt traumatization by a life stress, the transference neurosis may be replaced by a transference psychosis and/or a delusional transference, and more primitive states of mind may emerge. The therapist may be surprised at the patient's significant "change" and may be dumbfounded at having underestimated the depth of psychopathology. When such a patient is hospitalized, the course of treatment tends to be prolonged, dramatic, and character-ized by deep regressive needs for object attachments in the hospital.

Case Example

The patient, a recently married 25-year-old woman, entered analysis because of an obsessive fear that her husband's child from a previous marriage would haunt her and ruin her marriage. The patient was reared as an only child in Switzerland. Her parents divorced when she was three years old, and, because of the law of the country, she was placed in her father's custody. Her father then sent her to his own parents, who lived in a small village high in the Alps. The patient saw her mother frequently and regularly and loved her very much, but also loved her paternal grandparents. At the age of seven, her father took her back to Zurich for schooling. As a young woman, she got a job as a stewardess on a Mediterranean cruise ship. She met her future husband aboard ship; they had a whirlwind romance, married and came to the United States.

Analysis: Before the Psychotic Break

The first phase of analysis was characterized by a seemingly conventional development of a transference neurosis. The patient felt oedipally sexual toward me, and in the transference I became her warm, loving grandfather. Her husband became the reenactment of her more distant and authoritative father. We often switched roles; that is, I became the father and the husband became the grandfather. Feelings of oedipal jealousy were paramount at weekend and holiday breaks, and she had a proliferation of fantasies about my wife and children.

Ultimately, the patient was able to undergo a deepening of the transference neurosis to the point where she experienced a profound oral dependency on me, first as a father-grandfather figure, and then as a mother-grandmother figure. At this time, there emerged desires for me to mirror her exhibitionistic grandiosity; she also manifested an enormous idealization of me as her omniscient guide in her present world. She envied me because of her dependency, as evidenced by her playfully comparing me unfavorably with her previous therapist in Switzerland, whom she had originally contacted because of difficulties she had had while living with her mother during her late adolescence and early adulthood.

At this time, I felt that the patient was in a symbiotic transference state, one in which she felt inseparably attached to me on one level and only slightly separate on another. The weekend breaks became harder for her to handle. During this period, a most extraordinary thing happened which, in retrospect, turned out to be very fateful and highlighted a distinct change in the course of the analysis. About ten minutes into a session, the patient suddenly got up from the couch and sat in the consultation chair. She remained silent for ten or fifteen minutes, and I was so dumbstruck by the suddenness and unpredictability of her gesture that I also remained silent in my own chair. Then *I began to fantasize that I was dying*. Although

I could not explain it, I knew that I was experiencing something uncanny and preternatural. I sensed that these feelings must have been put into me, so to speak, by a projective identification from the patient, but I was unable to elucidate this strange event further.

Finally (it seemed eons, although it was actually no more than 25 minutes), the patient broke the silence and said,

> I had the feeling I was dying just then. I was remembering when my father came up to F—— (her grandparents' village in the high Alps) to bring me back to Zurich when I was seven years old. I was remembering my grandfather and grandmother at the train station as the train was pulling away, and how I felt they were dying and that I was dying by being separated from them.

I told the patient that she had caused me to experience the feelings of that dying girl and of those dying grandparents so that I could help her grieve for them and come back to life. She cried and then spoke some German, which I could not follow. She imagined herself talking to her beloved grandparents, but she could also visualize herself at the train station and was crying for that little girl too; I felt my interpretation was close to the mark. I also felt relieved from a great countertransference burden—which may be more appropriately called an experience of projective counter-identification (Grinberg 1957, 1979). I realized the following year that my interpretation had only scratched the surface and was far from complete. I did not yet know what had precipitated this strange event, but I was certain that I had introjected an important primitive experience. Immediately after I made the interpretation and felt relief from the burden of my own feelings, I remembered why she had initially consulted me: she was obsessively fearful that her husband's child would return to haunt her and ruin her marriage. I was not able to make an interpretation about that then because I was not clear about the connection; I merely felt certain that there was a connection.

Only with hindsight did I come to believe I had been introduced to a twin self or a split-off double during this session. This split-off double subsequently became more intrusive in the analysis. It consisted of a "dead twin," a deeply buried fantasy about an aspect of herself that seemingly "died" at the time of her parents' divorce and "died" again when she left her grandparents in the Alpine village. One might call it a deeply depressed, "endeadened" aspect of her personality that was split off from the main course of her development. This "endeadened" aspect of her personality was later displaced by the fantasy that her husband's child would haunt her and ruin her marriage. This child was "dead" on one level, but hauntingly eroded her life on another. It (she) corresponded to what Rosenfeld (1965) referred to as the polarized, dissociative splitting of the ego in borderline personalities, adumbrating Kernberg's highlighting (1975) of borderline dissociation. The double, or "dead twin," of this patient conveyed the highly dramatic imagery of the "double conscience" (double consciousness) that Breuer and Freud (1893–1895) considered the central core of hysterical neurosis. The episode I experienced could best be described as an *hysterical trance.*

Following that strange event, the analysis proceeded to unravel the patient's feelings about her parents' divorce and the breakup of the family unit. She talked about her idealization of her life in the Alps; her love, resentment, and envy of her mother, whom she contrasted with her highly idealized grandmother; and her feelings about her idealized grandfather, whom she contrasted with her nonidealized, stern father. The transference experience recapitulated the splits between a good father and a bad father, and a good mother and a bad mother. At this time, these splits were very much like the splits that take place in a neurotic transference neurosis. The patient was so engaging that for quite some time I overlooked the presence of what I later discovered was a psychotic twin who surfaced from time to time in dreams or treatment episodes such as the "hysterical trance" previously described. This twin was experienced as a "dead," specterlike presence who "haunted" the patient. During the hour immediately following the "hysterical trance" episode, the patient reported a dream in which she attended the funeral of a girlfriend from her youth. As she approached the casket and looked in, she saw that the casket was empty. Terrified, she woke up in a sweat. Her associations led back to her obsessive fear of being haunted by her husband's child. I then linked it up with the "dead" child of the "hysterical trance" episode and interpreted to her that there was a split-off child within her that she wished to keep dead because she could not bear her feelings. (The adjectival pronoun "her" was purposely ambiguous.) The patient, relieved by the interpretation, began to cry and then talked about children for the first time.

One day she followed me home in order to find out where I lived. She then began parking her car there regularly when she attended her classes at the university, which was very near my home. She fantasized and dreamed frequently either of being a member of my family who was invited to parties in my home, or of being a waif looking in at the parties from the outside and feeling sorry for herself because she had not been included. In her dreams, she confused herself either with one of my children, my wife, or myself. I interpreted her merger fantasies as a projective identification of herself into my family—her wish to be identified as my daughter, for example. The purpose of this fantasy was to deny the weekend and holiday separations. During this time, she related that when her husband arose to go to work, she would roll over and lie in his place with loving feelings about him. Her merger fantasies, which were part of the deepening of the transference, were attempts to achieve a virtual symbiosis with me. I began to believe more and more that the purpose of these merger fantasies was to undo her feelings of disruption caused by the several breakups of her early infantile and childhood home life.

Despite the merger fantasies and the deepening of the transference, an observing ego remained that was able to understand the interpretations and cooperate with me in a therapeutic alliance. Nevertheless, her sense of separateness became increasingly precarious during this stage of the analysis. She alternated between awareness of her deep passionate need for me and unawareness of any relationship to me. This latter feeling amounted to a denial of her awareness of her needy self and the object of those needs. Yet I had interpreted this defensiveness about dependency earlier and was puzzled as to why this tendency returned at this time. I was not aware of any perturbation in her external life which might have inspired this growing fretfulness in her relationship to me. On one occasion, she imagined being a member of my family, sitting on my lap, and then disappearing. I interpreted her desire to sit on my lap as a consequence of my being like a grandmother. She desired, and at the same time feared, falling backwards into me, merging into a primary, unborn at-one-ment with me in which she would lose her sense of self.

Thus the transference first deepened to the point where she acknowledged her primitive dependency feelings toward me, but then, as a defense against those feelings, she merged with me in fantasy to the point where she experienced loss of her identity. This led to claustrophobic anxiety when she was with me and, conversely, to agoraphobic anxiety when she left me. I showed her that her claustrophobic anxiety involved her fantasied transformation of me into a very needy, possessive, suffocating object who was engulfing her. I interpreted her agoraphobic anxiety as the fear of her having pushed her mind into me and then feeling denuded and disoriented without it when she was separated from me.

These interpretations seemed to help her to a lesser degree than I had anticipated. Later, I learned of a growing dissension between her and her husband which she had failed to report to me—or of which she herself was not aware. As a consequence, her overwhelming projective identifications were less atempts to control me than attempts to merge with me so as to escape from the painful reality of yet another anticipated disruptive separation in her life.

The patient took a vacation about two months before I took my own. I received some strange letters from Switzerland in which she reported that she felt cut off from me and had no feelings for me whatsoever—in marked contrast to her feelings in the transference immediately prior to that time. When she returned from abroad, she seemed dispassionate, sober, and detached from me. I slowly realized that she was making me feel "left out," much as I had felt in that uncanny "hysterical trance" scene reported earlier. I felt as if I were in the presence of the "dead" twin, as she acted as if she were dead to the world and especially to me. I experienced our relationship as lifeless, a remarkable change from the warm, friendly engagement I had experienced before she took her vacation.

I do not know when the transference neurosis ended and the transference psychosis began, but I think that the vacation break was significant. In the two months following her return, the detachment from me seemed slowly to deepen and she was resistive to all interpretations.

Then I left for a three-week vacation, but I made arrangements for her to contact another analyst in my absence if she felt the need to do so. When I returned, she manifested gross psychosis. She staggered into my office confused and disoriented; her speech was very loosely associative and subject to blocking. She disjointedly told me that, during my absence, her husband had told her he was having an affair with another woman and wanted to leave her. Shattered by this information, she began to show signs of mental disintegration. She contacted the analyst in charge of my practice in my absence, saw him for two visits, but did not return to him. Upon my return, the frankly psychotic (delusional) phase of the analysis began. I hospitalized her and arranged for another therapist to manage the case so that I could conduct the analysis with a minimum of deviations from standard technique (Boyer 1961).

Analysis: After the Psychotic Break

The patient had been in treatment for almost two years prior to the psychotic break. I had believed that the therapeutic alliance was strong enough, and that my interpretations were sufficiently in touch with her feelings, to prevent such a break. How could I have been so wrong? One possibility, of course, was that I was wrong altogether, and that the patient had misled me, but I had sufficient evidence to dismiss that notion. I then realized a second and more important alternative which I found true not only of her but of many patients afflicted with severely disturbed mental states: the therapist's interpretations to a patient are more understandable to their normal or neurotic personality than they are to their psychotic personality.

I realized that I had been conducting the analysis of a neurotic personality, based on an infantile neurosis, only to find that now, virtually without warning, I was confronted by a psychotic person-

ality that I suspected had emanated from an infantile psychosis. I
slowly realized that the earlier analytic progress with her neurotic
personality had caused a separation between her neurotic personality and her more primitive or psychotic personality, creating an
ever-greater vulnerability to the psychotic personality, which felt
that it had been "deserted" by her more normal personality. I
suggest that the "successful" analysis of the neurotic personality
was not altogether authentic insofar as it left the personality in a
pseudoadult state rather than an integrated one. Thus, when she
learned of her husband's affair and his desire to leave her, she
decompensated all the more because the so-called analyzed neurotic
personality was not strong enough to withstand this shattering
news.

As I sought to understand the psychotic break, I reconsidered the
"hysterical trance" episode that had occurred two years earlier. I
now believed that the episode had reflected her bringing into the
analytic situation her deep experience of containing an "endeadened" child who had undergone an infantile catastrophe at age
three when her parents divorced and she was sent to the high
Alps. This event may very well have been exacerbated by her
father's taking her back to Zurich. The catastrophe she suffered
after leaving her grandparents at the station to return to Zurich
occurred when she was about seven years of age and therefore,
chronologically, cannot be called infantile. Yet, it had a strongly
disorganizing effect on her development and maturation and may
even have had a retroactively explosive effect on her primitive
psychic structure so that an infantile psychotic state could have
developed along the fault lines of a "basic fault" formed in her
earliest years (Balint 1958).

Although there is no overt evidence to support my hypothesis,
I assume that the patient underwent silent psychotic breaks when
she was taken from her mother at age three and again at age
seven when she was separated from her grandparents. Such
silent psychotic breaks could have had similar effects on the
primitive depths of her personality and might have been personified by a psychotic and "endeadened" infant. As a result of deep
regression, the traumatized primitive parts, or basic fault, of this

personality emerged, making her especially vulnerable to the concomitant external catastrophe at age seven. Because of her ability to believe in at least a pseudonormal fashion, the family could have ignored or been unaware of her inner turmoil. Upon her return to Zurich, she had lived with her mother and had developed a strong symbiotic attachment. The tenacity of the symbiotic attachment to her mother, to her husband, and to me in the transference constituted the missing link in my understanding of the depth of her experience. Her object relations, although seemingly mature on the surface, were actually pseudoadult. Behind her engaging facade was a frightened, clinging little girl.

In retrospect, my three-week vacation was unwittingly ill-timed because of the resonating effect with her husband's sudden declaration that he was having an affair with another woman. The patient, wounded by his treachery, was hurt all the more because of her deep analytic involvement with me, which made her more vulnerable to trauma. Moreover, it recapitulated the breakup of the parental family and her move to the Alps to live with her grandparents, as well as the subsequent breakup of that family and her return to the isolation of a premature adulthood in the city. I then realized that being forced to leave her mother and then her grandparents corresponded to sudden disruptions of her primary identification linkages. First, there was a sudden disruption of her primary at-one-ment bond with her mother. Second, following this, there was another disruption of what amounted to a primary at-one-ment bond with her grandparents when her father took her back to Zurich for schooling. These disruptions had the cumulative effect of precipitating the formation of a "false self" (Winnicott 1952). I had been analyzing her superficial personality rather than her deeper one; the deeper personality had been obscured by the superficial personality's apparent "regression" to early stages of development.

The psychotic twin (personality), which had lain dormant from the time of the original disruption of the patient's merged state, emerged with her husband's revelation while I was on vacation. Here, the term "twin" denotes a phenomenological event: the patient's splitting off, personification, and repression of an overwhelmingly frightening, archaic experience of herself. Thus, this experience was never integrated into her normal course of development.

The phenomenon of the imaginary twin is normal for children but undergoes repression at the time of the resolution of the Oedipus complex (Grotstein 1980d). In some patients, especially borderline and psychotic patients, the imaginary twin persists. According to Gazzaniga and LeDoux (1978), both the normal and abnormal mind contain two distinct hemispheres that process the data of experience from their respective points of view; however, in the normal mind, they constantly inform each other of the results, creating an apparent unity. In the abnormal mind, this harmony of communication breaks down, and the different hemispheres appear as "dis-integrated" selves—or, phenomenologically, as incompatible "twins." Thus, the term "twin" designates the presence of incompatible, "dis-integrated" personifications loosely held together under the rubric of selfness.

I saw my patient six times a week in the hospital. She remained delusional, in a state of acute confusional excitement, and had auditory hallucinations. She was frequently distracted by imaginary voices in the consultation room with me, but had difficulty telling me about them. At the beginning of each interview, she would say, "Oh, you say you are Dr. Grotstein? You're not Dr. Grotstein, but you look just like him. He was here yesterday, but you are not the one who was here yesterday." It dawned on me that she saw me as the "twin" of Dr. Grotstein. My twinship probably constituted a projective identificatory assignment of her twinship alienation. This meant that my constancy as an object-representation had disappeared and had been replaced by ad hoc disconnected images of me as a projected internal object subject to massive splitting. This fragmentation of her representation of me had been caused by her belief that I had been destroyed during the vacation break because of the loss she had sustained in her object world. This fragmentation undoubtedly was due in large part to her anger at my not being there when she had suffered such a loss. Freud (1911) called such fragmentation of object-representations "decathexis of objects." Pao (1979) uses the term "disconnection" in place of "fragmentation."

The transference neurosis vanished and was replaced by a transference psychosis. Although in most regards it conformed to the notion of a delusional transference (i.e., one in which the therapeutic relationship is characterized by a delusional misperception without a therapeutic alliance), I felt that a therapeutic alliance still existed and that the patient's psychosis still had "meaning" for her. However, at this stage and later stages of regression, the patient crossed over the border into delusional transference (without therapeutic alliance) on many occasions.

Her misperception of me as an imposter was related to projections of her own lifelong feelings of being an imposter or impersonator. She felt herself to be a pseudoadult or "false self." Analysis had already revealed that although others found her very engaging, she felt ill at ease and frightened in contacts with strangers because of the fear of "discovery." Before her psychotic break, she admitted that she felt uneasy with people but was not sure why. The analysis during the psychotic period answered this question; she feared being discovered, engulfed, impinged upon, and "petrified" (Laing's [1960] term meaning the turning of the self into a robot by the controlling object). Upon her husband's betrayal, her pseudoadult self collapsed as it had in childhood with her father's desertion and subsequent disruptions.

I told her that I was indeed Dr. Grotstein who she felt had "cut up" her time and her self by taking the analysis away with me on vacation. I had left her in fragments and, insofar as I had taken her mind and her capacity to feel away with me, I had left her denuded of her mind and feelings. She had confused me with the bad husband who had betrayed her; she felt that because I no longer had found her desirable, I had "left" her (to go on my vacation). The patient accepted this interpretation, felt relieved, and then talked realistically about her feelings of shock over her husband's behavior. She remembered how much she had longed to see me while I was gone.

I later realized that my interpretation had covered only part of the story. That is, I recognized that once the patient had felt the full impact of the tragedy of her husband's desertion, she had defended herself by denial. In terms of her inner experience, this had been her only means of negating the impact of her loss. In the process, she had lost her memory of me as well. She had projected her split-off mind and feelings into me so that I contained the knowledge of her husband's betrayal; for this reason, when I returned, she had feared me all the more and had split me up into disconnected pieces.

Interpretations of splitting and projective identification normally depend upon the presence of a relatively intact mind that can understand interpretations. When a patient is in an acutely psychotic phase, interpretations of any kind, especially of splitting and projective identification, can be hazardous as they can be experienced as attacks against whatever sanity remains. I focused upon another aspect of projective identification, that of symbiotic relatedness (Searles 1961). Projective identification can involve leaving one's separate self behind and "disappearing," or merging into, the image of the object for protection. Such fusion with the object can be a beneficial experience conducive to healing (Searles 1961). The therapist must be able to tolerate or contain this merging experience. In the case of my patient, her thinking mind was no longer "safe" in her, so I had to become her mind, as she later told me articulately. I felt separate from her on one level and projectively identified with her on another—following the paradigm of the Siamese twin.

The patient was frequently catatonic, walked manneristically as though taking part in a serious religious pageant, and was dominated by hallucinatory voices who commanded her. There was no negotiation, dialogue, or conversation—there was simply control and being controlled. Her ego boundaries had vanished and been replaced by a cursorily improvised, diabolically reorganized domain of hallucinosis.

The catatonic phase of her psychosis emphasized another aspect of projective identification. Once she was able to recognize that she had thoughts, she believed them to influence external objects; on the other hand, actions by others strongly influenced her (delusions of reference). At this point, interpretations were very useful; I informed her that she feared both that I had no separate self or skin boundary to defend myself against her and that she had no skin boundary to keep my powerful thoughts outside her. These interpretations reinforced her ego boundaries. When she was obviously resistant to seeing me, for instance, I would point out that she had a mind of her own and could disagree with me, thus confirming that she was a separate person. I would repeat such interpretations when she seemed to be keeping secrets from me. I would tell her that she could construct a boundary to keep me outside and prevent me from knowing what she contained inside.

As the analysis progressed, she became paranoid, experiencing me as someone who was trying to harm her and influence her malevolently. Later in the analysis, she acted indifferently toward me, her surroundings, and her state of mind. She frequently pointed out how flat she felt and how flat the world seemed. During one period, her catatonia worsened as she regressed even more deeply in terms of instinctual and ego functions. She became severely anorexic and had to be tube fed. I conducted her analysis while another therapist was responsible for her management on the ward. The ward manager finally gave her antipsychotic medication, which had little or no effect. I learned in a letter from the patient many years later that she had been distressed by these drugs and had believed that they were of no benefit to her. Only my interpretations about her trying to get rid of her needy self seemed to have any effect during the anorexic phase of the treatment. I also discussed her desire to attack her controlling conscience. Her anorexia demonstrated control over her conscience and me. By not feeding herself, she asserted passive-aggressive mastery over our fused controlling consciences and emphasized my inability to influence her.

After the catatonic period, she became more and more blocked and silent. During this second phase of her psychosis, she occasionally talked to herself and considered my interpretations intrusive interruptions. I interpreted that she was trying to reestablish a close relationship with her silent, dead "twin" from long ago. The patient became angry but maintained contact with me for long moments in between her silences. At first, I thought that her imaginary twin had "forbidden" her to talk to me, but later I realized that she was trying to seal herself off from me so as to establish a mental boundary between the two of us. Bion (1962) found that psychotic patients reconstruct an abnormal ego boundary after experiencing a psychotic catastrophe. This abnormal boundary is an invisible, delusional shell surrounding them which keeps interpretations as well as experiences in the external world from having any effect. I keenly felt this abnormal boundary; it made me feel shut out and inconsequential. My interpretations seemed to bounce off an invisible wall without having any effect whatsoever.

I felt even more discouraged when she lost confidence in her protective skin boundary frontier that I had tried to help establish through my interpretations. Eventually, I realized more about her need to install a boundary of her own, which I interpreted. For instance, when I came to the hospital and heard from the nurse that she did not want to see me, or when she spoke a private language that I was unable to understand, I pointed out to her that she was trying to tell me that she was a private person who could not be understood or seen by me without her permission. Control of the treatment was in her hands, in that she could keep me and my words out or could let them in as she saw fit; this was contrary to the part of her that believed she was denuded of mind and boundaries. I told her that the accuracy of my interpretations depended upon her cooperation and the associations she gave me. Without them, I would have little knowledge about what was going on within her; I certainly could not read her mind, although part of her believed otherwise. Thus, in the silent phase, she tried to build up a skin boundary frontier representation. Although it was a psychotically restitutive representation, it offered her a semblance of confidence.

The silent phase continued, but she became less obstinate. She seemed happy in my presence; sometimes she talked and at other times she was quiet. I viewed this as symbiotic relatedness. Though I continued to interpret the psychotic transference, she seemed most intent on being with me and pretending that we were joined. At this juncture, contact was being re-established. I realized that she had been in an autistic state. Now I could keenly feel both fusion with, and separation from, her. I alternately pictured sitting behind her as a mirroring object and carrying her behind me like a papoose. I constantly interpreted her desire to enter into me and become one with me in order to get rid of her disturbing, crazy feelings.

The silent phase developed into a more cooperative phase in which the patient experienced a rebirth from a state of pathological fusion with me. She was very tentative, vulnerable, and frightened. I then understood her vulnerability as the consequence of the negative therapeutic reaction of the psychotic self, which was attacking her cooperating self because of its fear of being left behind. The more aware she became of her deep dependency on me, the more frightened she was of making any progress whatsoever. Whenever she made progress and understood interpretations, she feared that I would take her progress for granted and ignore her needy self.

During this phase, material emerged which later helped me formulate some ideas about the universality of demoniacal possession in psychotic illness (Grotstein 1979b). She told me that as a child she remembered pretending that she was somebody else in order to get rid of her sadness about not being with her mother. She also denied her mother's existence, wanting to believe that her grandmother was her mother. She had believed that her disavowal of her real being was something very bad for which she could never be forgiven. Her husband's current betrayal linked up with her earlier betrayal of herself.

She felt cursed because she was an impersonator rather than a real person and believed she had given her soul to the devil. My role as analyst was that of an exorcist—to relieve her from damnation. I told her,

> You fear listening to my interpretations and allowing yourself to progress because taking in my words and growing with them is yielding to my treachery of growing up so I can get rid of you. Therapist-mother-me will not leave you until you are ready for me to leave. I know that when you make progress part of you dreads progress because of its fear of change and its fear that it cannot change and will be left behind and deserted once more.

These interpretations powerfully affected her and eventually enabled her to leave the hospital. Unfortunately, the analysis and the hospital treatment were interrupted before they could be properly concluded because her mother summoned her back to Switzerland to complete her treatment there. Her husband, who had visited her less and less frequently, finally divorced her. I regretfully concluded that it was a wise decision for her to resume treatment in her native land, which she did.

CONSIDERATIONS OF TECHNIQUE

I was aware early in her hospitalization that this patient's deep regression would necessitate a shift in my interpretative emphasis from "content" to "container." I suspended interpretations of her projectively identified fragmented psyche and instead "allowed" her projective identification in me to exist in reparative repose (symbiotic relatedness). At times, I treated her projections as if they really were part of me so that she could maintain a comfortable distance from them. For instance, she sometimes talked about how childish and petulant I was. Further tactful inquiry elicited her picture of me as a frightened, helpless, easily irritated person who became very upset when I did not get my own way. I frequently allowed myself to be a "play doll" for her projections so that I could see her more clearly; she could safely reveal herself in this fashion. This technique seemed to work at these critical times (see Grotstein 1977a). I had to wait to interpret the *content* of her projective identifications until her recompensation was sufficient to withstand the return of her lost self fragments.

Giovacchini (1972) believes that interpretation with psychotic patients is different than that with neurotic patients. For instance, he says that resistance has been a pejorative concept in psychoanalysis that "creates an atmosphere, a moral tone that is antithetical to the analysis of many patients. . . . Analysis of resistance . . . is not the same as overcoming resistance" (p. 291). In a later contribution, he states,

the purpose of interpretation is antithetical to autonomy. It is an attempt to control the patient's behavior and at a deeper level it represents an intrusion, a prohibition and a demand that the patient relinquish a particular ego state for one with which the analyst will feel comfortable. . . . The patient feels the analyst's anxiety and intrusion and responds to its impact in the same way he experienced infantile trauma. [p. 442]

Giovacchini pointedly states that interpretations to a psychotic or a borderline patient can be harmful insofar as they deal solely with the content of the patient's associations. Due consideration must be given to the fragility and vulnerability of the patient's mental apparatus and feeling state. An empathic sensitivity to the patient's capacity to understand interpretations promotes interpretations that are supportive as well as accurate.

SUMMARY

The case presented in this chapter is an example of the not uncommon patient who appears to be a neurotic patient and only later reveals a psychosis with massive regression of ego functions and dissolution of ego boundaries. Some of these patients undergo prolonged hospitalization characterized by deep regression (Wishnie 1975). My patient probably suffered from a borderline personality disorder, but had a neurotic personality strong enough to repress her psychotic personality. Thus, she existed in splits, and the split selves presented themselves dramatically as the analysis proceeded. Her hospital course exemplified regression not only of ego functions and the organization of the self, but also of her capacity to experience psychic space—the consequence of the dissolution of ego boundaries.

The treatment of this and similar cases requires alterations in the *emphasis* of technique. I maintained the analytic treatment during the psychotic state with the help of a psychiatrist-manager. The emphasis of technique shifted from content and transference interpretations to container interpretations in which I mirrored the symbiotic relatedness and helped to reinforce her confidence in her skin boundary frontier (ego boundary) through interpretations. The understanding of splitting and projective identification was of key importance in helping me find my way through the morass of her confusion.

REFERENCES

Abraham, K. (1924). A short study of the development of the libido. In *Selected Papers on Psycho-Analysis*, pp. 418–501. London: Hogarth Press, 1948.

Balint, M. (1958). *The Basic Fault: Therapeutic Aspects of Regression.* London: Tavistock.

Bion, W. F. (1957). Differentiation of the psychotic from the nonpsychotic personalities. In *Second Thoughts: Selected Papers on Psycho-Analysis*, pp. 43–64. London: William Heinemann, 1967.

—— (1962). A theory of thinking. In *Second Thoughts: Selected Papers on Psycho-Analysis*, pp. 110–119. London: William Heinemann, 1967.

—— (1977). Emotional turbulence. In *Borderline Personality Disorders*, ed. P. Hartocollis, pp. 3–14. New York: International Universities Press.

Boyer, L. B. (1961). Provisional evaluation of psycho-analysis with few parameters employed in the treatment of schizophrenia. *Internat. J. Psycho-Anal.* 42:389–403.

Boyer, L. B. and Giovacchini, P. L. (1967). *Psychoanalytic Treatment of Schizophrenic and Characterological Disorders.* New York: Aronson.

Breuer, J. and Freud, S. (1893–1895). Studies on hysteria. *Standard Edition* 2:1–252. London: Hogarth Press, 1955.

Cattell, J. P. and Hoch, P. H. (1959). The diagnosis of pseudoneurotic schizophrenia. *Psychiat. Quart.* 33:17–31.

Federn, P. (1952). *Ego Psychology and the Psychoses.* New York: Basic Books.

Freud, S. (1905). Three essays on the theory of sexuality. *Standard Edition* 7:135–243. London: Hogarth Press, 1953.

—— (1911). Psychoanalytic notes on an autobiographical account of paranoia. *Standard Edition* 12:1–82. London: Hogarth Press, 1958.

—— (1919). The "uncanny." *Standard Edition* 17:217–256. London: Hogarth Press, 1955.

Gazzaniga, M. S. and LeDoux, J. E. (1978). *The Integrated Mind.* New York: Plenum.

Giovacchini, P. L. (1972). *Tactics and Techniques in Psychoanalytic Therapy.* New York: Aronson.

Green, A. (1977). The borderline concept: A conceptual framework for the understanding of borderline patients. In *Borderline Personality Disorders: The Concept, the Syndrome, the Patient*, ed. P. Hartocollis, pp. 15–44. New York: International Universities Press.

Grinberg, L. (1957). Perturbaciones en la interpretación por la contra-identificación proyectiva. *Rev. Psicoanál.* 14:23–28.

———— (1979). Countertransference and projective countertransference. *Contemp. Psychoanal.* 15:226–247.

Grotstein, J. S. (1977a). The psychoanalytic concept of schizophrenia. I. The dilemma. *Internat. J. Psycho-Anal.* 58:403–425.

———— (1977b). The psychoanalytic concept of schizophrenia. II. Reconciliation. *Internat. J. Psycho-Anal.* 58:427–452.

———— (1978). Inner space: Its dimensions and its coordinates. *Internat. J. Psycho-Anal.* 59:55–61.

———— (1979a). The psychoanalytic concept of the borderline organization. In *Advances in Psychotherapy of the Borderline Patient*, ed. A. Capponi and H. LeBoit, pp. 149–183. New York: Aronson.

———— (1979b). Demoniacal possession, splitting, and the torment of joy. *Contemp. Psychoanal.* 15:407–445.

———— (1980). A proposed revision of the psychoanalytic concept of primitive mental states. Part I. Introduction to a newer psychoanalytic metapsychology. *Contemp. Psychoanal.*, 16:479–546.

———— (1982a). A revision of the psychoanalytic concept of primitive mental states. Part II. The borderline syndrome. *Contemp. Psychoanal.* vol. 18, in press.

———— (1982b). A revision of the psychoanalytic concept of primitive mental states. Part III. Narcissistic disorders. *Contemp. Psychoanal.* vol. 18, in press.

———— (1982c). *Splitting and Projective Identification*. New York: Aronson, in press.

Katan, M. (1954). The importance of the nonpsychotic part of the personality in schizophrenia. *Internat. J. Psycho-Anal.* 35:119–128.

Kernberg, O. (1975). *Borderline Conditions and Pathological Narcissism.* New York: Aronson.

Klein, M. (1946). Notes on some schizoid mechanisms. *Internat. J. Psycho-Anal.* 27:99–110.

Laing, R. D. (1960). *The Divided Self.* London: Tavistock.

Little, M. (1958). On delusional transference (transference psychosis). *Internat. J. Psycho-Anal.* 39:134–138.

Mahler, M. S., Pine, F., and Bergman, A. (1975). *The Psychological Birth of the Human Infant: Symbiosis and Individuation.* New York: Basic Books.

Masterson, J. F. and Rinsley, D. B. (1975). The borderline syndrome: The role of the mother in the genesis and psychic structure of the borderline personality. *Internat. J. Psycho-Anal.* 56:163–177.

Pao, P.-N. (1979). *Schizophrenic Disorders.* New York: International Universities Press.

Rosenfeld, H. (1965). *Psychotic States: A Psycho-Analytical Approach.* London: Hogarth Press.

——— (1978). Notes on the psychopathology and psycho-analytic treatment of some borderline patients. *Internat. J. Psycho-Anal.* 59:215–222.

Searles, H. F. (1961). Phases of patient-therapist interaction in the psychotherapy of chronic schizophrenia. In *Collected Papers on Schizophrenia and Related Subjects*, pp. 521–559. New York: International Universities Press, 1965.

Tustin, F. (1972). *Autism and Childhood Psychosis.* New York: Science House.

Winnicott, D. W. (1952). Psychoses and child care. In *Collected Papers: Through Paediatrics to Psycho-Analysis,* pp. 219–228. New York: Basic Books, 1975.

Wishnie, H. A. (1975). Inpatient therapy with borderline patients. In *Borderline States in Psychiatry*, ed J. E. Mack, pp. 41–63. New York: Grune and Stratton.

10

NONVERBAL COMMUNICATION IN THE SEVERELY DISTURBED REGRESSED PATIENT

Alfred Flarsheim

Editor's Notes

Dr. Flarsheim's chapter clearly demonstrates how a sensitive therapist intuitively responds to those basic primitive needs of patients that cannot be articulated. His reactions are spontaneous and not based upon any preconceived conceptual models or predetermined deliberations.

The author had a great deal of experience working with severely disturbed patients, both adults and children, and had special talents in this area. He had been consultant at the University of Chicago's Orthogenic School. His work also can be understood from a theoretical viewpoint, one that focuses upon early developmental processes and primitive structural levels. To some measure, Dr. Flarsheim introduces us to hypotheses based upon these early stages, but his conceptualizations always serve to expand his clinical perspective. He constantly thought in terms of relating to the patient's needs as part of the treatment procedure.

Although this chapter was incomplete at the time of Dr. Flarsheim's death, we have chosen to publish this rich source of clinical material as is. We can all learn from his compassion and concern about patients, which reflect an outlook that, in the view of the editors, represents the psychoanalytic perspective at its best. Dr. Flarsheim's perspective is applicable to all patients, especially those fixated at primitive mental levels.

The scientifically minded reader will miss a discussion section dealing with abstractions. Dr. Flarsheim avoided teaching didactic courses, limiting himself to the here-and-now interchange with patients; he collected many memorable experiences throughout his thirty years of very active practice.

Still, his clinical work easily lends itself to theoretical extension. Such elaboration is useful because it elevates the contributions engendered by Dr. Flarsheim's unique talents and sensitivites to a palpable body of information that can be integrated in the therapeutic armamentarium of all psychoanalysts and therapists who wish to understand and work with severely disturbed patients.

I have written a discussion of this chapter which attempts to supply formulations that will integrate Dr. Flarsheim's clinical data into a conceptual, developmentally based system, with the primary emphasis on a presymbiotic context.

P. L. G.

In this chapter, I hope to demonstrate that the processes underlying the therapeutic interaction of less disturbed patients can be illuminated by studying the treatment experiences of patients with severe emotional disorders. Many people believe that the severe disorders I am about to discuss are organically based, but Bettelheim (1967) has introduced considerable evidence that they are the result of environmental factors dating from earliest childhood. Winnicott (1952) also stated that early environmental influences can have profound effects on later development and discussed the difficulties of separating congenital factors from environmental influences. Freud (1938) indicated that the earlier an environmental trauma occurs, the more extensive its effects are. Unfortunately, we cannot simply assume that the pathology resulting from etiologically significant environmental factors can be "cured" via later, helpful therapeutic experiences. Nevertheless, many patients can be helped if the therapeutic environment is appropriate to the severity of their disorders.

CLINICAL MATERIAL

Patients with severe disorders have patchy subjective boundaries that exist in some areas but not in others. The existence of areas in which these patients feel merged with, or undifferentiated from, others leads to special problems for anyone in contact with them.

Case 1

Mary, a 14-year-old autistic girl in a mental hospital, was extremely sensitive to the subjective reactions of others, even when she was completely apart from them. She used nonverbal communication to relay the kind of special environmental adaptation that she required.

Mary had always been ill, according to her parents, and this illness had been expressed in abnormal behavior and signs of severe distress at every phase of development. Before Mary's birth, her mother had expected her to rescue her from depression. Of course this "rescue" failed. Cohler (Grunebaum et al. 1978) described this phenomenon in his study of depressed mothers and their children. He concluded that mothers' depression often severely disrupts the emotional development of children.

From birth, the patient had been inconsolable and cried in a manner that the mother described as "intolerable." She also had shown an exaggerated startle reflex from the beginning and supposedly had had colic. Her pediatrician had felt that her bowels did not move sufficiently freely and advised the family to stimulate her rectum with a thermometer.

In the early months, Mary had started rocking so violently that she "rocked her crib from one side of the room to the other." At six months, she had begun head banging and once knocked a hole in the plaster wall next to her crib. She had been bottle fed until five, when she gave it up voluntarily. She never securely mastered toilet training. She never made eye contact and seemed unaware of other persons except as physical objects. She had an overwhelming need for sameness and constancy. There had been no 8-month stranger anxiety. Since early childhood, she had held her thumbnails against the palmar surfaces of her index fingers so that the skin of those areas tended to be ulcerated.

At age 11, Mary was nonverbal, although she had made vocal sounds and used several words earlier. She had had much inpatient and outpatient treatment before coming to our hospital, all without observable effect. I first joined Mary at lunch and then went with her to the hospital schoolroom. I wrote my notes immediately after seeing her on three occasions, at one-year intervals. I have included all details in order to support my specific formulations.

Notes: First Meeting

I went to the dining room to have lunch with the children, which I do regularly, each time wanting to observe one particular child in the group. If we want to, the child and I can go into an individual session room after lunch.

Mary sat next to her teacher at the table, facing more toward her than the table. She rocked constantly for most of lunch and made repeated sounds, not words.

She scattered bits of bread crust around the table. On several occasions, her teacher gathered these scattered bits together and put them in front of Mary. She had eaten almost none of her food when the time came to clear the plates from the table. When the kitchen staff started taking the plates, Mary started eating. She tapped her lips and teeth with her hands several times.

After we left the dining room, Mary walked slowly, as she always does in transition from one place to another, and finally stopped altogether. The teacher and other children walked ahead to the classroom and I stayed behind with her. She put her hands into the openings between the translucent, colored bricks of an outside wall. I did the same thing to see how it felt to be Mary. I noticed that the spaces between the bricks felt comfortably cool. I wanted Mary to go toward the classroom where the rest of her class had gone, but she was reluctant to go until some other children walked by. A teacher was carrying another child, and I asked Mary if she would like me to carry her. She was unable to use words, but let me know very clearly that she did not want me to do this. She walked ahead in the same direction that the teacher carrying the other child had gone until we reached the drinking fountain.

Mary played in the drinking fountain. She pushed my hand toward the water handle and I held it for her. She had the remains of a cookie she had brought from the dining room and she played with this cookie in the water, using the cookie, her mouth, voice, and hands while I held the water on for her. We had an enjoyable time together. A group of boys was playing baseball in the corridor near us and I was at once concerned that the ball might hit Mary. I turned to look at the boys and noted that they were using a soft, lightweight ball, and a rolled newspaper for a bat, and this reassured me. Turning my attention to the boys had no effect on Mary. She seemed completely unaware of me as a person; she was only aware that my hand was holding the faucet on for her. After about ten minutes, I got tired and somewhat bored holding the faucet. I glanced at the boys playing baseball, this time viewing their activity with interest, interest I had withdrawn from Mary. I was still holding the faucet for Mary; my physical actions had not changed at all. Her face was down in the bowl of the drinking fountain, and I was unaware that she was paying any attention to me. As soon as I looked at the boys with interest, Mary reached out and forcibly pushed my hand away from the faucet, started screaming, and banged her hands against her forehead. She then reached out and pushed me away from her.

I immediately realized what I had done and felt sorry that I had withdrawn from her. But, at the same time, I was intrigued by this seemingly very withdrawn girl's amazing demonstration of her alertness to another person's feelings. I was stunned by her accurate perception of the quality of my feeling toward her.

I recalled that Mary's mother had not nursed her because she had not wanted to; instead, she had fed her pap for many years despite "not wanting to care for her at all." She had said that she "hated every minute of it."

I tried to effect a reconciliation with Mary by turning on the water and kneeling down so that I could look closely at what she was doing, but she pushed me away again. I assume that she did this because my interest at this point was somewhat contrived and stemmed from my guilt at having abandoned her in the first place. It was getting close to the end of our session, and I wanted to take Mary back to the classroom. I suggested this several times, but instead of coming with me, she played more frantically with the water in the drinking fountain.

Then an older girl came along with some of Mary's clothing that she had left in another classroom; she told Mary that she was going to leave if for her in her next classroom. As this girl walked toward that room, Mary took my hand and we followed her up some steps. When we were halfway up the steps, the older girl turned into a room and disappeared from our sight.

At this moment, Mary suddenly stopped walking and started mouthing the aluminum bannister on the stairway. She intermittently held my hands and I noticed that her hands were cold (from the water). I took her hands in mine and said that I wanted to warm them. She rejected this offer. Then she took my hand and put it into her mouth, between her lips but not between her teeth. She did not bite my hand. Nonetheless, I noticed that in reporting our session later at the staff meeting, I forgot this incident until I was reminded of it by another staff member who mentioned that she sometimes did this.

In reflecting on why I had forgotten Mary's action, I found that my associations were to the intimacy of her gesture. This was important as it fit in with another misperception I had had of Mary: my thinking that I was of no importance to her except as a hand holding the water on while she was playing in the drinking fountain. The latter espisode was striking in that Mary, who had appeared so withdrawn and unaware of me as a person, had been intensely aware of my feelings toward her all the time, and had reacted violently to a change in them. This episode was reminiscent of her childhood experience: she had fallen apart when I had continued doing something for her without wanting to do it. This correlated beautifully with her mother's feeding pattern. Could it be that Mary's intense preoccupation with the emotions of others, with nonverbal and preverbal signals, had interfered with her verbal speech development?

Eventually, she accompanied me into the classroom. When it was time for me to leave, I said goodbye to her. In typical psychotic fashion, she gave no indication that she was aware of my speaking to her, that she noticed my leaving, or that she cared whether I stayed or left.

Notes: Second Meeting

I met with Mary in the same setting one year later. As I sat down next to her, she gave no evidence of any awareness of my presence. She rocked forward and backward with wide movements, at a rate of sixty to eighty times per minute (approximately the frequency of the heartbeat; some children rock more slowly, approximating the respiratory rate). She continued to rock during almost all of lunch and ate practically nothing. Her teacher frequently offered to feed her, and she accepted two or three small bits of lettuce, preferring to take it from the teacher's fingers rather than from a utensil. Mary still kept the thumbnail and index finger of each hand pressed firmly together, but not so firmly as to cause excoriation of the skin. When it was time to clear the table, the teacher asked her if she would like to keep her plate, and she clearly signalled, without words, that she would. However, she ate almost no lunch.

On the way up to the classroom, she held the teacher's hand. She stopped several times to move her feet back and forth on the floor. She did this more frequently when we were close to transitional points such as doorways and stairways. In the classroom, Mary sat on an armchair and I sat on a couch on her left. I drew the couch up close to her chair.

She immediately started the wide forward and backward rocking that she had been doing in the dining room. After five minutes or so, I realized that if I just sat and watched her rock I would become bored and inattentive, as I had in our previous meeting when she played with the water fountain. I decided that I wanted to respond to her rocking in some way that might reach her. I took her left hand, the hand on my side as she sat facing me at an angle, and began to move her hand forward and backward in rhythm with her rocking movements. Our own feelings are of relatively greater importance as a source of information with nonverbal patients than with verbal ones. Other children were watching us, and I felt an inclination to hesitate lest I be seen as behaving in a "crazy" manner. I thought of myself as wanting to "join Mary where she was," but wondered what those watching would think of what I was doing. My discomfort disappeared when Mary started to include me actively in her rocking motions. After that, it felt natural and I felt that anyone watching would easily recognize that we were doing something together. From then on, I felt comfortable with her.

The rhythm of her motion varied; in order for me to follow it, I had to pay close and constant attention. I particularly wanted to maintain my concentration because I remembered Mary's violent reaction when I had failed to concentrate on her last year. At the same time, I was curious what reaction she might have if I failed to do so. However, I did not lose my concentration.

Every time Mary paused in her rocking, I stopped moving her hand with my hand for a moment. This "game" soon changed to one in which my hand was on the seat of the chair next to her with my palm down and her hand on top of mine. Whenever she rocked, I raised my hand, pushing her hand up in the air. I raised my hand four or five inches and she then continued raising her had for perhaps another six inches, separating her hand from mine. She would then bring her hand back down on top of mine. This was unquestionably a *mutual* "game" because, when I paused in my motion, Mary would signal me to begin again. If I stopped with my hand up in the air, she would push it down toward the chair; if I stopped with my hand lying on the chair, she would put her thumb under the palm of my hand and lift it up, clearly signalling for me to continue. She seemed to enjoy this activity, as much as it was possible for her to enjoy anything. While we played the "hand game," Mary used the only two sounds of hers that had been interpreted as possible words. These sounds were "you" and "do."

When the end of our time drew near, I told Mary I had to leave. She very clearly pushed my hand away. I felt that this was an important and valuable way for the session to end. It provided Mary with an ending in which she participated. To some extent, she "controlled" the ending by pushing my hand away, rather than letting us break off our contact in an incomplete way, such as had occurred at our first meeting.

Mary demonstrated a simple concept that was essential to her treatment and rehabilitation. She needed us to pay close attention to her rhythms and to follow them whenever possible. Without this foundation, Mary could not develop any lasting relationship of real value. Skills alone, without the underlying strength acquired in the context of a relationship based on having her primitive needs met, would be of little use to her in terms of her overall total personal and social adaptation.

Notes: Third Meeting

One year after the second meeting, I met with Mary again in the same setting. When I entered the dining room and sat down with Mary on my right, she immediately took my right hand, palm up, and put it over her soup bowl. She then put her soup spoon into the palm of my hand and tapped it against her mouth, as though my hand were a soup bowl and she were eating from it. She put my hand against her lips several times, pretending to eat it. I felt that she wanted and expected some response beyond what I gave her, but I did not know what that might be.

This seemingly promising activity suddenly ended, and there was no pattern or continuity in the actions which followed. She jumped up from the table and ran lurchingly around the room. Her teacher followed her and persuaded her to sit down again. She got up repeatedly and ran around. Then, a nurse came into the dining room and told her to sit down. She made eye contact with this nurse, the first time I had noticed her make eye contact with anyone that day. She reached toward the nurse's breast and the nurse took her hand and looked at her, following her manneristic gestures for a few moments. Mary seemed pleased with this, relaxed temporarily, and returned to the table.

While the teacher served the other children, Mary reached toward her arm and occasionally toward her breast. The teacher told her that she would have to wait until she was finished serving, but after she finished, Mary no longer reached toward her. I offered to feed her, and she clearly let me know that she did not want this.

After lunch, we went to her classroom. She stayed only a moment and then left. I followed her. She went to the drinking fountain, and I thought that perhaps she was going to repeat the drinking fountain game that we had played two years ago, but she did not. She splashed water in the fountain, spat in it, and reached into the back of her pants, rubbing her anus. She then smelled her hand and once again put it in the fountain. She gave no indication of wanting me to participate.

She kept pulling her shirt up around her shoulders, scratching the area over her sternum until the skin was excoriated. When I asked her not to scratch so hard that she hurt herself, she stopped. Then she ran toward the exit door, pushed it open, and put her hand through the opening as the door started to close. I caught the door so that it would not crush her fingers, but I had the impression that she probably would not have hurt her fingers even if I had not done this. After opening and closing the door several times, she suddenly ran outside. I felt uneasy because I thought she might do something self-destructive, such as running in front of an automobile. I ran after her, firmly took her hand, and told her that we had to go back inside the hospital.

She was compliant and docile about returning. Back in the hospital, she stood in a corner of the room licking the wall and again put her hand between her buttocks; then she rubbed her fingers against the saliva-soaked wall. She did not seem to enjoy this activity in the way that I had seen her enjoy activities that we could share.

When it was close to one o'clock, I indicated that I wanted her to return to her classroom. At first she refused, but then she went along with me. She lay down on a couch, sucked her thumb, and looked at me for perhaps ten seconds, the only definite eye contact we had during the entire time I was with her. Then she put my thumb against her closed right eye, but did not press so hard that she hurt herself. When it was time to leave, I said goodbye, but she gave no indication of being aware of me.

Mary's behavior was less organized than it had been on the previous two occasions I saw her. At the time, I felt this might have been due in part to my having missed some communication during the soup game, which made it impossible for me to give her the response she sought. However, after writing these notes, I received additional information that shed further light on this problem: Mary's teacher and both of her nurses were planning to leave the institution shortly after my session with Mary. After learning this, I reconsidered the events of the session. Mary's behavior with my hand, the soup, the soup spoon, and her mouth could have represented an attempt at oral incorporation. The unsatisfactory consequences of her attempts to internalize presumably reflected her inability to establish a sufficiently stable introjection of the staff members who were leaving to sustain the relatively integrated functioning she had shown previously. Smearing feces and saliva on the hospital walls and testing the capacity of the doors to contain her safely inside the hospital might have been regressive means of expressing her need for continuity of personal care.

Case 2

Donna, a 17-year-old girl who complained of apathetic hopelessness and suffered from a life-threatening anorexia nervosa, also communicated in a very primitive, nonverbal fashion. The following clinical episode clearly illustrates processes similar to those operating in Mary's case. (See Flarsheim [1975] for a detailed description of this patient's treatment.)

During the third year of her five-day-a-week treatment, the patient entered silently and lay on the couch as she usually did.

During the next half hour, neither of us spoke and she seemed fairly comfortable. I was comfortable sitting with her. Then I began to feel uncomfortable, and I noticed that she was squeezing her eyelids tightly together, as though the light bothered her. It made me uncomfortable to see her showing what seemed to be signs of discomfort, and I walked over and turned off the light over the couch. Then I told her that I had done this because I had felt she was behaving as though the light were too bright for her and it had made me uncomfortable to see these signs of apparent discomfort.

Donna replied that immediately *after* I had turned it off, she had become aware that the light was too bright and was bothering her; she had been unaware of it before that. In fact, she had been unaware of either her existence or mine. She said that at the moment I had turned the light off, she suddenly had become aware not only that the light had been bothering her but also that we both existed.

Patients' awareness—of a disturbing stimulus, of their own existence and that of the therapist—is not sustained after a single episode such as the one I have just described. It takes literally hundreds of such experiences to add up to deeply meaningful personality changes. Rarely is an episode so dramatic and easy to understand as this one, and I selected it because it clearly illustrates how therapeutic adaptation facilitates ego integration.

Donna recognized that the light had been too bright for her only *after* I turned if off. Likewise, Mary perceived my departure and participated in it so that it was partially under her control only *after* I adapted myself to the rhythm of her activity. Donna's recognition of her reaction to the light and Mary's acknowledgment of my departure are both examples of expansion of the patient's perceptual system, and both *followed* my active adaptation to the patient's needs. In both instances, the expansion of perceptual awareness was accompanied by increased awareness of both the self and the object: Mary actively participated in our separation at the end of our session while Donna stated that she had become aware of both of us after I turned off the light.

*   *   *

A particular constellation of defenses against painful feelings seems to be characteristic of patients with severe emotional disorders. These patients have a poorly defined self-concept, with patchy boundaries between the self-representation and the mental representations of other persons. When such patients experience intolerably painful feelings, they may temporarily or permanently destroy their capacity to experience these feelings; sometimes this destruction extends to all feelings. By way of explanation, some of these patients say that they prefer to experience "nothing" because any feeling might become painful. Other patients whose formerly completely intolerable feelings are becoming just barely tolerable defend themselves by trying to use someone else to experience their feelings for them (Giovacchini 1975). The treatment of patients with imperfect boundaries between themselves and others is affected by these structural defects, and necessitates deviations from classical psychoanalysis, particularly for those who define the latter in terms of the analyst's fictitious total neutrality.

Case 3

The therapist must sometimes experience feelings which, initially, are too painful for the patient to tolerate. The following two clinical vignettes illustrate the way certain patients defend against intolerable feelings of sadness by temporarily destroying their capacity to experience feelings at all and by using their psychotherapist as a container into which they project these painful feelings until they are ready to experience them as their own.

The parents of John, a 12-year-old hospitalized schizophrenic boy, stated that he had shown precocious development and premature independence as early as the first months of life. He had become suspicious of food when very young and could eat only if he divided the food into two portions, separating out the "bad" part and eating the remainder. For example, he would pick out pieces of cereal that had a slightly firmer consistency, put them aside, and then eat the rest. He also had shown exaggerated responses to certain sounds (Bergman and Escalona 1949, Boyer 1956). For example, he would become panicky and inconsolable from the

hum of a vacuum cleaner. His mother described him as "not a cuddly baby," but rather, "like a wooden doll." However, as a baby, he had been aware of other people and had established eye contact and the beginnings of speech. These were mostly lost when he withdrew from the world around the age of fourteen months.

It is prognostically favorable that some development had occurred in early infancy; even though it had been lost, there was at least the possibility of "finding" it again. This is in marked contrast to situations where there is little, if any, historical evidence of an early capacity for communication, as was the case with Mary. In the latter situation, treatment must provide the opportunity for a primary infantile developmental experience, a truly formidable undertaking, but one that sometimes succeeds.

By the time John was hospitalized at age eleven, he screamed in an eerie, singsong way that sounded like a stage imitation of crying during most of his waking hours, which were usually at night, when others wanted to sleep. As with Mary, I saw him in the classroom setting, where I took the following notes.

Notes

I have visited John's classroom on several occasions in the past year and he has never acknowledged my coming or going with any greeting or any apparent recognition of parting. Our sessions, which included some moments of communication from him, were broken off at the end, rather than terminated with some kind of farewell.

When I entered John's classroom to see him today, he was sitting as usual, rocking vigorously back and forth, and screaming in his typical singsong manner. Another child said, "Stop that fake crying." John did not indicate that he heard what was said to him. I said that John had real feelings, real sadness, and that his crying was not "fake" (not just a histrionic defense). He immediately screamed, "Shut up! You make me sad. I do not want to hear that! You stop crying!"

Then he shredded Kleenex into small pieces, put them into his mouth, and, when they were thoroughly saturated with saliva, stuffed them into my ears. At first, he used his fingers to push the

saliva-soaked Kleenex into both my ears; then he used the eraser end of a pencil for this purpose. He turned my head so that the right side was down and he could get at my left ear more readily. Since my right ear was down, the Kleenex fell out. He said, perfectly clearly, in a soft, well-modulated voice, "Please pick that up for me." Next, however, he turned the pencil around and started using the sharp point to force the Kleenex into my ears. This was dangerous and I asked him to use his fingers or the eraser end of the pencil, and he easily accepted this limitation. When the time came for me to leave, he said goodbye to me for the first time.

John could not tolerate hearing about his feelings of sadness. He reacted by disowning both his feelings and his ability to hear, and sought concretely to project these defenses into me. His success at mastering his fear of his feelings of sadness in these special ways made him able to acknowledge a separation.

Much of what we learn from work with sicker patients helps us understand patients who are less ill. We even learn something about healthy functioning, which is the most difficult to understand. The next patient was also severely ill, but much less so than the patients already described.

Case 4

Sara, a 28-year-old depressed woman seen on an outpatient basis, had a history of severe trauma in early infancy. Although she was often suicidally depressed, she managed to survive by withdrawing from others and avoiding all feelings, except for an all-encompassing, unlocalized pain. She had been in outpatient treatment for several years, and scheduling difficulties had caused me to cancel several of her appointments. This had led to her painful awareness of her need for uninterrupted care, the kind she should have had as an infant, and to her painful realization of what she already knew—that we could not turn back the calendar and literally give her a new start, a new and better infancy. She felt faced with what was almost a conscious choice—either to stay imprisoned in avoiding her feelings, or to grieve over what had

been lost. She had lived through so many years of withdrawal, without really experiencing anything; if only she could complete her mourning, she could be free, or relatively free, of the restrictions based on fixation to the past.

There were moments of what she called "infinite sadness," sadness so great that "it's not in me, I'm in it." After one session in which she experienced such a moment, she wrote a short "letter" for a writing course she was attending at the university. In it, she expressed nostalgia, sadness, and remorse over memories of her grandmother, who had died ten years earlier. She handed me this letter at her next session, stating that she had "no feeling" about it, and that she was "numb and far away" and "felt nothing." But this poignant expression of sadness and remorse made me feel so sad that tears actually came into my eyes as I read it. I felt the patient's sadness, and the tears that came to my eyes were tears of sadness that the patient could not yet experience as her own.

SUMMARY

I have presented examples of nonverbal communication in the therapeutic interaction to show how successful adaptation to nonverbal signals can facilitate maturation and integration of previously undeveloped ego functions. These examples show clinical situations in which the therapist is under a special strain to maintain objectivity while accepting and containing the patients' projections without acting on them. In this way, feelings that are too painful for patients to experience as their own can be brought into the therapeutic relationship. With such ego support, patients are gradually able to experience feelings as their own; they no longer need to deny or project them.

In his book, *Children of Time and Space, of Action and Impulse,* Rudolf Ekstein (1966) wrote that mothers' empathic understanding of infants' distress is the prototype of the psychoanalytic interpretation. We do not assume that newborn infants know anything about milk, breasts, bottles, blankets, etcetera. Even the change from warmth to cold and back to warmth again must be

learned. We assume that infants feel some kind of inchoate discomfort. Under favorable circumstances (circumstances very different from the extremely unfavorable ones that characterized the infancies of the patients described), mothers "interpret" infants' inchoate distress as meaningful; they realize that their babies need some environmental adaptation to relieve the distress. In this way, infants begin to integrate the source, aim, and object of instinctual impulses. They integrate memories, internal perception, external perception, and the relationship with the caretaking person. This integration of progressively remote signals forms the basis for healthy ego development in infancy and, when things go well, in psychoanalytic treatment.

REFERENCES

Bergman, P. and Escalona, S. K. (1949). Unusual sensitivities in very young children. *The Psychoanalytic Study of the Child* 3-4:333-352.

Bettelheim, B. (1967). *The Empty Fortress.* New York: Free Press.

Boyer, L. B. (1956). On maternal overstimulation and ego defects. *The Psychoanalytic Study of the Child* 11:236-256.

Ekstein, R. (1966). *Children of Time and Space, Action and Impulse.* New York: Appleton-Century-Crofts.

Flarsheim, A. (1975). The therapist's collusion with the patient's wish for suicide. In *Tactics and Techniques in Psychoanalytic Therapy,* vol. 2, ed. P. L. Giovacchini et al., pp. 155-196. New York: Aronson.

Freud, S. (1938). An outline of psycho-analysis. *Standard Edition* 23:139-209. London: Hogarth Press, 1964.

Giovacchini, P. L. (1975). Various aspects of the analytic process. In *Tactics and Techniques in Psychoanalytic Therapy,* vol. 2, ed. P. L. Giovacchini et al., pp. 5-95. New York: Aronson.

Grunebaum, H. et al. (1978). Children of depressed, schizophrenic, and well mothers: Findings from a follow-up study. *Child Psychiatry and Hum. Devel.* 8:219-228.

Winnicott, D. W. (1952). Psychoses and child care. In *Collected Papers: Through Paediatrics to Psycho-Analysis,* pp. 219-228. New York: Basic Books, 1975.

Winnicott, D. W. (1963). *The Maturational Processes and the Facilitating Environment.* New York: International Universities Press, 1965.

11

DISCUSSION OF ALFRED FLARSHEIM'S CHAPTER

Peter L. Giovacchini

Severely regressed patients operate predominantly at primary-process levels and may or may not use words as a principal communicative modality. Schizophrenics sometimes deal with words as if they were concrete objects. In his chapter, Dr. Flarsheim provides us with fascinating preverbal data he gathered from autistic children who, unlike typical schizophrenic patients, were not even able to talk.

Dr. Flarsheim was not a passive objective observer collecting interesting behavioral sequences. Instead, he was a participant whose approach and response to children evoked reactions that represented attempts to establish some contact with the external world. The reciprocity of responses created a new level of functioning that these patients had never been able to achieve.

For the most part, Dr. Flarsheim did not interpret these interactions; he worked primarily at an intuitive level. I believe that his case examples can be viewed from a variety of perspectives relevant to the psychic operations and deficits encountered at the earliest levels of emotional development.

I will begin with the first interaction in which Mary, a hospitalized autistic girl, was playing excitedly with water in a drinking fountain while Dr. Flarsheim held the faucet, his attention riveted on the patient. The moment his attention wandered, the patient's involvement suddenly ceased. The whole atmosphere of pleasurable excitement abruptly collapsed, even though Mary had seemed to have no awareness whatsoever of Dr. Flarsheim as he stood there holding the faucet. In view of his almost imperceptible wandering of attention, I conclude that the patient had been energetically aware of Dr. Flarsheim, that she had been fiercely holding onto a perception of him.

I will present an example of a similar situation in which a child appeared unaware of the presence of another person until that person left his perceptual field; then his reaction was catastrophic. As part of a longitudinal study of child development and infant-mother relationships, my colleagues and I were watching a mother and her toddler son through a one-way mirror. The mother was sitting quietly and unobtrusively in a chair placed on one side of the room. Her son was calmly playing with some toys as he crawled on the floor. He was obviously frustrated with some of them since he was unable to make various parts fit together. However, he did not turn to his mother; he seemed totally unaware of her presence. After several minutes, at a prearranged signal, the mother left the room. The child did not appear to notice that she was leaving. However, after she softly shut the door behind her, he seemed to explode in anger and terror. He had a tantrum, clenching his fists, screaming loudly, stamping his feet, and banging his head on the floor. A woman research assistant immediately went to him and picked him up, attempting to soothe him. He was absolutely inconsolable, arching his back and trying to catapult himself from her arms.

The assistant finally put him down and left the room. Then the mother came back in and sat down on the chair once again. There was an amazing transformation. The toddler stopped crying and went back to his play as if nothing had happened.

Although, on the surface, the mother seemed totally irrelevant to the child, she actually was vital for his integration. I believe that, like the mother in my example, Dr. Flarsheim had become incorporated as an integrating factor in Mary's psychic equilibrium. Yet, on the surface, his importance to her was imperceptible.

Experiences such as these are meaningful for understanding the large population of patients suffering from character defects on whom this book focuses. *I believe that the specific ego defect of Dr. Flarsheim's autistic patient was the inability to form and hold a mental representation.* This defect is also fairly common in adults and often leads to difficult transference-countertransference impasses.

Before proceeding further, I will elaborate briefly on the inability to hold mental representations. Investigators who have studied child development from both a clinical and a cognitive viewpoint distinguish various levels of ego integration. When infants first begin to recognize objects as external rather than part of the self, they still have very little capacity to have a memory of them. At this stage, they are not yet able to retain an internal image of the object unless it is in their visual field. That is, if they do not see the object, it no longer exists for them. Later, during the establishment of separation-individuation and object constancy, toddlers can release the external object from their perception and still retain it in memory. Various investigators have distinguished different types of memory, such as evocative and recall memory. In the former, activation (analysts would say cathexis) of an internal object-representation only occurs when it is reinforced by the actual presence of the external object; in the latter, it occurs without the presence of the external object. This developmental sequence is important for our understanding of psychopathology.

Dr. Flarsheim's child patient, and primitively fixated or deeply regressed adult patients, demonstrate this inability to hold a mental representation without external reinforcement. I have discussed clinical complications and countertransference dilemmas that may result from this lack of psychic integration in my chapter in this volume, especially in the section on "unreasonable" patients.

The drinking fountain incident can also be discussed in terms of even more primitive mental processes than the formation of mental representations. The patient was excited as she played with the water in the fountain and then her excitement abruptly stopped. In view of her past history, this could be understood as a repetition of early infancy, when she often had felt "dropped" by her mother.

The mutual pleasure derived from sharing excitement is a significant element of the mother-infant relationship which leads to the acquisition of higher levels of psychic structure. Dr. Flarsheim unwittingly became part of the repetition of the failure of the maternal relationship in creating pleasurable levels of excitement. As a result of such maternal failure, stimulation was painful for the patient; it could not be contained or brought to an end point that gradually faded into a state of soothed contentment.

Analysis often involves the reenactment of the repetition compulsion. This need not be harmful to the therapeutic process. Analysts must recognize how they have complied with the role patients have assigned them. Then they can analyze transference-countertransference elements.

Dr. Flarsheim next saw Mary one year after the fountain episode, and she was rocking in a sitting position. He held her hand but let both their hands rhythmically rise and fall in an arc. Their excursion increased in amplitude and seemed to be mutually pleasurable. The patient was energetically involved in what they were doing. They were in synchrony with each other from both a physical and emotional viewpoint. In this instance, the excitement was contained and nondisruptively resolved.

Afterwards, the patient acted self-destructively; Dr. Flarsheim feared for her safety and had to limit what she was doing. I believe he was illustrating the difference between the past and the present nonverbally. He not only let in excitement; he participated in it without dropping her. Unlike the patient's mother, he enjoyed what he was doing, whereas the mother had hated every minute of her caretaking. Dr. Flarsheim's intuitive resonance with this autistic child also led to her attempt to talk, or form some words, something that she did only rarely.

Their third meeting one year later indicated continuity and progression. As was Dr. Flarsheim's custom as a consultant, he spent considerable time in the dining room with the children as they ate lunch. As he sat next to Mary, she took his hand and placed it palm up over her soup cup. She then dipped her spoon into his hand as if it were a cup and put the spoon in her mouth as if she were eating soup.

In view of the severity of her psychopathology, this was a remarkable sequence. She had developed the capacity for expectation, a dramatic acquisition in view of her previous utterly hopeless and desolate orientation, her complete autistic withdrawal from the external world. She felt, at least for the moment, that Dr. Flarsheim could nurture her, which signified that she knew, in some indistinct way, what it meant to be gratified. This play-acting of a feeding experience could well be the precursor of the establishment of an endopsychic registration of the nurturing relationship, the structuring of a nurturing matrix.

Whereas, previously, Mary had had little or no capacity to form and hold mental representations, this behavior with Dr. Flarsheim indicated that, by controlling the nurturing elements of external reality, she might find it safe to internalize them. This would also mean that she had developed some sense of trust instead of equating all attempts at gratification with being hated and "dropped."

Unfortunately, this progress was all very tenuous. Subsequently, her behavior became chaotic and disorganized, perhaps indicating that even though she had made beginning attempts to master and feel confortable with a caretaking relationship, she had not integrated them. This was based upon the insecurity and disruptiveness of the maternal relationship, and was reinforced by the imminent departure of several staff members on whom Mary had become dependent.

A consultant who sees a patient once a year can have only a limited effect, especially on patients who are as primitive, fragile, and needy as Mary. There are many differences between a consultant relationship and an ongoing therapeutic or psychoanalytic one. As Dr. Flarsheim emphasized, autistic children require constant and continuous care. A primary task in their therapy is to create a setting that permits them to reach out for help rather than withdrawing into their rigid autistic shells.

However, it is clear that, regardless of the infrequency of their contacts, at times Mary was able to relate to the segment of the external world that Dr. Flarsheim created. He made special adaptations that permitted him to "tune in" to her needs. Of course, the staff of the treatment center had the same goal of creating a milieu that was both gratifying and nonassaultive so that Mary would not have to withdraw as fiercely as she had from the infantile environment. The consultant's visits served as a periodic catalyst for this process. The mutual interaction and reinforcement of staff and consultant helped to create the benign and affectionate milieu Mary so desperately needed.

In the treatment of primitively fixated or regressed adult patients, especially those who are hospitalized, therapists may encounter problems similar to those Dr. Flarsheim faced as a consultant. Such patients need to shut us out because we represent the traumatic infantile environment. Their psychic structure is so amorphous that they do not have mental representations of soothing and nurturing experiences. For the most part, they do know what it means to be gratified. They are in a state of privation. They cannot articulate their needs because they are unable to perceive them in an organized fashion. At best, these patients feel a vague, generalized tension without being able to discriminate its source (e.g., thirst, hunger, the need to defecate or urinate). Initial contacts may have to be limited to containing tension and soothing.

The principal goal of treatment with such patients is the acquisition of psychic structure rather than the resolution of intrapsychic conflict. Nonverbal interactions can facilitate this structuralization, as Dr. Flarsheim illustrated in his discussion of the treatment of a young woman patient. She used the couch in her five-times-a-week therapy. During one session, Dr. Flarsheim felt that the light over the couch was annoying the patient. The patient, however, was unaware of her discomfort. Instead of experiencing it as an organized sensory perception, she felt only a vague, generalized physical irritation. As Dr. Flarsheim noticed that the patient was squinting, he turned off the light. Only then did the patient recognize that the bright light had been the painful stimulus. Her therapist's sensitive concern and perception of needs helped her to structure her generalized somatic response so that she became consciously aware of the external world and how it impinged on her. Insofar as the therapist's actions elevated the patient's level of response and comprehension, they facilitated her acquisition of psychic structure. I believe that such episodes occur fairly frequently in the treatment of severely regressed patients.

Here is an example from my practice. The patient, an adolescent male, had felt abandoned and had undergone a deep regression when I took my vacation. He had to be hospitalized and for some days was in a catatonic stupor. By the time I returned, he had recovered enough to communicate minimally with the ward personnel.

The psychiatrist who was responsible for the patient's management believed that I should visit him while he was still in the hospital, to facilitate the transition from the hospital to his eventual return to my office. He asked the patient if he wanted to see me and, in a typical fashion, he shrugged his shoulders as if he did not care one way or the other. His reaction to my impending visit was the same as Mary's reaction to Dr. Flarsheim's departure. The surface indifference protected both patients from feeling helpless and vulnerable and at the mercy of an external world that they could not control. My patient had developed some dependence and trust prior to my vacation, but believed that I had deserted him when I left. In a similar fashion, when it was time to separate from Dr. Flarsheim, Mary could not acknowledge that he had any meaning for her; she could only maintain control through indifference.

I visited my patient in the early afternoon. He was still in bed, although it had not been his custom to remain in bed that late in the day. We greeted each other somewhat awkwardly and then I sat down. Since he was lying down, I relaxed into a psychoanalytic frame of mind. He started talking slowly and then seemed to gather momentum and spontaneity. Even though the setting was different, we both settled into an analytic interaction.

He first referred to events that had occurred several weeks before I left for my vacation. Then he moved forward in time until he reached the week before my departure. As he continued talking about these more recent events, he became increasingly agitated. This was apparent in the sound of his voice and in his anxious, tense movements. I also felt more and more tense and uncomfortable.

All of a sudden, he stopped talking and shut his eyes tightly. Without any deliberation, I slowly got up and left. That evening, he told the attending psychiatrist that he wanted to be discharged the next day. He was asked if he wanted to continue treatment with me. He indicated that it really made no difference to him, but he did not object when an appointment was made for him. When we resumed treatment, I was convinced that he was glad to be back. (Indeed, it was the beginning of a long and mutually rewarding treatment, which I have reported elsewhere [1979].) The following formulation of the meaning of our interchange, which is relevant to the "light" episode with Dr. Flarsheim's patient, was pieced together after many months of analytic work.

In the hospital, the patient regressed to very early psychic levels and almost totally withdrew from the external world as was evident from his catatonia with its waxy flexibility. During our hospital interview, when his memory approached the time of our separation, an extremely traumatic moment that had made him feel helplessly betrayed, he was seized by intense panic. His ego lost some of its previous organization; he regressed to an extremely primitive level. He was unable to structure his needs; the most he could feel was pain and discomfort. Shutting his eyes represented an attempt to shut out the memory of the traumatic external world that had deserted him. I was the embodiment of that dangerous infantile environment.

Flarsheim's patient also had shut out a painful segment of her environment (the light). In both cases, the patients were not aware of the internal or external circumstances responsible for their distress. The analysts' reactions were the vehicles that created the capacity to perceive in a more organized fashion. This was clear with Flarsheim's patient; she became aware of the bright light that had been bothering her. With my patient, the change was subtler and requires amplification.

Besides being a painful grimace, my patient's shutting of his eyes was a reaction to threatening memories stimulated by my presence. When I left, he had the illuminating realization that something he did (shutting his eyes and wishing that I would leave) could influence the surrounding world (me). What had begun as a vague sensation of distress had now become a way of changing a painful environment. He was no longer entirely at the mercy of outside forces, but had developed some control over them. Inner pain was elevated to a wish, the wish to send me away. Our interaction enabled him to structure a wish. The fact that

somatic distress, elevated to a wish, could effect a significant change in the external world that would alleviate that distress somehow achieved endopsychic registration, a psychic structure that he had lacked previously. It became an organizing, synthesizing force that could elevate somatic responses to psychological representations, which then could be felt as structured needs. A good portion of my patient's analysis was spent in reconstructing this sequence.

These interactions were, at the beginning, essentially nonverbal. Autistic children such as those described by Dr. Flarsheim, as well as deeply regressed adult patients, function primarily at a prementational level. Some clinicians believe that because of their basically nonverbal orientation, they are not capable of being treated in a psychotherapeutic or psychoanalytic context. These clinical vignettes stress that even with psychologically amorphous, physiologically focused psyches, therapists can make contact on an interpersonal basis that will lead to the acquisition of sufficient psychic structure so that the treatment process can be carried out on a more conventional basis.

These incidents also have implications for normal development. Both Dr. Flarsheim's patient and mine succeeded in changing the external environment even though the impetus for that change did not originate within them. This has a parallel with the optimally developing infant whose surrounding environment creates favorable circumstances for growth. Initially, the infant's internal processes cannot be verbally expressed. They are, for the most part, governed by internal rhythms that will establish a diurnal cycle as long as there is no interference. In other words, the best conditions for growth are created by environmental compliance with the neonate's needs, which includes the establishment of circadian rhythms. These then become the foundations upon which nurturing and soothing sequences are constructed. Developmental progression consists of an ever-expanding spectrum between internal physiological processes and higher mentational activities. This progressive emotional development can be recapitulated in the therapeutic interaction and defines its structure-promoting potential.

SUMMARY

In Dr. Flarsheim's chapter, he illustrated how meaningful a nonverbal interaction could be when the therapist "tuned in" to the psychic level of the severely disturbed patient. This is the essence of mutuality and reciprocity, experiences that these patients probably have never known. This basic contact should have occurred in the early mother-infant relationship but did not. Thus, these unfortunate patients did not form a foundation from which they could grow emotionally.

Therapy, especially psychoanalytic therapy, does not repeat neonatal and infant development in a corrective fashion. It is doubtful whether that can be done even with young children. Still, as patients tend to re-enact the traumatic infantile environment in the transference regression or, as is true of autistic children, carry it into the current setting, therapists who do not withdraw or otherwise defend themselves against patients' pain initially will have certain reactions stemming from a primitive psychic level corresponding to that of the patient.

To maintain the analytic perspective, one must have the ability to view these primitive parts of one's self as they interact with those of patients who have been subjected to traumatic assaults. These nonverbal interactions serve as the basis for preverbal communications; the latter become structuralized and, eventually, are verbalized as well as organized into affects. The analytic setting facilitates this structuralizing process.

REFERENCE

Giovacchini, P. L. (1979). *Treatment of Primitive Mental States*. New York: Aronson.

12

THE BASIC BOND AND EMOTIONAL GROWTH

Martin Fields

Editor's Notes

In this chapter Dr. Fields discusses in detail his experiences with a patient who was too primitively structured to be treated on an outpatient basis. Wishing to maintain a psychoanalytic perspective, he had to devise a treatment approach consistent with his understanding of intrapsychic forces, structure, and developmental hierarchies. As this patient's emotional disturbances antedated even the symbiotic level, Dr. Fields turned to the most recent empirical data from neonatal research. In particular, he focused on the establishment of the basic bond during the early neonatal period. The latter approach increases in importance as we further explore the severest forms of psychopathology.

It is difficult to think in terms of the familiar concepts of regression and fixation with the types of patients discussed in this chapter. When the effects of trauma are significant so early in life, there are gross distortions in the sequence of emotional development and the usual hierarchical structuralization that distinguishes various psychic levels is not established in the ordinary sense. Many psychoanalysts have not even tried to understand such primitive, and

---

I wish to express my gratitude to Dr. Peter Giovacchini for his help in preparing this manuscript.

largely preverbal, psychic orientations, but have ipso
facto assumed that psychoanalysis is not possible
with such patients.

For many years, I, along with many of my colleagues, have repeatedly emphasized the extended
application of the psychoanalytic method. However, I
have also recognized that this method has limitations
and that it would be clinically unwise to think in
terms of its universal applicability. Dr. Fields certainly does not discuss traditional analysis, but he
does use fundamental psychoanalytic principles to
draw conclusions about treatability and to construct a
therapeutic strategy.

The therapeutic process described in this chapter
has implications for hospital treatment in general—
that is, treatment designed to achieve higher levels of
psychic structure and integration rather than just
symptom remission. The interaction with the milieu
and the use of multiple therapists are of central
importance to the success of such treatment. The
author demonstrates how and why he uses both hospital staff/therapists and setting to help the patient
form new psychic structures. He discusses how the
hospital's intrinsic, hierarchically arranged structure
can be used to make up for early environmental
failures.

I believe Dr. Fields's approach is unique and innovative; it has achieved impressive results. Since his
proposals differ from those of traditional hospital
treatment, even that based upon psychoanalytic principles, there will be some resistance to his ideas. The
latter will be mitigated if the critics ask themselves
what alternative they can offer these severely disturbed patients who often are condemned to institutional custodial care for most of their lives. Dr. Fields
has constructed a conceptual system and a treatment
method that he believes will enable these psychically
crippled patients to function fully as human beings.

The eventual validity of any clinical approach finally
depends upon its usefulness and applicability over

time. If Dr. Fields's success with the multiple therapist approach is duplicated by other clinicians in
the hospital treatment of similar patients, then this
method will cause modifications in our current attitudes about hospital treatment. It is also possible that
this method could be extended to patients with predominantly prementational psyches outside of the
hospital setting. Dr. Fields's approach is yet another
example of extending the applicability of psychoanalysis without necessarily retaining the formal elements of the psychoanalytic procedure.

P. L. G.

INTRODUCTION

Freud (1923) developed a structural viewpoint in which the
psyche is organized into a hierarchy of levels. Each level is a
separate way of understanding and reacting to perceptions of
experiences. For example, a perception of a breast could be understood at an early narcissistic level as an extension of the self, or at
an oral level as a need-gratifying object. He believed that as
development proceeds, perceptions become increasingly organized
and structured.

In psychoanalysis, the treatment process begins with the most
structured levels and proceeds downward. The structural hypothesis implies a treatment approach in which patients react to the
analyst with greater emotional intensity at one level of intrapsychic structure than at others. If patients experience the analyst
at an early narcissistic level as a part of themselves and at an oral
level as a need-gratifying object, one of these orientations will be
dominant, depending upon the current state of the transference. In
this chapter, I will discuss patients who lack either the ability to
maintain more emotional investment in one level of intrapsychic
structure than in others or the capacity to move from one ego state
to another especially when they experience inner disruption.

For example, a paranoid patient was terrified that people were
following him. He frequently expressed his terror to his therapist

who was the head of the department of psychiatry in a teaching hospital in which he was hospitalized. His therapist would, on occasion, leave the door of his office open to reassure him that no one was standing outside spying on them. The patient was always mollified by this. Apparently he needed something concrete to give him relief. In contrast, when a resident left the door open as he was interviewing the patient, he became enraged and insisted that someone was going to blow the ward up. He became so upset he had to be put in a pack.

The patient had reacted to the resident and the head of the department at two different levels of intrapsychic structure. At the more advanced level he had been paranoid; at the more primitive level he had been in an amorphous state of terror. As the latter had been dominant, a concrete action had been necessary to reassure him that his fear had no basis in reality. This action had been an organizing experience. If the higher level had been dominant, its effect would have been disruptive in that such "reality testing" would only have fixated his conviction that there were persecutors and intruders in the outer world.

Some very seriously disturbed patients have not developed the structural hierarchy Freud described. Most likely, very early in life, neonates establish a principle for creating structure for themselves which serves as a template or model for all subsequent intrapsychic structure. Patients whose template formation is deficient develop very specific forms of psychopathology that may require multiple therapists who relate to and create different psychic levels. Such therapy may have to occur in a hospital setting, which has an intrinsic hierarchical organization that places staff members in specific echelons. In this way, patients are able to relate to each staff member on a different level, since they do not yet have the capacity to move between various ego states with the same person. In fact, they have not yet established a hierarchical sequence that would enable them to climb up or down the developmental ladder.

The establishment of intrapsychic structure can be compared to a chromosome template in biology. The latter contains the original biological message for the production of cell components for various groups of cells as the soma achieves higher levels of structuralization. An analogous structuralizing template of the psyche is established, perhaps at the time of mother-infant bonding (Klaus and Kennel 1956). Klaus et al. (1972) believe that in the first days after birth, the way the mother and child relate to each other has a profound effect on later maternal involvement. Klaus and Kennel call this early neonatal stage the "maternal sensitive period" because the mother and infant are extremely sensitive to each other. The degree of interrelatedness is so profound that infants move in a rhythm that is in cadence with the mother's voice (Condon and Sander 1974).

Winnicott (1956) describes an intuitive, almost biological maternal attachment to the infant that he calls "primary maternal preoccupation." He believes that this preoccupation begins during pregnancy. In many ways, it is similar to the mother-infant bond described by Bowlby (1958). The latter is formed after the child is born, but its strength and quality are determined by a sequence of events and feelings that begin after conception. However, the observation of Klaus and Kennel, and others, of the hypersensitive period between mother and infant in the immediate postpartum stage suggests that something occurs between them which makes the primary maternal preoccupation manifest.

The remainder of this chapter is divided into two sections. In the next section, I will discuss the basic bond that helps determine the course of psychic structuralization. In the second section, I will explore why some patients with basic-bond defects may need multiple therapists to help construct various psychic levels. I will present a treatment model based upon psychoanalytic insights that evolved during the treatment of a hospitalized patient.

THE BASIC BOND AND EMOTIONAL DEVELOPMENT

First, it is necessary to formulate some tentative hypotheses of mother-infant bonding so that the clinical data that follow will be easier to understand. Once I have discussed clinical material and the therapeutic interaction, I will return to these formulations to determine their usefulness for the specific type of psychopathology I am confronting.

I am one of those who believe that during the bonding period in early infancy, neonates are basically unaware of their environment. They react to stimuli reflexively and cannot distinguish basic inner states such as comfort and discomfort because they have not yet established a fund of perceptual experiences against which to evaluate fresh percepts. This sounds strange because we observe neonates in what appear to be extreme states of discomfort and comfort, but we cannot know what they are actually feeling. We comfort infants when *we* feel they are uncomfortable; our interpretations of their feelings are determined by our own fund of perceptual experiences. It is conceivable that our interventions do make neonates comfortable and that they then internalize that feeling and become aware of discomfort as a contrast. The warmth of a comforting relationship—even though the adult, rather than the infant, perceives it as comforting—creates a state of awareness against which to evaluate other feelings. While we cannot present evidence regarding the perceptual experiences of very young infants, these conjectures may help to explain the clinical data I will present.

Freud (1915) wrote that infants' muscular movements enable them to distinguish between external percepts and internal tension states. Through physical withdrawal, infants can avoid contact with a stimulus from the outer world, whereas they cannot remove themselves from an internal state. It is possible that neonates' first mentational self-awareness is of their own movements as opposed to a distinct, unchanging percept of their inner experience (Giovacchini 1979).

It is also possible that as an infant begins to experience this earliest awareness in terms of movement and change, his mother becomes intuitively sensitized to him. This means that she unconsciously experiences changes in herself that will stimulate her to care for her child. She is involved in a primitive feeling state without psychological content, a feeling that something has changed. I believe this sequence of events establishes a primitive bond between the mother and her baby. Winnicott (1956) has called these psychological changes, which begin early in pregnancy, "primary maternal preoccupation." However, primary maternal preoccupation reaches the mother's conscious awareness during the bonding period and is experienced as an internal change that cannot be logically defined. The mother can share her feelings through interactions with her infant and her husband, who has undergone parallel changes in himself in preparation for fatherhood.

The good mother feels changes within herself that are in resonance with those the infant feels. The baby conveys his vulnerability to the mother, and she responds to it in subtle ways, both in her general attitude and in the specific ways she relates to and holds the infant. Based on my own clinical findings, I believe that the neonate experiences such a mother as a truly responsive environment.

When the infant reaches a phase in which he needs the environment to play with, rather than just to soothe him, he somehow expresses this need. The mother responds by feeling an impulse to play with both her husband and child. She then creates a structured play situation enabling her child to create an endopsychic registration of the desire to play. The child requires mother's participation, which emanates from her observing changes in herself and causes her to develop her unique form of play. Both mother and child learn to structure a play situation that is mutually gratifying and enhancing.

Once the basic bond is established, the mother and child revert to it whenever a new level of structure must be created, that is, when the child progresses in his emotional development. At these times, the mother uses the basic bond to change her orientation toward her child from one consistent with the old level of structure to the new one. She uses cues supplied by her infant so that she can create a new environment. Her infant fits in with each new environment because it evolved from his input. We can envision this process as being similar to the formation of a genetic template which determines cellular organization. As each gene strand contains many individual genes that are translated into cell components according to a fixed order, the mother provides the infant with a sequence of environments that produce structural hierarchies.

Although it is impossible to know the neonate's inner experiences, I can infer them from my reactions with patients who are primitively fixated. For example, patients who have regressed to what I call the "basic bond level" believe that they are changing but do not know how. They are observing a percept of their inner state in transition rather than one based upon the content of that state.

For example, a patient described constantly seeing changes in a picture on my wall, as she kept shifting her focus from its foreground to its background. Later, in a less regressed state, she acknowledged that she had noted the content of the painting the first time she saw it. She had thought it was quite a pleasant picture.

The infant's level of inner awareness varies throughout the day; his emerging mentation is closely linked to his biological state and diurnal rhythms, which affect the intensity of sensory experience. At specific times, the infant is increasingly active, moving around more than usual, and observing his own movements. When the mother regresses to a state that approximates that of the neonate, she becomes sensitized to her diurnal rhythms as well. The mother's and child's diurnal rhythms may become synchronized with each other so that she relates to her child at what we perceive to be an intuitive level. The gratifications from this type of relationship are more primitive than those derived from relationships with better-structured needs and with endopsychic structures of need-satisfying experiences.

The following clinical vignette illustrates some aspects of the bonding process as it is recapitulated in the analytic situation.

Case Example

Pam, a 30-year-old woman entered treatment because she could not allow herself to have an intimate relationship. She fought with people when they resisted her desire for intense involvement.

From the outset, she was deeply invested in her analysis. She thought about it constantly and felt it was her only hope for a happy life. Yet, she missed many of her early sessions because she was preoccupied with helping her friends or with her work. Some of her experiences were disruptive, but she did not talk about them because she believed they would threaten her treatment. While she was silent for long periods of time, she also experienced considerable relief from these outside disruptions. Rather quickly she became dependent on me and felt protected. She accepted my interpretations without any resistance. I felt that she had succeeded in comfortably fusing with me.

As she became further engaged in treatment, it became increasingly difficult for her to split off her disruptive states and keep them separate from our fusion. Once again, she missed many sessions. I interpreted her withdrawal from treatment as transference related, that is, she was afraid of destroying our relationship with her inner disruption. She replied that she felt more connected to me when helping her friends than when actually with me in sessions. We concluded that the only way she could receive help in periods of disruption was by offering it herself.

After a year of treatment, Pam achieved the ability to make demands of both her friends and me. She had never considered having needs of her own before. At this time, she also decided to change her career to mental health. In part, she saw this as an identification with me, but she also had a deep personal interest in the field. Furthermore, she believed that working in this area would add a dimension to our relationship that previously had to be kept outside of treatment. Being able to share her professional experiences with me created a flexible atmosphere in which she did not feel emotionally rigid. Previously, in maintaining what she considered to be the strict rules of the analytic situation, she could not have a friendly dialogue about casual issues.

She discussed her cases with me, especially a young woman patient who had been hospitalized because of head banging and other autistic symptoms. There were remarkable parallels in the treatment process of this patient and the relationship between Pam and me.

For example, the autistic patient felt she needed to be recognized as a person with her own needs rather than just being a victim of hospital rules. At the same time, my patient had a similar need to be recognized by the hospital staff for the good work she was doing with her patient. Simultaneously, I was striving for professional recognition. It seemed that our parallel concerns with our development created bonds among the three of us, myself and my patient and her, in turn, with her patient. As Pam gained recognition for her work, her patient was able to get the staff to recognize her needs, and I began to feel I was achieving my goal.

Their dreams seemed to run in tandem with regard to how they were attaining their objectives. My patient had a dream in which she was stopped by a policeman for having accumulated parking tickets, but he was flexible and did not arrest her. A friend, however, offered to bail her out of jail if she were arrested. Interestingly, the friend was viewed as rigid in contrast to the flexible policeman. Undoubtedly, this dream refers to different aspects of superego rigidity and relaxation. She emphasized that she experienced the external world as flexible.

Pam's patient had a dream on the same evening. She was in a car going to a racetrack. She was stopped by a policeman for speeding, but he sensed her distress and let her go. When she arrived at the track, she lost money in betting, which she equated to not getting her needs recognized. She was beginning to feel that the world, that is, the hospital staff, could recognize her needs as the policeman had, but she was confused because the environment at large was not supposed to gratify her as the race track had not.

Both dreams contain two persons, one flexible and one rigid. In my mind, they represent different aspects of the outer world which we can think of as corresponding to a more specific, particularized environment and a larger general one. The policeman could refer to the therapist for my patient and to the therapist and hospital staff for the autistic patient. The world surrounding this more narrow environment is still viewed as disruptive and not one that recognizes their needs.

When Pam discussed her patient with me, she stated that she felt as she did when she observed the picture on my wall. She was preoccupied with moving from foreground to background in the picture rather than concentrating on its content. She experienced a change within herself similar to the shifting perceptions of the picture. This was in contrast to a structured feeling that could be related in terms of its content. Later, as she became aware of the more structured content of her feelings, she was able to notice the content of the picture. During this period in our relationship, we felt very attached to each other because of our mutually shared growth.

Our relationship was based upon a feeling that we were changing. The nature of the changes was irrelevant. Still, it was a remarkable coincidence that we both wanted to further develop our professional skills.

Paradoxically, as we became increasingly comfortable with each other, she also felt considerable panic. Apparently she was now bringing what she had once experienced as disruption from the outside into our relationship, into our fusion. To help her manage her pervasive agitation, I briefly talked to her daily on the telephone, and I knew when she needed me to call again. This was based upon my awareness of her inner tempo as I measured it alongside my own. I realize this is difficult to describe, but it had something to do with how rapidly she talked and her general level of excitement, a certain frenetic quality I could easily detect. Our appointments were, at her request, in the early morning. These times, although there were other factors involved, may have corresponded to peaks in our diurnal rhythm patterns and in our alertness. We both felt that the telephone calls were strengthening the bond we felt with each other. If I failed to call when she needed me to, she became enraged because she felt I was not as invested in the relationship as she was.

One day she became extremely upset. Her patient had complained that she had not been available when needed. My patient was filled with rage at her patient because of her constant complaints. Pam could not respond to all of them without neglecting her other patients. We concluded that she was repeating an infantile pattern, that is, she was enraged at her patient and me, at times, as she had been toward her depressed mother. She was disturbed by her unempathic attitude especially now when she was feeling internal changes which were associated with her conviction that she was adding new dimensions to her personality. She was afraid that her rage would also damage our relationship and the bond we seemed to have established. She feared that I would react to her demands as she had reacted to those of her patient.

However, she gradually learned how her reactions were a repetition of her traumatic past and were being repeated in her behavior toward both me and her patient. She discussed, for example, how her father had left for the army when she was two months old. For the next several years she was alone with a depressed mother who was not only insensitive to her daughter's needs, but demanded that the patient minister to *her* neediness. She experienced her relationship with her mother as tenuous because she feared that whatever minimal bond she might have established with her would be destroyed by her anger.

As she was able to make these connections, she saw the picture on my wall as a totality instead of experiencing it as a sequence of changes from foreground to background. Possibly she was now operating at higher structural levels in which the content of her inner experiences rather than the experience of inner changes was predominant.

Her treatment, as would be expected, dealt with many issues which were the outcome of structural psychopathology. The bond she formed with me enabled her to modify her character structure so that she could face her needs directly rather than relating to someone else's needs before acknowledging and gratifying her own.

There are, of course, many other factors involved in her background responsible for the complexities of her problems, some also based upon intrapsychic conflict. However, I have chosen not to emphasize them since I want to stress only one facet of her development as it was illustrated in the therapeutic interaction.

There is still much to learn about how mother and child—and, later in life, patient and therapist—communicate such primitive inner psychic states to each other. Neonatal research demystifies such communication as it uncovers subtle cues and clues. In the case of Pam, I believe that the peaks of our diurnal rhythms made us particularly accessible to each other.

THE HOSPITAL SETTING AND THE FORMATION OF THE BASIC THERAPEUTIC BOND

Treatment that is designed to help patients solve emotional problems due to defective bonding often requires a hospital milieu. Such a setting can provide patients with multiple therapists; one establishes the basic bond while others associate with separate, higher intrapsychic levels.

Milieu treatment began with the work of T. F. Main (1946), who was followed by Maxwell Jones (1953). The latter introduced the concept of the therapeutic community in which "treatment" occurs throughout the day instead of just during the patients' therapy hours. It is conducted by a variety of mental health personnel, including nurses and social workers as well as physicians. Stanton and Schwartz (1954) conceptualized patients' intrapsychic growth in terms of the entire "institutional process," or the therapeutic effect of the hospital environment, rather than the impact of patients' therapy hours alone. Maxmen et al. (1974) presented the concept of the hospital milieu as a reactive environment; they categorized the hospital staff members by their therapeutic function rather than their professional discipline. They advised using many therapeutic techniques, including medication and group therapy, emphasizing the practical goal of getting patients back on their feet. The therapists' roles were determined by the techniques they used.

In contrast to Maxmen et al., Kernberg (1975) considered the therapeutic techniques used by the milieu, such as individual and group therapy, in terms of their effects on the intrapsychic development of patients. Kernberg viewed group therapy as producing primitive emotional reactions in patients and individual therapy as producing more structured ones. He felt that treatment plans should vary with regard to the amount of each intervention in accord with different patients' emotional needs.

Bettelheim and Sylvester (1948) conceived of the therapeutic milieu as an environment that provides patients with a consistent frame of reference in which they receive constant psychotherapeutic treatment. Similar to Maxmen et al. and Kernberg, they subdivided the milieu according to the role of the individual therapist. They viewed the staff as providing patients with a well-defined hierarchy of interpersonal relations. For example, child patients learn that classroom teachers have a role separate from that of counselors, and they relate to them on the basis of that difference. A counselor can treat patients individually, whereas the teacher has to take all the children in the classroom into account. According to Bettelheim and Sylvester, patients' internalization of the school's organization helps them internalize inner controls as well; they learn that they can accomplish different things with different people.

Bettelheim (1974) based his psychoanalytic milieu upon a defense-need model. He conceived of constructing an environment that would understand and support patients' defensive adaptations. In this model, patients are allowed to regress to a primitive developmental level so that the therapist can help them repair basic developmental defects. For example, Bettelheim (1967) described the treatment of an autistic child who constructed mechanical instruments and electrical circuits to represent the inner workings of his body. The counselors helped him build his models because they viewed them as adaptations that protected him from his basic helplessness and vulnerability. After several months, he relaxed his defenses and began to regress. He defecated in public areas of the residential treatment setting and displayed his primitve self in other ways.

His counselors explored the meaning of this regressive behavior instead of prohibiting it. They felt that this attitude would enable the patient to understand his behavior rather than find it frightening and shameful. Since Bettelheim knew that the patient's parents made him afraid of his bodily functions, he contended that regression would reverse the developmental trauma. This treatment plan assumed the existence of a coherent psyche with a well-organized defensive superstructure, as evidenced by the patient's mechanical behavior and his ability to regress. The patient needed the staff to respond either to his mechanical defense or to his aggressive behavior, but not to both at once. By contrast, patients with a defect in their basic bond do not possess the degree of intrapsychic structure that would permit them to demonstrate a separate hierarchy of intrapsychic levels.

Bettelheim (1974) viewed the hospital itself as providing a structural organization. He felt that patients use the natural hierarchy of staff personnel to create an inner organization for themselves. This enables them to use their primary counselor more effectively because they can place the latter's function in the context of the work environment.

Unlike the Bettelheim model in which only one counselor is the primary therapist, the hospital environment itself may be used as the fundamental vehicle for treatment so that a patient may have many therapists (staff members). In such treatment, patients begin to see the hospital structure as a place in which understanding can occur, rather than a containing environment that enables the therapist to function effectively. If staff members are presented in this context, patients will tend to use each one to represent a different level of their own psyche. The level associated with each staff member will correspond to that person's place in the intrinsic structural hierarchy of the hospital. For example, in the case example that follows, the patient used me, the coordinator of his treatment, to represent his superego because I gave him commands and he obeyed them. He tried to use someone from the dietitian's office to deal with his oral gratification.

Patients with a basic-bond defect cannot connect a specific intrapsychic level with a particular need and interaction. When such patients feel hungry, they simultaneously experience a primitive excitement that is inappropriate to their hunger. They may wish to discharge their diffuse excitement, for example, by driving a fast car. By relating to individual staff members on various intrapsychic levels, such patients can acquire psychic structure much as they would through the establishment of the basic bond. In the hospital, each intrapsychic level seems to be integrated and consolidated through an interaction that, to a certain extent, parallels the construction of the mother-infant basic bond. This also means that, at these various levels, the patient and the staff member/therapist experience similar intense feelings and resonance that the mother and her baby feel. There are differences, of course, because a therapist does not have the same biological involvement that a mother does, and higher psychic levels are always operative to some degree; but the connections we can make between early development and the treatment process are important for our understanding of how psychic structure is acquired during treatment.

The following case example of an adolescent patient illustrates structure-promoting interactions. He had been totally unable to function in the external world.

Case Example

Jim, age 18, had been told that his intelligence was in the genius category. Nevertheless, he was unable to apply it. He said he was in the hospital because his girlfriend believed that he could learn to use his intelligence. However, he had no conception of how the hospital could help him.

Jim's mother was unusually candid with me in talking about the problems she had had in rearing her son. During his first year and a half of life, he had had numerous minor illnesses such as sore throats and stomach disorders. She constantly had sought medical advice, but it seemed that her primary motivation had been the relief of her own agitation. She had had little success until Jim was one and a half. At this time she had been referred to a doctor who "knew what he was doing." Although he had prescribed a placebo, she believed that Jim's health improved. In any case, she had felt better.

She had followed the directions of a book on child care to the letter. If Jim were still hungry after feeding, she would not give him more since he had already eaten the amount the book recommended. He would have to wait until the next feeding before he got any more food. He had cried a great deal and always seemed hungry.

Rivière (1973) has written that observations of the internal states of infants and severely regressed patients are experienced in a way that is so primitive that they are not translatable into words. In my experience with patients suffering from primitive mental states, my correct reactions are often based upon intuitions. When I try to specify the observations that have led me to my intuition, I often find the task impossible. I can find observations that are tangential to the cause of my reactions. These observations can lead to many conclusions, but not to the one that I am convinced is correct.

With regard to Jim, many of the hospital staff had the same intuitions that I did, but we frequently could not reproduce the data that led to our conclusions. Does this make our conclusions scientifically useless? If we assume that our intuitions are so closely connected to the observations upon which they are based that the two cannot be separated, then we are considering them a priori givens. However, a theory based upon a series of intuitions can be useful if it is able to predict the patients's behavior and lead to suggestions as to how the therapist's behavior can facilitate the patient's intrapsychic development. Then our intuitions gain a degree of validity.

During our initial interview, Jim told me nothing about himself. His concern was with hospital rules—whether he could have visitors and what his privileges would be. I sensed that he was reacting to me at a superego level and needed to test my flexibility. In subsequent sessions, I was impressed with his emotional intensity, which seemed unrelated to what he was talking about.

As an example, one day when I entered his room, he eagerly ran to me, took me by the hand, and sat down. He said he had something he had to read to me. He then began reading dispassionately from *The Tibetan Book of the Dead*. Even though his eyes were fixed on the book, I felt he was so aware of me that if I moved, it would upset him. He appeared to be more involved with me than with what he was reading. He read it with minimal inflections in his voice, which led me to conclude that he was not involved in the material. Even though I felt his intensity, I could not get involved in the content of what he was reading. The moment I left him, I forgot all about him.

Other staff members who saw Jim also were impressed with his intensity while they were with him and forgot him when they left. If he had been interacting with me in an object-related way, I do not believe I could have so easily wiped him from memory. Instead, it seemed as if I were having a conversation with a parrot. A parrot may give the appearance of involvement because it speaks, but there is no substance to what it says. When people convey their substance or essence, they reflect their state of being in the structure of their communications. Patients who believe they are in a state of nonexistence may convey this by speaking endlessly of irrelevancies or by withdrawing. Furthermore, we intuitively feel that such patients are "not there" and cannot be "found."

Jim succeeded in establishing relationships with several staff members, including a social worker, Ms. N., with whom he seemed to be having structured conversations about his past romantic encounters and books he was reading. Ms. N. commented on the content of his conversation and his anger-provoking behavior on the ward, but he did not seem to hear her. At best, he memorized what she said without really integrating it. On the surface, this relationship appeared surprisingly sophisticated in view of the severity of his psychopathology. Nevertheless, the patient had caused Ms. N. to get in touch with her own deeper psychic levels and this determined the nature of their reactions.

For instance, she held a longer than usual session with him. Ms. N. later stated that it had been unthinkable for her to cut that session short because the interchange had been so vital. However, what they had discussed—books and similar matters—did not seem at all vital. We concluded that she must have been responding to him at some primitive psychic level. Otherwise, if she had been participating in a truly structured interchange, she would not have felt compelled to prolong the session beyond the customary time.

They had been reading and discussing psychiatric literature as if they were colleagues. Jim never had a peer relationship based upon mutual respect. As colleagues, they were working together to establish higher psychic levels from an interchange that began at basic, primitive levels.

At first, Ms. N. reacted to Jim as I had: she could not connect his intensity with content. When they discussed psychiatric literature, this lack of connection markedly changed. They were both deeply involved in content and this became a mutually enhancing experience. In creating an environment for the patient suitable for the acquisition of new psychic structures, Ms. N. relied upon changes within herself which were in resonance with similar changes within the patient, as well as other cues he supplied. This is similar to the formation of the template for intrapsychic structure described earlier.

The patient became comfortable with Ms. N., and he credited her for his ability to sculpture a breast of clay, his first creative project. He made it for his art therapist. The creation of a breast, a symbol of nurturing, indicated that working with Ms. N. made it possible for him to conceptualize a nurturing relationship with her. We felt that this represented new psychic structure, in that perviously, his internalization of nurturing experiences had been poorly integrated and weakly cathected. There were many other positive and satisfying elements to the relationship that led us to believe that he was creating further endopsychic registrations of gratifying and nurturing interactions.

The art therapist had concluded that Jim was devoid of artistic interest and abilities, and she felt useless. After he sculpted the breast, her attitude changed dramatically. She became interested in and excited about his work. Now she felt he had placed her in a maternal protective role. She became concerned about other staff members intruding into their scheduled appointments. She also saw to it that his privileges were ensured and that other patients did not encroach upon his rights. She had adopted the function of a stimulus barrier for him (Boyer 1956).

At this time, Jim told the art therapist the following dream. He was in a department store. The basement was on fire, and a witch was chasing him up from floor to floor. When he reached the roof, he jumped off. He did not feel particularly anxious about this dream.

The dream seemed to illuminate the patient's behavior with the staff and allowed us to speculate further about his basic structural deficits. The department store with its various floors could reflect the organization of his psyche. He associated the witch to destruction. The fire reminded him of the intensity of his relationship with Ms. N. It is noteworthy that the fire occurred in the basement, the lowest floor of the store and perhaps the most primitive level of his psyche. The patient further indicated that although he found his intense feelings with Ms. N. gratifying, he was also frightened that he would be destroyed by his involvement with her.

Jim became increasingly aware of his fear of Ms. N. so that he tried to avoid seeing her. Before the dream, he was unable to explain why he feared her. Apparently, he sought a more structured relationship, which he found with the art therapist.

Still, he was dealing with very primitive psychic levels with both therapists. Ms. N. depicted a level of excitement, initially without psychic content, that could be equated with a basic-bond involvement. This relationship, rather than leading to psychic growth, was perceived as destructive, as Jim's associations to the fire in the dream indicated. He was able to make a clay model of a breast, but he could not keep his creation in the context of his interaction with Ms. N. He was afraid that his model would be demolished in their mutual excitement. He needed another therapist, the art therapist, to share what he had created. She became a nurturing and protective mother to him. Developmentally, this was somewhat, but not much, more advanced than his relationship with Ms. N.

When Jim first entered the hospital, he was not able to use relationships constructively. He might involve himself in relationships similar to that with Ms. N. but, eventually, he would feel anxious and distressed. Instead of using regressive defenses, he would behave like an "adult." He might think of getting married, finding a productive job, and buying a home. This was all meaningless, since he did not have the capacity to achieve any of these goals. Nevertheless, moments of misery and despair would be followed by such adult preoccupations, even in the hospital. On one occasion, when his feelings toward Ms. N. were most intense and he feared annihilation, he suddenly pulled himself together and seriously stated his intention to leave the hospital and marry his girlfriend.

It would seem that when facing psychic trauma, Jim progressed rather than regressed. The manifest content of the dream graphically depicted this reaction. The witch was chasing him from lower to higher levels. When he jumped off the roof, he was not anxious. He reported that he did not actually fall with an impact, but rather, felt as if he were floating. His reaction to trauma was moving upwards, just the opposite of what Freud (1916) described in his retreating-army metaphor.

The trauma, as symbolized by the witch, undoubtedly refers to the wicked destructive mother and Ms. N. In other words, a mothering relationship caused him to seek defensively higher structural levels. For patients as severely disturbed as this young man, a mothering relationship refers to something more primitive than nurturing. It suggests an interaction concerned with basic survival. What I have referred to as the basic bond is associated with the early feeling of mutual striving or changing. As I will discuss later, his mother was almost exclusively focused on her own existence and had very little emotional investment in her son as a separate entity.

Being chased by the witch and fleeing to higher levels would seem to make the concept of regression in the ordinary sense meaningless for the type of psychopathology this young man illustrates. However, if we do not confine our interpretation of regression to spatial movement, then we can understand the interplay between the patient's psychic structure and his defensive adaptations. Apparently, he had had to construct higher psychic levels to escape from his mother. This type of development represented a pseudostructure that prevented meaningful structuralization. This pattern was repeated in the hospital.

Ms. N. related to him at basic feeling levels. With her, he was able to feel comfortable excitement for the first time in his life. Because of his infantile experiences with his mother, establishing a bond with Ms. N. had to become a destructive experience. The next, more structured stage was characterized by a feeling of being nurtured and protected; it could not survive in such a setting.

Again, we see why multiple therapists can be so important for such patients. Jim needed someone else, the art therapist, to relate to him at the structured level, which was symbolized by the clay breast produced in the relationship with Ms. N.

Once patients such as Jim relive early traumas with one therapist, they may need another therapist sufficiently removed from the first therapeutic relationship to support the latter's constructive or potentially constructive aspects. This is especially significant for patients whose early nurturing experiences occurred in a destructive context.

As Jim needed to escape from Ms. N., he also had to distance himself from me since he saw me as her ally. However, at the time he told the art therapist the dream, she was only minimally involved in his treatment and therefore was relatively safe from being projectively contaminated with primitive destructiveness.

There are similarities between the multiple therapy approach and conventional analysis. In all analyses, both the negative and positive transferences have to be analyzed. The analyst sometimes represents the bad object and at other times represents the good object. Usually this can be contained in one treatment setting since the patient's and analyst's observing egos can work together to scrutinize the "good" and "bad" interactions. In hospital treatment, these various relationships may be concretized and represented by separate therapists. Further, the hospital itself serves as the integrative force that holds the various therapists together, depicted in Jim's dream of a department store holding various floors or levels together. This may be seen as the equivalent of the holding environment (Winnicott 1954) created by the psychoanalytic setting.

As we began to understand Jim in the terms that I have just described, we formulated a treatment plan to give some direction to the therapeutic course rather than just letting it evolve. We hypothesized that Jim would need specific therapists to represent structural levels higher than those characterized in his relationships with Ms. N. and the art therapist. Each therapist would maintain his or her integrity by not becoming involved with material that would be more appropriate for another therapist. Instead, Jim would be directed to the appropriate therapist. As already mentioned, he would discuss food with the dietitian. He would play games with another staff member, and he would come to me for "rules and regulations," that is, for evaluation and direction of his behavior. This plan was implemented, and Jim continued seeing the social worker and the art therapist in addition to his "new" therapists.

Once we established this approach, Jim demanded a container of milk every few hours. He also became agitated to a degree that we had never seen before. He believed that he was incarcerated in the hospital forever and would be unable to survive in the outside world because no one was preparing him to live in it. He became so angry that he required restraints for the first time.

I offered him a therapist outside of the hospital staff, hoping that this would provide him with a relationship that would serve as a transition to the external world. At first, he hated the new therapist, Dr. S., and refused to see him. When Jim finally met with Dr. S., he ignored him until Dr. S. felt so useless that he considered breaking off treatment. However, Jim's agitation ceased and his investment in the treatment with Dr. S. gradually, and then markedly, increased. He asked Dr. S. if he would get him a needle for his most valued possession, his stereo, which he just had brought into the hospital. Dr. S. brought him the needle and the patient took pride in his ability to fix his hi-fi equipment and in his knowledge of good music. We conjectured that the stereo represented an aspect of the self from which he derived considerable self-esteem. He then asked permission to sit in the room in which he saw Dr. S. He would sit in this small conference room when he felt inadequate and it soothed him and helped him regain tranquility. Sitting there quietly made him feel "like a person" again.

It seemed that Dr. S. had become an integral part of the treatment relationship. The patient apparently used him to bolster his self-esteem, which strengthened the cohesion of his self-representation. We might say that Dr. S. was at the self-representation level. Jim's pleasurable preoccupation with the hi-fi equipment was a concrete expression of the process of consolidating his self-representation. He felt he was gaining an identity that would enable him to face the outside world.

Shortly after Dr. S. was comfortably ensconced in the therapeutic process, Jim had the following dream. He was in a hospital room with a woman whom he identified as Ms. N. He then went down a flight of stairs to a second room where a black man was sitting at a dinner table. The man threatened him. In a third room, a playroom located on the same floor, he found a friend. The room was filled with dirty laundry and washing machines that separated Jim and his friend. Jim asked this friend to help him escape from the hospital but he would not listen. However, the friend did give Jim a coat, which made him feel protected and hopeful.

The manifest dream content consisted of three scenes, each with a distinct theme. From this we can infer that he was dealing with different psychic levels. His free associations referred to different modes of behavior including wishes to be fed and wishes for more sophisticated romantic attachments. We felt that his relationship was primarily based upon early psychosexual phases rather than later ones. Concerning the black man at the dinner table, he first thought of several staff members who had refused to bring the milk he demanded. He then said that the therapist would have fed him, rather than reject him as the black man did. This seemed to depict the traumatic aspects of his early nurturing. We later learned that escaping from the hospital had several meanings for Jim, but at this time he associated it to Dr. S.'s attempt to help him enter the outer world.

It is noteworthy that there had been a marked change in the staff's attitude by this time. Whereas previously we could not retain a memory of Jim after we left him, now we all felt intensely involved even when we were not with him. We were particularly aware of him when he had this dream.

In terms of direction, this dream seemed to represent a regression, as Jim literally moved from a higher to a lower level. We questioned whether he was regressing from the relationship with Ms. N. to other relationships; since we had postulated that these relationships were based upon more structured elements. However, in his associations, he saw the relationship with Ms. N. at a higher level. We also believed that the dream depicted an early attempt to regress from a weakly held sexual position, something we conjectured he had been unable to do in the past.

Jim's behavior on the ward also seemed to be more primitive, at least when it concerned certain issues such as nurture. He demanded milk from the hospital, rather than from any particular person. Instead of relating to objects, he used the hospital itself as an integrating element; the individual therapists and their consultation rooms represented aspects of that structure.

Jim then created a similar situation with Ms. N. which recapitulated some elements of his early relationship with his mother. He wanted to touch and hug her, and he wanted to discuss her problems. Ms. N. felt uncomfortable and at first withdrew from him, upsetting him considerably. When Ms. N. withdrew, Jim was in a state of diffuse agitation most of the time. He was often immobilized, sitting on his bed for long periods, whereas previously he had been a very active and gregarious member of the unit. He also evoked a state of diffuse agitation among the staff and other patients, though it was impossible to attribute their reactions to any specific aspects of his behavior. Then, he had the following dream. He was walking down the hospital corridor arm in arm with Ms. N. When he reached the nursing station, two elderly female patients were sitting at the desk. Ms. N. began discussing other patients with one of them. Jim was left standing alone outside the nursing station. He needed help but no one was aware of him.

The meaning of this dream was virtually self-evident. Walking with Ms. N. reminded Jim of his desire to touch and hug her. The nursing station represented an environment in which care was offered, but he was isolated from it. He stimulated needs in Ms. N., but then she turned away from him. She became involved with others and had a discussion based upon her needs, which did not concern Jim. His needs were ignored.

In general, I believe that patients with problems at the level of the basic bond need to evoke, and attempt to gratify, the needs of the therapist as Jim did. Searles (1975) wrote that, at times, patients have to be therapists to their therapists.

Because of the transference-countertransference interaction Ms. N. was able to get in touch with certain levels of her personality that allowed her to become more involved with Jim. Ms. N. also discussed her countertransference feelings in supervisory sessions. As she became more comfortable she no longer withdrew, and Jim felt relieved. A relationship based upon mutual growth is an essential feature of the basic bond. This was a constructive relationship.

Jim's relationship with Ms. N. recapitulated his relationship with his mother. His mother used him to evoke needs in herself and then isolated herself from Jim. He tried to repeat this pattern with Ms. N. This is the equivalent of his mother seeking out doctors because of her neediness.

As Jim's repetition compulsion was contained by the hospital, it was expressed in a recognizable fashion. He dreamed that he was floating in the middle of the hospital day room when he noted that he needed care. There were two women caretakers nearby who should have provided it. Even though he saw them, he felt they did not exist—only the day room existed. He emphasized that the caretakers did not exist. They were part of his past, in which all care had been an illusion; thus the two women caretakers were also illusions. He said that they were the same two women patients of his previous dream. He also associated them to Ms. N. and the art therapist, his primary caretakers in the hospital. In his dreams, they were both therapists and patients. The dream recapitulated his mother's caretaking, which had been an illusion; she had needed to care for herself at his expense.

Still, he was now able to let himself be taken care of in an object-directed way. He obtained relief from tension when particular staff members checked him at night; previously, he had gotten angry at them when they checked him. Thus, the hospital had become a structure in which the staff's involvement could relieve his distress and help him grow. The painful memory of illusory care was contained within the hospital environment, represented in the dream by the day room. We believed that the day room referred to a newly created intrapsychic structure, an environment that could support him and his painful memories.

Jim had been in the hospital for about five months. I now felt that I was talking to a reactive human being rather than a parrot. He was receptive to what I had to say, and I discussed how he was repeating with each therapist various facets of the infantile situation with his mother. I especially emphasized his feelings of isolation and neediness, and how he had to evoke neediness in others to reproduce the traumatic maternal relationship. For the next month, he felt very comfortable in the hospital and did not make any more demands. Then he became restless and stated that he wanted to leave the infantile world in the hospital and move into the outside world. Shortly thereafter he was discharged.

After leaving the hospital, he arranged to get his high school diploma. Then he went to college, where he achieved an outstanding record. He established a relationship with a new girlfriend, the first such relationship that he really valued. He was considering seeking psychoanalytic treatment.

Comments

The hospital's integrating presence enabled Jim to establish a series of hierarchically arranged relationships that we believe represented various intrapsychic levels. After the patient established this hierarchy with Ms. N., the art therapist, Dr. S., myself, and others, he began to feel a disruptive agitation. He could not explain why he was agitated or what provoked it. He was so amorphously disrupted that he believed he had to leave the hospital. Later he could attach his disruption to his relationship with Ms. N. and the art therapist, and he could be soothed by particular staff members.

What was most striking about this patient's hospital stay was his emergence from a parrotlike state to the human condition. At first, none of the staff members could feel his presence. In a sense, they could not hold his mental representation. By the time he left, all of his therapists believed that he had become a meaningful part of their lives and that their work together had been mutually rewarding.

From the patient's viewpoint, his most significant relationship was with Ms. N. He had formed a deep attachment to her which we compared to the basic bond of infancy. They both experienced this bond as a meaningful attachment; one that was exciting in both a satisfying and frightening sense. Jim could not immediately relate to Ms. N. at higher structural levels. Their attachment had been based upon infantile factors, as evidenced by the long session they had, that would not permit other forms of gratification. Other therapists, such as the art therapist and some ancillary staff members, were able to supply him with nurturing and soothing experiences.

We could discern a sequence to his developing capacity to achieve instinctual satisfaction. First, it did not matter who gave him what he needed. As time went on, only specific staff members could provide him with food. Simultaneously, he was forming a deeper relationship with the art therapist and Dr. S. Toward the end of his hospitalization, he was able to discuss the same topics with Ms. N. as he did with the art therapist. He revealed to me that he was no longer afraid that the "excitement" generated between himself and Ms. N. would destroy the clay breast he had modeled. I had the impression that he was trying to bring higher psychic structures, that is, constellations of object-directed gratifications, in apposition to the basic bondlike attachment he had formed with Ms. N. That way he could establish continuity between the primitive and advanced parts of his psyche.

SUMMARY

In this chapter, I have discussed the treatment of two patients, a woman whom I saw as an outpatient and a hospitalized male adolescent. Both patients had had severe traumas in the form of profound disturbances in the establishment of mother-infant bonding. I believe that many patients suffering from severe emotional disorders have similar backgrounds. In treatment, it is sometimes possible to form a relationship that in some way resembles this early mother-infant bonding. The treatment of these patients illustrates that the process of establishing and using such a bond for further emotional growth may require multiple therapists.

REFERENCES

Bettelheim, B. (1967). *The Empty Fortress.* New York: Free Press.
—— (1974). *A Home for the Heart.* New York: Science House.
Bettelheim, B. and Sylvester, E. (1948). A therapeutic milieu. *Amer. J. Orthopsych.* 18:191–206.
Bowlby, J. (1958). The nature of the child's tie to his mother. *Internat. J. Psycho-Anal.* 39:350–373.
Boyer, L. B. (1956). On maternal overstimulation and ego defects. *The Psychoanalytic Study of the Child* 11:236–256.
Condon, W. S. and Sander, L. W. (1974). Neonate movement is synchronized with adult speech: International participation and language acquisition. *Science* 183:99–101.
Freud, S. (1900). The interpretation of dreams. *Standard Edition* 4–5:1–751. London: Hogarth Press, 1961.
—— (1915). Instincts and their vicissitudes. *Standard Edition* 14:107–114. London: Hogarth Press, 1957.
—— (1916). Introductory lectures on psycho-analysis. *Standard Edition* 16:241–478. Longon: Hogarth Press, 1963.
—— (1923). The ego and the id. *Standard Edition* 19:1–60. London: Hogarth Press, 1961.
Giovacchini, P. (1979). *The Treatment of Primitive Mental States.* New York: Aronson.
Jones, M. (1953). *The Therapeutic Community: A New Treatment Method in Psychiatry.* New York: Basic Books.
Kernberg, O. (1975). Hospital milieu treatment of schizophrenia. In *New Dimensions in Psychiatry,* ed. S. Arieti and G. Shrzanowski, pp. 202–220. New York: Wiley.
Klaus, M. and Kennell, J. H. (1956). *Mother-Infant Bonding.* St. Louis, Mo.: Mosby.
Klaus, M. et al. (1972). Maternal attachment, importance of the first postpartum days. *New England Journal of Medicine* 286:660–663.
Main, T. F. (1946). The hospital as a therapeutic institution. *Bull. Menninger Clin.* 10:66–70.

Maxmen, J. et al. (1974). *Rational Hospital Psychiatry: The Reactive Environment*. New York: Brunner/Mazel.

Rivière, J. (1973). General introduction for *Developments in Psycho-Analysis*, pp. 1–36. London: Hogarth Press, 1973.

Searles, H. (1975). The patient as therapist to his analyst. In *Tactics and Techniques in Psychoanalytic Therapy. II: Countertransference*, ed. P. L. Giovacchini et al., pp. 95–151. New York: Basic Books.

Stanton, A. H. and Schwartz, M. S. (1954). *The Mental Hospital*. New York: Basic Books.

Winnicott, D. W. (1952). Psychoses and child care. In *Collected Papers: Through Paediatrics to Psychoanalysis*. New York: Basic Books, 1975.

——— (1954). Metapsychological and clinical aspects of regression in the psychoanalytical set up. In *Collected Papers: Through Paediatrics to Psychoanalysis*, pp. 278–295. New York: Basic Books, 1975.

——— (1956). Primary maternal preoccupation. In *Collected Papers: Through Paediatrics to Psychoanalysis*, pp. 300–305. New York: Basic Books, 1975.

Part III

Specific
Clinical Situations

13

PSYCHOTHERAPY OF THE PARANOID PATIENT

William W. Meissner

Editor's Notes

For Dr. Meissner, the paranoid patient represents a paradigm that enables him to formulate concepts about the analytic process in general and about various relationships between internal and external object-representations. He stresses the importance of the therapeutic alliance, especially in the treatment of patients suffering from primitive psychopathology. He discusses the difficulty in maintaining the therapeutic alliance with such patients. A major stumbling block in the treatment of many severely disturbed patients is the therapists' inability to make emotional contact with them. In such cases, the analysis does not create a holding environment and the patient cannot become invested in treatment. Usually this situation is the consequence of an ego defect that does not permit the patient to establish any relationships.

However, the situation is not necessarily hopeless. In spite of their primitive fixations and traumatically distorted emotional development, many patients eagerly seek a psychoanalytic relationship. With these patients, we often reach an iatrogenically created impasse; that is, we consciously or unconsciously reject them because of the overwhelming magnitude of their psychopathology. Thus, analysts may resist forming a therapeutic alliance with these

patients because it is too threatening to become so
deeply involved at such a primitive level of psychopathology. One patient told me she had seen three
analysts who covertly refused to analyze her. She had
been actively seeking an analytic relationship and had
stated explicitly what she felt she needed. While none
of the analysts had refused her request directly, they
all had started treatment with absolutely no analytic
intent. Instead, each analyst had attempted to be her
"friend," to be helpful and supportive in the management of her daily life, which was disorganized and
purposeless. She tactfully maneuvered herself out of
each treatment because she did not want to offend
her well-intentioned therapists. Still, she believed she
needed an analyst not a "friend."

Dr. Meissner raises the important question of how
the therapeutic alliance is established. He offers no
strict rules or fixed strategies for achieving the alliance; indeed, there are none. Rather, he offers a
general approach or stance; he believes that the analyst's active presence and respectful nonintrusiveness
are the essential factors that lead to the establishment
of a workable analytic relationship. Dr. Meissner
emphasizes that the analyst's attitude is more important than any one technique or intervention.

The beginning analyst may not feel that these conclusions are very helpful; usually he seeks something
tangible, perhaps a formula that will enable him to
react properly to difficult material. I remember during
my training and early days of practice I was eagerly
searching for such directives. My mentors were unable
to supply me with ready answers and there was a
paucity of literature on technique. Even Freud wrote
about general attitudes rather than specific strategies
and maneuvers. He beautifully illustrated his viewpoints when he compared psychoanalytic treatment
to a chess game. The novice can learn something
about opening gambits and final movements but the
bulk of the game cannot be guided by strict rules.

Once we recognize that responses to patients are appropriate or inappropriate, we are operating in a useful transference-countertransference context. Severely disturbed patients produce transferences that reflect the unique qualities of their infantile environments. These create predictable countertransference responses unless analysts are especially sensitive to patients' projections. Thus, analysts may use their reactive feelings to assess the traumatic constellations or adaptive defenses patients are reliving with them and to respond in a fashion that does not repeat or reproduce the assaultiveness or the abandonment of the early environment. Patients repeat, but analysts do not participate in that repetition. Analysts' responses will be determined by the form and content of patients' projections, which are based on the latters' unique developmental vicissitudes. Such responses reinforce the therapeutic alliance, or the holding qualities of the analytic setting.

To summarize briefly, the therapeutic alliance (or analytic setting) can be strengthened in two ways. As Dr. Meissner points out, the therapist instinctively adopts a general attitude and mode of relating which create a calm non-anxious attitude and foster the promotion of an observational frame of reference. These are general stances that define the analytic position and can be applied to all patients. In addition, certain patient-therapist interactions characterize the treatment of patients with structural defects. These patients distort the reality of the analytic setting so as to reproduce the failures of their early caretakers and, at the same time, maintain psychic equilibrium by clinging to archaic adaptations. The latter, however, are not vital for psychic survival in the consultation room, as patients gradually learn. After they relinquish their archaic adaptations, patients can avail themselves of the fundamental support the analytic relationship provides, assuming that therapists' countertransference understanding has kept them from becoming part of the infantile ambience.

Here, too, general attitudes are also involved. Once countertransference feelings, in a similar fashion to anxiety, act as a signal that the analyst has regressed and if his regression has continued unchecked, disruptively regressed, adaptive mechanisms are set in motion. I especially state adaptive instead of defensive, although defenses may also be adaptive, because the therapist gains analytic insight rather than uses repressive measures to handle his countertransference and thereby derives maximum benefit from it.

These severely disturbed patients are very skillful in creating an atmosphere of chaotic urgency. They attempt to draw the analyst into their turmoil. Often analysts begin to feel responsible for these patients and obligated to do something about their helplessness and misery. They can regain their analytic equanimity once they understand how they are being submerged into the environment the transference has created and how they have taken over the feelings and attitudes of an archaic object.

Regarding the infantile ambience, Dr. Meissner primarily focuses upon a particular type, an early environment that is essentially paranoid in its construction. He has gone considerably beyond the usual formulations about this common form of psychopathology. To some extent, he concentrates upon structural defects rather than aberrant drives, as Freud did. I want to emphasize special sensitivities and vulnerabilities that are the outcome of specific types of traumas and that are eventually expressed in paranoid symptomatology.

Many paranoid patients have exquisitely sensitive sensory acuities, especially in the auditory sphere. I have seen this acuity disappear after paranoid defenses were resolved in treatment and it became apparent that the acuity represented an overcompensatory adaptation. The underlying ego defect emphasizes the importance that Dr. Meissner has attributed to the paranoid state as a significant paradigm. I am referring to these patients' basic helplessness and how vulnerable and unprotected they feel.

In the backgrounds of paranoid patients, we often find a relationship that stimulated them without offering any protection from stimuli. These patients perceive feelings as dangerous because their modulating, regulatory mechanisms are not well integrated into the psyche and therefore function poorly. The protective shield, or "Reizschutz," that Freud postulated has not developed adequately because the mother was deficient in screening external stimuli. In fact, she herself was a source of disruption (see Boyer 1956).

Paranoid patients seek protection through projective defenses. Disruptive, assaultive internal forces or introjects are projected into the external world. In Dr. Meissner's formulation, such projections serve as defenses against depression. That is, he views the hated and threatening aspects of the self that have been projected into the external world by the paranoid patient as the essence of a self-destructive, depressive constellation. Clinically, the combination of paranoid ideation and depression is quite common. Dr. Meissner offers us innovative ways of understanding familiar but puzzling clinical phenomena.

P. L. G.

This chapter applies some of the aspects of the paranoid process (Meissner 1974, 1978) to the treatment of paranoid patients. The basic schema presented here derives from analysis of aspects of the paranoid process insofar as it is organized around the basic principle that the externalized elements of the paranoid process—specifically, the paranoid construction, with its inherent and contributing projections—must be traced back to the underlying organization of introjects from which they derive and on which they depend. After this has been accomplished, the organization and supportive forces contributing to the maintenance and shaping of the introjects can be worked through effectively. In a broader sense, then, this schema

can be envisioned in terms of the conversion of paranoid (projective) manifestations into depressive (introjective) issues, and the
subsequent working through and resolution of the latter.

Although the clinical and theoretical basis for the approach
outlined here is spelled out in detail elsewhere (Meissner 1978), a
word about the derivation of the notion of the paranoid process
from previous concepts may be useful. The basic concepts of
introjection (narcissistic identification) and projection, originally
advanced by Freud, were extensively elaborated on by Melanie
Klein and her followers (Segal 1964). The understanding of introjection, and its relation to projection and the building up of the self
with its correlative structures, comes not so much from Klein, as
from the work of Hartmann (1939) on internalization, Anna Freud
(1936) on identification with the aggressor, Rapaport (1967) on
structure, Jacobson (1964) on self-object relations, and Modell
(1968) on the relation to reality. The concept of introjection
employed here falls closely in line with the formulations of Schafer
(1968), but with greater emphasis on the structural aspects of
introjects as contrasted with Schafer's more explicitly representational account (Meissner 1976, 1981).

Just as the paranoid process is not limited to paranoid psychopathology, but rather, is found in a wide spectrum of clinical
conditions (Schwartz 1963, Shapiro 1965), the psychotherapeutic
schema organized around the dynamics of the paranoid process
may be applied not only to paranoid psychopathology, but also to a
wide spectrum of disturbances treated in insight-oriented, interpretive psychoanalytic psychotherapy.

The patterns of dynamic organization to which the schema
addresses itself can be observed more clearly in certain forms of
psychopathology than in others. Perhaps the clearest and most
striking expression of these dynamics can be found in primitive
psychopathology such as schizophrenia, manic-depressive psychoses, and psychotic depressions. In such severe psychopathology, the
organization and projective orientations of the paranoid construction are driven by powerful underlying needs and dependencies, and
can reach delusional proportions. Such powerful needs may serve to
maintain the paranoid construction and projective elements with a

rigidity and resistance that create considerable therapeutic difficulties (Polatin 1975). However, it is in explicitly paranoid psychopathology that the elements of the paranoid process display themselves with the clearest separation and definition. While the projective elements may dominate the clinical picture, we need to remind ourselves of their derivation from underlying introjects. The paranoid construction serves ultimately to sustain the introjective alignment.

In contrast, patients with borderline psychopathology function at higher levels of ego capacity and personality organization, but their rapid and often fragile oscillations between projective and introjective alignments give them a chaotic, frenzied quality (Kernberg 1967). In such cases, the paranoid manifestations serve as important defensive alignments against the underlying depressive core, which centers around the introjective configuration.

It is important to realize, however, that the interplay of projective and introjective mechanisms is decisive in both severe and relatively mild psychopathology. Thus, the elements of the paranoid (projective) construction and the derivation from underlying introjects play important functions in the organization of the character disorders, including the narcissistic personality disorders (Kohut 1971) and the schizoid personality (Guntrip 1968). For example, Kohut (1971) has pointed to the archaic narcissistic configurations of the grandiose self and the idealized parental image, which reflect the operation of introjective and projective mechanisms at quite primitive levels in the differentiation of primary narcissism. Similarly, schizoid withdrawal can be seen in terms of an immersion in severely pathogenic introjects. In Guntrip's terms (1968), this leads "to the creation of an object-world that enables the ego to be both withdrawn yet not 'in the womb', the Kleinian world of 'internal objects', dream and fantasy, a world of object-relationships which is also withdrawn 'inside' out of the external world. This, par excellence, is the world of psychoneurotic and psychotic experience (p. 82)."

A very clear manifestation of the function of introjects can be found in the forms of neurotic depression, as well as in the more severe and incapacitating psychotic depressions (Jacobson 1971).

Moreover, the same configurations can be identified even in relatively well-organized and well-functioning personalities (i.e., those
with neurotic, hysteric, obsessive-compulsive, or phobic disturbances). Consequently, the mechanisms of our psychotherapeutic
schema cut across all forms of personality organization, manifesting
themselves in a variety of ways (Meissner 1978).

A few words can be addressed to the overall nature of the
schema itself. It does not provide a paradigm of psychotherapy,
nor does it offer a basis on which technical conclusions or directives
can be made. Rather, it offers a logical progression for the therapist's thinking and orientation to the therapeutic process, based on
an understanding of the mechanisms and dynamics of the paranoid
process. Consequently, it should be stressed that the schema is in
no sense univocal or prescriptive. Rather, it must be individualized,
that is, adapted to the unique therapeutic problems presented by
each patient. Thus, the schema can provide no more than a general
orientation and a guide to the relevant therapeutic issues; even so,
it offers logical progression and organization to the levels of
pathogenic structure and helps us understand how they play themselves out in the therapeutic process. It emphasizes sequential
working through: that is, early issues and levels of function and
organization need to be worked through before subsequent issues
can be meaningfully and advantageously approached in the therapy.
Finally, the psychotherapeutic schema not only provides a frame of
reference for intensive, long-term therapy, but also serves to conceptualize and focus the difficulties encountered in short-term
therapy.

PSYCHOTHERAPEUTIC SCHEMA

Establishing the Therapeutic Alliance

The therapeutic alliance is a major part of any meaningful
therapy, as it provides the realistic basis for the therapeutic work
(Zetzel 1970). The therapeutic alliance takes place between the
working ego of the therapist and the part of the patient's ego

which is relatively unembroiled in conflictual tensions, is capable of self-observation, and can join the therapist in the work of the therapy. This observant ego of the patient enters into the therapeutic contract with the therapist's working ego; together they make the contract a viable and vital reality (Greenson 1967).

It is essential that the therapeutic alliance be established and sustained. This does not simply happen, but must be watched for, taken into account, worked at, and, at repeated and important junctures during the therapy, reinforced by the activity of the therapist. As we deal with increasingly primitive pathology, the task of establishing and maintaining the alliance becomes more difficult and the alliance becomes more central to the therapy. The alliance is particularly difficult and crucial with patients whose developmental defect or deviation lies at an early developmental level involving the issues of trust and autonomy that have not been adequately worked through (Boyer and Giovacchini 1980, Giovacchini 1979, Zetzel 1971). Such is usually the case with paranoid patients.

Most neurotic patients develop a therapeutic alliance relatively easily; however, when the therapy makes effective inroads on their neuroses, the therapeutic alliance may be threatened and disrupted temporarily. Further therapeutic work must sustain and reinforce it or, if need be, repair it. In more primitive patients, however, the work on the alliance may form the central core of the therapy. For example, with many borderline and psychotic patients, the therapeutic alliance remains fragile over extended periods of time and requires continual reinforcement and frequent repairs in the face of disruptions and formations of antitherapeutic misalliances. Nonetheless, the alliance is essential for therapy with all patients (Langs 1974).

The question then arises as to how the alliance is established. It is difficult to answer this question since our current knowledge about the alliance is far from sophisticated. The basic issues, insofar as we are able to define them at this point, center around trust and autonomy. That is, the alliance is stabilized to the degree that the patient can both develop meaningful trust in the therapist and sustain a sense of autonomy within the therapeutic relationship. The therapist's contribution to this development of trust and autonomy is not altogether clear. It is generally linked to the therapist's empathic responsiveness to the idiosyncratic needs, anxieties, and inner tensions felt by the patient, such that the therapist responds to the patient in terms of the latter's own individuality, rather than in terms of the therapist's own needs or some pre-existing therapeutic stereotype.

One important element of this responsiveness is the therapist's consistently attentive listening to the patient's productions. This involves a sort of active presence within the therapeutic situation and relationship. I am not talking specifically about activity, although in some cases patients' difficulties in relating to an object in a relatively unstructured context may call for activity on the part of the therapist. Active presence, however, is something different, more in the line of presenting the patient with a consistent, available, "present" object.

Another element is the therapist's empathic understanding of what the patient experiences and feels, what Schafer (1959) has referred to aptly as "generative empathy." The therapist's being attuned to the patient's feelings in this way gives the latter a feeling of being effectively understood and thus contributes to the meaningfulness of the relationship. The therapist's attitude is one of respectful unintrusiveness. It is difficult to explain such a concept in behavioral terms, since the unintrusiveness cannot be spelled out in terms of specific behaviors. Rather, the therapist must manifest an attitude of openness and availability without forcing himself on the patient's attention or invading the latter's inner world. The respectfulness and the unintrusiveness are both extremely important: the former in regard to the patient's individuality and fragile identity, the latter in regard to the patient's fragile autonomy. Respectful unintrusiveness is particularly important with paranoid patients, whose autonomy is extremely vulnerable and easily threatened (Meissner 1978).

In this vein, it is useful to recall Winnicott's notion (1963) of "holding" and its importance in psychotherapy. He commented: "You will see that the analyst is *holding* the patient, and this often takes the form of conveying in words at the appropriate moment something that shows that the analyst knows and understands the deepest anxiety that is being experienced, or that is waiting to be experienced (p. 240)." The "holding function" is all the more important for patients with primitive psychopathology, but it plays a central role—explicitly or implicitly—in all psychotherapeutic interactions. Khan (1972) makes this explicit in his description of his two distinct styles of relating to a patient:

1. Listening to what the patient verbally communicates, in the patently classical situation as it has evolved, and deciphering its *meaning* in terms of structural conflicts (ego, id, and superego) and through its transferential interpersonal expression in the here and now of the analytic situation.

2. Through a psychic, affective, and environmental *holding* of the person of the patient in the clinical situation, I facilitate certain experiences that I cannot anticipate or program, any more than the patient can. When these actualize, they are surprising, both for the patient and for me, and release quite unexpected new processes in the patient. [P. 99]

In addition to such empathic responsiveness, there are certain technical procedures by which the therapist can contribute to the shaping of the therapeutic alliance. First, the therapeutic situation and contract must be defined at the very beginning of treatment (Langs 1973). Second, it may be important to clarify and specify the respective roles of therapist and patient not only at the beginning of therapy but also at critical points during the therapeutic process. Third, the therapist must pay close attention to the often implicit and minimally expressed distortions on the patient's part of the therapeutic alliance itself (Langs 1974). These may be expressed in terms of the patient's fear of judgment or criticism from the therapist, sense of helplessness or impotent dependence on the therapeutic situation, or view of the therapeutic situation as "confessional," that is, as one in which the patient's recitation of sins and defects is responded to by the therapist's curing absolution. In addition, I have found that patients who are students will respond to the therapeutic situation as though it were a school

arrangement in which a certain standard of performance is expected
and in which an evaluation or criticism is to be delivered by the
therapist.

Another variant of alliance distortion is found in the narcissistic
alliance (Corwin 1972), in which the patient enters treatment and
submits to the process with the (often unconscious) intent of
gaining something from the therapist which will enable him to
attain a narcissistically invested and usually unrealistic objective.
The latter tends to represent some form of narcissistic wish fulfillment and may embrace omnipotent, grandiose, or magical
fantasies. It impedes the establishment of a more realistic or meaningful therapeutic alliance. In the process of establishing and maintaining the therapeutic alliance, it is important to remember that
actions speak louder than words. Therapists must maintain a
therapeutic consistency between their words and their behaviors.
Their task is to work constantly at building patients' trust and at
encouraging and fostering the latter's autonomy. With patients
who cling to a helpless and infantile position in many of their
behaviors, there is a constant temptation for therapists to step into
a parenting role and thus find themselves unwittingly undermining
their patients' trust and autonomy. Disparity between verbal
formulations and specific actions signals the presence of therapists' unconscious countertransference attitudes.

I would like to add a word here about the importance of therapeutic confidentiality. Paranoid patients will be exquisitely sensitive
to the least breach of confidentiality. Their therapists must be
constantly alert to any intrusions on the confidentiality of the
therapeutic relationship and must minimize them. No communications should pass from therapists to outside parties of any kind
(family, friends, concerned colleagues, government offices, insur-
ance companies, etc.) except through patients (insofar as possible)
and with patients' full knowledge and consent. Due to the variety
of individual and social pressures on and threats to confidentiality
(Meissner 1979b), this may not be an easy task. But therapists have
to do their best to keep all transactions with patients open, honest,
and above board—to lay all the cards on the table. This is mandatory

with all patients, but with paranoid patients its importance cannot be overestimated.

Therapists must constantly remind themselves that their consistency is of the utmost importance in establishing and maintaining the therapeutic alliance, and that they must do nothing to further undermine patients' sense of trust, autonomy, and self-esteem. This becomes particularly difficult in work on patients' resistances. Analysis of these resistances, insofar as it contributes to their dissolution, runs the risk of undermining patients' fragile self-esteem and autonomy. Consequently, therapists' interpretations of patients' resistances must be accompanied by attention to alliance factors. This same caution applies to other therapeutic interventions as well. Confrontations, whether routine or heroic, are effective only to the extent that they serve to establish or reinforce, or occur in the context of, a working alliance (Adler and Buie 1972, Buie and Adler 1972, Corwin 1972).

In fact, patients are constantly confronted with the question, can they enter the therapeutic relationship and process without losing their already minimal self-esteem and fragile autonomy?

When the therapeutic alliance enjoys a certain solidity and stability, the task of entry is vastly simplified. But when the alliance is fragile or contaminated by elements of misalliance, the task can often be extremely difficult and the entry tentative. In any case, establishing, sustaining, and continually reinforcing the alliance must be a constant therapeutic preoccupation, since the alliance is a prerequisite for all future therapeutic progress.

Defining the Projective System

The theoretical frame of reference for this schema is that of the paranoid process. This process sees patients' experience—both cognitive and affective—as structured around three important constituents, namely, their introjections, the correlative projections, and the paranoid construction (Meissner 1978). It is in terms of these three constituents that patients organize their experience of themselves and the ambient world around them.

The basic organization of the paranoid process derives from the structuring of patients' inner world in terms of introjects (i.e., internalized object relations derived from patients' developmental experience). It is on the basis of such organization that patients derive and externalize certain aspects of their own self-organization in projections, through which they order their experience of external objects and relate to them. Patients organize their cognitive view of the world so as to incorporate and sustain the projections and give them an integral sense of meaning.

The entire process is in the service of confirming, reinforcing, sustaining, and validating the prior introjective constellation, around which patients organize and sustain their sense of self. At this level of work within the therapeutic schema, we begin to "tune in" to patients' projective system. Our general tactic is to identify the elements of the paranoid construction, elicit and define their projective aspects, and then shift back to an inner frame of reference where the introjective organization is a central therapeutic issue.

In our first approach to the projective system, the task is primarily one of listening to patients' accounts of their experience of themselves and the world in which they live. This is equivalent to a descriptive account of their paranoid construction. It is within that construction that we will be able to identify the projective elements. This aspect of therapy is essentially passive. There is no need to confront or refute the elements of the projective system. Our primary objective is to learn about that system, to find out what is in it, and to become as familiar with it as we can.

Patients tell us about their projective system and its correlative paranoid construction from the start. There is little in their demeanor, verbalizations, and expressed opinions that does not provide us with data about their view of the world and themselves. For example, the student who tells us how anxious he becomes when he feels he might be called on in class, how he stutters and becomes confused in conversation with his professors, and how he becomes anxious and impotent when intimately involved with a date is telling us something about his image of himself and his perspective on the world around him. We are not surprised to learn that he was the baby of the family, anxiously and obsessively hovered over by an insecure mother, that he always felt he was a "messy kid" who would never grow up. Consistent with this is his persistent enuresis until about age fifteen. These details blend into a picture of a helpless child-victim lost in a hostile and threatening world of powerful grownups. Consequently, his reaction to the therapist as threatening, intrusive, and powerfully controlling seems perfectly consistent.

Such patients may present the world of their experience as fact, that is, as the way things are. A fairly attractive and very intelligent young professional woman stoutly maintained that she was worthless and inadequate because she did not have the sort of physical attributes that men found attractive. No amount of questioning or contrary evidence would dent her conviction. She plainly displayed her construction of the social environment, which reinforced her own feelings of inadequacy and her perception of herself as unlovable and lacking as a woman. Quite consistently, she saw her male therapist as devaluing her in the same way.

The critical elements in these patients' organizations were related to their projections which, in turn, were related to the modification of object relations (Meissner 1971, 1978, 1979a, 1980, 1981). The relationships of both the student and the professional woman were contaminated by their convictions, based on projection, that significant others were critical, demeaning, malevolent, and the like. In each case, projective elements were related to significant introjective components derived from parental imagoes.

There are certain techniques that help us to define patients' projective systems. First, it is important to get as much explicit, concrete detail about patients as possible. This includes specific events, interactions with others, expressions of affect, and—most important—patients' perceptions and feelings. Second, it is useful to elicit as many parallel accounts as possible, within both interpersonal and historical frames of reference. Again, details are important, since they often reveal patients' patterns of behavior and attitudes. Historical accounts that suggest similar patterns in patients' early life are particularly helpful.

It should be noted that, at this level of the schema, we are not dealing solely with the elements of the paranoid construction; patients also may introduce direct expressions of the introjects. They may tell us in a variety of direct and indirect ways how they see themselves, feel about themselves, and think others regard and react to them. It often happens that in the process of eliciting the details of patients' feelings, hidden affects of depression, fear, shame, inadequacy, weakness, and vulnerability are manifested as direct expressions of the pathogenic sense of self.

A more important aspect of this stage of defining the projective system is the focus on the therapeutic relationship. The therapist must bear in mind the fact that the projective system operates in all spheres of patients' experience, particularly those which are affectively important and in which patients have some stake or investment. Thus, the projective system can be presumed to operate within the therapeutic relationship and, as the therapy progresses, will be manifested most dramatically within the transference neurosis. As the latter is usually the most vivid manifestation of the projective system, it becomes the primary vehicle for the therapist's recognition, definition, and handling of the system.

Several points can be made. First, the most important vehicle for the expression of the projective system is the patient's affect. Affective channels of communication carry the heaviest information load. Second, the therapist may get signals from the patient's affect—sadness, bitterness, regret, anger, fear, etcetera—but the therapist's own affective response may also provide important signals for identifying projective content. That is, the therapist's feelings of boredom, irritation, incompetence, inadequacy, or even hatred (Winnicott 1947) can provide important signals for the reading of a patient's stance. And third, it is important to remember in this realm of the countertransference-transference interaction that patients not only distort their perception and representation of the therapist, but frequently even work to elicit responses from the latter that will confirm their own distortions and misrepresentations (Boyer 1978, Shapiro 1978).

Testing Reality

The phase of reality testing, which follows the definition of the projective system, marks the first stage of the therapeutic approach to the projective system. It would seem obvious that the elements of patients' projective systems need to be tested against the hard stuff of reality, but the question is how this is to be accomplished. Our basic tactic here is to shift the focus of the therapy from the projective system back to the underlying introjective constellation from which it derives. It is usually not wise to test the projective system by challenging or confronting it. This is not to say that confrontation may not be useful elsewhere (Corwin 1972), but in this context it runs the risk of playing into the projective system. Rather, the undermining of the projective system, which carries within it so many residues of patients' pathology, is undertaken by following the tactic established in the previous step of defining the projective system. That is, the system is tested against reality by the process of detailed accounting. As patients fill out the details of the picture, they, in effect, confront themselves with more and more of the specifics, or concrete elements, of reality.

There are also some important specific techniques whose intent is to call into question elements of the projective system and to create a sense of distance between the projective elements as such and the emerging reality perspective. The first important technique involves the "tagging" of feelings. That is, when the patient expresses some content in terms of feeling, it is useful for the therapist to simply "tag" the content as a feeling. Thus, when the patient says, "I don't feel that I can ever do anything right," it is useful for the therapist to tag the feeling quality, rather than the specific content, of the statement: "That seems to be how you feel."

The tagging of feelings as such may need to take place over a long period of time and embrace many concrete circumstances and details of patients' affective experience. The tagging technique, however, has an intention and a direction. The intention is to establish the distinction between feelings (and their intimate connection with fantasies) and reality. Thus, this technique forms an important aspect of the reality-testing phase of the schema. The direction of tagging is toward the gradual amplification of patients' awareness of their feelings as a coherent and consistent pattern of their experience of themselves, and toward the gradual establishment of a connection between the pattern of organization of feelings and specific fantasies. Again, the feelings tend to relate more directly to introjective elements, so that the direction of the tagging approach seeks to establish the fantasy proportions of both patients' perceptions of reality and their perceptions and appreciation of themselves as human beings.

The second important technique for testing patients' reality perspective has to do with defining the specific areas in which their knowledge is lacking. Patients frequently offer interpretations, explanations, conclusions, hypotheses, or attitudes as if they were accepted facts. Quite often, these expressions imply areas of inadequacy or defectiveness. The therapist must not challenge the evidence or try to refute patients; such an approach would only meet with staunch resistance and a rigidifying of the latter's position. Rather, the therapist can tactfully point out the areas in which patients' knowledge is uncertain. For example, if a patient offers the opinion that people at work do not like him, the therapist would elicit further details on the situation at work, particularly those which might suggest that indeed other people at work do not like the patient. When the latter fails to provide such details, as is usually the case, the therapist can point out that the patient feels unwanted (tagging), but that he really doesn't know whether people at work want him there or not.

It is important to note that in the above example, the therapist's position is neither pro nor con. He does not say whether the people in the patient's work setting want to get rid of him. He is merely saying that the patient really doesn't know; carrying it a step further, where the patient does not have real knowledge, his tendency is to fill in the blanks, to fill the empty spaces with something that comes from someplace else. The someplace else, of course, is the patient's own head. By inference, the therapist carries the therapeutic process a step further by making the point that what fills in the blanks in the patient's experience of his reality comes out of his own head, namely, out of the constellation of introjections which form the substance of his inner world (see also Boyer 1971).

I can remember this process vividly in a young man in his mid-twenties who came seeking help because of total paralysis in his life. He had had a paranoid schizophrenic episode about two years before, followed by a profound clinging depression. His life was paralyzed by fear. Everywhere he went he met hostility; people stared at him, laughed at him, thought he was a sniveling weakling with no backbone or guts—"a worthless creep." He could not shop at his local grocery store because the clerk had given him a funny look, presumably thinking that he was a worthless degenerate. The patient fulminated against the capitalist system, social values, corporations, and the American government because he felt victimized and impotent in his dealings with them. His posture was one of helpless rage.

It was hardly difficult to discern the dimensions of this paranoid construction and the introjective configuration from which they derived. It was only after repeated and prolonged testing of many situations that he was able to grasp the projective nature of his reactions and turn his concern to an internal frame of reference. As this shift evolved, his capacity to tolerate social situations gradually increased to the point that he was able to hold a steady job and have a sexual relationship.

As this patient strikingly dramatized, reality testing occurred through progressive delineation of the realm of the patient's fantasy life—both in its external and internal referents—which had functioned by and large at an unconscious level. Further clarification of these introjectively derived fantasy systems and their role in early object relations, as well as in any current transference relation, helps to specify the introjective configuration and progressively delineate it from reality.

It should be noted that the present schema does not represent a conflict-focused approach. Rather, it is concerned with the critical pattern of introjections that underlie and give rise to intrapsychic conflicts. The severely phobic and paranoid young man just discussed was extremely conflicted, but the origin of his conflicts lay in the pathogenic introjects derived from highly ambivalent and narcissistically disturbed relationships with his parents.

Thus, the testing of the reality of the projective system—or rather, its testing against reality—is an extremely important juncture in the therapeutic progression. As the elements of the projective system increasingly come under detailed examination, their stability and utility for the patient become diminished and important therapeutic elements become mobilized. As the therapeutic process engages with the projective system more and more meaningfully, that system is increasingly undermined and the patient's needs to defend and maintain it are mobilized, often to an intense degree. The therapist has to deal not only with the systems as such, but with the defensive responses of the patient to the increasing pressure put on the system. It must be remembered that the projective system is not simply there as a matter of chance. It is an intensely invested, cognitive, affective, and defensive organization whose purpose is essentially the preservation of the patient's sense of self and narcissistic needs. It focuses on the preservation of the introjects as core elements around which the patient's sense of self is organized. Consequently, the defensive titer in the face of the gradual undermining of the projective system can become quite intense.

However, as the projective system is gradually modified, there is a progressive affective shift, so that the underlying (usually repressed) defended-against affects that motivate the system become increasingly available to the patient. Usually, either depressive affects or affects related to underlying guilt and shame are mobilized. The therapeutic alliance is crucial in the working through of defenses and in the tolerance of the painful underlying affect. These operations become possible only to the extent that the therapeutic alliance remains firm and intact, and allows the patient sufficient room and distance within the therapeutic relationship to engage with the therapist with a sense of alliance and supportive assistance.

Nonetheless, the therapist needs to be mindful that in the face of such intolerable depressive affects, the patient may regress to a more projective defense and may reinvest the projective system or modify it so that it is more readily sustainable in the face of therapeutic pressures. It should also be noted that the undermining of the projective system and the emergence of painful depressive affects carry the therapeutic process on to its next stage, insofar as the depressive affects are intimately tied up with and dynamically related to the organization of the underlying introjects. It is these depressive affects that bring the introjects into sharp relief and make them increasingly available for therapeutic intervention.

Clarification of Introjects

Recalling for a moment the organization of the paranoid process, it becomes immediately obvious that the undermining of the projective system and the paranoid construction shifts the focus from the projective system, as such, to the introjects from which the critical projections derive. The projective system, including the paranoid construction, consequently can be seen explicitly in terms of its defensive function in simultaneously avoiding the impact of the pathogenic introjects and sustaining them.

Consequently, the undermining of elements of the projective system leads to an unveiling of the introjects. The focus shifts from the external world to the internal one, and patients begin to give us an account of that internal world. Usually, in paranoid patients, the content of this inner world is depressive; these patients see themselves in terms of overwhelming weakness, inadequacy, helplessness, inferiority, defectiveness, worthlessness, and vulnerability. Just as a detailed process of definition was used to expose the projective system, here the definition of the introjects becomes the focus of the therapeutic process.

The therapist thus seeks to know the concrete and specific details of patients' inadequacy, helplessness, inferiority, etcetera. Again, the reality of these elements must be tested, moving toward the vital insight that, just as the elements of the projective system had more to do with fantasy than reality, so the elements of the introjective system have more to do with patients' fantasies about themselves than with the reality. Here again, the presumption is that patients do not know their own reality, so that the conclusions, attitudes, and feelings that they generate about themselves are based on an unknown quantity.

The introjective organization is manifested primarily within the therapeutic relationship, where patients tend to play themselves off against the therapist in a variety of ways. Most typically, within the therapeutic relationship patients see themselves as weak and inferior and the therapist as powerful, strong, and competent. They also may see themselves as victims of the therapist who are subject to the therapist's evaluation, criticism, and control.

Thus far, we have addressed ourselves to only one half of the economy of introjects. Frequently, patients will be easily in touch with the inferior and inadequate, or helpless and victimized, aspect of their introjects, but we know from experience that there is a parallel but opposite side that bespeaks patients' destructive power. Thus, one part of the introjective economy expresses patients' feelings of worthlessness while another equally strong part holds out for their specialness and entitlement.

What comes into perspective in this context is the inherent polarity of the introjects, which relates to the splitting of introjective elements on both sides of the middle ground of reality (Meissner 1978). In relation to important objects, this works in two ways. If the self is seen as inferior, the object is seen as superior; conversely, if the self is seen as superior, the object is seen as inferior. Correspondingly, if the self is seen as helpless victim, the object is seen as powerful aggressor; on the other hand, if the self is seen as powerful and destructive, the object is seen as victimized and helpless.

Thus, the polar aspects of the introjects tend to focus on one side or the other of the self-object differentiation and often shift back and forth between the two. This vacillating of the introjective elements is like an emotional seesaw. If my end is up, yours is down; if your end is up, mine must be down. Latent in this introjective polarization and the implicit seesawing are all the dynamics of narcissism and, particularly, envy. A similar pattern can be played out in the aggressive determinants, in terms of identification with the aggressor versus identification with the victim.

In this phase of the therapeutic process, it is critical to recognize that both aspects of the polarity derive from patients' own introjects. Thus, the vacillation between the self as superior and special, on the one hand, and inferior and worthless, on the other, is intrinsic to patients' introjective organization. Hence, if one polarity of the introjective economy escapes repression and is available to patients' awareness, the therapist knows that the opposite polarity is lurking somewhere under the surface and will emerge eventually. Thus, the young man whose life was a continual paroxysm of persecutory anxieties and fears saw himself as weak, impotent, helpless, and victimized. But only reluctantly did he unveil the opposite polarity of the introjective configuration: his sense of cold, ruthless superiority, his contempt for those around him, his profuse fantasies of humiliating, killing, or reducing to rubble most of the people who crossed his path.

It is important to note that the organization, dynamics, and functioning of the introjects are based on patients' inherent narcissism. Thus, as the correlative and polarized aspects of the introjects become more clearly defined, it becomes apparent that they operate very much in an all-or-nothing fashion. If patients see the therapist as superior and competent and intelligent, they see themselves as totally inferior and abject, without any competence or worth at all. When therapists hear this unmitigated logic of extremes—the logic of all or nothing, black or white, either/or— they know that they are closing in on introjective territory.

A further important point is that the polarized aspects of the introjects are locked together in a reciprocal defensive organization. Understanding this provides a critical insight into patients' depressive dynamics. Patients' intense clinging to a perception of themselves as inferior, inadequate, helpless, vulnerable, and victimized, a perception that resists therapeutic intervention so stoutly, only becomes understandable when one looks at the opposite polarity in which patients view themselves as special, entitled, exceptional, etcetera. Although only one aspect of the introjects may be visible, it is critical to remember that the polar opposite is irrevocably and unquestionably present and operative. The therapist must understand and help patients to see that the polarized opposites are irrevocably linked together, that they feed off each other, and that they are bound together by the iron clasps of reciprocal defense and cannot be separated. After patients see this, they are in a position to accept and integrate, or reject and surrender, the whole package.

Parallel to the process of defining the introjective economy is the continuing process of testing. For example, patients' feelings of weakness, inadequacy, and helplessness can be repeatedly tagged as feeling elements, and the gradual understanding can be developed that such elements relate to a fantasy that reflects the organization of the underlying introjects. Patients either know only the fantasy or have accepted the fantasy as a part of their real self for so long that they no longer know what their real self is like. Again, the primary testing ground for distinguishing between these introjective fantasy elements and the real self is the therapeutic relationship—most specifically, directly, and powerfully in the distinction between the transference neurosis and the therapeutic alliance.

The Derivation of Introjects

Clarification of the pathogenic introjects, including the gradual delineation of the component elements themselves, requires identification of the introjects' polarized aggressive and narcissistic dimensions. It entails awareness of their reciprocal defensive involvement and interlocking functioning as a unit. While these factors contribute to the gradual delineation and undermining of the embeddedness and investment in the introjects, they rarely provide sufficient ground for effective therapeutic intervention. The next logical and necessary step in determining the organization of the introjects is the exploration of their derivation.

It must be remembered that in this context the introjects are equivalent to internalized object relationships; therefore the exploration of their derivation has to establish and clarify specific ties to patients' past and present objects. With some patients, adequate exploration of this area of their experience can be done fairly actively, but this is not often the case. Usually, this information must be acquired in subtler, more indirect ways that require a considerable degree of self-discipline and patience on the part of the therapist.

Little by little, the picture of patients' past relationships, particularly with parental figures, emerges and takes shape. There are many pitfalls, as any experienced therapist knows. It often takes considerable time before reliable information about past experiences becomes available. One cannot assume that the early reminiscences and the first, or even second, rendition of patients' past experience have unquestionable validity. The initial rough sketch that patients make of their past will be progressively filled in, resketched, refined, and recast as the therapy progresses. It should also be remembered that none of this recounting is simply a recapturing of past reality. Rather, it is a recapturing of patients' experience, which may be overlaid and permeated with elements of fantasy, wish, desire, and defense.

The task at this level of the therapeutic schema is to retrace patients' experience, to establish links between the present organization and structure of the introjects and patients' past experience of object relationships. The critical objects in this context are the parents, though other important figures may enter in, depending on each patient's unique life experience. Siblings often play a vital role, and other relatives or even nonfamily figures also may play a significant part.

One finds that the polarized aspects of the introjects are derived from patients' ambivalent relationships with significant objects. To illustrate this point, let us examine the derivation of the primary polarities organized around the dynamics of aggression and narcissism. In terms of aggression, the "victim" introject derives from patients' relationship with and attachment to a victimized object. This "identification with the victim" is based on the sadomasochistic relationship of the parents; the mother is usually identified as the victim by both male and female children, but the father also may be included in this internalization insofar as he alternately functions as a victim. The "identification with the aggressor" relates to the attachment to and dependence on a relatively aggressive object, and here the father tends to be the primary figure. However, one frequently runs into aggressive, hostile, and destructive elements within the mother's character which form the basis for the child's emerging identification with the aggressor. Similarly, if we turn to the narcissistic elements of the introjective polarity, we find that the content of the introject derives from the narcissistic elements involved in the relationships with the same significant objects. Thus, the child may introject the depressive and devalued aspects of the parental object, on the one hand, and the parallel elements of narcissistic grandiosity, special-ness, and entitlement, on the other.

Thus, patients' introjective accumulation can be seen as a re-creation within themselves of elements derived from important early objects. The introjects can be understood as a form of depend-ent, narcissistically motivated clinging to the infantile past that serves to preserve the level of infantile fantasy and involvement with these objects.

This derivation of the introjective configuration was dramatically demonstrated in a young housewife who started treatment because of chronic depression and dissatisfaction with life. Underlying her overt feelings of worthlessness and inadequacy were the correlative feelings of specialness and entitlement, as well as the sense that she was different from and superior to other people. She felt she had been doomed to a life of suffering in which her extraordinary merits went unrecognized and unrewarded. An important deter-minant of these feelings was her intense penis envy, directed particularly at a much older brother who had been a brilliant student, concert pianist, and the apple of her mother's eye. Even more critical, however, was her mother's attitude: she saw herself as one mistreated by the fates and held herself apart from others, to whom she felt superior. She reveled masochistically in her victimization and suffering and jealously reviled the world for its failure to pay her her due and acknowledge her superiority. The introjective configuration in my patient was derived directly and dramatically from the mother. Mother and daughter had formed a special magical bond, a union of narcissistic glorification through suffering, solidified by the constant expectation that true worth and superiority would have their day. The bond was motivated by the intense and continually frustrated yearning of this young woman for closeness with, acknowledgment by, and acceptance from a narcissistic mother whose pathology allowed her to acknowledge little merit in her daughter.

At times, the parallels between the organization of patients' introjects and the source objects are striking, but often they are more obscure. After all, introjection is a dynamic process. The product of introjective internalization comprises not only elements derived from the object but also dynamic determinants from patients' subjective inner world. Together these elements interact to constitute a realm of internalized object relations that remains essentially transitional (Meissner 1971, 1978, 1981, Modell 1968).

It must be emphasized that the therapeutic relationship is one of the most critical, vital, and forceful areas where the pattern of relating to significant objects manifests itself. Patients' increasing dependence on and involvement with the therapist give rise to regressive pressures that activate infantile projections, serve as the basis for the infantile distortions of the therapeutic relationship, and represent the core elements of the transference neurosis. In the elaboration of the transference, the patient described above saw me as a powerful and all-knowing wizard who would finally bring about a magical change in her life, which would bring her the acknowledgment and admiration that she so desperately sought.

The exploration of the derivation of introjects also serves to clarify patients' understanding that the pattern of their present experience of themselves and the world around them—and particularly their relationship with important figures in their environment—is dependent on their infantile pattern of experiencing and responding. Consequently, the difference between patients' past and present experience underlines the essential insight into the fantasy quality of the experience generated around the introjects and clarifies the distinction between elements of that experience and the real world of patients' present life and activity. In the transference neurosis this understanding and realization are borne in upon patients with particular force, since it is in this critical relationship that they can see most clearly and vividly that the patterns of infantile relating play themselves out in inappropriate and unrealistic ways.

The Motivation of Introjects

The progressive clarification and exploration of the derivation of introjects lead to the next logical question, namely, what are patients' motivations for retaining these introjects and, in fact, clinging to them with such dire tenacity? This is a critical juncture in the therapeutic process and often gives rise to the most vigorous resistance. Up until this point, the primary therapeutic focus has been on clarifying elements involved in patients' pathology and on attempting to understand their organization along a number of important parameters. At this juncture, however, we begin to tap patients' motivations for their psychopathology.

This is a very difficult stage of therapy. One begins to approach not merely what is involved in patients' pathology, but their own inner reasons for clinging to it. I say "clinging," because my experience has shown that only rarely do patients easily surrender their neurosis. Rather, patients *cling* to their introjects, defend them in a variety of ways, and fight off the therapist's attempts to make any inroads on them. The question that naturally arises is, "Why are the introjects so intensely invested and so important to patients?" The answer lies in the inherent narcissistic dynamics of the introjects themselves. It must be remembered that for many of these patients the introjects provide the essential core around which their inner world and sense of self are organized. It is this threat to the patients' organization of their sense of self that creates the often rigid and intense barriers to therapeutic intervention.

What emerges from this reflection is that the introjection represents an adherence to the now internalized objects of patients' experience; it serves to prolong the infantile dependence on and attachment to those objects. Thus, the most important parameter of this dependence is narcissism. The introjection preserves patients' infantile narcissism and is bound up in the often repressed or split-off feelings of omnipotence, superiority, and specialness. The dynamics of the paranoid process operate in such a way that patients—often in hidden, subtle, and difficult-to-elicit ways—see themselves as exceptional, in Freud's sense (1916) of the word. The working through of this level of patients' narcissism is absolutely essential to the success of the therapy. This stage of the therapeutic work encompasses all the difficulties of work with pathological narcissism, a subject that has aroused great concern and controversy recently.

In addition to preserving patients' infantile narcissism, the clinging to introjects also preserves patients' attachment to infantile objects. This clinging to infantile objects tends to prompt a repetition of elements of patients' past experience with those objects. In such patients one frequently finds a frustrated yearning for the acceptance, love, closeness, and caring of the introjected objects. The introjection thus serves as a sort of defensive repossession of the object which cannot be achieved in reality. At the same time, it serves as an important defense against the underlying rage, disappointment, and disillusionment about the relationship with these objects.

The paradox in this infantile involvement and its derivatives is that they serve to preserve and sustain the objects at the cost of the subject. This is true not only of the external aspects of the relationship with objects, but also of the patient's inner world, since the internalization of these pathogenic introjects serves to distort and impair patients' self-organization and autonomous self-identity. For example, the cost to the depressed young housewife described above was monumental in terms of her chronic dissatisfaction, depression, and sense of tormented worthlessness and envy. She was willing to pay this exorbitant price to gain the golden fleece— a sense of specialness, superiority, moral hauteur, and entitlement. The idealized and aggrandized image of her mother was preserved at the cost of considerable neurotic impairment and unhappiness.

But the dynamics also preserve objects within the realm of patients' external experience. For example, one frequently finds hidden loyalties in the family involvements of such patients that reinforce and sustain patients' introjective alignment while protecting family relationships and members. In this context, one often finds family myths that represent adherence to a family projective system that usually is organized so as to preserve the introjective alignment of family members and maintain a delicately balanced narcissistic equilibrium. Frequently, then, patients' introjective alignment actually serves as a vehicle for the preservation of elements of threatened parental narcissism. To return to the young housewife, from this perspective, her adherence to the narcissistically embedded code of specialness and superiority through suffering was calculated to reinforce and sustain her mother's highly vulnerable and fragile narcissism.

The Mourning of Infantile Attachments

Thus far, we have articulated the introjects, clarified their elements, and examined their derivation and motivation. We have focused on the intrinsic relatedness and unity of the introjective polarities and understood that they are locked together in mutual and reciprocal defensive interaction. Because of their inseparable unity, patients are forced to make a radical choice: they must either accept and work with, or surrender, both sides of the polarity. They cannot have one without the other.

The inevitable issue generated by these progressive insights is the surrender of the introjects. This requires some form of confrontation or working through of the infantile dependence and the narcissistic investment in the introjects. Not infrequently, as the narcissistic defenses are diminished, one begins to meet patients' intense rage and envy against the significant objects, which frequently have a highly oral character. Patients' rage and envy often play themselves out in the relationship to the therapist and become a significant phase of the therapeutic work. They constitute another manifestation of the narcissistic dynamics that divide the world into haves and have-nots, and view the distribution of goods in terms of all or nothing. Thus, patients' envy of the therapist's "goods"—whether they be worldly goods, social position, intelligence, or even a penis—must be worked through in terms of the underlying narcissistic dynamics.

This working through sets in motion an important mourning process in which the attachment to the infantile objects is gradually given up and their loss accepted and integrated. As the mourning process is worked through, and the potency and influence of the introjects diminish, autonomous ego capacities gradually emerge in these patients.

The Emergence of Transference Dependence

As the underlying determinants of the introjective economy become increasingly apparent, and the mourning process of the immature and largely narcissistic attachments takes place, patients' infantile dependence on past objects gradually wanes. As that dependence wanes, however, the therapeutic dependence may begin to wax in important and problematic ways. In other words, patients often try to replace infantile attachments with a dependent attachment to the therapist.

The motivational basis for this process needs to be explored, clarified, and focused in the same terms as patients' now explicit and recognizable narcissistic needs. Dependence on the therapeutic situation and on the therapist thus needs to be resolved on its own terms, independent of the working through of infantile attachments to past significant object relationships. This new dependence operates in terms of the same "emotional seesaw" that characterized earlier attachments. Most typically, the visible aspect of this seesaw is the inferior, weak, vulnerable, victimized side of the introjective organization—the equivalent of the victim-introject. However, the therapist must not forget that the powerful, superior, special, entitled side of the introjective economy remains latent in this condition.

The residual elements of the introjective dynamics express themselves in terms of patients' feelings of inadequacy, their difficulty in dealing with interruptions of the therapy or absence of the therapist, their apprehension over the apparent therapeutic progression and the possibility of termination (separation from the therapist), and so forth. All of these issues must be worked through in the therapeutic relationship and must be seen specifically in terms of the resolution of the residual aspects of patients' introjective dynamics—particularly the narcissistic dynamics.

As the pressure of these dependency needs increases, drawing patients progressively into replacement of the objects of infantile dependence with the object of therapeutic dependence, there may be a defensive denial of such dependence and a retreat to a position of artifactual autonomy and self-sufficiency. This may take the form of a narcissistic self-sufficiency that defends against the pressure of dependency needs by denying the need for the therapist and possibly even belittling both therapist and therapy. Thus, the powerful, superior, grandiose aspect of the introjective economy may be activated—leaving the inferior, inadequate, needy aspect of the victim-introject out of the picture.

Underlying this pressure toward narcissistic withdrawal and self-sufficiency or pseudoautonomy, there may be residual defenses against patients' sense of narcissistic affront, with accompanying rage and envy directed toward the therapist. The rage and envy may be accompanied by anxiety and guilt, along with a longing for love, caring, and acceptance on the part of the therapist. These reenactments of infantile concerns serve as important defensive maneuvers against the working through of immature attachments and dependencies.

Transference Resolution

Thus far, we have clarified and illuminated patients' introjective dynamics and the narcissistic and other motivations that support and drive them. We have seen how the dynamics underlying the introjects shift to the transference relationship, where the issues of dependency are worked through on a different level. The therapeutic resolution of these issues constitutes the next step of the therapeutic schema. When patients' dependence on the therapist becomes sufficiently intense, the infantile dependence must be worked through and surrendered within the therapeutic relationship. Thus, the mourning over the loss of infantile attachments to past significant objects is now extended and reworked in regard to the infantile attachment to the therapist. Patients must be helped to work through a variety of regressive infantile pressures that keep them in a position of dependency and serve to satisfy underlying narcissistic needs. As these elements are gradually worked through, patients establish an increasing degree of autonomy and sense of initiative and industry. Finally, there is the clear and decisive emergence of patients' sense of identity.

The resolution of the transference dependency requires the reactivation and extension of the mourning process, which deals specifically with the loss of the transference object. During this mourning process, patients' reliance and dependence on the therapist are gradually surrendered. The therapeutic relationship, particularly in regard to its transference elements, is gradually replaced with a more real relationship based on the more mature and autonomous aspects of patients' developing personality. Thus, the mourning of the transference object is made possible by the gradual enlargement of the therapeutic alliance, which takes place through the latter's increasing absorption, reworking, and reintegration of the infantile aspects of the therapeutic relationship—most acutely with regard to the transference neurosis.

Termination

The working through of the mourning over the loss of the transference object and the resolution of the transference elements set the stage for termination. The erosion of the infantile underpinnings and motivations of the introjective organization makes possible patients' introjection of aspects of the therapist and the therapeutic alliance, which offers the possibility of a more reasonable, realistic, and adaptive organization of the self.

The latter introjections are considerably less susceptible to regressive drive influences and drive distortions than were the earlier introjections. They also are correspondingly less involved in defensive narcissistic investment. Patients' increasing capacity to model themselves on the realistic, adaptive aspects of the therapist opens the way for emerging identifications that enhance patients' autonomy and structural capacity to resist drive derivatives. The termination work enhances the critical internalizations that form the basis of inner structural changes—specifically, changes in the ego and superego—which serve as the basis for long-lasting, adaptive therapeutic change (Meissner 1981). Thus, there is a shift from defensive to adaptive concerns, a refocusing of patients' interest and investment from the past to the present and future, and a general unleashing of developmental potential which leads toward the growth of a stabler, more reasonable, more adaptive, and more mature personality.

SUMMARY

The foregoing schema sets forth a logic of the therapeutic progression based on the paranoid process. It does not solve the dilemmas of psychotherapy, nor does it substitute for the hard knocks of therapeutic experience and the guidance of good supervision. It does provide a helpful frame of reference for the logical progression of the therapeutic process. Paranoid patients offer an infinite variety of problems and difficulties which challenges any approach to the understanding of therapy. I would hope that the above schema, compressed and condensed though it is, may help to orient and guide the clinician through perplexing and frustrating phases of treatment.

REFERENCES

Adler, G. and Buie, D. H. (1972). The misuses of confrontation with borderline patients. *Internat. J. Psychoanal. Psychother.* 1: 109–120.

Boyer, L. B. (1956). On maternal overstimulation and ego defects. *The Psychoanalytic Study of the Child* 11: 236–256.

Boyer, L. B. (1971). Psychoanalytic technique in the treatment of certain characterological and schizophrenic patients. *Internat. J. Psycho-Anal.* 52: 67–86.

―――― (1978). Countertransference experiences with severely regressed patients. *Contemp. Psychoanal.* 14: 48–72.

Boyer, L. B. and Giovacchini, P. L. (1980). *Psychoanalytic Treatment of Schizophrenic, Borderline and Characterological Disorders*, 2nd ed., rev., New York: Aronson.

Buie, D. H. and Adler, G. (1972). The uses of confrontation with border-line patients. *Internat. J. Psychoanal. Psychother.* 1: 90–108.

Corwin, H. (1972). The scope of therapeutic confrontation from routine to heroic. *Internat. J. Psychoanal. Psychother.* 1: 68–89.

Freud, A. (1936). *The Ego and the Mechanisms of Defense*, rev. ed. New York: International Universities Press, 1966.

Freud, S. (1916). Some character-types met with in psycho-analytic work. *Standard Edition* 14: 309–333. London: Hogarth Press, 1957.

Giovacchini, P. L. (1979). *Treatment of Primitive Mental States*. New York: Aronson.

Greenson, R. R. (1967). *The Technique and Practice of Psychoanalysis*, vol. 1. New York: International Universities Press.

Guntrip, H. (1968). *Schizoid Phenomena, Object Relations and the Self*. New York: International Universities Press.

Hartmann, H. (1939). *Ego Psychology and the Problem of Adaptation*. New York: International Universities Press, 1958.

Jacobson, E. (1964). *The Self and the Object World*. New York: International Universities Press.

Jacobson, E. (1971). *Depression: Comparative Studies of Normal, Neurotic, and Psychotic Conditions*. New York: International Universities Press.

Kernberg, O. (1967). Borderline personality organization. *J. Amer. Psychoanal. Assn.* 15: 641–685.

Khan, M. M. R. (1972). The finding and becoming of self. *Internat. J. Psychoanal. Psychother.* 1: 97–111.

Kohut, H. (1971). *The Analysis of the Self*. New York: International Universities Press.

Langs, R. J. (1973). *The Technique of Psychoanalytic Psychotherapy*, vol. 1. New York: Aronson.

——— (1974). *The Technique of Psychoanalytic Psychotherapy*, vol. 2. New York: Aronson.

Meissner, S. J., W. W. (1971). Notes on identification. II. Clarification of related concepts. *Psychoanal. Q.* 40: 277–302.

——— (1974). Correlative aspects of introjective and projective mecha-nisms. *Amer. J. Psychiatry* 131: 176–180.

——— (1976). A note on internalization as process. *Psychoanal. Q.* 45: 374–393.

——— (1978). *The Paranoid Process*. New York: Aronson.

—— (1979a). Internalization and object relations. *J. Amer. Psychoanal. Assn.* 27: 345–360.

—— (1979b). Threats to confidentiality. *Psychiatric Annals* 9: 54–71.

—— (1980). The problem of internalization and structure formation. *Internat. J. Psycho-Anal.* 61: 237–248.

—— (1981). *Internalization in Psychoanalysis.* Psychological Issues, monogr. 50. New York: International Universities Press.

Modell, A. (1968). *Object Love and Reality.* New York: International Universities Press.

Polatin, P. (1975). Psychotic disorders: Paranoid states. In *Comprehensive Textbook of Psychiatry,* vol. 2, ed. A. M. Freedman et al., pp. 992–1002. Baltimore: Williams and Wilkins.

Rapaport, D. (1967). *The Collected Papers of David Rapaport,* ed. M. Gill. New York: Basic Books.

Schafer, R. (1959). Generative empathy in the treatment situation. *Psychoanal. Q.* 28: 342–373.

—— (1968). *Aspects of Internalization.* New York: International Universities Press.

Schwartz, D. A. (1963). A review of the "paranoid" concept. *Arch. General Psychiatry* 8: 349–361.

Segal, H. (1964). *Introduction to the Work of Melanie Klein.* London: Heinemann.

Shapiro, D. (1965). *Neurotic Styles.* New York: Basic Books.

Shapiro, E. R. (1978). The psychodynamics and developmental psychology of the borderline patient: a review of the literature. *Amer. J. Psychiatry* 135: 1305–1315.

Winnicott, D. W. (1947). Hate in the countertransference. In *Collected Papers: Through Paediatrics to Psychoanalysis,* pp. 194–203. New York: Basic Books, 1975.

—— (1963). Psychiatric disorder in terms of infantile maturational processes. In *The Maturational Processes and the Facilitating Environment,* pp. 230–241. New York: International Universities Press, 1965.

Zetzel, E. R. (1970). *The Capacity for Emotional Growth.* New York: International Universities Press.

—— (1971). A developmental approach to the borderline patient. *Amer. J. Psychiatry* 127: 867–871.

14

HELPLESSNESS IN THE HELPERS

Gerald Adler

Editor's Notes

Although this paper was first published over a decade ago, it fits in well with the currently written chapters in this book. Dr. Adler discusses disturbing situations that are familiar to all analysts who treat severely disturbed patients. He is a prominent member of a small but growing group of analysts who place a heavy emphasis on their countertransference reactions.

In the analytic tradition, Dr. Adler tries to understand his reactions in terms of patients' psychopathology—specifically, as repetitions of the patients' past archaic object relationships. Patients defeat their analysts and take pleasure in doing so. Often they are repeating a life-and-death struggle with an important person from their past, this time, however, taking an active role, whereas previously they were passive, helpless, and vulnerable victims. As Freud taught us, the repetition compulsion is adaptive in that it attempts to achieve active mastery of a passively experienced trauma; similarly, the patients Dr. Adler discusses repeat infantile abandonment by provoking their therapists to reject them. They are in control this time in that they are manipulating their analysts and forcing them to feel helpless by projecting their feelings of vulnerability into them.

Although Dr. Adler describes very sick patients, these patients have sufficient structure to experience considerable gratification as well as intense frustration and rejection. His patients do not have a relative absence of helpful introjects; instead, they fear that such introjects will be destroyed by negative introjects. As their egos are capable of forming endopsychic registrations of both helpful and destructive experiences, their psyches maintain a precarious balance.

Patients suffering from structural psychopathology commonly demonstrate an intense fear of intimacy. There are many reasons for this crippling fear, which prevents meaningful and loving relationships and leads to a profound, desperate, pervasive loneliness. Such patients do not feel completely human since being connected with another person is frightening and painful. Even in the analytic relationship, they have to preserve isolation to such a degree that therapists often feel frustrated because it is difficult to reach out to help them.

This mutually frustrating situation in the consultation room may be the outcome of a defense that Melanie Klein has described in different clinical contexts. To allow oneself to be helped imposes a feeling of obligation in the person who is the recipient of such help. As higher levels of psychic structure are achieved, being nurtured and soothed leads one to feel grateful. It also forces one to acknowledge that there is someone in the outside world who is capable and powerful and can minister to painful feelings of neediness. Therefore, the recipient is weak and vulnerable and the caretaker is strong and competent. Avoiding intimate relationships enables patients to avoid acknowledging their vulnerability and, as Dr. Adler candidly discusses, is a way for patients to create a power struggle and reverse roles.

The author explores the interplay between good and bad objects, which are the products of splitting mechanisms. He emphasizes that keeping bad objects inside and good objects outside causes patients to feel empty. Obviously, it would also cause them to feel self-destructive as well as destructive. To become close to the good object might mean destroying it. Therefore patients have to keep their distance and not allow themselves to be helped because they wish to protect the therapist from their destructiveness. Dr. Adler notes a common and disturbing outcome of this type of relationship, namely, that the analyst feels destructive toward the patient.

In dealing with such countertransference reactions, we tend to focus on the changes occurring within analysts as provoked by patients' psychopathology. Implicit in this exploration is the attitude that analysts have to explore their psyche with the intention of changing their orientation so that they can once again function in the analytic frame of reference. That is, analysts must regain the therapeutic perspective. Little, if anything, is said about patients losing the "patient's perspective." We do not ordinarily think about patients having obligations in a treatment setting. I am not referring to issues of analyzability, but rather, to certain qualities of all patients, regardless of psychopathology, that are necessary for therapists to feel sufficiently comfortable to maintain the analytic perspective. Dr. Adler describes a group of patients lacking in these qualities. We may not admit it even to ourselves, but we require some encouragement from our patients, minimal though it may be.

I recall without any particular effort, several patients who plodded on month after month and year after year making no apparent progress whatsoever. Nothing ever changed. I felt heartened the few times they reported a change for the worse since this signified some movement. This chapter reminds me of such sad moments and I remember further how often I thought of giving up the treatment.

With one patient my discouraged attitude rapidly vanished after a conversation with a colleague. The patient was a personal friend of my colleague who congratulated me on how well she was doing. Her husband and friends were extremely pleased with her progress. I had had no evidence of her increasing adaption to the outer world from the material she presented to me. Everything I heard made me feel useless but then I realized that apparently she had a need to present herself in a fashion that would not reveal what she had accomplished. In retrospect, this would be perfectly obvious but I had failed to maintain my analytic deterministic perspective because she had succeeded in making me feel hopeless. Since then I have received a sufficient amount of subtle signs and cues of encouragement to enable me to maintain some analytic equanimity.

Dr. Adler makes the point that we feel particularly vulnerable when we first start practicing analysis inasmuch as we are relatively young and inexperienced. This is undoubtedly true, but feelings of helplessness are also found in the most experienced analysts who work with severely disturbed patients. Dr. Searles's chapter bears this point out.

There is something intrinsic in the transference of the type of patient Dr. Adler describes that will create essentially similar countertransference reactions in most of us. However, there are also intrinsic elements in the analytic setting which mitigate the intensity of our feelings. Dr. Adler's construction of the analytic setting seemed to have helped him survive his patient. When he asked the patient to use the couch and increased the frequency of sessions from one to five times a week, the patient was easier to tolerate. I know that I find that the couch permits me to react less personally to patients. This does not mean that I am less involved, but that I find it easier to view their devaluations of me as clinical material rather than something I have to take to heart.

Quite clearly, a basic therapeutic task with the group of patients Dr. Adler describes is to survive both their attacks and our reactive anger. There are times we wish to kill them, most likely the same feeling a parent had toward them. The transference is a reliving of important infantile constellations and relationships. I sometimes wonder whether it is a necessary part of the transference interaction actually to feel the same way the parents did toward their child. That is, I question whether analysts who have seen many helpless, provoking patients can profit from their past experiences and understanding, and therefore not react. Could patients then deal with the fantasy of having caused changes in their analysts through their projections rather than the reality of such changes? Perhaps analysts might gain understanding of these projections without any affective upheaval. Or, they might react with a slight affect that would permit them to reconstruct the elements of the repetition compulsion and infantile relations. This would be similar to the signal function of anxiety.

Dr. Adler offers thought-provoking insights into treatment issues that analysts deal with daily. The significance of these contributions have become even more apparent since the time they were first published.

P. L. G.

Traditionally, clinical descriptions of psychoanalytic work have elaborated a "one-person psychology." The sparsity of material about analysts' feelings and comments has supported the fantasy of the classical image of the "analyst as a mirror." We can certainly understand analysts' reluctance to let others know that they can be very uncomfortable with specific feelings within themselves during periods of work with a patient, not understand what is going on for long stretches, or even make mistakes. Many of us reserve a few close, trusted relationships with colleagues for the mutual sharing of distress in our work with problem patients. Yet the careful and honest reporting by such workers as Boyer (1961), Greenson (1967), Little (1960, 1966), and Searles (1965) has demonstrated the importance of analysts' personal attitudes and feelings towards their patients for the understanding of the analytic process and the limitations of patients and/or analysts in their work.

In this chapter, I want to describe problems analysts and therapists and their patients face when confronted with feelings of
helplessness and hopelessness that both feel with conviction during
the course of psychoanalysis and psychotherapy. I believe that such
feelings in patients and their therapists are inevitable companions
in the treatment of many patients, and especially manifest in work
with certain difficult ones. And the inability of the therapist to
understand and stand these feelings is an important limitation in
the successful therapy with such patients.

My discussion of feelings of helplessness and hopelessness is an
attempt to broaden our understanding of some obstacles in the
empathic psychotherapeutic and psychoanalytic work with certain
difficult patients, some of whom have been described as "unwork-
able" by traditional psychotherapeutic methods. I hope it will also
contribute to better work with neurotic patients who can arouse
these feelings in therapists as elements of their pregenital conflicts are relived in the therapeutic encounter.

My interest in problems of helplessness and hopelessness in
psychotherapists arises from my attempts to make sense of some
of my own experiences. As a first-year psychiatric resident, I
became aware of a reaction when I worked with some difficult
patients and felt particularly lost and helpless. I would have the
thought, "If only my supervisor were here; he'd tell me what to
do." I then would try something he had discussed or demonstrated
with a patient. Sometimes, to my relief and delight, it would work,
but often it would not. I then might feel angry that his advice had
not been good, or probably, more often, depressed and hopeless
that I wasn't my supervisor and could not do what he could do. As
my training proceeded, the syndrome I am describing continued; in
fact, it got worse, for more names were added to it. But the essence
of the syndrome was the same: my helplessness with a patient, the
summoning of an image of the omnipotent teacher who in his own
work with such a patient would have no trouble doing what I could
not, and my gratified, depressed, or angry responses after my
attempts to carry out his fantasied intervention.

Years of struggling with these images have led me to put things
in better perspective. I began to see my omnipotent teachers more

as people as I came to know them personally, found some almost as helpless as I was when confronted with a difficult patient, heard some disagree with each other on the treatment of a specific patient, and even disagree with what they themselves had said to me the week before. Also, as part of my evolution as a therapist, I discovered that there was an occasional person in training who would summon up my image idealistically and ambivalently to rescue him—even while I was still having episodes of feeling helpless in my own work with patients.

I finally had to conclude that feelings of helplessness and hope-lessness were part of the burden I had to bear as a therapist, and that I was not alone in experiencing them. I also began to see that these feelings tended to come up with greatest intensity with certain kinds of patients. And, in spite of my best intentions, I found myself repeatedly hopeless, helpless, and furious with those patients and fantasying different ways to get back at them or get rid of them.

PATIENTS WHO ELICIT HELPLESSNESS IN THERAPISTS

Let me now define the kinds of patients that I feel tend to elicit the most marked feelings of helplessness and hopelessness in their therapists.

These patients may present as insistently and urgently demand-ing, clinging, or empty on an intense or low-keyed level and yet find that any response of the therapist does not give them the answer or relief they seek (Giovacchini 1970, Giovacchini and Boyer 1975). If something the therapist does or says helps, it is usually for a short period of time, followed by an increasingly justified plea for further relief. When these patients begin therapy in a positive way, they usually maintain a view that their therapist is omnipotent (Kohut 1968) and capable of gratifying and "curing" them. After the inevitable disappointment of these wishes, they may regress to the demanding, unsatisfied position. When ques-tioned about the details of what they really want, they often become vague. But usually they can allude to a therapist who understands them fully and does not have to question them, who intuitively knows what they feel and want. And of course their specific therapist is not that person. No matter how much he may try, the therapist hears that his responses are off the mark, not enough, or just plain stupid. And no matter how hard the therapist works, this kind of response from the patient seems to persist.

Helplessness and hopelessness begin to appear in the therapist as he finds that he can do nothing right (Giovacchini 1970). In addition, patients may repeatedly attack and devalue the therapist, supporting the therapist's feeling of inadequacy and inability to give anything of worth. If the therapist gets increasingly angry, patients use it to confirm their initial conviction that the therapist was basically inadequate from the start. At the same time, if the therapist can stand back for a moment to look at it, he can sense a certain delight in patients when they finally see the therapist helpless and hopeless in fury and depression. The barrage of demands and attacks may subside for a while, until the therapist is convinced that he is forming a good relationship with patients and that they are making progress at last. But then patients have a disappointment in life or in the relationship with the therapist, and the angry, demanding, clinging assaults return, as if the lull and positive relationship had never existed.

If we look at this group of patients in more detail we find that they are usually fixated at, or have retreated to, a position involving a life-and-death battle with the important people in their lives (Adler 1970, Kernberg 1967, Little 1960, 1966). Their concerns in this struggle are whether they will devour or be devoured, destroy or be destroyed. As part of this struggle they can alternate between swallowing and merging, or destroying the person completely through their biting, tearing anger, or by rejecting him. In therapy they can live out a constant expectation of abandonment and provoke the therapist to reject and hurt them. Helplessness and hopelessness, accompanied by severe depression and suicidal preoccupation, are often seen in these patients. Inevitably, they can involve their therapists in their life-and-death, helpless and hopeless dilemma.

Depending upon complex constitutional factors and environmental experiences, these patients may exhibit varying capacities to test reality, to relate on higher levels with another person, to work productively, and to maintain control of their impulses. Diagnostically, these patients include psychotics, borderlines, and severe character disorders. In addition, relatively healthy psychoneurotic patients with a walled-over, unresolved, oral ambivalent conflict can show some of the manifestations outlined as this conflict is reopened in therapy, though rarely with the intensity that I am describing. In these neurotic patients, the therapist is often faced with a choice of opening these areas based on whether he believes it is necessary for the achievement of mutually agreed-upon goals.

How can we understand the helplessness and hopelessness of these patients? And why does it have such an impact on us? Let me first summarize what I believe are some major factors in this understanding, and then amplify and illustrate them.

I feel that on the deepest level, these patients have a firm conviction that they will ultimately find themselves alone and empty, having been abandoned and disappointed by the person they depended on, or having driven away or destroyed that person (Adler 1970). The experience is akin to that of annihilation and nothingness (Little 1960, 1966). This conviction is also based on the state of their internal objects: these patients cannot maintain an internal image of a basically helpful person without it being overwhelmed or lost because of negative introjects or feelings. In addition, I believe that these patients re-experience in the transference a situation of early, overwhelming abandonment, loss, and fury, with a repetition of very early helplessness and hopelessness felt alone and/or perceived as really present in an important early figure. Ultimately, these feelings of helplessness and hopelessness have to become part of the psychotherapy as similar feelings are experienced with the therapist as object.

The intensity of the feeling of loss and abandonment experienced by this group of patients has been described and illustrated by Bowlby et al. (1952) and Robertson (1956) in their observations of very small children separated from or losing a mother, and by

Winnicott (1960) in his writing about the early mother-child relationship. The very small child depends upon the "good enough" mother to respond to his needs often enough, and to sense the limits of his capacity to stand frustration at a specific time and age. The "good enough" mothers are not particularly afraid of their own or their child's anger, and can be firm when they have to frustrate. They can do this because they have confidence in their basic goodness and capacity to care and give without having to hurt and retaliate for old hurts. These mothers have clearly been able to internalize relationships with the good objects in their lives and make them a solid part of their identity. Children raised by such mothers are ultimately certain they can depend on them and trust them; as they grow they can carry away within themselves this basic solid relationship. When such a relationship with a "good enough" mother has not occurred or been adequate enough, the frightening helplessness of the very small child remains, or reappears when a loss is threatened. Repeated experiences of lack of sensitivity to the child's needs can turn the child's or adult's rage at abandonment into helplessness, a state of feeling annihilated, and then hopelessness and despair. The global rage of such a small child is never significantly modified, and can reappear after disappointments as a primitive, frightening, rejecting hate. The overwhelmed mother, in addition to her lack of sensitivity and relative or actual abandonment of her child, also presents the model of helplessness and inability to cope with her own emptiness and anger.

I have mentioned these patients' difficulties with internalization of objects. I have stressed it because of my experience that this is a major factor in their long-standing helplessness and hopelessness, and in their difficulties in psychotherapy. Kernberg (1967) has described the problem of "splitting" in the borderline. I feel that splitting is an important defense mechanism in this entire group of patients and also is present in neurotic patients as pregenital conflicts emerge in psychotherapy and psychoanalysis. In Kleinian terms, people who use splitting as a major defense are still in the paranoid position, and have not achieved the capacity to tolerate loving and hating toward the same person at the same time. In splitting, the loving and hating may alternate over time, i.e., the patient may love the same person one minute, and immediately thereafter relate to that person with hatred as if the loving relationship never existed. Such patients may be aware of the splitting intellectually, but the alternations remain a vivid and dominant affective force in their life.

As part of splitting, patients sometimes can be aware of emptiness, helplessness, hopelessness, and despair. They are empty when they have only badness within themselves with all the good gone and perhaps only visible outside in someone else. They are helpless in the face of the storm of good and bad around and within them, but with goodness not permanently inside. If they act at a moment when they are in touch with good, loving interactions with earlier people in their life, they cannot count on their permanence. In a period of lack of gratification which may follow their positive action, and which arouses their fury, all the good can be lost. They then are helplessly buffeted by the badness inside as well as their projections of it outside. Their hopelessness, depression, and despair can occur with the feeling that they are in the midst of an insoluble dilemma that permits them no consistent core experience of self-esteem and of the constancy of good internal objects. Nor can they count on current people in their life because they have projected their destructive and aggressive feelings onto them or provoked them to treat them so as to justify their distrust of them. And they may destroy, devalue, or reject anything others attempt to offer them.

This is often the situation between therapist and patient in the heat of involvement. The therapist's helplessness and hopelessness in seeing these alternating states in the patient or a persistence of anger and devaluation with little evidence that there is any internalization of anything good from therapy mirrors the patient's own similar but usually more intense experience. And the therapist's helplessness is compounded by the patient's need to reject or destroy anything the therapist tries to offer during much of this time. Inevitably the therapist's rage is aroused, resulting in possible serious consequences: for example, the therapist may sadistically attack the patient, angrily confront the latter's narcissistic entitlement, withdraw emotionally, terminate, switch the patient to another therapist or kind of treatment, or find some way to get the patient to leave therapy.

Part of the therapist's rage can be understood as follows: we are willing to give, understand, and be helpful, but we expect something back as a reward (Racker 1957). What may be a major distinction between one therapist and another is what and how much each can give and what and how soon each expects something back from the patient. With the group of patients I am discussing, that part of all of us is stressed, even in those of us who feel we have achieved high levels of altruism. And there is no better way to bring it out in us than our work with patients who repeatedly tell us they are helpless and hopeless; and demonstrate that our giving is not enough, is valueless, or is nonexistent, even minutes after it was previously acknowledged; and ultimately reject and destroy all our giving attempts.

In addition, the therapist's feelings of helplessness and hopelessness may be a countertransference empathic response to patients' experience of annihilation and wish for fusion in the presence of the therapist. The helpless rage of patients that can lead to the experience of annihilation can empathically frighten and enrage the therapist. When not understood by the therapist, it can lead to the described ways the therapist turns off or gets rid of patients.

In examining and reconstructing these patients' histories, it is striking how often their turmoil and helplessness, as well as that of the therapist, were a part of these patients' early lives. Their mothers were either emotionally unavailable or alternately smothering and depriving. Frequently, the mothers themselves were severely depressed and felt helpless during the child's early years. Precipitants for this depression in the mother include death of a parent, loss of an earlier pregnancy, death of a child before the patient was born, or threatened or actual breakup of the marriage. These mothers sometimes had severe postpartum depressions or psychoses. The conflicts of this group of patients may remarkably parallel those of their mothers at that time. And the manifestations of helplessness that arise in the patient and therapist may be recreations of this early mother-child relationship. Occasionally the overwhelming helplessness experienced by the patient in childhood can be projected onto the mother and is experienced as coming from her. But I suspect that, more often than not, the helplessness was a real part of these mothers. The re-experiencing of this early mother-child helplessness may be an inevitable part of the psychotherapy with these patients, and can become an important part of the therapeutic work.

I have described this theoretical model before giving a detailed clinical example because I have found it important for me in my work with such patients. It provides me with the understanding and distance that make work with intense feelings of patients tolerable to me. I hope that it is also theoretically correct.

The patient I want to discuss presents another question that derives from my previous remarks: how important is it for a therapist to like such a patient from the beginning? The therapist may be able to anticipate the hard times ahead while still in the evaluation period. Should he agree to continue to work with a patient if he has serious or some doubts about his capacity to have a genuine liking and respect for the patient? And what happens if the therapist is not sure, but increasingly has doubts about his caring, respect for, and interest in the patient as therapy proceeds? And is a similar feeling important in the patient, i.e., should the latter feel, early in therapy, that the therapist has the "right" qualities? Is a basic mutual liking and respect an important early ingredient? And how can both patient and therapist exercise this choice in their early and later negotiations?

Case Example

The patient was a 28-year-old accountant who came for treatment because he felt he was not advancing in his work, but primarily because he could not form any lasting relationships with women. Though of average height, he was thin, awkward, and adolescent in his gestures and voice. His sitting position from the start was characteristic of how he related to me for years: he would slouch and practically lie on the chair, talking to the overhead lighting fixture, the picture to the left of my head, or the window to the right. He spoke with a soft Southern drawl in a way that was aloof and distant, yet at the same time could summon up articulate and bitingly humorous descriptions of his work, his past, and the few people in his current world. He could readily define the major disappointment in his life which had determined his responses to people ever since: his mother, who had held, hugged, and hovered over him for the first five years of his life had abandoned him for his newborn sister. To him it felt like being an infant who was suddenly thrown off his mother's lap. He tried to woo her back by adopting her loving, smiling, fundamentalist religious position, which included a denial of jealousy or anger. He also tried turning to his brusque, busy father who scorned him for his awkwardness and weakness. He struggled to love, but at the same time found himself vomiting up the lunches his mother packed for him to eat in school in the first grade. Gradually, the vomiting included food he ate at home. His friend-ships at school were jeopardized by his need to report to his mother the nasty things the other children said and did; he agreed with her that he would never think such naughty thoughts himself. During his adolescence he became increasingly preoccupied with thoughts of inadvertently hurting people, which culminated in marked anxiety in his early twenties when he became afraid that he would stab pregnant women in the abdomen. This anxiety led him to his college health service and his first experience with psychotherapy.

In spite of these difficulties, he did well academically in high school, spent two years in the navy, where he felt liberated, and was able to complete college successfully. His relationships with women consisted of looking at them from afar and actively fantasizing closeness and hugging; actual contacts were awkward and brief. He could form more sustained but distant relationships with men, but was transiently concerned that he might be a homosexual at the time he was discharged from the navy.

His previous psychotherapy had occurred during his last year at college. He had felt frightened and desperate, and quickly saw his therapist as his rescuer. His therapist was a psychiatric resident whom the patient described as large, athletic, and "like a football player," smoking big fat cigars, and actively giving advice. He was very real and direct with the patient. In looking back at this therapy, my patient felt that it had helped to diminish his preoccupations and anxieties, but had left him still unable to form lasting, satisfying relationships with people. It had stopped before he felt ready, because, after one year of work with the patient, the therapist had finished his training and left the area. When I first saw the patient six years later, he defined his problem as a chronic one which he felt he could not solve alone. Yet he felt pessimistic that anything could be done to change things.

This patient was one of my first private patients and really puzzled me. I was impressed by his wish to work, his loneliness and isolation, and the frightening quality of his anger implied by his earlier symptoms. I was concerned about his aloofness and distance from me; I did not feel we were making contact with each other, but did not know what to do about it. At that point in my experience I could not even formulate the question of how much I liked him and whether that was important. However, I did recognize that he had a choice of whether he wished to see me regularly and offered him that opportunity at the end of our first meeting. He replied that he was willing to see me, and felt that one hour a week was what he had in mind.

From my perception of the first few months of our meetings, nothing much seemed to happen. He gave me more history to fill out the outline of his life and told me more about the emptiness of his current existence, but all with a manner that shut me out and maintained an amused distance. Because of my distress and increasing boredom, I began to point out as tactfully as I could the way he was avoiding contact with me and keeping me out of his world. His response was a quick glance, and then a slow unfolding over a number of months, with an insistent sameness, that he had made a mistake. He did not know how to tell it to me, but I was not the right therapist for him. In addition to my soft voice and mild manner, I probably had never been in a bar in my life, had never been in a fist fight, and did not smoke cigars. He would then speak with affection about his previous therapist, and again spell out the vast differences between us.

When I could sometimes recover from what occasionally felt like a devastating personal attack, I would try to help him look at the meaning of what he was saying. I would relate it to his relationship with his mother, his fury at her abandoning him, and his wish to turn to the other parent, who also let him down; and often I could point to specific parallels. Usually he rejected these interpretations as incorrect, irrelevant, and worthless. He would also deny that he felt any anger at me when I would point out the obvious attacking quality of many of his statements. He would ask, how could he be angry when he wasn't even involved and didn't care?

Over a nine-month period I went through stages of boredom, withdrawal, fury, depression, and helplessness. I gradually began to feel like a broken record, and had run out of any new ideas except the increasing acknowledgment that maybe he was right: I probably was not the therapist for him. With relief I suggested that he see a consultant who would help us make that determination. I also had to acknowledge to myself that my narcissism was on the line. To fail with one of my first private patients, and also because of so many alleged personal inadequacies, was more than I wished to face at that time. Also, I had chosen a consultant I greatly respected, adding to my concerns about revealing my inadequacies as a therapist. The consultant felt that therapy had certainly been stalemated, but largely because of the infrequency of the visits and the lack of confidence I had in the worth of my work with the patient. He minimized my insistence that the patient did not feel I was the right therapist. He stated that in his interview with the patient the patient had talked about what he did not like, but also had conveyed a respect for our work and some willingness to continue with me. After the consultation, I ambivalently negotiated with this patient for psychoanalytic treatment involving the use of the couch and five meetings a week. With the reassurance that at least my consultant loved me, I arranged to have him continue as my supervisor.

Psychoanalysis with this patient lasted four years. The position he had taken in our earlier therapy was maintained, but this time it was amplified and understood by dreams and memories that verified previous hypotheses. Clarifications about his murderous rage that appeared in dreams made it somewhat safer to talk about his fury with me. Gradually he could speak intellectually about the possibility of an involvement with me, but it was something he never really felt. Only on two occasions did he feel real anger at me, both leading to near disruption of the analysis. One followed my inflexibility when he wanted to change an appointment, and led to his calling the consultant in order to request a change of analysts.

The other occurred toward the end of analysis, when I pointed out his need to maintain a paranoid position in relation to people. It resulted in his storming out of the hour and phoning that he was never returning—which lasted through one missed session.

Gradually, I became personally more comfortable with this patient, though seeing him was always hard work. I felt much less helpless and hopeless as I saw his attacks, isolation, and distance in the context of a theoretical framework, as part of the transference and a defense against it. My supervisor's support and clarifications helped me to maintain this distance. But my helplessness was still present when my interpretations were rejected for long periods of time and I was treated as some nonhuman appendage to my chair. I often felt hopeless that we would ever achieve our goals. I say "we," but usually there was little sense of our working together. I frequently had to ask myself whether I liked him enough to suffer with him all those years, but had to grudgingly acknowledge that, in spite of everything, I did. Somehow, the process of long-term work with him had made me feel like a parent with a difficult child who could finally come to accept any change at all in that child with happiness. And the changes that occurred were presented to me casually and minimized. They consisted of passing comments about his increasing ability to date women, and led ultimately to his marrying a woman with whom he could share mutual tenderness.

I feel that certain aspects of this patient's defensive structure and the transference that emerged in analysis made working with this patient particularly difficult for me. He was reliving a relationship of helplessness and hopelessness with his mother. Not only had he felt abandoned by her when his sister was born, but he had been allowed no direct expression of his anger and jealousy. He chose to comply on the surface, but maintained an aloof, disparaging distance with her that protected him against his fury, helplessness, and despair. Since he did this with his mother to stay alive, he understandably repeated the same pattern with me—complying on the surface, but vomiting up and rejecting what I attempted to give. In a sense, he never left that position with me; he was able to change the quality of relationships outside of analysis, but maintained his aloofness with me to the end. He would say that to show real change with me was to acknowledge that he had taken something from me and kept it as part of himself; he just did not want to do that openly, for he would have to admit the importance of our relationship and how grateful he was. His compromise was to remain very much the same with me: to change significantly outside, and then ascribe the changes to things he could take from the new important people in his life.

Though I feel satisfied with the results of my work with this patient, I still sometimes wonder whether I was the right analyst for him. Perhaps if he had seen someone who could remind him more of his father as his first therapist had, the intensity of the mother transference would have been less and he would have found it safe to feel more about his mother with the analyst.

THERAPEUTIC USE OF REGRESSIVE COUNTERTRANSFERENCE

How does a therapist avoid the difficulties I have described when feelings of helplessness and hopelessness arise in therapy? Since I believe that intense feelings of helplessness are inevitable in both patient and therapist in the treatment of this group of patients, we deny the human qualities of people to expect a therapist to maintain a therapeutic position throughout his work when he feels so much. What then can we say about the therapeutic position with these patients and how can we help a therapist remain useful as much as possible in his work with them?

In the heat of battle, a tendency toward countertransference regression is inevitable. The ultimate ability of the therapist to recover some distance and an observing ego is a crucial ingredient in such stressful work (Adler 1970). The therapist's capacity to grow during his own analysis and use his countertransference responses diagnostically and empathically is crucial with these patients (Heimann 1950, 1956).

The therapist has to accept, as part of his human frailties, that hatred within himself for these patients is expectable, and can be put to therapeutic use in assessing what the patient is experiencing. Though the hatred is obviously the therapist's own, it is often experienced at that moment because of a projection or provocation on the part of the patient. This awareness can support the therapist in exploring what the patient feels and why.

The regressive countertransference situation often places the therapist in a position of feeling he literally has to rescue and comfort the patient (Heimann 1956, 1957). The patient demands and expects the rescue from the omnipotent parent, and the therapist, as that parent, feels he has to respond. The inability of the therapist to see this as an essential part of the transference experience with such patients leads to his tendency to respond with a rescuing, smothering, gratifying, yet frightening message. For many patients this provides temporary relief. But, ultimately, this response provokes increasing regression in patients, who perceive that the therapist sees them as the helpless child who has to be held and saved from disaster. Inevitably, demands increase, patients regress more, and ultimately they often reject and devalue the therapist in their increasing fury. The therapist who began as the rescuer ends up feeling as helpless and furious as the patients. The capacity of the therapist to anticipate this transference-countertransference situation, as well as variations of this theme, is crucial. But once he sees it, the therapist is more able to control his helpless and angry feelings so that he does not attack the patient sadistically in what he feels is a useful clarification, interpretation, or confrontation. It is at such times that the therapist may confront patients with their narcissistic entitlement or infantile wishes rejectingly and sadistically while feeling that he is trying to help patients see something important. The mechanism is poorly defined by which a therapist transforms his sadistic hate into a useful, productive therapeutic tool. But those therapists who can do it use their regressive countertransference tendencies as a signal to convert their helplessness and fury into a force to help patients understand and stand what is happening, so that together they can master it. In effect, the therapist is also providing patients with a model for identification in the constructive use and mastery of unbearable feelings, and with a corrective emotional experience, in contrast to the mutual helplessness of the original mother-child setting. And a major part of the corrective emotional experience very much follows Winnicott's beautiful description (1969) of patients' finding that they cannot destroy the object. As part of this work, the therapist ultimately assists patients to recognize that they have increasing choices as they master and understand.

Yet for certain patients at certain times, a concrete physical expression of concern and caring is necessary to provide the setting for a corrective emotional experience. Little (1966) and Balint (1968) describe such instances and at the same time discuss the dangers of poor timing and indiscriminate use.

CONCLUDING REMARKS

It is obviously easier to talk about the issue of rescuing patients versus helping them see the choices they can have than to do it successfully with this group of patients. The art of being a good therapist consists in part of a sensitivity to how much patients are genuinely overwhelmed and need to be fed symbolically, and how much they can stand and examine at a specific moment. The "good enough mother" aspect of the therapist ultimately determines whether patients have a corrective emotional experience as part of therapy or a pathological experience similar to that of early childhood. As many authors have described, limit setting is an important ingredient in a group of patients whose wishes are enormous, and whose impulse control is often tenuous, and may become even more so in the heat of the transference. But the vicissitudes of the therapist's helplessness and fury determine whether the limits are part of a firm, caring, facilitating operation, or a punitive, attacking, rejecting, and envious assault.

Should the more difficult patients I have described be seen in more than once weekly therapy, and should the therapist ever make the transference manifestations an important part of their work? Zetzel (1971) has stressed the regressive potential of these patients in intensive treatment. In my experience, such patients do not necessarily regress behaviorally when they are involved in intensive psychotherapy and psychoanalysis, i.e., two-to-five-times-a-week treatment. Whether or not they regress depends in part on whether their therapist can respond and give when they genuinely need it, with clarifications and interpretations on the appropriate developmental level (Little 1960, 1966), and withhold when patients can stand it. As I have described, therapists who only give, and then do not recognize patients' increasing strengths at a later time, communicate to patients that they are only in touch with their infantile side. The result is often increasing behavioral regression and disorganization. Therapists must be able to frustrate patients maximally, but never more than they can stand.

Transference clarifications and interpretations do not necessarily lead to behavioral regressions in psychotherapy and psychoanalysis with these patients. These patients have varying capacities to look at elements of the transference and make use of it. It is important for sufficient material to be present for the therapist to be certain of his statements before the transference is discussed, and then in a tentative, supportive way as the transference, especially the negative transference, emerges. The therapist can be certain only in this way whether it facilitates or impedes therapy. Exceptions about waiting involve patients who develop massive regressive reactions practically in the first session. Then active work with transference material may be the only way to preserve the possibility of treating the patient.

Many of these patients can be treated in once-a-week therapy with some success. I feel that more intensive work can help many of them achieve significant changes in the quality of their object relations, as described by Balint (1968) and Little (1966), that less intense, more supportive work does not permit. Of course, the danger of opening issues that cannot always be shut off is a risk. The patient's and therapist's mutual decision to take these risks should be a factor in defining the frequency and intensity of the work.

How is the therapist to assess whether real changes are occurring in therapy as the patient attacks, rejects and devalues? Is the rejecting by the patient only part of the therapeutic process, while assimilation is taking place on a deeper level, or is the patient genuinely rejecting the therapist and their work? I am not certain of the answer. But I do know that there is a real danger in agreeing with the patient that all is hopeless and that the therapy is essentially worthless. The patient I have discussed is one with whom I could easily have stopped with the feeling, even after two or three years, that he was correct. It was only in the last year of therapy that I was convinced that a genuine assimilation of our work was occurring. The therapist's awareness that patients can use their defensive structure and the transference repetition to present the hopelessness of the task insistently can alert the therapist that he may be missing genuine therapeutic growth which is occurring simultaneously. Little (1966) described a similar experience of initially not recognizing the growth of her patient during long barrages of hopelessness and devaluation.

I have tried to stress that treatment of these patients is a task that requires an empathic understanding as well as a theoretical model to provide the structure and distance to make the work possible. And I have presented part of a theoretical model that has helped me intellectually and emotionally to pursue this work. I hope that this chapter's focus on the treatment of difficult patients will be used to foster understanding of certain elements of treatment of *all* patients.

SUMMARY

Feelings of helplessness in patients and their therapists can limit the possibility of successful psychotherapy and psychoanalysis. The patients most likely to elicit these feelings in therapists with greatest intensity are usually those who are reliving the helplessness of a very early unsuccessful relationship with a maternal figure. This helplessness is experienced by patient and therapist as the defenses, conflicts, and feelings of that early period become manifest in the transference; the therapist's helplessness probably repeats the helplessness the patient's mother experienced during that time. In addition, problems of internalization of new objects and experiences in these patients contribute to this helplessness as the therapist's attempts are rejected, destroyed, or devalued. A detailed clinical example illustrates the difficulties of the therapist in work with such patients.

REFERENCES

Adler, G. (1970). Valuing and devaluing in the psychotherapeutic process. *Arch. Gen. Psychiatry* 22: 454–461.

Balint, M. (1968). *The Basic Fault: Therapeutic Aspects of Regression.* London: Tavistock.

Bowlby, J. et al. (1952). A two-year-old goes to hospital. *The Psychoanalytic Study of the Child* 7.

Boyer, L. B. (1961). Provisional evaluation of psycho-analysis with few parameters employed in the treatment of schizophrenia. *Intern. J. Psycho-Anal.* 42: 389–403.

Giovacchini, P. L. (1970). Characterological problems: The need to be helped. *Arch. Gen. Psychiatry* 22: 245–251.

Giovacchini, P. L. and Boyer, L. B. (1975). The psychoanalytic impasse. *Internat. J. Psychoanal. Psychother.* 4: 25–47.

Greenson, R. R. (1967). *The Technique and Practice of Psychoanalysis,* vol. 1. New York: International Universities Press.

Heimann, P. (1950). On counter-transference. *Internat. J. Psycho-Anal.* 31: 81–84.

——— (1956). Dynamics of transference interpretations. *Internat. J. Psycho-Anal.* 37: 303–310.

——— (1957). A combination of defense mechanisms in paranoid states. In *New Directions in Psychoanalysis,* ed. M. Klein et al. New York: Basic Books.

Kernberg, O. (1967). Borderline personality organization. *J. Amer. Psychoanal. Assn.* 15: 641–685.

Kohut, H. (1968). The psychoanalytic treatment of narcissistic personality disorders: Outline of a systematic approach. *The Psychoanalytic Study of the Child* 23: 86–113.

Little, M. (1960). On basic unity. *Internat. J. Psycho-Anal.* 41: 377–384, 637.

——— (1966). Transference in borderline states. *Internat. J. Psycho-Anal.* 47: 476–485.

Racker, H. (1957). The meanings and uses of countertransference. *Psychoanal. Q.* 26: 303–357.

Robertson, J. (1956). A mother's observations on the tonsillectomy of her four-year-old daughter. With comments by Anna Freud. *The Psychoanalytic Study of the Child* 11: 410–433.

Searles, H. F. (1965). *Collected Papers on Schizophrenia and Related Subjects.* New York: International Universities Press.

Winnicott, D. W. (1960). Ego distortion in terms of true and false self. In
    The Maturational Processes and the Facilitating Environment, pp.140–
    152. New York: International Universities Press, 1965.
——— (1969). The use of an object. *Internat. J. Psycho-Anal.* 50: 711–716.
Zetzel, E. R. (1971). A developmental approach to the borderline patient.
    Amer. J. Psychiatry 127: 867–871.

15

THE MEANING OF PLAY IN CHILDHOOD PSYCHOSIS

Rudolph Ekstein
Seymour W. Friedman

Editor's Notes

Dr. Ekstein and his coworkers have been pioneers in the treatment of psychotic children. Their work has been especially impressive because of their sensitive understanding as to how both the primitive mind and the primitively distorted mind function. We felt that in a book about severely disturbed and primitively fixated patients we should include a chapter on children. We chose to reprint Ekstein's and Friedman's work because it was one of the first that made subtle investigative explorations while also illustrating technique in this area.

Dr. Ekstein has written a considerable amount about play. In this chapter, he and Dr. Friedman are not dealing with play in the traditional sense, but rather, in the sense of the playing out of psychopathological processes. Furthermore, as is typical of the psychoanalytic method, the unfolding of psychopathology cannot be separated from the therapeutic interaction.

The analyses of primitively fixated adults confront us with the same type of functional impairments and structural defects that the authors describe in the treatment of psychotic children. However, psychotic

children express themselves in a much more forth-
right fashion, revealing with only minimal disguise
and covering defenses the operations of a primitive
mind. Later in life, these observations are harder to
make, the transference-countertransference axis is
considerably more complex, and the mind reveals
itself in more devious fashions.

The first patient discussed, Robby, had the peculiar
habit of stealing door stoppers and removing doorknobs with a dexterity and agility that would be
amazing in an adult, let alone in a 5-year-old boy. His
extraordinary skill in manipulating a screwdriver was
unfortunately associated with destructiveness; he
would literally dismantle a room rather than using
his ability to construct and build. Drs. Ekstein and
Friedman view such activities in terms of various
psychic operations. For example, doorstops and knobs
are functional components of a structure, a door,
which controls entrances and exits, that is, access.
Robby's violent behavior can be compared to a chaotic
force bursting into a room. A closed door, or even a
fixed door (i.e., one held by a stopper) would slow
him down, thereby exerting some control over his
actions. Robby had a poorly developed capacity for
control. However, by stealing these stoppers and
knobs, he was collecting trophies which he could
make part of himself. Thus his destructiveness paradoxically represented an attempt at control. In a
similar fashion, Robby's behavior could also be
thought of in terms of putting into the external
world various actions that were initially directed
toward his body. As the authors stated, when he
annihilated a room, he could be annihilating the
inside of his body. The latter might be associated
with a variety of delusions regarding attacking and
consuming introjects that manipulated and controlled
him. This is not uncommon among psychotic children.

The second patient discussed, Nick, a 13-year-old
boy, slavishly and almost automatically did whatever

his peers told him to do, no matter how humiliating their commands might be. His responses resembled echopraxia, insofar as he seemed to be fully controlled by external objects. However, experience with psychotics has taught us that the most extreme forms of passivity (i.e., echopraxia and catatonia) are also extreme forms of control. The outer world is almost totally excluded and disavowed, which reduces it to a state of having no significance or impact.

Nick's treatment resembled traditional play more than Robby's did. The therapist helped construct and share a fantasy with Nick much in the same way children play out certain pretend situations. By adopting their play roles, Dr. Friedman and Nick "set up" an observational platform from which they could observe the therapeutic relationship. This is an excellent example of how play can become an integral part of a therapeutic interaction whose formal elements may differ from those of traditional psychoanalysis, but which nevertheless retains the latter's principles.

Other chapters in this book devote considerable space to destructive play (the authors prefer to avoid the negative connotations of the term "acting out"). Undoubtedly, Robby was expressing his psychic state through actions rather than words, but then the extent of his psychopathology did not permit him to do otherwise. He did not have enough secondary process organization to express the manifestations of such primitive psychic states in a verbal fashion. There was no other way Robby could express himself. In fact, one of the goals of therapy was to achieve the capacity to communicate in a less destructive fashion. Robby could not free associate in the conventional sense, but he was eminently capable of revealing the inner workings of his mind.

By assuming the role of his ego-ideal, Nick was able to examine various aspects of the therapeutic relationship and reveal how he felt about himself. There was no assignment of roles, as in psychodrama. Rather, the participants fell into their respective identities in an almost spontaneous fashion. The similarity to the spontaneous unfolding of the transference was obvious. In the transference, the analyst was viewed as a figure from the infantile past and the patient reverted to an archaic ego state, sometimes being vulnerable and helpless, and sometimes adopting an overcompensatory grandiose stance. Nick's play in treatment was the vehicle for expressing the transference. As was the case with Robby, transference could not be contained in a free association context.

Drs. Ekstein and Friedman have provided us with a rich clinical chapter that yields important insights about psychotic children. They illustrate that even in very difficult cases, it is possible to establish a holding environment that promotes insight and, eventually, psychic integration in a transference context. In other words, even when dealing with such primitive minds, the essential principles of psychoanalysis are still applicable.

P. L. G.

Victor Tausk's classic contribution, "On the Origin of the 'Influencing Machine' in Schizophrenia" (1919), in spite of its now partly outdated conceptualizations, continues to stimulate many investigators in our field through its richness of ideas. The nature of Natalija A.'s "influencing machine" was then understood primarily in terms of paranoid projections. Tausk speaks about the "infantile stage of thinking, in which a strong belief exists that others know of the child's thoughts" (p. 535). He suggests that "a striving for the right to have secrets from which the parents are excluded is one of the most powerful factors in the formation of the ego, especially in establishing and carrying out one's own will" (p. 535). He speaks of "the loss of ego boundaries," a concept which is frequently used in the work of Federn (1952), and suggests that "this symptom is the complaint that 'everyone' knows the patient's thoughts, that his thoughts are not enclosed in his own head, but are spread throughout the world and occur simultaneously in the heads of all persons. The patient seems no longer to realize that he is a separate psychical entity, an ego with individual boundaries" (p. 537). We recall that the ego concept here does not derive from the tripartite model of psychic organization, and is used somewhat loosely in terms of the self-concept.

Freud discussed Tausk's contribution in a meeting of the Vienna Psychoanalytic Society in 1918 (Nunberg and Federn 1975), and he "emphasized that the infant's conception that others knew his thoughts has its source in the process of learning to speak. Having obtained his language from others, the infant has also received thoughts from them; and the child's feeling that others know his thoughts as well as that others have 'made' him the language and, along with it, his thoughts, has therefore some basis in reality" (Tausk 1919, p. 528). Freud's comment, as well as Tausk's discussion, would have to be considered an oversimplification of the genesis of paranoid projections, in the context of more modern concepts of psychic organization.

Natalija A.'s "influencing machine" represents a regressive phenomenon within a psychic organization which is characterized by rudiments of a mature psychic apparatus. Her fantasy of the "influencing machine" constitutes a restitutive element, the psychotic's attempt to reconstruct the dramatic past and to describe inner experiences which run parallel to the infant's lack of developed capacity for differentiation of self from object, and struggle to maintain a world of omnipotence while growing toward awareness of self and objects. During this stage, primary narcissistic omnipotence, as it prevails in a comparatively undifferentiated psychic organization, shifts at times by means of narcissistic projection on to the object, which is then experienced as giving thoughts or knowing all thoughts, and as thus influencing the other. The "influencing machine" characterizes the fluctuation of fantasies of omnipotence from self to object and back again to self. This struggle attempts to restore symbiosis, and thus to overcome fragmentation of body image and to restore the "oceanic feeling," the oneness with mother, in which she has the executive function of the controlling ego.

These newer assumptions which attempt to describe the development of the psychic organization before individuation has taken place were earlier expressed in terms of the *content* of fantasies.

Only later were attempts made to infer from the content the *state* of the psychic organization. For example, when discussing Tausk's contribution, Freud also suggested that the "significance of the mode of burial of Egyptian mummies [placing the mummy in] a case resembling the human body suggests the idea of the return to 'mother earth,' the return to the mother's body in death." He continued that "as a compensation for the bitterness of death, man takes for granted the bliss of existence in the uterus." The fantasy of the return to the uterus is "then an atavistic one, a preformed fantasy;" and as such, "this fantasy appears symptomatically in schizophrenia as the pathological reality of the regressing, disintegrating psyche. The mummy returns to the mother's body by physical, and the schizophrenic by psychical, death."

The "psychical death" of the schizophrenic constitutes an attempt actually to restore an early unity in order to gain safety. It usually fails to do so, since the symbiotic experience often signifies the threat of loss of identity, the fear of being devoured, and of being dominated by the other. The "influencing machine," then, represents both the wish to return to an undifferentiated, symbiotic phase and the lonesome struggle against the loss of precarious identity.

As we trace the literature for contributions in which psychotic mechanisms of childhood are described and note particularly the use such children make of machines (e.g., Elkisch 1952, Mahler and Elkisch 1953, Rank 1949), we face a variety of problems of a different order. These children, particularly the younger ones, have never advanced to states of maturity characteristic of the premorbid adjustment of Natalija A. Rather, we find in them personality organizations which frequently are better understood in terms of psychotic fixations than in terms of psychotic regressions. In this regard, we must remember that the application of these dynamic processes towards the characterization of the essential nature of the state of personality organization of psychotic children is a way of speaking, a convenient shorthand generalization, as it were, for a complex situation, rather than a scientific conclusion reached as the result of valid evidence. For these processes merely refer to the importance of developmental factors in the evaluation and understanding of the various problems of psychosis in childhood. They stress the need to make qualitative as well as quantitative distinctions between the psychotic processes of adults and children, and between the psychoses of younger and older children.

Thus, in the very young children of preschool age, we find ego fragmentation, symbiotic and autistic conditions, an extremely impaired capacity for reality testing, and primitive precursors of object relationships which characterize their specific adjustments. The dynamic considerations which define the dimensions of the play of psychotic children are derived from factors which characterize the archaic structural aspects of the developing ego. Significant and relevant components of the ego organization which determine the patterns of psychotic play concern the concept of distance as a function of defense; the vicissitudes of impulse organization during the development from primary- to secondary-process control; language development and object relationships; the problem of identity; and the adaptive functions of the ego, especially its motor and synthesizing functions.

Similarly, qualitative differentiations can be made between the play of neurotic and psychotic children. For example, in the play of neurotic children acting out, play action, and play serve the functions of recollection, mastery of conflicts, and the search for identity. But in the play of the psychotic child, the functions of mastery, pleasure, and motor expression are less important as the end products of ego development. They interest us rather as diagnostic indicators of the functional state of the ego and as the means of communication about the conflictual problems confronting the ego in its particular developmental state.

The foregoing considerations are among the many subjects dealt with in an enormous body of literature that the present authors and their coworker, Bryant, have described and integrated (see Bellak 1958). Other publications deal with the relationship of play patterns and diagnosis in childhood psychosis (Loomis et al. 1957, Shugart 1955).

Our purpose here is to study the play of such children in order to find answers to two sets of questions. Their play constitutes the royal road to an understanding of certain aspects of the available psychic organization. The understanding of the structure of available psychic organization can then be used in order to develop therapeutic techniques. Children's play, their royal road to the unconscious (Erikson 1940), can be considered their dominant

language and thus their most powerful means of communication
with the therapist.

The word "communication" must be understood in terms of the
available psychic organization of the child. Even the assumption
that play be considered a substitute for free association in the
treatment of the psychotic child needs amplification, since the
effectiveness of language, of interpretive work, would depend
upon the nature of the psychic organization, the available capacity
for differentiation of self and nonself, and the fluctuating state of
affairs concerning object relationships. Consequently, we must
question what communication and interpretation really mean
when psychotic "transference" prevails. We would like to ascertain
how psychotic play can teach us to make contact with such children.
And we wonder how it might be possible to develop "sending
power" (Erikson 1950) in profoundly psychotic children in spite of
the deficits in their psychic organization. It might also be wished
that Natalija A. had been able to teach us how to develop "influencing machines" for those autistic and mute children who possess
only a rudimentary capacity for play, the nature of which is so
different from the play of children within the neurotic range.

An analogue of Natalija A.'s "influencing machine" was experienced by a 5-year-old boy. He felt all noises to be intrusive,
penetrating tormentors who, by gaining entrance into his body,
could simultaneously discover his secret forbidden wishes and
destroy him. Upon hearing loud noises, he would cringe and cower
as if in pain, whimper in terror, and, in mounting panic, clap his
hands over his ears as if to block out the hideous frightening
sounds that were attempting to invade his head. For this psychotic
boy, the threatening noises and sounds were equated with the
frightening voice of his enraged father, threatening to send him
away if he were naughty again. And like Natalija A.'s "influencing
machine," they represented a monstrous but impersonal delusional
force which the boy had introjected in order to achieve symbiotic
union with the omnipotent father. At the same time, the boy
struggled against introjection of the father's violent image and
enraged voice which would have separated him from home and the
needed father.

While the "influencing machine" of both Natalija A. and this
psychotic child dealt with their common struggle around the con-

flicting wishes toward symbiosis and individuation, one essential difference between them lay in the capacity of their respective egos to internalize and stabilize parental introjects. In a sense, Natalija A., having internalized the object, could create a completed machine which could function without the external physical object and could derive its driving power from the force of her delusional fantasy. The psychotic child, not having succeeded in internalizing the introjected image of the omnipotent father, could create only a precursor of the "influencing machine." The machine could not function independently of the real, external object-voices and object-sounds, around which he wove a delusion of the ambivalently viewed father who could both destroy and protect him within the same fantasy. Reality is the "nutriment"—as Piaget (1954) puts it— for the ego of the child, without which the inherent patterns cannot be mobilized and evolve.

The successful achievement of identity depends upon the ego's capacity to internalize its introjects; without the latter, it never comes to fruition, as in the severely psychotic child. Waelder (1933) has suggested that the play of the child can be understood as fantasy woven around external objects. Although he refers to physical objects which the child employs for his play activities, he nevertheless assumes a capacity for differentiation between outer and inner world, a primitive form of thinking which, however, has moved toward a more mature developmental stage. Natalija A.'s "influencing machine" might be considered such an external object around which she wove fantasies. Its nature, however, was such that no differentiation was possible between her own body image and the fantasy image of the "influencing machine" in the hands of her alleged tormentors. Winnicott's (1953) conception of the transitional object provides us with intermediate stages of object formation in which part objects may also become the hub around which delusions may be woven by the child's ego.

It may be said that often when young psychotic children weave fantasies around external objects, they cannot identify these external objects as being a part of the outside world. We might paraphrase Waelder and suggest that the play of the psychotic child is explicable as hallucinatory and delusional fantasy woven around external objects. The adult psychotic, having once in the past internalized but having later lost the introjected object, can create a psychotic fantasy through autistic thought processes without the help of actual external objects. The psychotic child, never having been able adequately to internalize the object, must weave hallucinations and delusions around external objects which are not experienced by the child as differentiated from the internalized object. Abortive attempts at differentiation between internal and external objects (also, the child's interrupted struggle toward individuation and identity formation), are regularly followed by regressive moves for the maintenance of symbiotic union with the parental object. The psychotic child's play very frequently characterizes the conflictual struggle to maintain symbiosis and to wipe out the difference between the self and the outside world, in order to avoid painful insight and to remain one with the world.

This brings to mind the play of the psychotic child who had to twirl constantly and who reacted with violent displeasure to attempts to interrupt her twirling. She suggested that she did so because she wanted the world to be confused and topsy-turvy, so that it would be exactly as she felt within herself; she would no longer be able to sense that she was different from others. No doubt, this child could make such an observation only at the point when her symptoms no longer completely possessed her, and after she had started to experience them as an alien part of herself. She needed to rationalize these symptoms in order to make them ego-syntonic.

We are indebted to Williams (personal communication) for these data. This psychotic girl, whose play so vividly demonstrates the need of the child to maintain a sense of oneness with the outer world, started intensive treatment in the early latency period. Her outstanding play activity during a long period of treatment centered around her fascinated love for incinerators which she attempted to control by magic gestures and to which she was endlessly attracted. During many therapy hours her fantasy life was woven around one special incinerator. The incinerator, as the representation of the fragmented maternal introject, separated the negative, engulfing, and threatening aspects of the maternal object from the positive, nourishing, and protective components of the maternal image. The child's endless play around the incinerator and her fascination with it contained both precursors of obsessive mechanisms and related instinctual derivatives, witnesses to the ceaseless but unsuccessful struggle of the rudimentary ego to establish a stable, adaptive, defensive organization. This child attached her psychotic thought processes to a mechanical object. In situations that are characteristic of a somewhat higher psychic organization, actual persons are used as the nucleus of the psychotic fantasy.

CLINICAL MATERIAL

Our case illustrations serve as models for the type of thinking necessary to reconstruct the psychic organization characteristic for the child and to develop modes of intervention derived from a better understanding of the nature of the psychotic child's "communications," i.e., play activities. Once more we wish to call attention to our meaning of "communication" in psychotherapy with a psychotic child. Within this context, we differentiate between that aspect of communication which is derived from the child's activity, and the alternate pole of communication which refers to the therapist's interventions. Psychotic play activity, if properly understood, might yield insights necessary for a fuller understanding of the process of communication, as well as of a number of other mental processes, which, we hope, will enrich our understanding of the psychic organization. In turn, this might enable us to develop more effective therapeutic techniques which could further the development of the patient's psychic organization.

Case 1

Robby was almost 5 when he was brought for psychiatric treatment. For the past two and a half years he had posed the most difficult management and discipline problems to his parents, who felt themselves caught in an impregnable trap created by his incomprehensible behavior and wild emotional outbursts. They complained of his severe temper tantrums that erupted with volcanic fury at the slightest frustration and sometimes with apparently trivial provocation. They felt desperately helpless that they could not reach him or make themselves understood to him. They were deeply concerned and frightened over his failure to mature along normal developmental lines, thus leaving them with the fearful expectation that he would be diagnosed as an organically damaged child for whom there was no hope of cure or improvement. Robby's father particularly despaired that the child's intellectual development would remain permanently retarded. He found himself inextricably enmeshed in his own struggle between his despair for Robby's future and his own violent rage toward his son when provoked by the boy's uncontrollable behavior.

The one area in which the parents found a glimmer of hope, agile motor development, proved to be a mixed blessing for them. For although this precocity gave them the one ray of hope that he was not retarded, it also provided the most excruciating provocation for their anger and helplessness. They could not prevent Robby from using his motor skills and his singular mechanical aptitudes to dismantle the doors, locks, and mechanical appliances in their home. Sporadically, the parents frantically felt that they could only stand by in paralyzed impotence and watch their house literally taken apart, piece by piece. In frenzied, excited forays, Robby would leave the doors hanging loosely from their hinges, the moldings separated from the walls, the carpet torn up to expose the bare floors, and every object sufficiently loose to become vulnerable to his prying tools, torn from its moorings. Robby's parents feared that his infantile verbal development must mean hopeless mental retardation. Robby's language consisted of very few words, which were difficult to comprehend, and bizarre sounds and fragments of words to which only his parents, eager to understand him, could attach meaning.

For the first few months of psychotherapy, Robby did not display the unusually frantic behavior that plagued his parents. At best, his play was fragmentary and impulsively interrupted, but never impetuously frantic. From fragmentary house building with blocks, Robby slowly turned his interest to the door stoppers in the therapist's office. Quickly, all other play activities were pushed into the background as Robby became obsessed with collecting every door stopper within his visual and tactile reach. His speech would rise in an excited crescendo as he would gleefully repeat the phrase, "want a door stopper," and impulsively pounce with either hand or foot upon every door stopper accessible to him. He would tug and pull, jump and pounce upon the door stoppers, until he either broke them off or unscrewed them from the wall. He carried a large collection of door stoppers of every variety with him and, at one time, posed a difficult problem for the therapist. He ran through the corridor of the medical building in which the doctor's office was located, dashing into every office, and pounced upon the door stopper in each office that he had already precisely located, until he was apprehended and removed. With lightning speed in one foray he dashed away from the therapist and, bursting into a strange office, quickly broke off the door stopper and slammed the door against the wall, cracking the plaster and leading to a socially difficult situation for all concerned.

The interpretation that Robby was looking for a stopper that would keep him from destroying his house when he could not prevent himself from flying open like a door and breaking the wall, eventually diminished his compulsive, frantic need for the door stoppers, as both therapist and parents assumed more effective forms of external control for him. But as he slowly gave up his need for the door stoppers and yielded to the authority of adults as stoppers of his lightning impulsivity, Robby's compulsive preoccupations centered around a collection of screwdrivers and doorknobs which he skillfully and with lightning rapidity removed from every available door. At home, in the therapist's office, wherever there was a door, no doorknob was safe from his frantic clutch. With one swift movement of the screwdriver, he could remove a doorknob before he could be stopped. The one word "knob" formed the nucleus of his verbal expressions.

During the phase of his compulsive attachment to doorknobs, Robby's father was absent from home for several weeks. Robby's need to dismantle the doors and to remove the doorknobs heightened in intensity until his mother found herself desperate and unable to cope with his impulsive destructiveness. Prior to one therapy hour, the mother had told the therapist that Robby had had quite a scare. He had suddenly burst into the kitchen where the mother was working, and in wild excitement threw his screwdriver into the air and cracked the ceiling fixture so that part of it came tumbling down to the floor, crashing between Robby and his mother. Robby had become so frightened that he had dashed in wild panic from the room while his mother dashed after, both to comfort and to scold him. She angrily took the screwdriver away and threatened him with its loss forever unless he learned to refrain from using the tool as a dangerous weapon. Robby erupted into wild hysteria and could not be comforted for two hours until, in exhaustion, he lapsed into a tormented sleep.

During this period, when Robby arrived for his therapy hours, he usually dashed to the drawer where his favorite screwdriver lay waiting for him, hastily went to the playroom, and removed the doorknobs and the plates from the two doors there. The therapist, whom Robby called "Friend," interpreted Robby's need for the doorknobs as his need for Mama who left him with Friend.

For many weeks, Robby went through the ritual of demanding numerous kisses from his mother when she left him, whereupon with reassurance that she would return, he went flying to the doors with the therapist's screwdriver. Dismantling the doorknobs would leave Robby with a smile of satisfaction, mischievous cunning, and an almost ecstatic pleasure in which the therapist could feel Robby's great relief from his anxiety over the mother's leaving. As the end of the hour approached, Robby went through the ritual of replacing the doorknobs with the help of the therapist's interpretation, insistence, and encouragement that now he could put the knobs back and leave them with Friend since Mama was coming to take Robby home.

At this point in one session, Robby became quite anxious and repeated with almost tearful pleading that he needed the doorknobs and did not want to put them back. "Why put doorknob back?" he cried in repetitious, frantic excitement. "Don't want to put doorknob back," he asserted with a defiant gesture. As the therapist tried to allay Robby's anxiety, he told him that he knew that Mama had taken the screwdriver from him and that he was very frightened that he would be without his screwdriver and could not have his knobs. Maybe he was even more frightened without his knobs when Daddy was away, especially since Mama had taken his screwdriver away. Robby confirmed this interpretation by displaying mounting anxiety and by more intensely repeating his pleas for the knobs. The therapist told him that he knew that Robby needed the knobs in order not to be afraid that Mama would leave him and sometimes he needed the knobs so that he would not be afraid of Mama. But Friend wanted to help him so that he would not have to be afraid and he would feel big and strong even without Friend's knobs. Although

Robby listened and betrayed a fleeting, satisfied smile, he maintained his insistence that he must have the knobs and could not put them back, repeatedly asking why the doors needed the knobs. When it became clear to him that he could not take the knobs with him but would have to replace them on the doors and leave them with Friend, his anxiety mounted into panic proportions. He looked at Friend and in a terrified whisper confessed, "Don't want to be girl."

Robby's strange, repetitive play, the compulsivity of which was also characterized by uncontrollable passion, moved through a number of phases. The first phase of the game concerned the ceaseless removal of door stoppers and the prevention of the locking of doors, the deeper purpose of which was to fight against isolation and separation, and to secure access to the parental figure. Availability of the mother had to be fought for through the struggle for the open door. The removal of the door stoppers could be understood as an expression of his uncontrollable impulsivity, with no holds barred. Thus he told the world—that is, his therapist—about the deep conflict between his uncontrollable impulsivity, which had to be stopped and governed and which threatened him with the punishment of isolation and separation from the protecting and nourishing mother, and his deep wish to be reunited with her and to keep his access to her open. One could hardly think of a better symbolic presentation for the struggle between the autistic and the symbiotic position. The removal of the door stopper portrayed the eruptive quality of Robby's impulsive life which then actually threatened the desired accessibility. The parents were driven away by his lack of control, lack of boundary between self and nonself, and ceaseless passionate yearning for unification. The constant threat to the home, the literal physical annihilation of the inside of the home, destroyed the very basis for the emotional security Robby needed. It was characteristic and most certainly a symbolic presentation, also, for the state of the personality organization of the child, in which neither the boundaries between different psychic organizations nor the identity of separate functions could be maintained. The regressed and fluctuating ego of this child was deprived, if we may use the metaphor of the play, of its door stoppers, its doors, its walls, and its separate entities. The struggle against walls and doors, motivated by the wish for unification, for togetherness with the mother, actually achieved the opposite and threatened the very foundations of the child's life.

While the first phase of the play characterized the archaic conflict, the regression to a state of uncontrollable impulsivity, the second phase aimed at restitution, at the solution of conflict for which the psychotherapy was preparing. The removal of the door stoppers, the removal of all controls, was followed by the passion to remove doorknobs from all available doors, to collect them and keep them. They assumed for Robby the purport of a quasi fetish. This play assumed different meaning at different points, and at times maintained different meanings at the very same moment. Whenever Robby found himself in a phase where higher functions of personality organization were available, where there was some availability of differentiation between object and self, the knob symbolized parts of the mother or the father which the child wished to make accessible to himself. By holding on to the knob he had access to the open door, and he could maintain the connection between himself and the parent. At most moments, though, as was expressed so clearly in Robby's frantic and terrorized plea that he did not want to be a girl, the knobs referred to his own body. It would be incorrect to see the knobs only as symbolic representations of the male genitalia. The dominant meaning of these knobs referred to his inability to maintain a clear body image. The loss of the knobs, identity with the loss of the mother as an accessible object—as an introject that could be maintained—referred to the threat of loss of identity, a threat particularly powerful whenever separation was threatened.

The ending of each psychotherapy hour, when Robby had to give up the knobs of the office doors, created a new threat for him, in the separation from the therapist and the necessity to take along the quasi fetish. The function of the fetish was not only to replace the lost love object—which explains the reference to "quasi fetish"—but to secure narcissistic cathexis, so that the body image could be maintained and precarious identity insured.

The external knob, not dissimilar in function from the "influencing machines" described earlier, was the external object around which delusions and inner perceptions concerning body and self-identity were woven.

If our interpretation of the play is correct, we should be able to draw conclusions for therapeutic technique. In this instance the use of a quasi fetish for symbolic representation and gratification became a part of the therapy. The therapist could not treat the doorknob simply as a utensil, but had to think of it as part of an important ritual without which communication could not succeed. Zulliger (1952) made use of a talisman which he gave to his girl patient as a symbolic representation of the father image. Sechehaye (1951) used symbolic gratification in the gift of an apple to her schizophrenic girl patient. The use of the knob here, above and beyond verbal interpretations, insured communication and contact with the child.

The end-of-the-session ritual in which the knob was finally returned to the therapist, as was the screwdriver which was used to control the different knobs, became for Robby the symbol of security. It was as if Robby and the therapist had agreed that the means of control were safe as long as they were left with the therapist, and that the child would trust the therapist in terms of accessibility and in terms of a guarantee for restitution. As long as he was with the psychotherapist he borrowed, as it were, the strength of the therapist by taking his doorknobs, the guarantee of parental supply. When he left, he was willing to restore the therapist's wholeness, and felt secure in the knowledge that the continuing process was guaranteed. The quasi fetish was returned to the psychotherapist, a form of undoing of the fantasied destruction of the therapist. This was the child's first indication that he aimed to master the problem of impulsivity and would replace the primary process with higher mental functions which would make available to him a new capacity for delay.

During an interim phase of this play, Robby would bring old battered doorknobs from home and try to exchange them for the therapist's shiny new doorknobs. Such an exchange could have been the symbolic representation of an attempt to get well by introjecting the therapist and also to get rid of introjects from earlier phases of life which were experienced as damaged, powerless, and undesirable.

The compulsive behavior of Robby's play differed from compulsions on higher levels of development in that it was accompanied by unbridled affect and was dominated by uncontrollable impulsivity.

Three months later, Robby's therapy hour had assumed a new compulsive and ritualized form. Every hour would start with his bursting into the therapist's office, his hands filled with an odd assortment of tools. He would go through an anxious procedure of bidding goodbye to his mother with demands for more and more kisses, gradually decreasing in intensity as he seemed more re-assured that she would return for him. He would dash to the drawer for the screwdriver and urgently remove the doorknobs in the therapist's playroom with obvious relief and satisfaction in his prowess, and then quickly explore the office for more available doorknobs and loose hingepins. These he would quickly remove if he were given the freedom to do so. Then he would gather up his screwdrivers and tools and place them in Friend's pocket, as he exclaimed, "Want to go out." He would lead the way into the corridor. The familiar trek along the corridor followed. Robby would compulsively touch the doorknob of every office door. Then, with one hand in the therapist's, he would almost happily walk down the stairway and out into the alley to look for abandoned pipes, bulbs, hinges, and doorknobs in the piles of rubbish con-veniently left by workmen who were remodeling offices in nearby buildings. The journey would lead to a parking garage in which Robby had come to know the location of every door and of every doorknob. At the doorway to the stairs, Robby would inspect the door which for a long time was without a knob: Robby had dismantled and thrown it away rather than have it taken away from him. Finding the knob missing, he would rapidly ask where the knob was. On being told that Robby had thrown it away, he would smile with a satisfied, cunning expression on his face, and with that would lead the way to the second level, where he would inspect the doorknobs of the door leading into the garage. Noting that the knobs were present, he would immediately proceed to the third floor where one knob was still absent as a result of his prior activities. Demanding that the therapist hold this door open, he would wrap his legs around the door and hold on to the protruding part of the lock as he swung back and forth and emitted a loud, excited, shrill, "EEEEE," and rapidly ask where the doorknob was. When told that Robby seemed happy that the doorknob was gone but that maybe he was really frightened to see that there was no doorknob after he had thrown it away, he would give up swinging, slam the door shut with great gusto, and proceed down the stairs into the alley. The therapist could interpret to Robby that he seemed happy to see the doorknob gone, but he must be afraid that every time he saw a doorknob missing, it must make him think that the same thing would happen to him. And without his doorknob, Robby was afraid that he had no Mama, no Daddy, and no Friend. Robby would characteristically respond with a satisfied smile and place his hand in the therapist's as they walked together to a building under construction. Here Robby found a windfall of doors, doorknobs, wooden paneling, molding, and building equipment of all kinds.

During one hour, a door that had not been fixed to its hinges but was leaning against the wall became the center of Robby's frantic compulsive activity of removing its doorknob. As he deftly and swiftly removed it and looked for other knobs to place in his collection, the therapist remarked that Robby seemed very happy when he could have his bright, shiny doorknob. It must make him feel very strong and big so that he would not have to be afraid that he would be left alone. A pleased smile crossed Robby's face as he went on to explore a pile of rubbish for more doorknobs and hinges. As the time approached to return to the therapist's office, Robby went through the struggle of returning the doorknob at the therapist's request. With the therapist's interpretations that he knew how hard it was for Robby to leave the doorknob on the door when Robby thought he needed it to make him feel like Robby and as big as Friend and Daddy, Robby went through an obsessional struggle with the doorknob. He replaced it and then quickly removed it, until the therapist remarked that he knew how hard it was for Robby to leave the doorknob with the door. Robby didn't like to see that the door had a better doorknob than Robby had. And Robby was afraid to return the doorknob when he was always afraid that he would not have his knob and that he would have no one to belong to, while the doorknob belonged to the door. For a moment Robby seemed satisfied and replaced the doorknob, but as he started to walk away he quickly removed it with one sure turn of his screwdriver and a tug of his hand—and stood still, as if transfixed. He looked at the therapist and rapidly repeated the question, "Who took doorknob off? Who put knob in Robby's hand?" The therapist remarked that Robby needed Friend to tell him that Robby took the doorknob and that Robby had put it in Robby's hand. Robby needed Friend to tell him what he did, because Robby did not know Robby, and he did not know what Robby did. But now he could put the knob back and Robby could go back with Friend to the office, to Robby's and Friend's house, where Mama would be waiting for Robby.

When Robby seemed at first unable to return the knob, the

therapist suggested that maybe he would be able to help Robby put it back. Robby quickly remonstrated that he would do it, which he did at once, saying, "Friend, I fix it."

On the trek back to the office, he followed the familiar path down the stairway into the basement of the building, where more doors and knobs were quickly explored and given up after a struggle. The route then led into the alley past the parking garage and up the back stairway of the building. Here Robby, on hearing loud noises, would suddenly close his ears and appear frightened. The therapist would remark to him that the noises frightened Robby whenever he thought that he was bad. He was afraid the noises would jump out and carry him away from Mommy, Daddy, and his home. Sometimes Robby felt like the knobs that he took from the doors, alone and not belonging to Mommy and Daddy, and when he took the knobs he was afraid that Daddy would scold him and make big noises like the noises that he now heard. Apparently satisfied with this interpretation, Robby would remove his hands from his ears and place his arm in front of his eyes as he put one hand in the therapist's hand. Blindly, he would again lead the way up the stairs, but with the assurance that the therapist was shadowing him. In this manner he would reach the therapist's office where he would dash into the office and inquire in a loud questioning voice, "Where Mama?" Upon her arrival, he would happily entwine his legs around the door and, with one hand on each knob of the door, swing back and forth in gleeful excitement. Then, on his mother's request, he would pick up his screwdrivers and other paraphernalia and bid goodbye to Friend before rapidly dashing down the hall to the elevator.

In this play sequence, which began after several months of therapy and repeated itself hour after hour for many weeks, there was a new development in the ritualistic play around the door-knob. First of all, we realized that the patient could cope with the threat of the psychotherapy situation only if he could control it through the ritualistic play. The compulsive control and collection of doorknobs guaranteed his mastery over the object and reduced anxiety. The meaning of the play was overdetermined inasmuch as his control of the doorknobs guaranteed him both accessibility and an avenue of flight. He could get to the object without having to be afraid of it, and could leave it at will. The doors, physical symbols of the object, were deprived of their controlling mechanism and thus could be controlled by the child. His collection of doorknobs, combined as it was with the passionate glee of victory, could be compared to headhunters' trophies; the latter's collections indicate not only mastery of the enemy but also incorporation of the enemy's virtues and strength. These trophies are not only the sign of victory but a protection against deep-seated anxiety.

As the play continued, Robby struggled with the therapist, but actually attempted to resolve his inner struggle about control. Hour after hour, as he incorporated aspects of the psychotherapist, who continued to show him the meaning of the play, he gathered strength. This can be compared to a headhunter who feels that everybody is afraid of him when they notice all his trophies of victory. The child therefore could discontinue this attack and might even be able to discontinue the exhibition of his "trophies."

This struggle concerning the incorporation of introjects as it was exhibited in the play with physical objects led Robby to the beginning of individuation. As he incorporated the therapist, or rather the therapist's well-meaning and helpful intentions, he could raise the question as to "who did it." In the mind of the child, the loss of body function might be caused by the threatening, castrating, negative introject. This introject created a paralyzing fear, which, if recognized and given up, might lead to the restoration of function. It was during this period of the hour that Robby, in raising the question, permitted the therapist to help him see that he (Robby) himself had taken the doorknobs off the door. By thus destroying the function of the door, he had tried to undermine the functioning of the therapist, had symbolically destroyed him. Even though he expected retribution, he also found out that he might safely ask the question since separation and individuation had become less frightening.

As Robby understood that he himself was the one who took the doorknobs off, and as he started to sense his own will, the first recognition of individuation, he was overwhelmed by fear. As the play, the ritualistic repetition of the hour, proceeded week after week, he found himself confronted by terrible noises as frightful as the vengeful chorus of the Erinyes. He interpreted the noises, actually the acceptance of the therapist's earlier interpretation as to "who did it," as voices of doom and danger. He tried to deny their existence, shut his ears, but nevertheless worked through on

that Nick was doomed to an incurable illness for which there was no
real help, but parental conscience and duty required her to arrange
futile gestures of medical treatment.

Although there had always been an open question regarding the
etiology of Nick's disturbance and there were grounds to suspect
some organic brain damage, it was clear from an evaluation of
Nick's illness that he had been psychotic for many years. Further,
there was reason to believe that his intellectual retardation was
more in the nature of a pseudostupidity than a genuine organic
type of dementia. At the age of 13, Nick displayed a grotesque
masochistic compliance in relation to his peers, which manifested
itself in bizarre ways. He had long become known to his schoolmates as a clown who would do the most ridiculous things in order
to make other boys laugh. Nick never saw humor in these situations,
only a desperate need to comply with the tormenting provocations
of his peers and to offer himself as a helpless victim of their abuse
and ridicule. Nick described these situations with an air of remoteness about them, as if he were talking of the exploits of another boy
rather than of himself. Actually, he did speak about a dissociated
part of himself. A favorite pastime of his schoolmates was to gather
around Nick, shout various orders to him, and humiliate him. When
they would order, "Nick, piss on the wall," Nick would immediately
comply by urinating on the wall. When the boys would shout at him,
"Shit in your pants," Nick would go through the motions of having a
bowel movement and would sometimes be so compliant as to
succeed. When the boys would torment him with the command to
kiss their shoes, Nick would get down on his hands and knees and
obediently kiss the shoes of his tormentors. Nick's parents were
confused and mystified by his behavior, since to them his most
cardinal problem seemed to be that he never obeyed them. They felt
that the most difficult thing about him was the negative attitude he
had towards them, that of not accepting their authority, an attitude
manifested most provocatively in his constant clownish attacks on
his sister.

Although the parents vaguely recognized that there was much
that was immature in his development, they were never really aware
of his illness. They complained only of his "badness" and the
irritation that he aroused in them. Nor did they realize to what
extent Nick suffered an invisible panic lest he be deserted and

abandoned. For Nick literally forced his mother to do his bidding at all times lest he become aware that he no longer controlled her and therefore had no assurance of her continued presence and attachment to him.

During many early therapy hours with Nick, the therapist felt the extent of the unbridged chasm that lay between himself and Nick. Nick would withdraw to a corner and read the therapist's medical books or ply him with a number of questions related to the manufacture of drugs used in psychiatric treatment. Nick wanted to know how Sodium Pentothal was made and why the therapist did not use it on him. He carried a pharmacy manual with him and repeatedly asked the therapist whether he knew what the drugs were for and why he did not use drugs. He brought numerous books with him that he obviously could not understand and perhaps could not read. He gave the impression at all times that he was interested only in what was useless to him. He seemed to imply in his behavior that he felt that he could expect from the therapist only what was useless, just as all his life he had received only futile gestures of help from the many different types of treatment he had undergone in his pediatric and allergy care. In his unguarded moments, he broke out in bizarre clownish behavior in which he attempted to shadowbox with the therapist in such a manner as to convey the deepest anxiety and the most pathetic kind of humor that would inevitably lead to his ridicule and humiliation.

On one occasion, the therapist remarked how much Nick would like to be a tough guy but that he was having a terrible time as he was always so afraid of everyone. Nick liked being called a tough guy and said, "That's my name." The therapist told him that it was fine with him that Nick wanted to be a tough guy and maybe he even wanted to be the leader of a gang. Nick thought this was a great thing and when the therapist offered his services to him in the gang, Nick, now christened "Tough Guy," referred to the therapist as "Red."

Tough Guy and Red formed the nucleus of an invisible gang which had no apparent purpose for its existence. Tough Guy, as the leader of the gang, had no desire to be a criminal. But he needed Red to accompany him on his explorations through the streets of Beverly Hills, first to discover the whereabouts of the residences of famous movie stars and then to trace a familiar route along the streets, apparently in search of nothing. But as Tough Guy and Red pursued their aimless wandering, Tough Guy cautiously confessed to Red that he had heard that Nick was having a lot of trouble. He heard that he must have many disorders. He even heard that Nick had shit in his pants at school. He hated Nick; he thought he was crazy. Red said that he, too, had heard about Nick. He heard that he had many troubles and that he was looking for someone to help him but that he never could find anyone who could understand him. Tough Guy snorted and said that he hated Nick anyway. Red said that he heard that whenever Nick heard that anyone hated him, he got plenty scared because he couldn't stand being hated. He especially got in trouble when Tough Guy hated him. He really wanted Tough Guy to like him. Tough Guy said that he could never like Nick because he was so crazy. He even kissed the boys' shoes when they told him to. Red said that maybe Nick had to do this because he thought that the more he did crazy things, the more he made the other boys laugh at him, the more he thought they liked him. Tough Guy looked at Red, and suddenly the vacant and incomprehensible look on his face faded slightly, and a faint smile of recognition with genuine feeling appeared as he turned to Red and said, "Red, you're a good psychiatrist."

Red turned to Tough Guy and snorted, "Do you mean like that crooked quack, Friedman [the therapist's own name]?" Nick laughed cautiously and asked Red if he knew Friedman. Red said he had heard about him; he had heard that Friedman was one of the biggest crooked quacks in Beverly Hills. Tough Guy turned and said, "Red, do you know what that Friedman does?" Red said he thought Friedman probably did a lot of crazy things, too. Tough Guy said he had heard that Friedman sent big bills to Nick for his treatment. Red said he had heard about that, too, and then snorted in disgust, "That dirty, crooked quack, Friedman. He's a crooked crook. He pretends to be a doctor and is supposed to cure Nick of his disorders, but all he does is sit in his office and doesn't give Nick any medicine to cure him. He just sends big bills and makes Nick's parents pay out all their money so that there is nothing left for them."

Tough Guy looked at Red with questioning but vacant eyes. His suspiciousness of Red was quite apparent and the look of incredulity remained with him as he seemingly became more embarrassed and anxious. Timidly he said, "Friedman's all right, Red. He's a nice guy." Red again snorted in disgust, "If you want to think he's a nice guy, that's for you to think, Tough Guy. But all I ever hear about Friedman is that he is supposed to treat Nick, but all he does is charge so much money that Nick thinks that there is nothing left for his family. He just talks to him, doesn't give him any medicine, and doesn't cure him. He just keeps him coming and sometimes he doesn't even see him in his office. No wonder Nick always disappears as soon as he comes to see him. He would probably get more help if he joined our gang than if he came to see that quack, Friedman."

Tough Guy said, "Yes. Maybe you're right, Red." And then he musingly remarked, "But I don't want Nick in this gang. He does crazy things. He has a lot of disorders. I hate him."

In becoming "Tough Guy," the patient strove for the ego ideal, and for support from the therapist, actually the "Red" part of the therapist. At the same time, he tried desperately to keep out his pathological counterpart, the masochistic child who had no identity of his own and lived on borrowed identity, usually the disgracing "orders" of his contemporaries. This despicable part of himself was matched by the despicable part of the therapist who was experienced as not helpful and as charging too much, and who thus seemed to express what the child did not want to be true, but what he might hear the parents say as they expressed discouragement about the slow treatment, the lack of visible success, and the tremendous expense involved in trying to help their child. The negative version of the therapist was also the projection of the parents' own negative attitude towards the child. This was experienced by the youngster as the hated parent who was to be kept out of the therapy, just as he attempted to keep the hated child-patient out of the therapy. This seemed to maintain the collaboration of the positive aspects of patient and psychotherapist, and thus provides a vivid example of schizophrenic ambivalence.

One could look at this situation as one of a divided-identity struggle. The therapeutic situation could be maintained only by the forceful seclusion of the other aspect of the personality. It was as if Dr. Jekyll were not allowed to know about Mr. Hyde but finally came to the point where he might be able to go through life with the identity of Dr. Jekyll and with the added knowledge of a role belonging to Mr. Hyde who was to be kept out of the treatment situation.

Our metaphor actually could be understood in reverse, since what was accepted consciously were the negative aspects, if we were to look at them in terms of contemporary values. The conscious value of the patient was complete obedience and masochistic pleasure. The rejected value, which was rescued in the sanctuary of the psychotherapy situation, was the strong boy, the "Tough Guy." As such, he was then supported by something in the therapist's personality which was experienced by the patient as forbidden, as a secret to be kept from the parents; the positive concept of the therapist, the psychiatrist with the doctor's title, was experienced as unwelcome and unacceptable to the child.

One might well wonder how the psychotic illness of this child must have looked when he was five years old. Instead of using schizophrenic play-acting, he might have used physical toy objects as Robby did. We would like to make the point that the prevalent modes of expression depend upon the patient's stage of development, and that the schizophrenic process finds different expressions at different times of the child's life. The disease process makes use of different "channels" in the ego organization as they become available through age-bound maturation which, though distorted, nevertheless follows a chronological sequence.

The convenient assumption, in the case of the adult personality, is that the psychotic process finds similar expression regardless of age. This example permits us to raise the question concerning certain quantitative and qualitative differences in the psychic organization of the psychotic ego. If correctly understood, these would suggest appropriate methods of communication with the sick child rather than force acceptance of mere abstract understanding of the disease process.

SUMMARY

"Influencing machines," inventions that control perpetual motion, frequently play a part in the inner life of certain adult schizophrenics. Physical objects that are utilized as toys or as transitional objects by children as they slowly develop the capacity for adult thinking seem to be the infantile equivalent of these machines. The play of psychotic children indicates a special use of physical objects, which are the external crutches, as it were, supporting the delusional and hallucinatory ideation that characterize the inner life of such children. Certain qualities of the psychotic play of children, such as stereotyped repetitiveness, fragmentation, and condensation, are striking and outstanding features, the observation of which permits inferences about the nature of the psychic organization of the patient. In our case illustrations, play is used as a springboard toward an understanding of the fragile and fragmented ego organization of these children. With such understanding, therapists are better equipped to develop rational treatment techniques for this patient group.

The questions we have raised concerning certain elementary processes that characterize the psychotic child's ego indicate the desirability for formalized research into the nature of the psychotic child's play. Such research would require the study of both the different stages of the illness and also the nature of the ego organization and its changes when certain maturation takes place. Peller (1954) has provided us with such a study of play patterns in normal development. Such research regarding the psychotic child will contribute towards increased flexibility in approach. Older formulas may be useful for initial contact, but they fail in different stages of the therapeutic process. Psychotic play, then, constitutes the royal road not only to unconscious mental process and conflict but to an understanding of primitive ego organization and its developmental course in childhood psychosis.

REFERENCES

Bellak, L., ed. (1958). *Schizophrenia: A Review of the Syndrome.* New York: Logos Press.

Elkisch, P. (1952). Significant relationships between the human figure and the machine in the drawings of boys. *Amer. J. Orthopsychiatry* 22: 379–385.

Erikson, E. H. (1940). Studies in the interpretation of play disruption in young children. *Genet. Psychol.* monogr. 22: 557–671.

—— (1950). *Childhood and Society.* New York: Norton.

—— et al. (1957). Childhood psychosis. II. Play patterns as nonverbal indices of ego functions: A preliminary report. *Amer. J. Orthopsychiatry* 27: 691–700.

Federn, P. (1952). *Ego Psychology and the Psychoses.* New York: Basic Books.

Mahler, M. S. and Elkisch, P. (1953). Some observations of disturbances of the ego in a case of infantile psychosis. In *The Psychoanalytic Study of the Child,* vol. 8, ed. R. S. Eissler, A. Freud, H. Hartmann, and E. Kris, pp. 252–261. New York: International Universities Press.

Nunberg, H. and Federn, E., ed. (1975). *Minutes of the Vienna Psychoanalytic Society.* New York: International Universities Press.

Peller, L. E. (1954). Libidinal phases, ego development, and play. *The Psychoanalytic Study of the Child* 9: 178–198.

Piaget, J. (1954). *The Construction of Reality in the Child.* New York: Basic Books.

Rank, B. (1949). Adaptation of the psychoanalytic technique for the treatment of young children with atypical development. *Amer. J. Orthopsychiatry* 19: 130–139.

Sechehaye, M. (1951). *Symbolic Realization: A New Method of Psychotherapy Applied to a Case of Schizophrenia.* New York: International Universities Press.

Shugart, G. (1955). The play history: Its application and significance. *J. Psychiatric Soc. Work* 24: 204–209.

Tausk, V. (1919). On the origin of the "influencing machine" in schizophrenia. *Psychoanal. Q.* 1933, 2: 519–556.

Waelder, R. (1933). The psychoanalytic theory of play. *Psychoanal. Q.* 2: 208–224.

Winnicott, D. W. (1953). Transitional objects and transitional phenomena. *Internat. J. Psycho-Anal.* 34: 89–97.

Zulliger, H. (1952). Child psychotherapy without interpretation of unconscious content: A theoretical exposition of pure play. The use of a child's talisman as a psychotherapeutic agent. *Bull. Menninger Clin.* 1953, 17: 180–188.

16

A YOUNG WOMAN'S INABILITY TO SAY NO TO NEEDY PEOPLE AND HER IDENTIFICATION WITH THE FRUSTRATOR IN THE ANALYTIC SITUATION

Vamik Volkan

Editor's Notes

Dr. Volkan is a dedicated clinician who adheres to the formal elements of the psychoanalytic process more so than most clinicians who treat severely disturbed patients. At seminars, in his writings, and in private conversations, he takes a position that is close to the classical one. Nevertheless, he does not hesitate to treat patients who would be rejected out of hand by the classical analyst. The structurally defective patient presented in this chapter used the couch in five-times-a-week treatment that was conducted within an interpretative transference context. The analysis of this young woman incorporated some structural formulations.

This needy patient had to "rescue" others; she needed to relate to the mourner who could not give up the lost love object. Dr. Volkan describes the patient's relationships with needy persons who were, in fact, mother displacements, as examples of projective identification. The external object was a suitable receptacle for the patient's projected neediness, which she could then introject and, in Melanie Klein's sense, repair. The author formulates that the patient represented a "linking object" for the mother: she had become a substitute for the mother's lost love object.

Rescuing, repairing, and giving represent attempts at integration and structuralization. For patients suffering from severe ego defects this may mean that the caretaking person has to be constantly available. Dr. Volkan's patient put herself in that position, giving anything and everything that needy persons demanded. She was trying to create a world for them that she never had, and, of course, through projective identification, to create such a world for herself, too.

Dr. Volkan depicts a clinical situation where the usual boundaries that define a person and keep her separate from others are blurred; either they have been imperfectly formed or they have been disrupted in the regressive flow. How far regressed or primitively fixated Dr. Volkan's patient was could be the subject of another discussion.

This interpenetrability of boundaries was beautifully illustrated by Dr. Volkan's seemingly impetuous response of "No!" to this patient, as he felt himself in the position of having to respond to her neediness. In a sense, he resisted or, better still, refused to accept her neediness, which she was trying to put inside him. This countertransference response became a crucial focus for the remainder of the analysis.

Dr. Volkan discusses the ramifications and subtleties of the transference–countertransference interaction. He would not let himself use or be used by the patient as her psychopathology dictated. This very valuable analytic experience was *not* based on the analyst countering the patient's primitive, maladaptive needs. Rather, the analyst's countertransference responses became the vehicle by which he could both feel and understand the essence of the patient's traumatic infantile past as she repeated it in the analytic setting.

This chapter contains formulations about various clinical and technical issues, and implications about the developmental process. Transitional phenomena and the lack of prohibiting introjects (the frustrator who says "no") are important elements for the development of specific types of psychopathology. Their implications for ordinary psychic development need further exploration. Consequently, besides being a stimulating clinical exposition, this chapter points to areas that can enhance our understanding and treatment of patients.

P. L. G.

In the eleventh month of the psychoanalytic treatment of a young woman with seriously regressed ego organization, I responded uncharacteristically to the emotional-ideational flow between us: I felt she was depositing something unpleasant in me, and I said "No" aloud, adding that she was to take back this unpleasantness. This chapter is the story of my unusual response, and an examination of the way it was included in the analytic process, becoming the central theme of this patient's treatment for the following seven months and, fortunately, leading to useful new psychic structures within her. These included a positive identification with the frustrator in the sense in which this concept was originally described by Spitz (1957, 1965).

Poor results in the treatment of seriously regressed patients with defects in their ability to integrate a cohesive self-concept can often be traced to therapists' failure to use their "emotional responses" to patients in their formulations. Boyer (1977) wrote that "Success results not only from accurate, empathic, and timely maneuvers which lead to genetic interpretations, but also from the development of the patient's new object relations with the therapist" (p. 420). Such development of severely regressed patients, be they borderline or schizophrenic, occurs on levels similar to those of the early child/parent relationship (Loewald 1960), has the latter's accompanying affective states, and requires monitoring and appropriate utilization in treatment. Although analysts' emotional responses (i.e., their feeling/participation) are instruments to help such patients achieve a structural change, I oppose the indiscriminate voicing of these responses as they can turn the treatment into a "wild analysis." In this instance, I did not use my emotional response as a calculated technical maneuver; it came naturally. Its exaggeration was unusual and unlike my customary procedure, which might have been an interpretation, or silence until I further understood the psychological interaction. My abrupt utterance, "No! Take it back!" and the emotion in my voice surprised me.

Case Material

Margaret, 19 years old, was admitted to a psychiatric hospital after experiences with dangerous drugs, acute psychosis, promiscuous sexual activity, and suicidal gestures. For two years, she had been under the intermittent care of a psychiatrist, who gave her tranquilizers. Her parents, embarrassed by her behavior, offered environmental manipulations, such as sending her on vacations overseas with friends, in an attempt to solve her problems. After a bad LSD trip, her psychiatrist advised more intensive psychotherapy and she was hospitalized.

Margaret "collected herself" over the few months she spent in a protective hospital environment and was referred to me for psychoanalytic treatment. This tall, rather handsome young woman, came to our first meeting in a rebellious mood. She did not want treatment, but felt that she had no choice in view of her suicidal feelings and her parents' insistence that she "get straightened out." She initially told me that her mother had always thought of her as different from her other children—more "outgoing" and "more fun." Nonetheless, she had sucked her fingers until her early teens, and had carried little lint fuzzballs with her that she rolled between her fingers. Her childhood history was an unhappy one: she had been afraid of the night and of being alone. She had stolen from her mother's purse and from store counters since childhood. I began to see her five times a week, expecting that her analytic treatment might include the development of a transference psychosis and its resolution.

I immediately noticed two dominant themes threading through her relationships with others, one a form of pathological generosity, and the other its opposite—her belief that others had an obligation to meet her needs. She did not hesitate to take from others when she felt the need and, in this sense, made them into "instant mothers" (Speers and Lansing 1965) to meet her needs. This propensity led her to adopt a dangerous life-style. For example, regarding a food store as an instant mother, she felt entitled to pilfer whatever she needed from the shelves. Such stealing did not evoke conscious guilt.

Some clinicians have defined pathological generosity as an emotional state characterized by the profuse and overwhelming desire to give others not only material things but thoughts, interests, and care as well (Lewinsky 1951, Socarides 1977). It also can be used defensively to help a person frustrated by rejection to avoid despair and hate; in this sense, it involves the fear of refusing others. Coexisting with pathological generosity, "there is unconsciously a need 'to get something for nothing' in order to heal a narcissistic wound of childhood" (Socarides 1977, p. 206). Lewinsky states that giving, as it appears in pathological generosity, is rooted in oral and anal fixations.

Margaret alternated between giving and taking, functioning on a low level of "character pathology," to use the term Kernberg (1975) applies to "severe character pathology typically represented by the chaotic and impulse-ridden character, in contrast to the classical reaction-formation types of character structure and the milder 'avoidance traits' characters" (p. 12). She also identified both openly and covertly with those who received her "gifts." However, after scrutiny it became clear that her pathological generosity was specialized—she was generous only to those she considered "needy." Her giving to these needy people seemed to be a type of rescue, a way of nurturing them (emotionally and physically) and making them "forget their troubles." Such generosity was tied to her inability to say, or use the concept of, "no." Although she knew the vocabulary and gestures of negation, and used them toward those she considered "normal," her inability to say "no" to those she considered needy was most striking.

For example, she could not pass a shabby hitchhiker without

being impelled to pick him up in spite of her awareness of the inconvenience or danger this act might entail. During her first year in treatment, she gathered a group of emotionally sick or physically undernourished, suicidal, lonely people around her and allowed them to push their way into her life and her apartment at any time of the day or night with no remonstrances. When her inability to say "no" was gradually brought to her attention with gentle clarifications of her behavioral patterns, she bought a special lock for her apartment door, a symbolic gesture of blocking access to the breach in her ego boundaries. But, when one of her hangers-on broke the lock, she could not protest. Her behavior toward needy hitchhikers began to change in a parallel way. Her judgment now precluded her picking up everyone standing hopefully by the roadside, but she continued to feel "pangs of conscience" when she passed them by and would set her directional signal to make them believe she was not going their way.

Margaret was the third child of traditionally religious, middle-class parents from the rural South. By the time she became my patient, her father had established himself as the head of a food-processing plant and had become widely known throughout the area as a public speaker. He held idealistic and liberal views about helping the needy, and was interested in fighting malnutrition and hunger. An identification with her father's behavior toward the needy played a role in determining the dominant theme in Margaret's life, but certain other psychological processes were more important to its formation. At the outset of her treatment, Margaret reported seeing her father as strong and manly on the surface but without "anything but his size to impress everybody." The family had been financially hard-pressed before he became successful and Margaret had been born during a time when her father was away from home seeking higher education and providing little income for his family. As he advanced toward success, he continued to be away from home much of the time.

Margaret's mother had an identical twin. According to the family story, the mother of the twins had been injured during their delivery, and her death was attributed to this obstetrical difficulty, although she lived until the twins were ten years old. Margaret's mother had beaten her hands on her dead mother's bed and cried,

"Wake up! Wake up!" In later life, she showed signs of pathological grief (Volkan 1970, 1981), a state in which the bereaved individual is unable to move through the expected mourning stages toward ultimate internal adaptation to the suffered loss. Such an individual will maintain chronic hope, searching for the return of the lost one and, at the same time, dreading the success of this search. The bereaved person will continue to be preoccupied with the image of the dead one. As a child and a teenager, Margaret had overheard her mother praying nightly for her grandmother's return to life.

Margaret's mother, who was inseparable from her twin, lived near her even after they were both married. The first prolonged, real separation between them occurred when Margaret's family moved because the father had enrolled in a university. Margaret was conceived during this time, although her mother was romantically attached to another man, as she admitted openly later. As a young adult, Margaret suspected that her mother had conceived her in an effort to save her marriage. While pregnant, her mother was preoccupied with thoughts of death, depressed, and afraid of dying in childbirth or of bearing a deformed infant. Her moderate-to-severe depression continued throughout the first year of Margaret's life and for a short time thereafter until she was once again able to live near her twin sister.

Margaret's mother had unconsciously seen her baby daughter not only as a link to her sister, from whom she was temporarily separated, but also as a link to her dead mother. Thus Margaret was a *living linking object* (Volkan 1981, 1982), a version of a replacement child (Cain and Cain 1964, Poznanski 1972) or the "vulnerable child" (Green and Solnit 1964). In the early mother-child interaction, the mother may deposit the image of the lost one into the child's self-representation through the mechanism of projective identification. The aim of such projective identification is to avoid separation from the lost one. Then, as the child grows, he must make internal adaptations to what has been conveyed to him. These adaptations can lead to creativity or even to psychosis. In any event, the child becomes the meeting place of the representation of the mourner and the mourned one; being thus linked to the "living dead" perpetuates the child's omnipotence. Such children desire to save the mourner. What at first seems to be altruism is actually a selfish hope that if the grieving mother can be purged of her grief, the child's push for individuation can be realized (Volkan 1981).

When Margaret became my patient, her mother seemed to sublimate her oral needs. She supported her husband in their shared concern for feeding the needy. In fact, I thought that her husband's liberal career, which had focused on taking care of the needy, had been initiated as well as supported by the psychological needs of his wife, who nonetheless betrayed remnants of her continuing effort to ward off depression by her interest in vitamins and health foods. Margaret focused upon her mother's preoccupations and described how she carried pills in her purse wherever she went and stocked a bathroom cabinet full of them. Margaret had stolen some pills for herself.

The whole family tended to pair off, to form "twinships." Margaret, the third girl, was three and a half years younger than the younger of the two other girls, who had been born a year apart. The brother, born three and a half years after Margaret, was quickly followed by another child. Margaret felt that the family had two sibling pairs, and that her lack of a partner was compensated for by a special closeness to her mother, on whom she was chronically dependent. At the same time, she was determined to "save" her.

The mother's fears of pregnancy and childbirth, ingrained by the oft-repeated family story that the grandmother had been injured in childbirth, accounted for the daughters' counterphobic tendency toward pregnancy at an early age. Both older sisters conceived and had abortions while in their teens. Margaret followed suit, becoming pregnant at the age of fifteen by a depressed teenager who had survived a suicide attempt with severe shotgun wounds. Since he was needy, Margaret was unable to refuse him. In a sense, he represented her depressed mother, and she felt obliged to fuse with him in intercourse to relieve his depression. During the incredibly bloody, criminal abortion which resulted, she saw the fetus flushed down a toilet. Disorganized, she fled into excessive drug abuse. She stayed in a regressive state for the next four years, during which time early pathological internalized object relations were activated. She became the generous savior while identifying with the needy she hoped to save. Only after hospitalization for a "bad trip" was she referred to me.

The First Eleven Months of Treatment

After a few initial face-to-face interviews, I began to see Margaret for analysis five times a week. I asked her to tell me whatever came to mind and describe her emotional and physical sensations. I told her I would talk whenever I thought it useful and that if she came to my office under the influence of drugs there was very little I could do for her. She accused me of being "square" and unable to understand her generation, and wanted to withdraw from treatment. I confidently indicated my awareness of her problems, some of which actually endangered her life. Within two months, she recognized my commitment to her welfare and stopped behaving arrogantly. She said that until then she had not been able to see the various items in my office as discrete and differentiated. Then she asked if I could absorb her "bad feelings" through "osmosis." I gave no direct verbal reply. During the following sessions, she confided that she and her mother could know each other's inner feelings without talking about them, and that she felt able to communicate with others (by implication, those she thought of as emotionally ill and needy) by means of osmosis, thought waves, or a "third eye."

Some time after acquainting me with her notion of this magical communication, she undertook an "upward refuge" in seemingly rather open oedipal material that arose from conflicts of simultaneous desire and dread connected with merging the needy with the needed. Although her words dealt with oedipal matters, her nonverbal communications, conveyed by rolling lint fuzzballs between her fingers, referred to object-relations conflicts. The precursor of the fuzzballs had been the transitional object of her childhood, a red security blanket. Her transitional object and transitional object relatedness (Modell 1968) were reactivated on the couch. By reactivating the transitional object, over which she had the illusion of absolute control, and bringing it to my office, she sought to control the psychological distance between herself and her analyst. In this way, she provided an illusionary solution for the anxiety provoked by the simultaneous experience of wanting to merge with the "other" and dreading to do so.

I customarily pay little attention to the oedipal preoccupations of patients like Margaret at this phase of treatment, as they represent "upward resistance." Instead, I concentrate on following the pathology of internalized object relations as they evolve in treatment. I agree with Boyer (1961, 1977, Boyer and Giovacchini 1967), the Ornsteins (1975), and Rosenfeld (1966) that premature oedipal interpretations, and even direct attention to such issues, preclude the development of pre-oedipal transference states. As Boyer insists, these states must be worked through before the patient can reach a classical transference neurosis, or a version of it. Only after the patient develops a stable self-concept differentiated from object-representations, as well as a stable internalized object world, do I expect the analysis to parallel the classical analysis of a neurotic patient, in which oedipal issues become the central theme. At this point in Margaret's analysis, I was more concerned with establishing a firmer therapeutic alliance. When she indicated that she thought I was able to read her mind, I gently insisted that I had no such magical ability. I also clarified her inability to say "no" to needy people whenever she brought accounts of her daily life to our sessions. This repetitive pattern became evident.

In the fifth month of analysis, Margaret found a special boyfriend, a rather depressed young man who habitually lived at others' expense and thus could be seen as needy. Her inability to deny him was clearly observable, and occasionally she merged with him during her rescue attempts. She reported fantasies of this young man's depression being lifted after being with her. During sexual intercourse, she could never be sure which legs were his and which hers. I was perceived as a split-off intruder upon this unity she enjoyed with her boyfriend, but the idea that I would save her despite her "distance" from me was hidden within the transference manifestation.

At the outset of psychoanalytic treatment, Margaret rented an apartment in the city where I practice. Her mother, who lived elsewhere, visited her often. During these visits, the two women would lie side by side while the mother asked Margaret to press her body close to hers so that they could fit together in a type of twinning. Her analogy was one of an apple cut in two pieces; when the pieces were put together and fit well, it was possible to maintain the illusion that the apple was intact. I made the formulation, which I did not share with her, that this physical "twinning" of split or fragmented pieces was a return both to the illusion of a good breast and to the good mother-child relationship in which savior and saved would fuse, leaving no room for grief or depression.

On occasion, Margaret would lose her body boundaries while lying with her mother and would merge with her, much as she merged with her needy boyfriend during intercourse. Clarifications of the split between her relatedness with me and her relatedness with the boyfriend/mother, as well as the shifts between the two, helped her. She began to observe her reactions to her mother when she came to visit. Whenever her mother set up an appointment to meet her at four o'clock for a movie that Margaret knew began at three, she was unable to correct her mother and explain that four would be too late. By observing this kind of behavior and then reporting it to me, Margaret became capable of making some flimsy attempts at saying "no" to her mother. Her mother began to experience anxiety and began psychotherapy at the beginning of Margaret's tenth month of psychoanalysis. Around the time her mother began treatment, Margaret began fully and intensely to bring her relatedness to the early depressed mother into the transference. For example, instead of exhibiting a preoccupation with saving the depressed boyfriend, she talked more openly and directly about her images of me and her wish to save me.

During this phase of treatment, her dreams gave us both further evidence of the nature of the transference relationship and helped to authenticate the belief that her having had a depressed mother during her early infancy and childhood accounted for her significant current behavior pattern. During the eleventh month, she dreamed of Dr. A., a psychiatrist friend of mine who, like myself, speaks English with an accent, and who has hair like mine. Margaret had met him briefly once, but knew nothing of our relationship, only that his office was near my own. In her dream, Dr. A. was depressed and needy. In reporting her associations, she concluded that Dr. A. represented me. After realizing this, she acknowledged that she had been secretly convinced that I needed her as a patient to make a name for myself since she was the daughter of a widely known man. She would look me over intently before taking her place on the couch, examining my face for signs of distress. She would then declare that I was clearly ready to be sent to a state hospital for the mentally ill. I thought this reflected her expectations of her early environment, in which a depressed mother had played a central role.

During one hour toward the end of the eleventh month, Margaret's slow, monotonous voice was so suggestive of depressive affect that I felt paralyzed with heaviness and could hardly keep my eyes open. I recalled noting that this indicated ingestion of something "bad" associated with a depressive affect that I could not shake off. Although uncomfortable, I did not lose the ability to observe my firsthand experience of how she felt in receiving such feelings in infancy from her depressed mother; she was her early mother, and I was the infant Margaret. The experience also occurred in reverse since, in this shared regression, both of us, the depressed principal and the one affected by her depression, merged through projective identification and projective counteridentification. Nevertheless, it was not my secondary-process thinking that led me to utter an abrupt "no" toward the end of the hour and demand that she take back the "bad" feeling that belonged only to her; it was a spontaneous strong response that surprised me since, after my long experience with severely regressed analysands (including Margaret), I considered myself able to absorb any externalized self- or object-images that might be contaminated with exaggerated hate or love, and return them piecemeal to the patient in a tamer form. I then realized that I had given a personal emotional response in the midst of my empathic regression, responding to what was going on psychologically between me and my patient. I examined this, but by then the empathic regression and the awareness of the "bad" feelings were gone.

During previous sessions, my patient and I had experienced enough of my tolerance of such relatedness, and I thought I had used my ability to refrain from too hasty an interpretation of projections and externalizations. Refraining from either constant or untimely interpretations of projections and externalizations is a technical maneuver to be considered, especially when dealing with a regressed patient. Giovacchini states (Boyer and Giovacchini 1967) that when restraint is not exercised and projections are interpreted, an internalization of conflict is likely to occur. "The analyst's purpose is to focus on the intrapsychic, and when the patient succeeds in doing likewise, he has gained considerable security" (p. 224). Since I had waited long enough without interfering, my counter-response of "no" actually had been correctly timed from the therapeutic point of view. But I soon realized that I was intellectualizing and hoping, through this intellectualization, to rid myself of the guilt for making a technical mistake. Further self-analysis suggested the possibility of my jealousy and dread of Margaret's symbiotic relatedness to her mother and my abrupt wish to rid myself of such symbiotic relatedness and deny my jealousy and dread because such symbiosis contained a flow of unpleasant feelings. I then realized that my unusual response was not to be evaluated in terms of good or bad—it happened and it made me a frustrator in Spitz's sense (1957, 1965) of the term.

The Concept of the Frustrator

The term frustrator was used by Spitz in his description of how the concept of "no" and the ability to express this concept by word and gesture develop. The formation of this concept is a true milestone in the child's development, presupposing the capacity for judgment and negation. Spitz demonstrated how the rooting reflex (the rotary motion of an infant's head searching for food at the nipple) is affirmative behavior in the neonate. It is without the intent to signal or communicate while the infant is in the "object-less state," and it rapidly recedes as the infant matures. It reappears at six months of age, but with a "change of function." At this stage, rotation of the head is used to refuse food by a gesture not directed toward any object. Spitz further proposed the outline of a comprehensive explanation as to how the motor pattern of head rotation at the age of fifteen to eighteen months becomes the matrix of the semantic gesture of negative headshaking.

As soon as the infant is capable of locomotion, the communication between mother and child suddenly changes to that of prohibition or response with the mother's use of the word "no," accompanied by headshaking as she prevents her child from carrying out his intentions. But more than imitation of the mother is involved in the acquisition of the concept of "no." Spitz connects it with the biological urge to replace passivity with activity, since the child will not tolerate being forced back into passivity without resistance because of the aggressive thrust of the id when every "no" the mother utters represents emotional frustration for the child. By the end of the first year and throughout the second year, the child uses the concept of "no" through the mechanism of identification, especially identification with the frustrator. Identification with the frustrator is a variant of "identification with the aggressor" (A. Freud 1936), which plays an important role in the formation of the superego, or at least its precursors.

The child's ability to grasp the concept of "no" can signal the appearance of stubborn behavior. In this phase, which corresponds to the anal phase of the psychosexual development scheme, the child's attention is focused on eliminative functions, which are condensed upon activities connected with intake. The child exhibits stubbornness in the struggle to control what goes in and comes out of his or her body. The concept of "no" also appears in interpersonal activities and in the internal representations of interpersonal relations, i.e., relations between different introjects. Some regressed patients display the motor aspects of the gesture of "no" during psychoanalytic sessions (Volkan 1976). They may also reactivate frustrator introjects and shout restraining orders such as "Shut up!" or "Stop!" when they experience primitive disruptive anxiety states.

Olinick (1964) suggested that the child's "no" initially might be a means of resisting, or aggressively warding off, excessive stimulation. At this point, the anxiety signal leading to "no" could be seen as "too much to be safe." The concept of "no," which binds aggressive energy with aid from the synthetic activity of the ego (Nunberg 1931), is also a focal point of the more sophisticated, later concept of assertiveness.

Kohut and Seitz (1963) provided an example of one mother's harsh "no" and another's kindly "no" to demonstrate the difference in degree of traumatic and optimal frustration. When the child's original frustrator within the early mother-child interaction is not likely to help the child reach the milestone of grasping "no," the child will experience subsequent difficulties in understanding and employing negative responses when they are appropriate. The nature of the child's aggressive endowment also plays a part in such mother-child interactions. Khan (1969) wrote about the mother's task as "the provider of phase-adequate aggressive experience." When this task is not performed, "exaggeration of positiveness interferes with her weaning from the child and thus leads to a failure to enable the child to distance itself from her" (p. 143). Khan further suggested that what patients who have not had adequate frustrators "*need* is an aggressive encounter and experience in the analytic situation, through which they will be able to experience the validity of their own aggression and hate as well as that of the non-self (the analyst)" (p. 145).

The role of her mother's depression during the first years of Margaret's life is of special interest here insofar as the mother was "not good enough" as a frustrator. The depressed mother may appeal for rescue and thus sow the seeds of a savior fantasy in the child. The developing child wants to save the mother, not for altruistic reasons, but to enable her to provide adequate mothering. In 1969, Searles stated that one of schizophrenia's main determinants is the effort to keep other depressed family members alive. (I [1981] have reported a similar finding.) In 1975, Searles further stated that man has a powerful and innate "psychotherapeutic" striving, and that patients like Margaret attempt to be therapeutic even for their analysts.

While the depressed mother may unconsciously invite her child to rescue her, on the one hand, her superego demands punishment and may cause her to accept aggressively tinged behavior from her child, on the other. She is unable to say "no" to her child effectively and appropriately when the child is aggressive toward her. The result is that the child is left with rescue fantasies as well as an identification with one who could not say "no" effectively. Thus,

the child is doomed to rescue the depressed mother and her representations—in Margaret's case, the needy people—since frustra-
tions in these efforts can not be stopped with "no." Such a child has
failed to grasp the use of "no" as "a suitable vehicle to express
aggression" (Spitz 1957) and to be assertive. The child may perceive every assertive act toward the mother, especially any attempt
to achieve psychic separation from her, as a derivative of the raw
aggressive drive. The child lacks the benefit of an effective "no" to
tame aggression and limit the pull toward symbiosis. A tendency to
merge remains, since it now includes a defense (Volkan and
Akhtar 1981) against the aggressive drive. By being one with the
mother, the child may keep an illusion of not being capable of
"killing" the mother.

Margaret appeared to be trapped in and regressed to a state in
which she required the continual presence of a needy person. She
could not say "no" to needy persons since she had no adequate
identification with a frustrator. She wanted to rescue the needy in
order to be rescued by them in turn. Moreover, she had to have
them nearby and sometimes merge with them in order to assure
herself that they were not "killed" and that someday they would be
rescued.

My unusual response occurred while I was identifying with
Margaret as she was identifying with her depressed mother. I
placed a "no" between us (between the child and the depressed
mother representation) that could initiate assertion for the sake of
separating the two representations. She identified with my "new"
image as one who was able to say "no" and who thus was a
frustrator in her fantasy.

The Inclusion of the Analyst's Unusual Response
and Identification with the Frustrator
in the Analytic Process

The day after my unusual response, Margaret related the following dream: "A young woman was standing by the window with a
man who tried to touch her breasts and kiss her. She said 'no' to
him." Her associations to this dream triggered her recall of an
actual incident, which she had related to me at the beginning of her

analysis. She had been on a bus one night returning home from a neighboring city. She had sat next to the window beside a black man who, in the darkness, began running his hands over her body. She had allowed him to do so for several hours. Her report of this incident at the start of her analytic work indicated that, in her own way, she was telling me for the first time how she would lose the concept of "no" when she perceived a needy person. This man's blackness was tantamount to neediness as far as she was concerned. The dream's day residue had come from our previous hour in which I had said "No!" In the dream, she identified with me as a frustrator and became able to turn a passive stance into an active one by crying "No! No!" As she told how the young woman in the dream represented herself, she was surprised that she could say "no" under such circumstances.

The next day she reported another dream and I thought that she continued to respond to my unusual verbalization of "no": "A bird came to my room and I fed it milk and baby food." The day residue of this dream came from her feeding some birds after going home from her previous hour with me. She described feeding the birds as they perched outside. She believed that they had received "waves" from her. She pitied the birds for having to depend on an anxious, "freaked out" woman for food. She realized she had identified with an aspect of the depressed mother in feeding the birds and in being "freaked out" because, in reality, her mother did take pleasure in feeding birds. Moreover, as I pointed out, she had identified with the birds who got food and "waves" from a depressed mother. I explained that this dream referred to a time when there was no "no" between the two representations, and bad images and feelings could flow from one to the other. Her curiosity was stimulated to re-examine her "boundary problem" with her mother and her surrogates.

Two weeks later, during the twelfth month of her analysis, she brought in the following dream: "You and I were walking when you put your arms around me. There was an opening in my dress, and you put your hands there, trying to touch my breasts. You said, 'Do you mind?' At first I thought I wouldn't mind but then I was able to say 'no' to you." This dream was another version of her experience with the man on the bus, but now I was the needy man who wanted to touch her breasts. Her account of this dream led her to continue examining her early childhood environment and the unfavorable circumstances for her acquisition of the concept of "no." After reporting the dream, she began talking about a movie in which two sisters bought a pig to eat. One sister left home with a lover while the other sister stayed at home, sick and faced with the dead pig on a plate.[1] When I showed curiosity as to why the movie came to mind soon after her dream report, she indicated that the theme of the movie reminded her of aspects of her early childhood as well as problems of separation.

The pig reminded her of her aborted fetus, which had been laid aside in a medical basin to be flushed down the toilet. She also recalled the family story about her "sick" mother remaining at home with her newborn child while the "healthy" mother's mind was concerned with the man with whom she was romantically involved at the time. The sisters in the dream also represented the maternal twins. Margaret remembered that at one time during her childhood, her family had shared a home with the family of her mother's twin sister for the sake of economy. She recalled being cared for by her aunt while her mother worked. Margaret believed that while her aunt was pregnant, she had provided Margaret with inadequate, even pathological child care. When the baby arrived, Margaret was jealous.

Margaret said that the basic theme of the movie was one sister driving the other crazy—a theme that has received Searles's attention (1959). I reminded her that family twinning was preserved in her relationship with her mother, and that she and her mother would lie down on a bed as if to put two pieces of one whole together. I agreed that the two sisters in the movie could represent the maternal twins, but might also represent her and her mother. I stated that although the sister's attempt to drive the other crazy

[1] When I presented this case later to a professional group, a colleague in the audience who had seen this film noted that the dead creature on the plate was a bird instead of a pig. Since I did not know this when she reported the dream, I did not investigate why Margaret had changed the bird into a pig. A bird would clearly have been more consistent with her earlier bird dream.

might be one side of the coin, its other side might well be an attempt to rescue the other. My attempt to touch Margaret's breast in her dream might focus the conflict arising from twinning with her mother. The insertion of "no" into this dream seemed to be a wish to deal with this conflict.

After our discussion of the movie, Margaret busily recalled childhood memories and put them in order. I felt she was trying very hard to integrate the meaning of her dominant behavior patterns, those that had originally arisen from her relatedness to a depressed mother.

Three weeks later, Margaret's mother called my secretary just before Margaret's appointment and left a message for her. My secretary wrote the message out, put it in an envelope, marked it "urgent," and delivered it to me before Margaret arrived. I put it on the couch without reading it, and called it to Margaret's attention. The incident was unusual since no such urgent message had come for her before and I had never passed a note to her. After lying on the couch, Margaret read the message, which informed her that her childhood friend's mother had died. The friend, who lived in the same city as Margaret's mother, asked her to come and stand by her in her grief. Margaret had been fond of the dead woman and grieved for her on the couch. As the hour progressed, she fantasized that her aggression might kill her own mother. I explained that the death of her friend's mother had occurred at an unfortunate time, since she was actively attempting to separate herself from me, her mother, and her boyfriend. I explained that such efforts can sometimes appear to be aimed at doing away with those from whom one seeks separation. (In reality, after the transference-countertransference intensified and was used to work through the conflicts of her early object relationships, Margaret's relationship with her needy boyfriend cooled and they parted in her twelfth month of treatment.)

Margaret attended the funeral and cared for her needy, grieving girlfriend in a realistic manner, without becoming a savior. She listened to her friend and made remarks to soothe the pain of her grief. Afterwards, Margaret returned to analysis and reported the following dream: "I was sitting on a stool when you passed by. We went to a little bathroom where you gave me feces on a plate and asked me to eat them. I began eating them and was surprised to find that they didn't taste bad at all." She recalled telling me earlier about a dead pig on a plate. Then her associations returned to my saying "No!" to her and telling her to take back (eat) her own bad feelings. She held that this scene had also been repeated when she received the message about the death of her friend's mother. She had opened the note and read it in front of me on the couch. Although she had felt sad and had experienced great anxiety about her own murderous fantasies (of killing her mother), I had not taken her "bad feelings" away from her. Instead, I had allowed her to "eat her own shit." She felt that because I had not responded to her difficulty by immediately absorbing her "bad" feelings, I had again taught her to say "no."

She recalled that I had once told her that her feces represented untamed aggression. I had made this interpretation when we talked about her peculiar behavior of defecating on restroom floors in movie houses and then returning to her place in the theater, excitedly awaiting the fearful screams from whoever discovered the filth. I told her that her dream showed that the fear of feces no longer evoked fear of annihilation. I stated that some taming of her aggressive drive had taken place and that she could say "no" and assert herself without killing anybody.

During the thirteenth and fourteenth months of analysis, Margaret showed increasing interest in the circumstances of her birth, her grandmother's death, her mother's depression, and the unavailability of adequate mothering. She gathered historical data about these early events on a visit to her father and used the acquired knowledge to integrate her analytic experience. Her activities reminded me of Novey's concept (1968) of the "second look." Novey speculated as to why some patients in psychoanalysis or psychoanalytic psychotherapy have an urge to explore old diaries and papers and return to the physical settings and persons important to them in an earlier phase of life. Such behavior may constitute acting out in some instances, but it also may represent the furthering of the collection of affectively charged material and the advancing of the treatment process.

I had to cancel two hours in her fourteenth month of analysis. She fantasized that she was driving me crazy, and she became terrified about coming to her sessions because she saw me as emotionally fragile. When her aggressive drive derivatives were taken into her in an opposite direction, she felt an emotional flooding, saw her skin changing color, and felt herself growing hair and turning into an ape. I interpreted that the ape stood for her untamed aggression.

She then reported that she now said "no" to the demands of all her needy people, although doing so still made her feel like a criminal. An increase of introjective-projective relatedness occurred between us. On one day, for example, she would think of herself as depressed, while on the next she would see me in that state. She not only observed her fantasy of an affective flow between us, but she was capable of observing in it a repetition of her childhood relationship with her depressed mother.

The most important event she reported at this time was kicking her cat (Volkan and Kavanaugh 1978). She had stolen the cat while traveling through a strange town where she had seen a child with his pet and appropriated it. She named this female cat after her father, thus contaminating it with bisexual fetishistic qualities. She treated it as a fetish, but also used it as a reactivated transitional object, as evidenced by her associations. It thus was another version of her red security blanket and fuzzballs. She became "addicted" to the cat and could not sleep without it. She made the cat curl around her body on the bed, just as her mother did when they "twinned," and occasionally lost her self-boundary. The cat became a bridge between not-me and mother-me (Greenacre 1969). By kicking the cat, she attacked this link for the sake of further individuation, observing and naming her feeling state as she kicked. She said to herself, "This is anger!" and her emotional storm subsided.

At the end of the fourteenth month, she offered two dreams in one hour: "My mother is dead," and "I was looking in the dictionary for a definition of integrity and integration, and I wondered whether there is moral as well as emotional integration." I told her these dreams indicated her wish to separate her self-representation from the representation of the childhood mother in order to find her own individuality and integrity. She readily agreed, and also agreed that she might be perceiving such separation as the death of her mother. After hearing these interpretations, she experienced the sensation of "floating in the air" away from the couch. I thought that the couch in this connection represented the analyst/ mother image, but then the couch itself floated in the air and stayed with her. Thus she could not yet fully separate from the representation of the childhood mother. She continued to feel afloat during the following hours and could not recall the content of her dreams, but described the sensation connected with her dreaming: "Last night I dreamed again; I don't remember what I dreamed about, but I was connected with my dreams by an um- bilical cord."

During the fifteenth month of analysis, she began leaving her fuzzballs behind on the couch. I thought this was a symbolic effort to rid herself of the bridge that connected her with the childhood mother. I did not mention it for some time, but after she left the room, I put the fuzzballs in an unused ashtray near the couch. She did not notice this growing collection for a long time.

In the sixteenth month of analysis, she consciously observed her mother's reactions on social occasions and compared them with her own. I thought of this as an attempt to mark differences between her mother and herself in what was, in effect, an exercise in separation.

She then reported dreaming: "I saw a body of water with a rope ladder rising out of it. I and my younger siblings climbed the ladder. They climbed higher than I. I was stuck at a certain place. Would I go upward or would I go back into the water?" This dream reminded her of her experience of floating over the couch; the rope was associated with the umbilical cord. The day residue of this dream came from her repetition of an old behavior pattern the day before. During a visit from her mother, the two women planned to attend an important meeting at ten o'clock, but when the mother insisted that the meeting would take place at eleven, Margaret refrained from correcting her, although the concept of "no" came to mind. They were late for the meeting and Margaret felt irritated. "Why couldn't I say 'no'?" she lamented. She seemed determined to say it the next time she found herself in this situation. She thought the dream represented her progression in analysis, and I agreed. Would she separate herself from the representation of her mother, or would she remain in danger of being engulfed by her (fall back into the water)?

Margaret practiced saying "no" as if her life depended on it and, in a sense, it did. At this time I had to take a week's leave from my office. I shrank in her mind; she would come to my office, look at me before lying on the couch, and then report that she perceived my body to be getting smaller. By the time of my departure, I represented her fetus. She went into an abreaction over her abortion, shaking with fear, sadness, and anger. She was still trembling when the hour ended, but I felt—as it turned out, correctly—that she could tolerate the separation and I left her for the week according to schedule. I did not give her the name of any colleagues to call if she felt the need during my absence, although I have done this with some of my regressed and disorganized patients during interruptions in their treatment. She found a new apartment and separated from her needy friends during the next month. She had attended school on and off while holding temporary jobs, but she now found appropriate employment.

In the eighteenth month of analysis, during which time she still left fuzzballs on the couch after each session, she said, "I don't want to bring my chaotic little balls into your organized life." This rather peculiar statement came after her account of still feeling confused whenever she said "no" to her mother. Then I called her attention to the growing pile of fuzzballs in the ashtray. After becoming aware of having left them behind, she grew nervous. She told me that they no longer soothed her anxiety. When the hour ended, she took the pile of fuzzballs with her.

A month later, she reported that she had tried to relax by rolling a fuzzball between her fingers and masturbating, but she finally had collected all her fuzzballs and flushed them down the toilet. Three months later, she gave her cat away. Much later, she took it back, but by then it no longer had magical properties for her. Her analysis continued for three more years. After disposing of the fuzzballs, she moved increasingly toward more mature object relations and a genuine oedipal transference. Only on rare occasions of particular stress did she return to making and using fuzzballs for transitional object relatedness. She gave even these up upon analysis of the meaning of the stressful situation. What was most interesting was that a remnant of a fuzzball, condensed with other symbolic events (her acceptance of womanhood, in particular) appeared a week before our work terminated. She "accidentally" cut her finger, bandaged it, and began rubbing the bandage as she previously had rolled her fuzzballs. She noticed this activity in the middle of the hour, and spontaneously told me that she thought it was an effort to revisit the fuzzball relatedness because separation from her analyst lay ahead.

SUMMARY

One of the major behavioral patterns in this case of a severely regressed young woman was her inability to say "no" to needy people. This pattern was linked to the interaction between the patient as an infant and her depressed mother. Toward the end of her first year of treatment, I spontaneously frustrated the introjective-projective relatedness of the infant and her depressed mother; I had become a frustrator. The data I gave about the ensuing seven months of treatment emphasized her dreams, showing how my unusual emotional-verbal response that made me a frustrator affected the flow of her analytic work, resulting in her successful identification with the frustrator.

Patients such as the one described in this chapter are apt to evoke intense feelings in analysts due to what they externalize onto them. Analysts' monitoring and utilization of these feelings are important not only for keeping an eye on the nature of the therapeutic process but also for keeping the therapeutic process moving. When analysts respond unusually to the emotional flow between themselves and their patients—not as a technical maneuver, but spontaneously—it is possible to work through this response in analysis. Even if the unusual response is a "mistake," analysts must carefully monitor patients' responses as well as the psychological process between themselves and the patients. Eventually the unusual response and any events it may have precipitated are assimilated into treatment. As was the case with my patient, the assimilation of an unusual response can further therapeutic progress significantly.

REFERENCES

Boyer, L. B. (1961). Provisional evaluation of psycho-analysis with few parameters employed in the treatment of schizophrenia. *Internat. J. Psycho-Anal.* 42: 389–403.

———— (1977). Working with a borderline patient. *Psychoanal. Q.* 46: 386–424.

———— and Giovacchini, P. L. (1967). *Psychoanalytic Treatment of Schizophrenic and Characterological Disorders.* New York: Science House.

Cain, A. C. and Cain, B. S. (1964). On replacing a child. *J. Amer. Acad. Child Psychiatry* 3: 443–456.

Freud, A. (1936). The ego and the mechanisms of defense. In *The Writings of Anna Freud*, vol. 2. New York: International Universities Press, 1966.

Green, N. and Solnit, A. J. (1964). Reactions to the threatened loss of a child: A vulnerable child syndrome. *Pediatrics* 34: 58–66.

Greenacre, P. (1969). The fetish and the transitional object. In *Emotional Growth*, vol. 1, pp. 315–334. New York: International Universities Press.

Kernberg, O. F. (1975). *Borderline Conditions and Pathological Narcissism.* New York: Aronson.

Khan, M. M. R. (1969). On symbiotic omnipotence. *Psychoanal. Forum* 3: 137–147.

Kohut, H. and Seitz, P. F. D. (1963). Concepts and theories of psychoanalysis. In *Concepts of Personality*, ed. J. M. Wepman and R. Heine, pp. 113–141. Chicago: Aldine.

Lewinsky, H. (1951). Pathological generosity. In *The World of Emotions: Clinical Studies of Affects and their Expression*, ed. C. W. Socarides, pp. 205–217. New York: International Universities Press, 1977.

Loewald, H. (1960). On the therapeutic action of psychoanalysis. *Internat. J. Psycho-Anal.* 41: 16–33.

Modell, A. H. (1968). *Object Love and Reality: An Introduction to a Psychoanalytic Theory of Object Relations.* New York: International Universities Press.

Novey, S. (1968). *The Second Look: The Reconstruction of Personal History in Psychiatry and Psychoanalysis.* Baltimore: Johns Hopkins University Press.

Nunberg, O. F. (1931). The synthetic function of the ego. *Internat. J. Psycho-Anal.* 12: 123–140.

Olinick, S. L. (1964). The negative therapeutic reaction. *Internat. J. Psycho-Anal.* 45: 540–548.

Ornstein, A. and Ornstein, P. H. (1975). On the interpretive process in schizophrenia. *Internat. J. Psychoanal. Psychother.* 4: 219–271.

Poznanski, E. O. (1972). The "replacement child"—A saga of unresolved parental grief. *Behav. Ped.* 81: 1190–1193.

Rosenfeld, H. A. (1966). Discussion of "Office treatment of schizophrenic patients" by L. B. Boyer. *Psychoanal. Forum* 1: 351–353.

Searles, H. F. (1959). The effort to drive the other person crazy—An element in the etiology and psychotherapy of schizophrenia. In *Collected Papers on Schizophrenia and Related Subjects,* ed. H. F. Searles, pp. 254–283. New York: International Universities Press, 1965.

——— (1969). Discussion of "On symbiotic omnipotence" by M. M. R. Khan. *Psychoanal. Forum* 3: 150–152.

——— (1975). The patient as therapist to his analyst. In *Tactics and Techniques in Psychoanalytic Therapy,* vol. 2, ed. P. L. Giovacchini et al., pp. 95–151. New York: Aronson.

Socarides, C. W. (1977). *The World of Emotions: Clinical Studies of Affects and their Expression.* New York: International Universities Press.

Speers, R. W. and Lansing, G. (1965). *Group Therapy in Childhood Psychosis.* Chapel Hill, N.C.: University of North Carolina Press.

Spitz, R. A. (1957). *No and Yes: On the Beginning of Human Communication.* New York: International Universities Press.

——— (1965). *The First Year of Life.* New York: International Universities Press.

Volkan, V. D. (1970). Typical findings in pathological grief. *Psychiat. Q.* 44: 231–250.

——— (1976). *Primitive Internalized Object Relations. A Clinical Study of Schizophrenic, Borderline and Narcissistic Patients.* New York: International Universities Press.

—— (1981). *Linking Objects and Linking Phenomena: A Study of Complicated Mourning, Internalization, Externalization, Generational Continuity and Re-Grief Therapy*. New York: International Universities Press.

—— (1982). Immortal Ataturk: Narcissism and creativity in a revolutionary leader. In *The Psychoanalytic Study of Society*, vol. 9, ed. W. Muensterberger and L. B. Boyer, pp. 221–256. New York: Psychohistory Press.

Volkan, V. D. and Akhtar, S. (1981). The symptoms of schizophrenia: Contribution of the structural theory and object-relations theory. In *Integrating Ego Psychology and Object Relations*, ed. G. D. Goldman and D. S. Milman. New York: Kendall-Hunt.

—— and Kavanaugh, J. G. (1978). The cat people. In *Between Reality and Fantasy: Transitional Objects and Phenomena*, ed. S. A. Grolnick, L. Barkin, and W. Muensterberger, pp. 291–303. New York: Aronson.

17

THE BORDERLINE PATIENT AND ACTING OUT

León Grinberg
Juan Francisco Rodriguez-Perez

Editor's Notes

The authors of this chapter practice psychoanalysis in a culture that differs in some respects from the milieu here in the United States. At the time they wrote this chapter, they both lived and worked in Buenos Aires. Furthermore, their conceptual framework differs from ours in many ways. The study of their case material permits us to differentiate constants inherent in the psychoanalytic process from more variable analytic phenomena. Most notable, however, is the lack of cultural relativism.

The authors tell us that at the time the patient Alice was in treatment, the "hippie" movement was just beginning in Argentina. Her joining the movement, as well as other actions, caused them to view her behavior as acting out. Acting out has become a term of opprobrium. Although psychoanalysts in general are increasingly accepting their patients' overt manifestations of psychopathology, acting out still carries a pejorative connotation and is something that a "good patient" is not supposed to do. Drs. Grinberg and Rodriguez-Perez emphasize how Alice's acting out behavior became psychoanalytic material, acquired transference significance, and facilitated the treatment process. They believe that this acting out behavior was indispensable to therapeutic progress.

The problem of evaluating behavior is even more complex when we turn our attention to adolescents. Regarding Alice in particular, there is little that would set her apart from adolescents in our country. She expressed herself through fairly familiar symptoms and her character problems, although severe, do not seem unusual in view of the patient population we encounter. As other cultures become more and more similar to ours, they seem to produce psychopathology that resembles that of our patient population. For example, since Morocco achieved independence from France and began to strive for the same material standards as the French, Moroccan youth have begun to chafe under Moslem restrictions. At the same time, the manifestations of their psychopathology have also changed. Instead of encountering primarily classical hysteria with somatic conversion symptoms, which was the most common emotional illness prior to independence, psychiatrists now note an immense increase in borderline states and other forms of character disorders. There has also been some increase in the number of schizophrenic patients.

It would seem then that practice in Buenos Aires does not differ significantly from psychoanalytic practice in any large city in the United States. Thus we would not expect to see a conceptual system radically different from ours. Drs. Grinberg and Rodriguez-Perez do not present us with any such system. However, many analysts who reside south of our border adhere strictly to the doctrines of Melanie Klein without paying any attention whatsoever to the numerous findings and observations gathered in the last decade about early developmental stages. Of course, there are also many analysts who share our authors' viewpoint and who have creatively blended and modified Melanie Klein's formulations with more recent concepts.

Apart from some theoretical reflections, this is primarily a clinical chapter. The authors candidly reveal how they work with and what they feel about patients. In this instance, they focus on a late adolescent female patient. We can all learn from their experience as they skillfully guide us through the confusing maze of the patient's characterological defects and masochistic acting out.

P. L. G.

Let us imagine a primitive human being, so primitive that in fact he can hardly be classified as *homo sapiens*. In such a situation, it is possible to imagine that his being is, up to a point, an animal in which the normal tendency in him is to act first and, if he is sufficiently developed, think afterwards. In such a situation, one would say that the acting out is normal and the thought abnormal. Acting out means security; thought can lead to death.

Bion, 1968 seminar in Buenos Aires

In this chapter, we shall examine some technical aspects of the psychoanalytic treatment of a borderline patient who frequently acted out and also had a negative therapeutic reaction.

The criteria regarding the analyzability of patients with serious emotional disorders such as schizophrenia, narcissistic personalities, and borderline personalities have been modified. In spite of his initial pessimism, Freud did not dismiss the hope that these patients could be reached, as he pointed out in "An Outline of Psychoanalysis" (1938b), where he said that in many acute psychic disturbances, a normal person is to be found in a corner of the patient's mind. In his papers "Fetishism" (1927) and "The Splitting of the Ego in the Process of Defense" (1938a), Freud postulated that when the ego is faced with a threatening conflict, it may use the defense mechanism of splitting and thereby simultaneously recognize and rebuff the demands of reality and avoid displeasure or pain. This viewpoint has been tremendously fruitful for the investigation and psychoanalytic treatment of psychotic phenomena. Bion (1957) postulated the coexistence of two mental states, the "psychotic personality" and the "nonpsychotic or neurotic personality." Many analysts apply this concept when treating borderline patients, as they analyze the negative and positive transferences, as well as the psychotic transference.

Grinberg (1977) believes that borderline patients can be placed in the following two categories: (1) schizoid borderline patients and (2) melancholoid borderline patients. In the first category, we find patients who are characterized by isolation, a sense of futility, withdrawal, feelings of strangeness, occasional episodes of depersonalization, intolerance of frustration, identity disturbances, and low self-esteem. They are preoccupied with compensatory omnipotent fantasies and a need to denigrate others. Frustration creates intense feelings of envy. Among the principal defense mechanisms are splitting and pathological projective identification. The latter produces reactions of projective counteridentification (Grinberg 1962). There is also a marked tendency to act out.

Melancholic borderline patients are usually intelligent and emotionally sensitive, but at times appear delayed in their intellectual development due to conflict-laden links with their primary objects. These conflicts are based upon the lack of an emotional bond with the mother, who has failed in her function as a receptacle capable of containing the child's projections. Because of maternal failure, these personalities react to frustration and separation with deep depressive reactions that are experienced as catastrophic. They usually have enormous sensitivity to both internal and external stimuli. Sometimes they have an insatiable desire for "skin to skin" contact, for example, through sexual promiscuity. In this way, they try to recapture the very primitive, tactile elements of a symbiotic relationship. At times, they may demonstrate a peculiar type of passive disorganization similar to Meltzer et al.'s (1975) "dismantling" of objects and ego. External objects are perceived as they were during infancy; compared to adult perceptions, they appear fragmented. These patients give the impression that their mental apparatus is "falling to pieces." This temporary suspension of ego functions results in a primitive state of "mindlessness" in which it is difficult for patients to discriminate between subject and object, fantasy and reality, animate and inanimate.

Boyer (1977) describes a borderline patient who had "a very complicated concatenation of ego structures. She apparently retained from very early childhood split maternal introjects that she then sought to project into various people in her environment" (p. 416). The persistence of this patient's need to fuse represented a wish to regain the mother of the symbiotic phase. Furthermore, "although it was very easy for her to identify with her autistic son, [the patient] did not become an autistic psychotic. She had the capacity to develop a hierarchy of defenses, including rationalization and repression, and object relationships that varied in their levels of maturity" (p. 416).

Finally, Boyer believed that "a case could also be made for schizoaffective psychosis, with masked depression stemming from the incomplete mourning of her lost grandfather, combined with cognitive regression" (p. 417).

It would appear that Boyer's patient had a mixture of schizoid and melancholoid aspects, as demonstrated by the intensity and frequency of her pathological projections, her tendency toward fusion and adherence to the object, and her depression. Most borderline patients show both schizoid and melancholoid characteristics, but one will dominate the clinical picture.

Alice, the patient we will present, was in analysis for seven years with Dr. Rodriguez-Perez and she presented aspects of both types of borderline patients. She was pathologically jealous and felt tremendous rivalry and envy toward her brother. She was aggressive and rebellious, particularly during her "hippie" period. Her magical fantasy that abandoning the object would end with its death, and her almost delusional conviction that she would either devour or be "devoured" by the object, are "schizoid" characteristics. On the other hand, her view of herself as a helpless child, her shallow emotions, her search for a "skin to skin" relationship, her depressions, and her incomplete mourning for her father were clear melancholic symptoms.

Clinical Material

Alice was 24 years old and had finished her formal study of educational sciences when she first sought analysis. Her "hippie" attire was both daring and shabby and suggested a maladjusted personality.

She stated that she wanted to be analyzed because it would be a training experience. The problems she presented were vague and varied; she was both aware of and denied the need to be helped. She had been in psychotherapy for two years. Her therapist had terminated her treatment because he had felt it was adequate. Then he had had an intermittent sexual liaison with her which persisted for many months.

Alice was the second of two siblings, a year younger than her brother. She was born and reared in a suburb of Buenos Aires. Throughout her psychoanalytic treatment, she stressed her difficult relationship with her mother and brother. From earliest childhood, she had felt that there was no place for her because her mother was always occupied with her brother. To Alice, "being occupied" had a physical meaning since she could not remember ever being held by her mother. By contrast, her brother, because of a long series of minor illnesses, never left their mother's arms. Alice did not remember her mother being in the house despite her conviction that her mother was totally dedicated to household tasks. Her mother simply was not there for her.

As a child, Alice had devised certain rituals to gain love and attention from her mother. For example, she would become docile, spending endless hours in bed. In a passive and suffering way, she would imitate the movements of her mother rocking her elder brother in her arms. This behavior, which seemed autistic, apparently had stopped when she realized that her mother was not responding. As she became older, she found herself at war with her brother for the mother's love and affection. Her father became increasingly important as an ally. He was a teacher and thus was better able to evaluate Alice's intellectual progress and victories over her brother.

When her brother would ask for something as simple as a glass of water, she would also ask for one, demanding that she be given it first. Her brother still wet the bed after she had stopped. He was always ill; she never was. If he had trouble learning something, she learned it immediately. In fact, she learned to read and write before he did.

These experiences and patterns of behavior were detrimental to her psychic development. They did not allow contact with her own self, her own potentialities and genuine desires. If she asked for a glass of water, it did not necessarily imply that she was thirsty; this was her brother's need. They also intensified her penis envy. She ascribed to the penis the privileges and attentions the brother was accorded, and devalued and hated her femininity, which she saw as responsible for her failure to capture her mother's attention.

This jealousy of and rivalry with her brother was still very intense when she started analysis. It was so fierce that they occasionally attacked and hurt each other. For example, Alice and her brother were to take a university examination that he had repeatedly failed. She helped other students in their preparation for the test; she and they passed it while her brother failed once again. Naturally, this action weighed heavily on her already guilty conscience.

The death of her father when she was 12 was particularly traumatic for her, as he had been her only ally against her mother and brother. The father's death had a tremendous emotional impact upon the mother and brother, as well as resulting in the family's social and economic bankruptcy. Her mother became depressed with distressing physical symptoms, and her brother developed serious learning problems and behavioral disorders which made him give up his studies. He became a social misfit.

The family felt the loss of the father's leadership grievously. After his death, the sibling rivalry became much worse. The brother tried to assume the role of the father, which was intolerable for Alice. During her mourning, she was somewhat stuporous and perplexedly submissive. Then she quickly changed into a hostile child who rebelled against all authority and insisted on going her own way. She would be away from home without letting anyone know where she was for practically the whole day. She would wander through fields, sleep there, and return home late at night. Subsequently, she became somewhat obsessional and her infantile rituals returned, this time colored with religiosity. This allowed her to reorganize herself through rigid control and intense repression.

She managed to enter a university, graduate, and establish her first relationship with a boy. Nevertheless, her precarious adjustment became evident when she discovered that her boyfriend was having a sporadic relationship with another woman. She left him abruptly and entered the hippie world, which had just formed at that time in Buenos Aires. This movement's philosophy fitted her like a glove; she emerged again as a rebellious vagabond adolescent. She behaved as if nothing mattered. She indulged in indiscriminate and superficial social and sexual contacts. For example, she would walk into bars alone, approach groups of strangers, and ask if they minded if she sat with them; on one trip to New York, she arrived in the early hours of the morning and knocked on the door of the first person who came to mind.

When she started analysis, her reactions were somewhat toned down, but her inner disruption and her tendency to discharge her tensions in behavior was quite evident. Because of this tendency and her previous psychotherapeutic experience, her analyst had to be firm in order to establish an analytic setting. She tried to exasperate him. Session after session, she would lie on the floor, sit at his side, lie prone, look at him, or threaten to touch him. She would even inspect his library and, on occasion, leave the consultation room. The analyst believed that the patient was being provocative and rebellious, bringing the hippie world into the treatment. He did not react by becoming upset as she had expected. He simply viewed her behavior as clinical material and intervened only when he experienced her as disruptive to analytic equanimity. When it became evident that he was going to maintain the analytic setting at all costs, Alice protested at length that she was in a straightjacket, where she "could not move, or think, or feel, or do anything." But underneath this protest, the analyst was gradually being transformed into a strange authoritarian and idealized figure with a certain sanctity. As she was allowed to stay by his side, she would share his greatness. Interpretations were unimportant in terms of their content. She just cherished being close to her analyst. We wondered if she were repeating her infantile longings of being at the mother's side, a mother from whom she could not receive anything.

Nevertheless, this relationship with her therapist led to some psychic integration. Her therapist did not abandon her and she was able to find employment in a public institution. She also stopped living with her mother and brother and rented an apartment. She lived alone, far away from her tremendously intrusive and controlling mother. However, moving away caused tremendous anxiety and highlighted the disturbances in the relationship with her mother.

She revealed that close relationships were impossible because they were based upon the premise that she or the other person would be devoured. In order to stay alive, one person in the relationship had to be controlled and dominated. Being abandoned meant dying, since the relationship was life sustaining. On the other hand, the person who did the abandoning was also in a precarious position since his intense guilt would destroy him.

During this period, she and her mother reproached and threatened each other constantly and the patient suffered intolerable guilt. Her anxiety was so intense that, at times, it interfered with her reality testing. She had difficulties in distinguishing between fantasies and events in the external world. Nevertheless we were able to understand that her "happy-go-lucky hippie" demeanor was a defensive superstructure protecting her from a demanding superego, terror, shyness, shame, and insufferable feelings of impotence.

Her sexual behavior was an example of how she covered up her neediness and vulnerability. She seemed to be uninhibited. Actually, she was terrified of any encounter with a man in which he was to any degree aggressive. She perceived submissiveness as being brutally raped. Consequently, she regularly took the initiative and kept herself in control of the situation, removing the threat—or, as she viewed it, the nightmare—as quickly as possible.

Her self-image of an abandoned, fearful child conflicted with her phallic wishes to be an invulnerable male. She was angry that she had not been born a boy. She also wanted to be a sage, a sainted teacher—her view of her father and her analyst—without feeling inadequate, anxious, or needy.

As she reviewed her capabilities, she spent many analytic hours despising and attacking herself. The picture she was developing of herself was markedly different from the hippie role she had un-comfortably assumed. The attacks were directed toward her parents, as well as her analysis and analyst, because the treatment had not turned her into the intrepid, guiltless male she had wanted to be. Throughout this long period, her analyst wondered whether she would be able to face her sense of vulnerability without suffering a depressive collapse and perhaps committing suicide. Suicidal fantasies would suddenly emerge without any warning; sometimes she would obey her impulse to dash across busy streets against heavy traffic.

Nevertheless, she made painful progress and gradually was able to face her psychic reality. Her previous psychotherapy had, as she thought, only served to strengthen her manic defenses. Her image of her analyst also changed. Now she saw him as "capable of being" and "capable of being there." We believe that, for the first time, Alice began to understand that a person can exist in his own right without wanting or needing to be someone else. This insight, combined with an improvement in her living conditions and the achievement of a degree of stability in her relationships with her mother and brother, made us less fearful of sudden and disruptive regressive shifts. Progress, however, was equated with abandon-ment; that is, her mother would desert her if she were "the only one in the family to be saved." At the end of her fifth year of treatment, she tried unsuccessfully to get her mother and brother into treatment. She reasoned that if they improved, then she could continue improving. In spite of her obvious anxiety about being abandoned, interpretations about separation were meaningless to her. Still, during holidays and weekends, she would develop a rash over her abdomen and arms.

In general, she had improved. She was no longer associated with hippies and was able to form love relationships, albeit sporadic and short-lived ones. Her analyst was pleased with her progress, but he now felt that she had entered a period of stagnation. He feared that her unconscious sense of guilt would provoke severe melancholic feelings and create manic defenses. He did not foresee the strange twist of events that we shall now describe.

By this time, Alice was having a sporadic relationship with a fellow worker who appeared to have serious emotional problems. During the summer holidays, she became pregnant. Against everyone's advice and even her better judgment, she moved in with her boyfriend. Her analyst, because of intense countertransference feelings, also opposed this move, since it was obvious to everyone that the relationship was basically sadomasochistic.

On reflection, the diversity of the elements condensed in this acting out seems almost unbelievable. Alice took more than a year to "rescue" herself from this nightmarish relationship and even then retained a feeling of unreality, as though she had lived through a terrible dream. We shall enumerate here only the aspects that are relevant to this chapter.

It was at first difficult to sift out the meanings of various aspects of the relationship, but it became apparent that her partner was a jealous, controlling, possessive man who could not tolerate her having any relationship with anyone else; he was even upset by her involvement in her job and analysis. After she gave birth to a son, he became so jealous of the latter that at times he would insist she stop breastfeeding the baby and pay attention to him instead. She was to devote herself wholly to him. He stopped giving her money and demanded that she be available to him at all times, regardless of her needs. Her response to these demands was curious. She indicated that, in some way, she had provoked them. More seemed to be involved than extreme dependence and masochistic needs. She unconsciously wanted to subject herself to so much pain and humiliation that she could assert herself without feeling guilty.

When she finally reached that state, she began to feel that she also had the right to have objects, needs, feelings, and her own life. However, she was far from secure, since she had been so totally needed and dominated. As she emerged from the submissive, masochistic phase of this relationship, she gradually accepted the fact that she was justified in having claims of her own and a place in the world. When she had been born, there had been no place for her. During the submissive phase of the relationship, she relived that early period of her life. To be sure, she was able to tolerate such abuse because she had projected her own sadism, jealousy, possessiveness, and need to control onto her partner, who acted them out for her.

Alice had identified with her mother taking care of her brother. She then allowed herself to be attacked in the same way she wanted to attack her mother. However, this identification was adaptive in that it enabled her to set limits to her voraciously devouring and hateful feelings. This probably occurred because she had been able to introject some of the positive, integrative qualities of her mother, which had permitted her to take pride in her own motherhood.

Alice also obtained a considerable dependent gratification by caring for her son, inasmuch as she made him part of herself. She voraciously enjoyed the attention she gave him, and a passive receptive experience became one of active giving.

We need not further pursue the course of Alice's treatment. The analysis of the situation just described was crucial and enabled her to achieve states of higher ego integration.

Case Discussion

Shallowness as an Adaptive Defense

Alice appeared shallow; her emotions and feelings seemed flat. She frequently responded to interpretations with such comments as "those are nothing more than words" or "that sounds as if it came out of a book." She seemed to regret not having had a more vigorous, fuller, and deeper experience.

Without warning, after an interpretation she would shut her eyes, clench her fists, and violently shout "Shut up!" or "I'll thump you!" We conjectured that Alice had been invaded by feelings and emotions so overwhelming that she lost her capacity for self-observation and analytic reflection. This was the diametric opposite of shallowness, but it constituted a transference psychosis that was disruptive to treatment. This sudden eruption of violent impulses and fantasies explains in part her maintaining distance from her feelings and her forming a shallow but idealized transference relationship. She was similar to the patients described by Meltzer and his colleagues (Meltzer et al. 1975): people who are constantly involved with others, but only on a superficial level, without any true intimacy. Such patients tend to have a poorly developed sense of time. In fact, for years Alice refused to wear a watch.

The shallowness of this patient's object relationships had at least two meanings. Literally, it meant that she had to relate at a surface level. In infancy, she had felt deprived of "skin to skin" contact, the soothing and comfort of being held in her mother's arms. This is mainly a kinesthetic experience. From an intrapsychic viewpoint, the shallowness of her object relationships protected her from being devoured by her envy and hatred. In the transference, she was terrorized by intimacy because it could lead to either her or her analyst's destruction.

In treatment, this created a dilemma, because she could not incorporate or internalize anything that would lead to integrating and structure-promoting identifications. She complained that she could not really learn; she simply "held" information on the surface of her mind. This included analytic interpretations.

She complained of feeling empty; at the same time, she became intensely preoccupied with differentiating between people's appearance and their true self. She wondered about the emotional masks other people wore—their as-if qualities. Alice was aware of her hollow, synthetic self. She knew that she had only a semblance of being, which was maintained by what Bick (1968) called an "adhesive identification," a sticky surface attachment to a supportive person.

It was important for Alice's treatment that her analyst remain in touch with all parts of her psyche and not deny any of them. His comfortable, autonomous presence provided her with a model for a deeper identification, enabling her to reintegrate in a harmonious fashion the split-off parts of the self.

Acting Out

As is characteristic of many borderline patients, Alice displayed a marked tendency to act out. Instead of condemning her behavior as detrimental to analysis, it has to be understood in terms of her severe emotional problems and its adaptive purpose.

Acting out can occur on a neurotic or a psychotic level. At the neurotic level, the self and external objects remain relatively intact and the acting out represents a repetition of infantile experiences. Alice recapitulated her early behavior with her brother in the sadomasochistic relationship with her lover. Both her boundaries and her lover's boundaries remained intact.

Her masochistic submission also represented a negative therapeutic reaction. Freud (1938a) formulated that such a reaction is a resistance against recovery. With Alice, this proved to be a regressive expression of guilt for having abandoned her mother and brother. Her associations indicated that she had strong urges to save the mother; she felt she had damaged the mother by leaving her. This fits in with Rivière's belief (1936) that the negative therapeutic reaction is associated with a compulsion to repair the damaged object. If Alice became psychically healthy, she would have the power to destroy the objects of her hatred and envy.

Alice also acted out at the psychotic level. Infantile objects and primitive parts of the self could not be contained simply by dealing with them verbally. When she was acting out at the psychotic level, her boundaries and those of the external object were no longer intact. Her inner and outer world were invaded with archaic introjects and split-off parts of the self. She used her lover and other persons and situations in the external world as receptacles for her early feelings and conflicts. She replaced the current reality with the infantile world.

This behavior seemed self-defeating, since she was so immersed in keeping her psychopathology outside the consultation room. Insofar as she seemed inaccessible to an analytic interaction and kept the analyst at a godlike distance, the psychotic acting out could also be considered part of the negative therapeutic reaction. It became clear, however, that she kept her inner chaos outside of the treatment in order to maintain her bond with her analyst.

This is an interesting paradox. Acting out at the neurotic level was obviously self-defeating for Alice. Acting out at the psychotic level had the appearance of a negative therapeutic reaction but actually was a positive therapeutic reaction. Pontalis (1979) described something similar when he stated that the negative therapeutic reaction represented a "hope for change and rebirth." Alice's treatment causes us to question the pejorative connotation of "unproductive resistance" usually associated with the terms "acting out" and "negative therapeutic reaction."

We feel that acting out should be viewed with the same analytic attitude we reserve for dreams. Naturally, we cannot overlook the obvious differences between the two phenomena, particularly regarding the possible dangers of acting out and the tactical changes it may require in therapy. Here, we prefer to stress the similarities between them. To repeat, analysts usually point to the resistive nature of acting out, but do otherwise with dreams, in spite of the fact that dreams, too, may be largely a product of resistance.

Grinberg (1968) discussed the way dreams can function as a container that frees patients from increased tension. This can be the principal function of a certain type of dream, stronger than and independent of wish fulfillment. Such dreams typically are associated with weekends and other periods of separation from the analyst. They have been called "evacuative dreams" and "dreams of discharge." Grinberg and his collaborators (Grinberg et al. 1967) found that the incidence of these dreams is inversely proportional to the amount of acting out; that is, the more "evacuative dreams," the less the tendency to act out, and vice versa. Grinberg (1968) concluded that acting out is an "evacuative dream" taking place during waking hours.

Returning to Alice, we must remember that her acting out occurred just before her summer holiday. She later referred to that period of her life as a dream, a nightmare that she had once lived through. She knew it had actually happened, but she remembered it more as belonging to dream space than to external space. Her oral-sadistic impulses had been stimulated and mobilized in the transference, but she was prevented from living them out in the analytic setting because of the summer vacation. (It was not only the vacation that prevented her from living out her conflicts in the analysis; in addition, she was afraid of destroying the idealized image of her analyst.) She was unable to contain these impulses in dreams, even evacuative dreams, so they spilled into the external world.

Furthermore, we wonder whether Alice even had the capacity to express her internal state in dreams. Her severely limited capacity to introject would result in a similarly limited ability for dream symbolization. In fact, prior to her acting-out relationship with her lover, Alice had reported very few dreams.

Ekstein (1966) expressed a similar viewpoint regarding acting out. In discussing an adolescent patient, he pointed out that acting out revived the patient's past conflicts with his parents and increased his insight into the latter, contributing to their effective resolution. He added that, from this point of view, acting out could be seen as a positive attempt toward a new resolution.

Freud (1937) referred to some instinctual conflicts as "sleeping dogs" and wondered whether it was judicious to awaken them. He answered his own question by stating there are two ways to get to these "sleeping dogs": "The artificial production of new conflicts in the transference . . . and the arousing of such conflicts in the patient's imagination by talking to him about them and making him familiar with their possibility" (pp. 232–233). According to Freud, the first method, "artificial production of conflicts," would arouse hostile feelings in the patient because the analyst would have to be provocative and this would disturb the positive transference and thus therapeutic cooperation. The second method, which concerned the production of future conflicts, would be meaningless to the patient since he could not feel them. "The patient," wrote Freud, "hears our message, but there is no response. He may think to himself: 'this is very interesting, but I feel no trace of it.' We have increased his knowledge, but altered nothing else in him" (p. 233). Freud's point is that it is not possible to work analytically on an unexperienced conflict. Recall Alice's regret and sorrow when, time and time again, she repeated that everything was "words, just words" or "things from a book."

Freud (1937) added: "The patients cannot themselves *bring all their conflicts into the transference*; nor is the analyst able to call out all their possible instinctual conflicts from the transference situation" (pp. 232–233, our emphasis). On the other hand, Freud tried to prohibit acting out. He asked his patients not to make any important decisions such as getting married or changing their profession. This position, in our opinion, is both technically and pragmatically incorrect. However, the length of analyses today would make such prohibitions untenable. Patients cannot suspend living and we cannot expect the transference toward the analyst to contain all of their projections.

Children endlessly repeat in analysis, either in play or in behavior, material which has not been properly understood or interpreted. This also applies to adults in which a single episode of acting out may be insufficient. Rodriguez-Perez (1967) reported a patient who, in the first years of her analysis, was faced with the frustration that her analyst could not "surgically remove horrible and monstrous" parts of herself which had become deposited in her nose; thus she underwent surgery. Her behavior was partially analyzed, but four years later, she symbolically castrated her husband. She became the family breadwinner while her husband, a highly qualified professional, remained at home and took care of the children. Then she developed a mysterious crippling infection of a big toe and once again sought surgical treatment. She went through all of the terrors of being castrated. She was certain that the surgeon would amputate her big toe and the surgical scar in the interdigital space would become a vulva; she was disconsolately anxious and certain the wound would never heal.

SUMMARY

Analysts' fear of confronting patients' psychotic fantasies and anxieties can force them to deal in a nonobjective way with acting out and its overdetermined meanings. As long as analysands behave like "good patients" (i.e., do not act out), the analysis may appear to proceed normally. However, the patient and analyst may share an "avoidance alliance" that prevents primitive, hidden parts of the personality from emerging. In fact, such a course would have been characteristic of Alice's analysis if she had colluded with her analyst's countertransference feelings. Had she done so, she would have behaved like a submissive child, sitting at her mother's side, receiving nothing but "words, words, words." This would have saved her, her relatives, and her analyst a good deal of strife but it would have prevented her from facing the primitive feelings and parts of herself that had interfered with her emotional development.

In conclusion, we should not forget Freud's discovery (1911) that action makes thinking possible. Thought appears in the human mind only after motor discharge can be delayed. For this reason, all thought retains an aspect of action. In certain patients, some psychic elements can only become recognizably mental through actions that later become thoughts.

REFERENCES

Bick, E. (1968). The experience of the skin in early object-relations. *Internat. J. Psycho-Anal.* 49: 484–486.

Bion, W. R. (1957). Differentiation of the psychotic from the non-psychotic personalities. *Internat. J. Psycho-Anal.* 38: 266–275.

Boyer, L. B. (1977). Working with a borderline patient. *Psychoanal. Q.* 46: 386–424.

Ekstein, R. (1966). *Children of Time and Space, of Action and Impulse.* New York: Appleton-Century-Crofts.

Freud, S. (1911). Formulations on the two principles of mental functioning. *Standard Edition* 12: 213–226. London: Hogarth Press, 1958.

———— (1927). Fetishism. *Standard Edition* 21: 149–158. London: Hogarth Press, 1961.

———— (1937). Analysis terminable and interminable. *Standard Edition* 23: 209–254. London: Hogarth Press, 1964.

———— (1938a). Splitting of the ego in the process of defense. *Standard Edition* 23: 271–279. London: Hogarth Press, 1964.

———— (1938b). An outline of psycho-analysis. *Standard Edition* 23: 144–206. London: Hogarth Press, 1964.

Grinberg, L. (1962). On a specific aspect of countertransference due to the patient's projective identification. *Internat. J. Psycho-Anal.* 43: 436–440.

———— (1968). On acting out and its role in the psychoanalytic process. *Internat. J. Psycho-Anal.* 49: 171–178.

———— (1977). An approach to the understanding of borderline disorders. In *Borderline Personality Disorders*, ed. P. Hartocollis. New York: International Universities Press.

———— et al. (1967). Función del soñar y clasificación clínica de los sueños en el proceso psicoanalítico. *Rev. Psichoanál.* 24: 749–789.

Meltzer, D. et al. (1975). *Explorations in Autism*. Ballinluig, Perthshire: Clunie Press.

Pontalis, J. B. (1979). The negative therapeutic reaction: An attempt at definition. Paper presented at the European Psychoanalytic Federation, Third Conference, London, October.

Rivière, J. (1936). A contribution to the analysis of the negative therapeutic reaction. *Internat. J. Psycho-Anal.* 17: 304–320.

Rodriguez Perez, J. F. (1967). Histórico clínico de una paciente asmática. Paper presented before the Argentine Psychoanalytic Association.

18

AN OBJECT-RELATIONS PERSPECTIVE ON MASOCHISM

Theo L. Dorpat

Editor's Notes

This chapter deals with masochism, a phenomenon that has always puzzled clinicians. We find it inexplicable and mysterious because we instinctively avoid pain. We find the pleasure principle much easier to understand. Still, the seeking of pain is a common enough occurrence, especially among patients suffering from character disorders.

Dr. Dorpat views his patient's masochistic perversion in terms of its adaptive potential. He is able to explain it in the context of the repetition compulsion, by which the patient attempts to control the pain and the person who is inflicting it. Whereas in infancy, the patient had to submit passively to his sadistic mother, a mother who both understimulated and overstimulated him, as an adult he can recreate and control the infantile situation. As Freud pointed out, the purpose of the repetition compulsion is to achieve active mastery over a traumatic situation in which one was formerly passive and vulnerable.

Dr. Dorpat goes into considerable detail about his relationship with the patient. He emphasizes that many of the patient's associations indicated a striving toward autonomy. I specifically refer to this because, at first glance, these interchanges did not seem to be transference interpretations; yet they were effective. Let us explore the matter further. The patient had created a situation in the consultation room similar to the infantile one with his mother, that is, a master-slave relationship. To understand the transference, the patient had to be aware of his need for autonomy, which was in opposition to his "slave" position. Without this awareness, he would have no frame of reference, no observational platform from which to view and feel infantile impulses as distinct. If he did not recognize his autonomous strivings, then there would be no contrasting background against which the transference could stand out in bold relief. Thus, Dr. Dorpat's interpretation about autonomy was, in effect, a transference interpretation as it provided the contrasting background so that the transference could be used therapeutically.

Dr. Dorpat emphasizes the difference between masochistic phenomena in patients suffering from characterological problems and those with psychoneuroses. He formulates that primitively fixated patients' self-punishing behavior is the outcome of a cruel maternal introject, whereas neurotic patients suffer because of a punishing superego. In the former, patients are responding to someone else's sadism and in the latter, they are responding to their own sadism.

I believe that these are quantitative distinctions. A sadistic introject is an unintegrated psychic element as long as it retains its introject status. Once it becomes assimilated into the psyche, it exerts its influence through an ego-subsystem, the superego. There is a sequential development between an endopsychic registration, a mental representation, an introject, and an ego system such as the executive system or the superego. Clinicians may differ as to terminology, but there is a progression from incorporation into the psyche to a smooth integration into various ego systems. Freud worked this out in detail when he discussed the formation of the superego. Today we are accustomed to thinking in terms of introjects becoming assimilated into the ego.

Dorpat emphasizes what he calls an object-relations model. I believe some may be confused by his contrast of this model with what he calls a structural conflict model. The latter refers to conflicts between different areas of the mind which demonstrate defects in structure. The object relations model emphasizes behavioral disturbances and faulty relationships with external objects. However, these are not mutually exclusive entities; defective structure is reflected in disturbed object relations. The treatment dealt with structural, or characterological, problems that affected how the patient related to external objects.

The clinical example in this chapter highlights how primitive parts of the ego express themselves in part-object relations. These adaptations, the outcome of defective integrations and executive responses, are reflected in the transference as the patient attempts to recreate the traumatic infantile ambience. Dr. Dorpat demonstrates how he managed to work within a psychoanalytic frame of reference even though the patient suffered from a masochistic perversion.

P. L. G.

This chapter presents clinical data to illustrate and discuss an object-relations perspective for understanding masochism. Object-relations theories are probably the most critical and essential aspect of psychoanalytic clinical theory (G. Klein 1976). Klein distinguishes between clinical theory, which is derived from psychoanalytic data, and metapsychological theory, which expresses Freud's philosophy of science. In contrast to metapsychological theories, object-relations theories are testable by clinical psychoanalytic methods.

Clinical Material

Mr. A., a 39-year-old C.P.A., worked for a large corporation when he began analysis. He was married, but separated from his wife and three children. He had low self-esteem, frequently felt depressed, and experienced a long-standing dissatisfaction with his job and marriage. He complained that his wife did not respond to him either emotionally or sexually and that he had not had sexual relations with her for several years. He alluded to having engaged in abnormal sexual acts with prostitutes, but was unable to divulge the details of these practices until he had been in analysis for over a year.

Mr. A. had grown up in a large Texas city, the second son of an Armenian family. Both sets of grandparents had emigrated to the United States early in this century. He described his father as an easy-going, intelligent owner of a small business firm, and his mother as a hot-tempered woman who, although rarely affection-ate, was fiercely loyal to and protective of her family. When Mr. A. was 13, his father died of a heart attack.

In the first weeks of analysis, the patient would discuss some problem and then ask, "What should I do?" or "Don't you have some advice for me?" It became abundantly clear that he wanted me to give him directives on how he should lead his life and behave. Initially, I used the customary methods of silence or turning the question back to the patient to deal with his questions and demands. When his questions intensified, I explained the analytic contract and frame to him, telling him why I thought it would not be helpful to him or the analysis for me to provide answers. My efforts were fruitless and he became more demanding of marital advice. Finally, I told him, "You feel so anxious and uncertain about your relationship with your wife that you are trying to control and pressure me into giving you an answer about what you should do." He then relaxed and talked about how troubled his conscience was about his marriage. However, this interaction did not resolve his need to control the analyst and seek magical answers to his problems.

The patient's relative lack of psychological separateness from others characterized many of his important interpersonal rela-tions. In the 13th month of analysis, Mr. A. became disturbed over the learning difficulties his 10-year-old daughter was experiencing in her language class. She spoke and wrote in fragmented, incomplete sentences. After her teacher pointed out this problem to her parents, they noticed that the other two children and the mother also talked in this fragmentary manner. They would typically wait for each other, and especially the father, to finish the sentences they had begun. For example, the wife would start to say something and hesitate. Her hesitation served as a cue for Mr. A. to finish her sentences. In this way, all of the family members shared in maintaining pathological symbiotic (or self-object) relationships in which they thought and spoke for each other. The same interaction was transferred to the analytic situation, where, for the first three years of analysis, the patient persistently wished, and even demanded, that I think and speak for him.

Childhood Trauma

One of the major causes of Mr. A.'s chronic depression was an unresolved and pathological mourning reaction to the death of his father. As his attachment to me became more stable and important, long-repressed memories of his father and his death came to the fore. Mr. A. had not completed the "work" of mourning; he had not grieved for his father and had been unable to accept the reality of his death fully.

Even on the day of his father's death, he had been unable to cry over the loss. Limited space does not allow full documentation of the hypothesis that the death of his father and his pathological mourning response to the loss severely blocked the patient's psychosexual development. For studies on how denial of death and pathological mourning reaction retard psychosexual development, see Altschul (1968), Dorpat (1972), and Wolfenstein (1966, 1969).

The mobilization and reactivation of the mourning process for the death of his father had two positive consequences, both involving progressive steps in his development. Whereas formerly he had repressed memories of his father, he was now able to remember his father as a warm, affectionate man. Memories of sitting in his father's lap and talking and playing with him came back. He identified with this loving aspect of his father and became much closer to and more affectionate with his own children. To some extent, identification with this loving imago supplanted his defensive identification with the hostile, controlling aspects of his mother.

While working through his mourning, the patient unconsciously and pathologically identified with his father's illness and mode of death. Early in the analysis, he talked seriously about his fears that he would not live beyond 52, his father's age when he died. One day Mr. A. came to an analytic hour breathless and tired from playing racquetball. He feared that he would have a heart attack, as his father had. "Living means more to me now," he said. "Before, I didn't think I would live a longer life." The above vignette and other clinical evidence indicated some working through of his pathological identification with his father's age at death. Such pathological identifications with the illness or death of a lost loved one are frequently found in unresolved mourning reactions (Anderson 1949, Krupp 1965).

The revival and gradual working through of grief for his father had another constructive outcome. He began to identify consciously with his father as a trader and businessman. For over fifteen years, Mr. A. had carried out a double work life. By day he worked as an accountant; at night, he quietly and secretly did what he really enjoyed—investing. In the second year of analysis, he confided that he had accumulated a small fortune through investing, mainly in real estate. He had never liked being an accountant, and he especially disliked filling out tax forms and taking orders from his superiors. In the 21st month of analysis, he resigned his position in the corporation and opened a private office as an investor and real estate developer.

His move to a business career also marked another forward step in his emancipation from his mother. She had wanted him to be an accountant, and one of the principal reasons he had pursued that career was to please her and comply with her wishes.

Masochistic Perversion

Over a year of analysis elapsed before the patient could disclose the details of his sexual perversion. In one extremely tense and dramatic hour, he revealed in a halting, tremulous voice that for over 18 years he had regularly and frequently used prostitutes for sadomasochistic practices. I said little in that hour because he seemed too vulnerable and ashamed to tolerate any intervention; beads of perspiration ran down his face. The general perverse pattern began with Mr. A. giving specific instructions to prostitutes to insult, denigrate, and punish him. Sometimes he had them spank his bare buttocks with a leather belt. Sexual intercourse or masturbation would follow these carefully planned, controlled episodes of punishment and humiliation. The most humiliating and submissive perverse act involved his lying on the floor with the woman squatting above him and urinating on his head.

What are the important meanings of these sadomasochistic practices? Although humiliated and punished during these acts, Mr. A. still controlled the situation because he gave precise instructions to the prostitutes. He would unmercifully berate and scold them if they deviated in any way from what he ordered them to do. The anxiety he experienced in relating his perversion and the need for absolute control over the situation were the important clues I used to understand the unconscious meaning of the perversion: it was an unconscious attempt to master and control traumas the patient had suffered in the relationship with his extremely controlling, cruel mother.

The evidence for the mother's sadistic control of the patient surfaced not only from a reconstruction of past events revived and remembered in the transference situation, but also from the patient's gradual awareness of his mother's current tyrannical oppression of her children, grandchildren, and others. The patient's unconscious need to repeat continually the sadomasochistic quality of his early relations with his mother was a manifestation of what Freud (1920) called the "repetition compulsion"—the unconscious need to repeat traumatic experiences in order to overcome and master them.

Some trauma was specifically sexual. After the death of Mr. A.'s father, the mother had insisted that he sleep in the same bed with her, "spoon" fashion, with the son behind the mother. This practice stopped at age 15 when he had an erection. His irate mother accused him of depravity and pushed him out of her bed. From the age of 6 until he left home to attend college, the patient dressed and undressed his mother. His assignments included fastening and unfastening her corset and brassiere and if he did not instantly and correctly obey these assignments, she slapped his face and scolded him.

After considerable analytic work on the sadomasochistic relations with his mother, the patient was able to say, "I was her personal slave." In the third year of analysis, he spontaneously interpreted that his mother had made him her slave just as she, the youngest of a large family, had been enslaved to her own mother for many years.

One crucial difference existed between his ritualized experiences with the prostitutes and the earlier traumatic experiences with his mother. With the prostitutes, he was in control; with his mother, he had been painfully helpless. The traumatized subject became the agent rather than the victim of the unpleasurable activity. Unconsciously, he attempted to master the slave relationship with his mother and the associated feelings of sexual arousal, helplessness, and rage by replicating the sexualized slave relationship with prostitutes. Before analysis, he had no awareness that he repeated with prostitutes the same type of eroticized master-slave experiences he had endured earlier in the relationship with his mother.

The sadomasochistic, master-slave qualities of his perverse sexual practices also occurred in his other relationships. In most interpersonal relationships, he played either the role of the dominating tyrant or the complementary role of the abjectly submissive, obsequious one. He often spoke of trying to "force" or "make" his wife become more emotionally responsive to him and had no awareness that his need to control her actually provoked her withholding and withdrawn behavior.

During our analysis of these early experiences and their relation to his perversion, he had a recurrence of a nightmare he had experienced many times in his adolescence. In the nightmare, he is home alone in his parental family room, hiding because he has done something wrong. Two policemen come to the door of the house to catch him and he awakens from the dream in a state of terror.

The death of the father, the going to bed with the mother, and the punishment dream are, of course, reminiscent of the oedipal situation. I made an oedipal interpretation, stating that he feared punishment for what must have seemed a frightening victory over his father. My interpretation had no impact whatsoever on the patient. His polite and detached response was, "That's a very interesting idea, doctor. I read something like that somewhere." I was obviously on the wrong track, and returned to my hypothesis that his sexual disorder stemmed from his traumatic relations with his mother.[1]

Self-Object and Whole-Object Relations

The major transference configurations during this period of Mr. A.'s analysis involved variations on the master-slave relationship. At moments, he perceived me as the slave, but more frequently the focus of transference interpretations was upon his wishes, fears, and especially unconscious fantasies of being my slave. With the gradual working through in the analytic transference of the master-slave relation, his visits to prostitutes decreased. In the 23rd month of analysis, he stopped the practice entirely, after having a startling and revealing experience with one of them. Instead of programming a prostitute to carry out his masochistic fantasies, he decided to talk to her. He found that they had common childhood experiences of growing up in the South. This led to what he described as the amazing discovery that she was a real person with thoughts and feelings of her own. Previously, he had denied the personhood of prostitutes and had related to them solely as the depersonalized vehicle of his wishful fantasies (as his mother had so often treated him).

Clinical evidence strongly suggests that perverse masochistic behavior is based on pre-oedipal, or self-object, relationships.

[1]The effects of making oedipal interpretations prematurely have been discussed by Volkan (chapter 7, this volume). See also Boyer (1967), Ornstein and Ornstein (1975), and Rosenfeld (1966).

Prior to analysis, the patient viewed and treated prostitutes only in terms of sadomasochistic wishes, and any qualities of the prostitute that seemed discordant with his wishes were denied or simply ignored. When he attained a growing capacity for whole-object relatedness through analysis and his conversation with the prostitute, the perverse masochistic desires disappeared.

Homosexuality is also often based on pre-oedipal self-object relationships in which the sexual object is viewed almost entirely as the embodiment of the subject's conscious or unconscious perverse fantasies. During the fourth year of analysis, the patient became obsessed with homosexual fears and fantasies for a brief period. While driving to his office one morning, he picked up an athletic black youth who seemed to epitomize his sexual desires for a young and virile sexual partner. When the young man appeared interested in a sexual affair, the two drove off to a secluded area with a six-pack of beer. While talking with his companion, he noted that his sexual ardor gradually waned. He learned that the young man was the same age as his own son. With intense and mixed feelings of resignation and regret, he realized that his homosexual desire was founded on the fantasy of incorporating through fellatio the imagined masculine strength of the black youth. While thinking over this fantasy, he remembered an interpretation I had made about his wish to incorporate the idealized virility of other men through sexual intercourse. Recognizing the difference between this previously unconscious fantasy and the man beside him led to the collapse of any desire for sexual relations.

The major point of this vignette is the same as the one made earlier about the role of self-object relations in perverse masochistic behavior. Conversation with his companion made him aware of a developmentally higher form of reality testing and he was then able to view the companion as a whole object. The decisive difference between pathological self-object relations and whole-object relations in that the whole object is represented and related to as a person distinguishable from the wish-fulfilling projections of the subject.

Different modes of reality testing are linked with different modes of object relations. In self-object relationships, patients manipulate the external object so that it conforms to their wishes and expectations (Brodey 1965). They do not perceive aspects of behavior that cannot be used to verify their projections.

Mr. A. was both understimulated and overstimulated by his mother. Childhood and adolescent experiences of dressing her and sleeping with her stimulated intense feelings of helplessness and sexual wishes that could not be acknowledged or gratified. Boyer (1956) discussed the relationship between maternal overstimulation and the early development of ego defects. Chronic states of overstimulation were manifested in Mr. A.'s tense hyperactivity and initial difficulties relaxing on the couch. Over time, he developed trust in me and was able to use the couch as a "holding environment" that supported him and made it possible for him to relax. After he learned to use the couch and the analytic situation for relaxing, he observed that he had never before realized how tense and overstimulated he had felt for nearly all his life. The analytic regression to a self-object transference and his trust in me allowed him to gradually relinquish his former pathological dependence on excessive amounts of alcohol and marijuana. Previously, these drugs were the only agents he found useful in relieving his chronic tension states of overstimulation.

Subjective states of understimulation alternated with the states of overstimulation. Episodes of sadomasochistic perversion were often triggered by uneasy feelings of understimulation, such as boredom, loneliness, or depression. In analysis, adult experiences of understimulation could be traced to their childhood antecedents, such as being alone at home after school. His mother worked full time after he was one and a half years old; the patient was often left alone as a child.

The same basic transference issue of trying to control and manipulate me into giving him directives and advice surfaced repeatedly throughout the analysis, albeit in different forms. In the second year of the analysis, when he was again uncertain about whether he should terminate his marriage, he wanted me to tell

him what he should do. I told him, "You think of me as having the
perfect answers about your marriage, and you wish for me to tell
you what you should do." Mr. A. broke down and cried. He said he
felt sad that I did not have a magical and perfect answer for him.
My interaction revived the still incompletely resolved mourning
for his father. After his father's death, he felt all alone, as if there
were no one alive who could help him. My response implied that I
did not have magical answers for him and temporarily disrupted
his idealizing transference.

Conflicts over Separation

In the third year of analysis, Mr. A. seriously planned to drop
his treatment and run away to another part of the country. His
pressing impulse stemmed partially from fears that he would have
to meet my fantasized expectations or face my rejection and abandonment. Living up to my expectations meant that he would have
to adopt my rigid, conservative, traditional values. The unconscious
fantasy underlying these fears was that I had controlled him and
molded him into my slave. This transference reaction involved
projecting onto me aspects of the master-slave introject—an introject formed and internalized mainly from his relationship with his
mother.

During this crisis, I made several transference interpretations
concerning his need to see me as the oppressive, controlling part
of himself or his mother. These interventions seemed to have no
effect, and he maintained his paranoid attitude that I was secretly
intent on controlling and directing his life. The crisis finally
passed, and he appeared more comfortable with the analysis. I was
puzzled about what had happened and anxiously speculated that
the master-slave transference manifestations had simply gone
underground, concealed by surface politeness. Was he merely acting
compliant and agreeable defensively in order to hide and preserve
the unspoken part of how he perceived our relationship?

Several weeks later, while discussing an interaction with his
wife, he told me that he had checked himself from giving her a
directive about her behavior. He stopped himself when he recalled
that a month before I had told him I would not direct him because I

would then be depriving him of his rights and capacities to choose his own way of life. He explained that my respect for his freedom had made a profound and lasting impression on him. This surprised me because at the time I made that statement, I had felt that none of my interpretations or interventions had any impact on his paranoid fears about me.

Thereafter, in his interpersonal relations he increasingly adopted the attitude that "everyone has the right to think and decide for himself." He recounted many interactions with others, especially his wife and children, in which he refrained from assuming his former dictatorial and pre-emptory control over their conduct. In the analytic situation, these changes were linked with a new understanding and cautious acceptance of my neutrality. He had not previously understood that my interpretations were intended as useful information; rather, he experienced them as overt or covert directives in which I communicated how he should feel, think, and behave.

Mr. A.'s adoption of my attitude of fostering autonomy is an example of what Giovacchini (1972, 1980) has called the "analytic introject" and waht I have referred to as the "analyst introject" (Dorpat 1978). Outside the analytic hours, the patient used fantasies and memories of me to comfort himself and to prevent himself from acting out destructively. The formation and use of the analytic or analyst introject does not in itself instigate permanent ego or superego structural changes; for this to occur, introjection must be followed by identification with the introjected relation with the analyst.

Mr. A. gradually identified with the analyst introject, and integrated these identifications into his improved ego and superego functioning. As a result of the gradual dissolution of the transference configuration, which involved both wishes and fears that I would provide magical directives and advice, he took another step toward autonomy. A new and major theme emerged, one that he called "learning to take care of myself."

One evening, the patient and his three children played pinball at their athletic club. Mr. A. interrupted his game to watch his daughter at a nearby machine. Meanwhile, his 17-year-old son,

John, having finished his game, took over his father's pinball machine. The patient mildly protested the intrusion and assumed control of the machine. John launched a tirade of verbal abuse at his father, but Mr. A. stood up to John and finished the game.

The patient was tense while recounting the above episode. I said, "You have been struggling with yourself here over whether or not you have the right to take care of yourself." Pleased, he relaxed on the couch. The idea of taking care of himself and protecting his own interests had not occurred to him before. He explained how he had struggled with two different impulses. Not only had he resisted the impulse to give in to his son and allow him to take over the pinball machine, but he also had restrained himself from becoming overtly enraged and abusive, as had frequently been the case in the past.

During the next analytic hour, he told me how he had set limits on his son's erratic and dangerous driving. John had been arrested several times for driving under the influence of alcohol and speeding. Mr. A. felt unsure and anxious about his capacity to stand up for himself and withstand his son's demands and manipulations. His next associations were to a frightening dream in which a policeman questioned him and accused him of some unspecified crime against a woman in another city. The dream had seemed acutely real to him and had frightened him. Then he recalled the recurrent nightmare of his adolescence in which two policemen came to his door to capture him. He thought that fear of the police might be connected with his adolescent shoplifting.

He recalled the pleasure he had received the preceding weekend by being with his two daughters. He compared the enjoyment he felt when he cooked for them with his father's happiness when he cooked for his family. His father had been an expert cook. He described a conversation with a friend in which he had talked about his sadness over the prospect of missing his children when he divorced his wife. His friend asked him why he had not considered obtaining either partial or full custody of his children, and this prompted him to consider some type of custody of his children for the first time.

I then interpreted the dream in which he was accused of committing a crime as his fear of being punished for looking out for himself. I told him, "It is true that the activities you talked about today—standing up for yourself to your son, wanting to have custody of your children, trying to find a condominium—are not crimes in any usual sense of the word. Still, to you they are crimes because you are doing these things for yourself. In the relationship with your mother, there was an unspoken but powerful rule that you were supposed to take care of her but not of yourself." Initially, he was flustered and surprised by my interpretation, but after a few minutes of verbally exploring the validity of my remarks, he stated that there was some truth in them. On the night before his punishment dream, he had gone to bed feeling good about what he had done for himself and his daughters.

About a week later, he anxiously related having lunch with a woman friend who had discussed her marital problems with him. She had held his hand, and he had felt that she wanted a more intimate, sexual relationship with him. He had told her that he liked her but was not sexually attracted to her. I interpreted his anxiety and conflict: "You have been in conflict between doing what you wanted—taking care of yourself—and another part of you that wanted to please your friend by having a more intimate relationship." He replied, "That's exactly right!" Again, when I understood and recognized his feelings, Mr. A. felt relieved and immensely gratified.

The theme, "taking care of myself," remained central in the analysis for several months. The notion that he could take care of himself and at the same time respect the rights of others to do the same proved to be novel and liberating for him. At the most basic level, this change represented a further differentiation of the self-representation from the representation of his mother. As always, recognition and gradual appropriation of new and improved ego and superego capacities were not carried out without concomitant interpersonal and psychic (mainly object-relations) conflicts.

In an apologetic and cautious manner, he reported success in a real estate venture. I interpreted his apologetic mode as stemming from his fear that I would appropriate and control his success, as his mother had. He responded with memories of how often he had felt that his achievements at home and school had really belonged to his mother.

In another session, Mr. A. recounted a disturbing encounter with a rude waitress. He was pleased with himself for being neither submissive nor combative with her, stances he had often taken previously in similar situations. His further associations suggested that he felt guilty while telling me about his growing capacity to regulate himself more independently. I told him that he felt guilty because he imagined that I would feel hurt and abandoned by his independent activity. His memories of his mother's desperate hold on him and her use of punishment to discourage his strivings toward autonomy confirmed this interpretation.

He felt guilty and feared punishment because his progressive movements in the analysis toward taking care of himself conflicted with the prohibitions of his introjected representation of his mother against autonomous activity. His normal strivings toward self-caring had broken the implicit rules of the pathological, symbiotic caretaking relation with his mother.

This object-relations conflict contains a specific structure and implicit rules governing the caretaking relation first organized and formed in the mother-child relationship and later displaced to others. The discovery of the structure of this introjected relation with his mother did not surface in a single flash of insight to either the patient or myself. Rather, the analytic reconstruction of this particular object relation was a cumulative and collaborative process in which the pertinent information was obtained more through the analysis of transference and countertransference than through a study of historical events or interpersonal relations outside the analytic situation.

It is both desirable and possible to analyze the structures of object relationships (past or present, actual or imaginary) in terms of the shared rules that regulate specific interpersonal interactions. The sociologist Goffman (1974) and Spruiell (1980) have advanced theories about the rules that govern social interactions. The system of rules defines the frame or structure of the object relation. An important aspect of resistance and transference analysis is the recognition and interpretation of the rules governing childhood object relations which have been unconsciously transferred onto the analyst or the analyst-analysand relationship.

Like other kinds of caretaking relations, the implicit contract between the patient and his mother included the shared rule of reciprocity, an arrangement by which each person would enjoin to take care of the other in return for the other's caretaking. But this mutual caretaking relation differed from more normal ones in that the recipient of the caring was tacitly prohibited from assuming any rights or capacities for self-caring. In the mutual caretaking relation with the mother, there could be only one mind, one center of power, intentionality, and decision, for the dyad. The one being cared for was not represented or recognized by either party as a whole person with rights and capacities for self-caring, self-control, and self-direction. The object of the caring blankly and mindlessly acted out the role projected upon him.

This is reminiscent of mother-infant symbiosis. However, it differs from normal symbiotic relations in that the mother's caretaking frequently was not regulated by the patient's actual needs. At times, he unconsciously lived out the role of being cared for when the role was not congruent with his immediate needs and wishes. For example, the mother would coerce him to accept gifts from her which he did not want or need.

Mr. A. obtained some insight into the unhappy discrepancy between his actual needs and his mother's perceptions of his needs when he remembered what had happened to him and his mother at his father's funeral and afterwards. He recalled how his mother physically had leaned on him at the funeral, ignoring his pressing need for comfort and solace. Afterwards, she had leaned on him in a more figurative sense and, in his words, had treated him more like a "husband" than an adolescent son. In this caretaking relation, the patient and his mother alternated roles, with first one and then the other assuming control and regulation for the other. The mother expected, and sometimes demanded, that he assume duties such as management of the family's finances, which had previously been his father's responsibility. His mother would assume a childlike dependent attitude and look to him for direction, guidance, and leadership.

At the height of the patient's concern and conflict over taking care of himself, he related a dream so frightening that it had awakened him. He dreamed there were two conveyor belts ("the machine") carrying dishes; one belt carried dishes of food from a kitchen, and the other returned the empty dishes. He had to unload the dishes of food quickly, serve them to people seated nearby, and load the emptied dishes onto the belt to return them to the kitchen. Anxiety developed when Mr. A. could not keep up with the machine and accomplish all of the assigned tasks. As a result of his inability to keep up with "the infernal machine," some dishes of food fell on the floor, making a huge mess. Another person, not fully recognizable in the dream (but whom he later identified as me), approached the machine to turn it off. He awoke with a sense of panic over the mess and his inability to serve the seated people.

At various times, I represented the different persons and objects in the dream, including "the infernal machine," but the main and abiding transference element was the vague figure who was going to shut off the machine. The nondescript figure represented the idealized analyst (or idealized parent imago) who would help him gain some relief from his compulsive need to please, take care of, and feed others, primarily his mother.

His dream vividly depicted the essential elements of the introjected caretaking relation with his mother. The machine's actions of rapidly and inexorably carrying dishes to and from the kitchen represented both his and his mother's urgent oral needs and demands. Above all, the impersonal and relentless movement of the Kafkaesque machine replicated early experiences with his unempathic, controlling mother. It represented the coercive pressures she exerted against him to meet her needs. It symbolized the rule that he was to relinquish any concern for his own needs in the service of caring for others. The working through of various meanings of the dream, and particularly the transferential aspects connected with the introjected caretaking relation, were lasting progressive steps made by the patient in taming, if not completely dismantling, the machine within himself.

The patient made several other important changes during his analysis; the most important steps have probably been in the direction of his individuation and gradual emancipation from the pathologic symbiotic relationship with his mother and others. The quality of his interpersonal relations and his capacity for object constancy and object love experienced a solid and enduring gain. He made some headway in transforming narcissistic rage into the nonviolent employment of aggression in the pursuit of personal aims. He gave up his compulsive use of alcohol and marijuana and no longer engaged in sadomasochistically perverse sexual activities. Psychoanalysis helped him to resume his personal development in areas that had been blocked by psychic conflict and trauma.

Object Relations and Masochism

Mr. A.'s punishing relationship with his mother was unconsciously repeated in his masochistic sexual perversion, his interpersonal relations, and his attitudes toward himself. For example, he was punitive toward himself about working. His unstable work pattern varied between loafing or daydreaming and working at a furious pace. When he managed to work productively, he required either conscious or unconscious fantasies of someone forcing or punishing him to initiate and sustain his efforts.

An object-relations perspective explains the self-punishing behaviors of masochistic patients. Freud (1924) distinguished between the self-punishment of masochists and that of obsessional patients. In the latter, the subject turns hostility against the self, but without the attitude of passivity toward another person that occurs in masochism. The masochist's passivity toward another's aggression implies an object relation. In masochistic patients, the need for punishment is linked with either real or imagined relations with an other. In contrast, the self-punishing actions of obsessional and other neurotic patients stems from superego guilt over unconscious forbidden sexual or aggressive wishes.

Psychoanalytic writings often ascribe the self-punishing and self-damaging behaviors of the masochist to a turning of the patient's own sadism upon the self. Although this familiar dynamic is often correct for neurotic patients, it is not a prevalent dynamic pattern in masochistic patients. Rather, in masochistic patients the central dynamic involves the introjection of the parents' sadism. It is not the patient's sadism that is turned against the self, but rather, the sadism of the introjected love object. Berliner (1958) held that the diagnosis of masochism should not be made unless the introjection of another person's sadism is the essential pattern.

Mr. A.'s use of introjects to punish himself and force himself to work developed from his introjection of his mother's punitive attitudes toward him. His need to invoke fantasies of someone punishing him or forcing him to work did not arise from a punitive or cruel superego. The demand that he work as a punishment arose from the introject of his mother, that is, his representation of a controlling authority figure.

In "The Economic Problem of Masochism," Freud (1924) differentiated "erotogenic" and "feminine" masochism from "moral" masochism. All three types of masochism were repeatedly demonstrated by my patient in his daily life and the analytic situation. My clinical observations are in accord with those of Berliner (1958), who believes that there are no sexual masochists who are not also severe moral masochists. The masochistic perversion is a superstructure over a character malformation that the moral masochist and the masochistic pervert share.

Berliner (1940, 1942, 1947, 1958), one of the first to interject object-relations concepts in studies of masochism, linked masochistic phenomena with pathogenic parent-child relationships. He provided clinical evidence for the hypothesis that masochism, in both its sexual and moral forms, constitutes a disturbance of object relations and a pathologic form of loving (Berliner 1958). In his view, masochism means loving a person who gives back hatred and ill-treatment. This was evident in my patient's sexual perversion and interpersonal relations. A frequent transference manifestation of this dynamic was the patient's wish to earn the analyst's love through humiliating and debasing himself.

Some parents of masochistic patients have been outrageously cruel to them as children (Berliner 1958, Bieber 1980, Panken 1973). Another common genetic pattern is that the parents' ambivalence tends more toward hostility, and the child enjoins in the ill-treatment or guilt imposed under the guise of love. Mr. A.'s profound longing for love through suffering stemmed not only from his mother's cruelty to him as a child, but also from the fact that her rare expressions of concern came when he humiliated himself or made himself the object of her pity.

Menaker (1953) also used an object-relations perspective to investigate masochism. She viewed masochistic behaviors as an outcome of traumatic deprivation at the oral level and as a means of perpetuating bonds, however, painful, to the mother. My clinical observations support her hypothesis that masochism may be viewed as an adaptive and defensive ego function that is used to maintain a vitally needed love relationship to a primary object.

Bernstein (1957) investigated the role of traumatic early parent-child relations in the pathogenesis of masochism. He found that the ego functions and qualities of such patients were made to serve the narcissistic needs of their parents. Their successes were not their own but their parents', and they were robbed of the gratifications that might have been derived had they been encouraged to accomplish things for themselves. Bernstein described their need to repeat original narcissistic traumas of disappointment, rejection, and humiliation. In adult life, masochistic relationships are repetitive re-enactments of traumatic childhood object relations; they give patients the illusion of actively controlling situations that they once endured passively.

Object-Relations Theory and Conflict

It is necessary to distinguish between psychic and interpersonal conflicts. Psychic conflicts are conflicts between conscious and/or unconscious motives of the subject. Interpersonal conflicts are conflicts between persons.

A hierarchical model of the mind is required for a more integrated understanding of psychic conflict (Dorpat 1976). I constructed such a pattern, following Gedo and Goldberg (1973); I placed the tripartite model at a higher developmental level than the object-relations format. Psychic conflicts were classified into object-relations conflicts and structural conflicts. The object-relations class of psychic conflict covered the pre-oedipal phase of psychic development prior to id-ego-superego differentiation. Object-relations conflicts are psychic conflicts between the subject's wishes and the ideals, injunctions, and prohibitions that are not experienced as his own, but rather, are represented in primary- or secondary-process representations of some (usually parental) authority.

There may not appear to be any difference between an object-relations and a structural conflict, because the content (e.g., wishes, prohibitions, injunctions) of the opposing parts of the conflict may seem the same in both types of conflicts. The crucial difference is that in a structural conflict, the subject experiences (or is capable of experiencing, if part of the conflict is unconscious) the opposing tendencies as aspects of himself. The subject's values, prohibitions, and injunctions conflict with the subject's sexual, aggressive, or other kinds of wishes. In the object-relations conflict, the conflict is between the subject's own strivings and wishes, on the one hand, and the subject's representations (mainly introjects) of another person's injunctions, prohibitions, and values, on the other.

The content of Mr. A.'s guilt was similar to what Modell (1965) described as "separation guilt." Separation guilt, unlike superego guilt, is not experienced as stemming from real or imagined transgressions against one's moral values. The patient did not consider the thoughts, feelings, or overt acts that evoked separation guilt as morally wrong in themselves. Rather, he felt guilty because he believed that his strivings toward self-gratification and individuation would displease his mother. The power of the prohibition against autonomous functioning was subjectively linked with his memories and fantasies of a disapproving mother who rejected his movements toward independence.

Separation and guilt feelings did not arise from structural conflicts (i.e., from real or imagined transgressions against an internalized and impersonal authority). He evoked guilt by feelings, thoughts, and overt actions which he considered displeasing to the introjected representation of his mother. Culpability and wrongdoing were implicitly defined as behaviors opposed to what his mother wanted of him. Guilt and anxiety over psychological separateness from his mother arose from unresolved unconscious object-relations conflicts and fixations at the separation-individuation phase of development. His gradual appropriation of other ego and superego functions in analysis (e.g., establishing ideals and goals, and regulating his self-esteem), were sometimes sources of object-relations conflicts. The most frequent overt indications of such unconscious conflicts were various manifestations of anxiety and guilt over behaving and regulating himself in an autonomous manner.

Transference and Self-Object Relations

Most clinicians view transference as a universal aspect of object relations (Loewald 1960). All human relationships contain an admixture of transference and realistic reactions (Fenichel 1938, p. 72). The analytic situation does not create transference by itself, but provides conditions for transference to emerge into consciousness in order to be understood and worked through.

The major transference reactions that developed in Mr. A.'s analysis were self-object ones. Self-objects are objects experienced as part of the self. Patients who develop predominantly self-object transferences have not fully differentiated their object-representations from their self-representations and, like young children, frequently experience and treat the analyst as an extension of themselves. Self-object relations and transferences should be distinguished from the more highly developed whole-object relations and transferences that are found in psychoneurotic and normal individuals. Whole objects are loved (or at least represented and recognized) for their own qualities, independent of the subject's needs. Wholeness also implies that the subject can sustain both positive and negative feelings for the same object. In contrast, more disturbed patients tend to divide their object-representations into good and bad, weak and strong.

An abiding characteristic of self-object transferences is the subject's need to control the self-object, who is perceived and treated as an extension of the subject's self. This type of omnipotent control is similar to the control 2-year-old children often attempt to exercise over their parents. Patients experience the self-object much as they experience control over their own limbs. Actual or threatened loss of the self-object incurs a sense of helplessness and rage similar to that incurred by loss of a body part or function. The threat of object loss or loss of control over the object triggers a reaction similar in quality, if not always in intensity, to the "catastrophic reaction" described by Goldstein (1939) as a typical emotional reaction of brain-damaged persons. The overwhelming anxiety experienced by brain-damaged persons is connected with their sense of losing a part of themselves, and their helplessness to prevent or defend against the terror evoked by the loss.

Many therapists tend to react adversely to such patients' need for control, and may mistakenly attribute hostile motives to the patient. The need of patients with pre-oedipal fixations to control their self-objects is not always or necessarily fused with hostile or destructive wishes. Viewed from a developmental perspective, their need to control the self-object may be a normal, expected aspect of development. For patients who have not developed more differentiated means of self-regulation, control over the therapist serves the dual purpose of avoiding external traumatic stimulation and maintaining a semblance of internal emotional equilibrium.

Patients with pre-oedipal disorders initially cannot understand or appreciate the psychoanalyst's neutrality and psychological separateness. They tend to perceive the analyst's communications as directives, rather than interpretations. These distortions stem from their unconscious need to project either their ego and superego functions, or the power to co-opt and regulate their own psychic functions onto the analyst. Patients with pre-oedipal disorders commonly project not only sexual and aggressive contents onto the analyst, but also one or more of their psychic functions. Classical literature on transferences involving projection emphasizes the projection of superego elements, but makes little mention of the projection of ego functions, onto the analyst (see Giovacchini 1967, 1975).

Patients with pre-oedipal disorders tend to project their unstable and poorly differentiated ego functions, such as reality testing, decision making, and judgment, onto the analyst far more than do patients with neuroses or neurotic character disorders. One of the most common technical mistakes in the analysis of such patients is the analyst's bending under transference pressures and acting out the role of the idealized parent by providing directives and advice. It is of primary importance that the analyst maintain an attitude and technique of neutrality in such situations (Dorpat 1977).

SUMMARY

An object-relations perspective provides a method for illuminating crucial processes in the pathogenesis and treatment of masochistic patients. In this chapter, I have examined clinical and theoretical differences between structural conflicts and object-relations conflicts. Object-relations conflicts refer to psychic conflicts between the subject's wishes and the ideals, prohibitions, and injunctions contained in introjects of some (usually parental) authority.

In the case example presented here, two critical childhood traumas, the death of the patient's father and a pathological symbiotic relationship with his mother, decisively contributed to the patient's masochism and his developmental fixation at the separation-individuation phase of development. As a child, the patient was compelled to serve as his mother's personal slave. This master-slave relationship was unconsciously replicated in sado-masochistically perverse sexual practices with prostitutes, and then in the transference situation with the analyst.

The patient suffered from intense object-relations conflicts and guilt over functioning independently of his mother. His masochistic perverse behavior was associated with a self-object relation with his sexual partners, who were perceived and treated solely as the embodied projection of his wishes. With the development of a more stable capacity for sustaining whole-object relations, the perverse sexual behavior disappeared.

REFERENCES

Altschul, S. (1968). Denial and ego arrest. *J. Amer. Psychoanal. Assn.* 16: 301–318.

Anderson, C. (1949). Aspects of pathological grief and mourning. *Internat. J. Psycho-Anal.* 30: 48–55.

Berliner, B. (1940). Libido and reality in masochism. *Psychoanal. Q.* 9: 322–333.

—— (1942). The concept of masochism. *Psychoanal. Rev.* 29: 386–400.

—— (1947). On some psychodynamics of masochism. *Psychoanal. Q.* 16: 459–471.

—— (1958). The role of object relations in moral masochism. *Psychoanal. Q.* 27: 38–56.

Bernstein, I. (1957). The role of narcissism in moral masochism. *Psychoanal. Q.* 26.

Bieber, I. (1980). *Cognitive Psychoanalysis.* New York: Aronson.

Boyer, L. B. (1956). On maternal overstimulation and ego defects. *The Psychoanalytic Study of the Child* 11: 236–256.

—— (1967). Office treatment of schizophrenic patients: The use of psychoanalytic therapy with few parameters. In *Psychoanalytic Treatment of Schizophrenic and Characterologic Disorders,* ed. L. B. Boyer and P. L. Giovacchini, pp. 143–188. New York: Science House.

Brodey, W. M. (1965). On the dynamics of narcissism. I. Externalization. *The Psychoanalytic Study of the Child* 20: 165–193.

Dorpat, T. L. (1972). Psychological effects of parental suicide on surviving children. In *Survivors of Suicide,* ed. A. C. Cain, pp. 121–142. Springfield, Ill.: Charles C. Thomas.

—— (1976). Structural conflict and object-relations conflict. *J. Amer. Psychoanal. Assn.* 24: 855–874.

—— (1977). On neutrality. *Internat. J. Psychoanal. Psychother.* 6: 39–64.

—— (1978). Introjection and the idealizing transference. *Internat. J. Psychoanal. Psychother.* 7: 23–54.

Fenichel, O. (1938). *Problems of Psychoanalytic Technique.* Albany, N.Y.: The Psychoanalytic Quarterly, 1939.

Freud, S. (1915). Instincts and their vicissitudes. *Standard Edition* 14: 111–140. London: Hogarth Press, 1955.

—— (1920). Beyond the pleasure principle. *Standard Edition* 18: 7–64. London: Hogarth Press, 1955.

—— (1924). The economic problems of masochism. *Standard Edition* 19: 157–171. London: Hogarth Press, 1955.

Gedo, J. E. and Goldberg, A. (1973). *Models of the Mind.* Chicago and London: University of Chicago Press.

Giovacchini, P. L. (1967). Frustration and externalization. *Psychoanal. Q.* 36: 571–583.

———— (1972). Summing up. In *Tactics and Techniques of Psychoanalytic Therapy*, vol. 1, ed. P. L. Giovacchini, pp. 697–727. New York: Science House.

———— (1975). Various aspects of the psychoanalytic process. In *Tactics and Techniques in Psychoanalytic Therapy*, vol. 2, ed. P. L. Giovacchini et al., pp. 5–95. New York: Aronson.

———— (1980). Epilogue. In *Psychoanalytic Treatment of Schizophrenic, Borderline and Characterological Disorders,* 2nd ed., ed. L. B. Boyer and P. L. Giovacchini. New York: Aronson.

Goffman, E. (1974). *Frame Analysis.* Cambridge, Mass.: Harvard University Press.

Goldstein, K. (1939). *The Organism: A Holistic Approach to Biology Derived from Pathological Data on Man.* New York: American Books.

Klein, G. S. (1976). *Psychoanalytic Theory.* New York: International Universities Press.

Krupp, G. (1965). Identification as a defense against anxiety in coping with loss. *Internat. J. Psycho-Anal.* 46: 303–314.

Loewald, H. W. (1960). The therapeutic action of psycho-analysis. *Internat. J. Psycho-Anal.* 41: 16–33.

Menaker, E. (1953). Masochism, a defense reaction. *Psychoanal. Q.* 22: 205–220.

Modell, A. H. (1965). On having the right to a life: An aspect of the superego's development. *Internat. J. Psycho-Anal.* 46: 323–331.

Ornstein, A. and Ornstein, P. H. (1975). On the interpretive process in schizophrenia. *Internat. J. Psychoanal. Psychother.* 4: 219–271.

Panken, S. (1973). *The Joy of Suffering.* New York: Aronson.

Rosenfeld, H. (1966). Discussion of "Office Treatment of Schizophrenia" by L. Bryce Boyer. *Psychoanal. Forum* 1: 351–353.

Spruiell, V. (1980). Classical psychoanalysis and frame theory. Paper presented at the Seattle Psychoanalytic Society, May.

Wolfenstein, M. (1966). How is mourning possible? *The Psychoanalytic Study of the Child* 21: 93–123.

———— (1969). Loss, rage and repetition. *The Psychoanalytic Study of the Child* 24: 432–460.

INDEX